mother panic

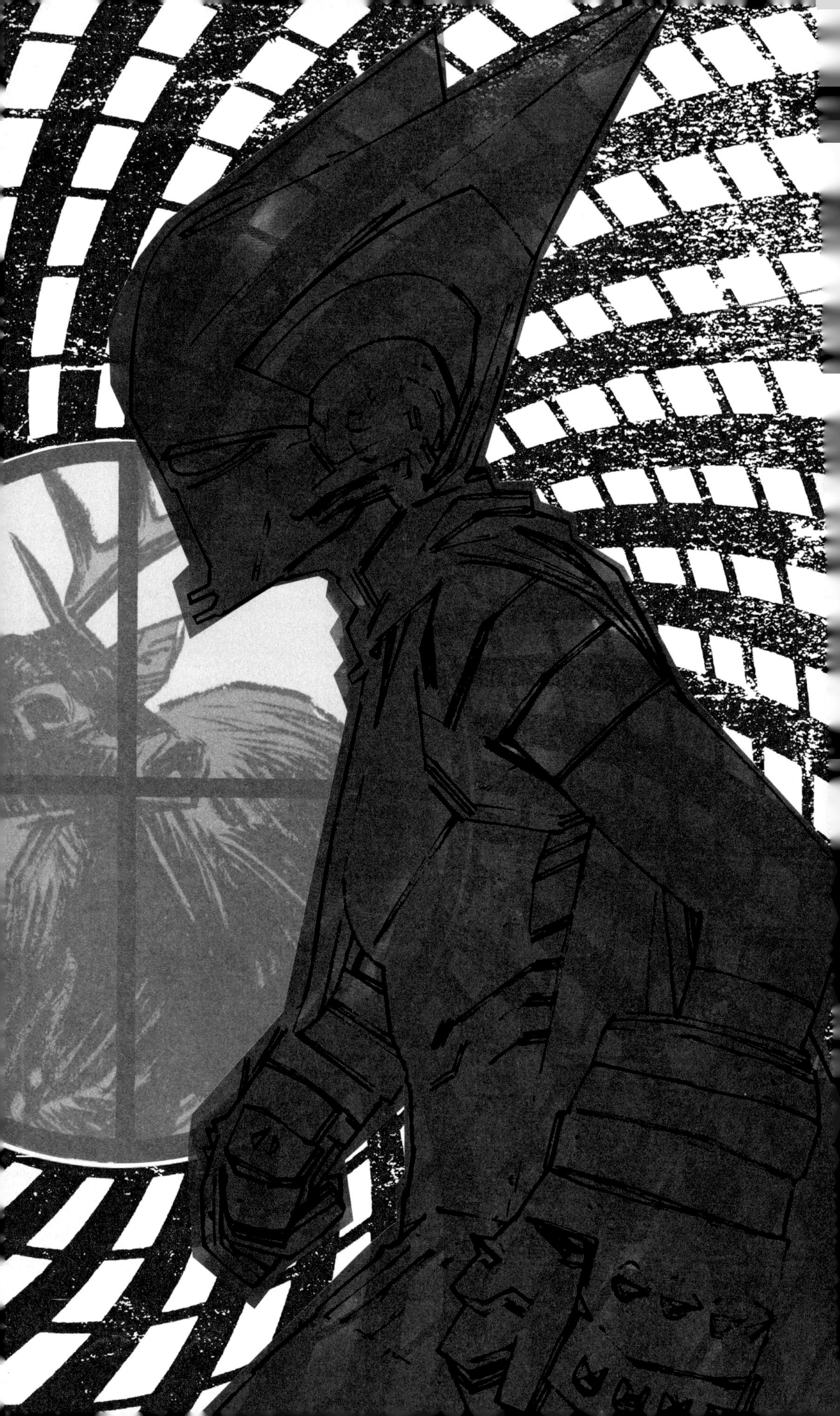

mother panic

VOL. 2: UNDER HER SKIN

JODY HOUSER Writer
JOHN PAUL LEON
SHAWN CRYSTAL Artists
DAVE STEWART JEAN-FRANCOIS BEAULIEU Colorists
JOHN WORKMAN SHAWN CRYSTAL Letterers
TOMMY LEE EDWARDS Cover Art
TOMMY LEE EDWARDS JOHN PAUL LEON Original Series Covers
GERARD WAY DC's Young Animal Curator
MOTHER PANIC CREATED BY GERARD WAY,
JODY HOUSER AND TOMMY LEE EDWARDS

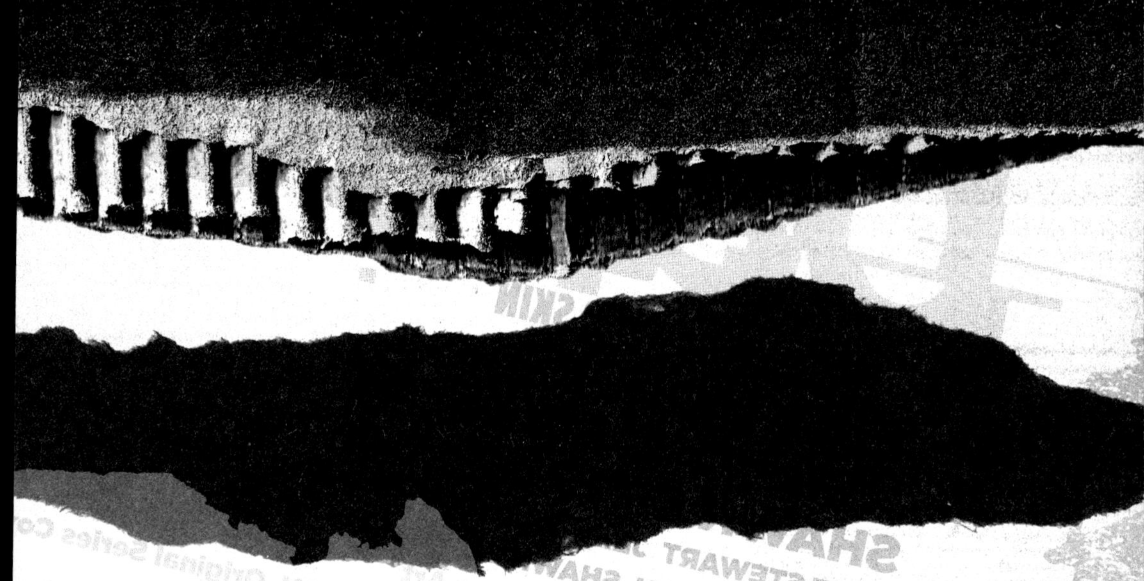

Molly Mahan Editor – Original Series
Jeb Woodard Group Editor – Collected Editions
Scott Nybakken Editor – Collected Edition
Steve Cook Design Director – Books
Louis Prandi Publication Design

Bob Harras Senior VP – Editor-in-Chief, DC Comics
Mark Doyle Executive Editor, Vertigo

Diane Nelson President
Dan DiDio Publisher
Jim Lee Publisher
Geoff Johns President & Chief Creative Officer
Amit Desai Executive VP – Business & Marketing Strategy,
Direct to Consumer & Global Franchise Management
Sam Ades Senior VP & General Manager, Digital Services
Bobbie Chase VP & Executive Editor, Young Reader & Talent Development
Mark Chiarello Senior VP – Art, Design & Collected Editions
John Cunningham Senior VP – Sales & Trade Marketing
Anne DePies Senior VP – Business Strategy, Finance & Administration
Don Falletti VP – Manufacturing Operations
Lawrence Ganem VP – Editorial Administration & Talent Relations
Alison Gill Senior VP – Manufacturing & Operations
Hank Kanalz Senior VP – Editorial Strategy & Administration
Jay Kogan VP – Legal Affairs
Jack Mahan VP – Business Affairs
Nick J. Napolitano VP – Manufacturing Administration
Eddie Scannell VP – Consumer Marketing
Courtney Simmons Senior VP – Publicity & Communications
Jim (Ski) Sokolowski VP – Comic Book Specialty Sales & Trade Marketing
Nancy Spears VP – Mass, Book, Digital Sales & Trade Marketing
Michele R. Wells VP – Content Strategy

MOTHER PANIC VOL. 2: UNDER HER SKIN

Published by DC Comics. Compilation and all new material Copyright © 2018
DC Comics. All Rights Reserved.

Originally published in single magazine form in MOTHER PANIC 7-12.
Copyright © 2017 DC Comics. All Rights Reserved. All characters, their
distinctive likenesses and related elements featured in this publication are
trademarks of DC Comics. The stories, characters and incidents featured in
this publication are entirely fictional. DC Comics does not read or accept
unsolicited submissions of ideas, stories or artwork.

DC Comics
2900 West Alameda Avenue
Burbank, CA 91505
Printed by LSC Communications, Owensville, MO, USA. 1/19/18. First printing.
ISBN: 978-1-4012-7768-0

Library of Congress Cataloging-in-Publication Data is available.

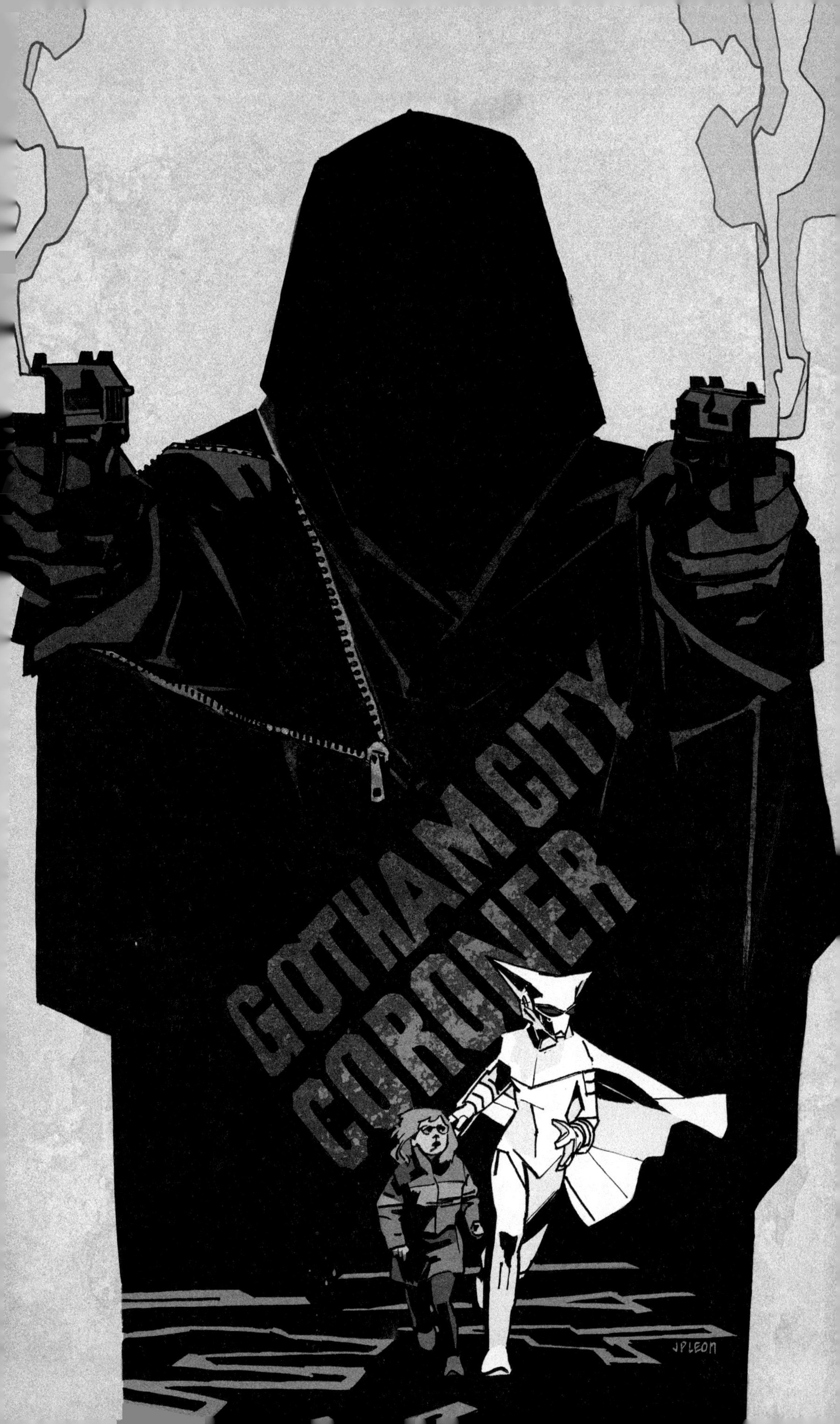
GOTHAM CITY
CORONER
JPLEON

Variant cover art by Tommy Lee Edwards

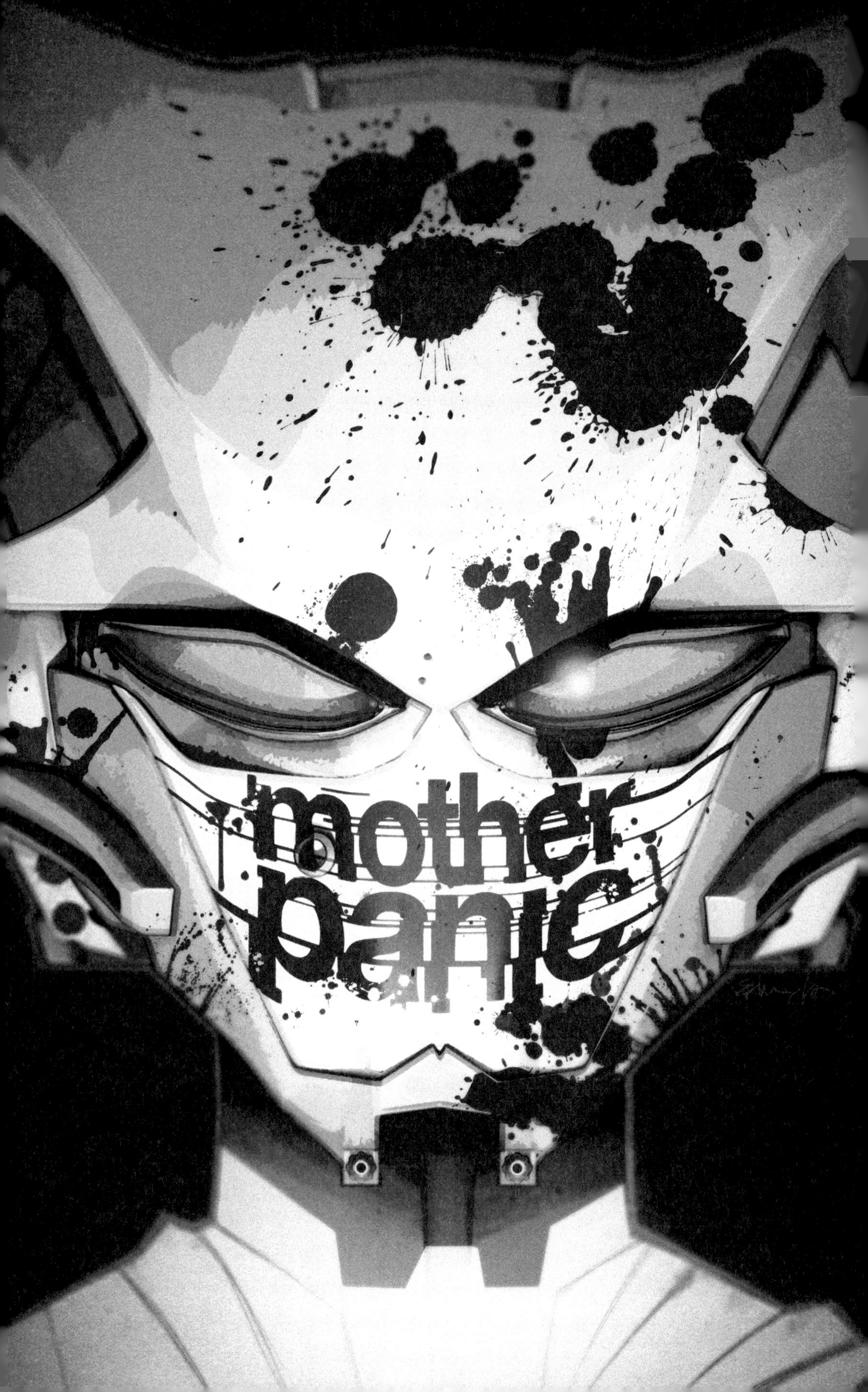
mother panic

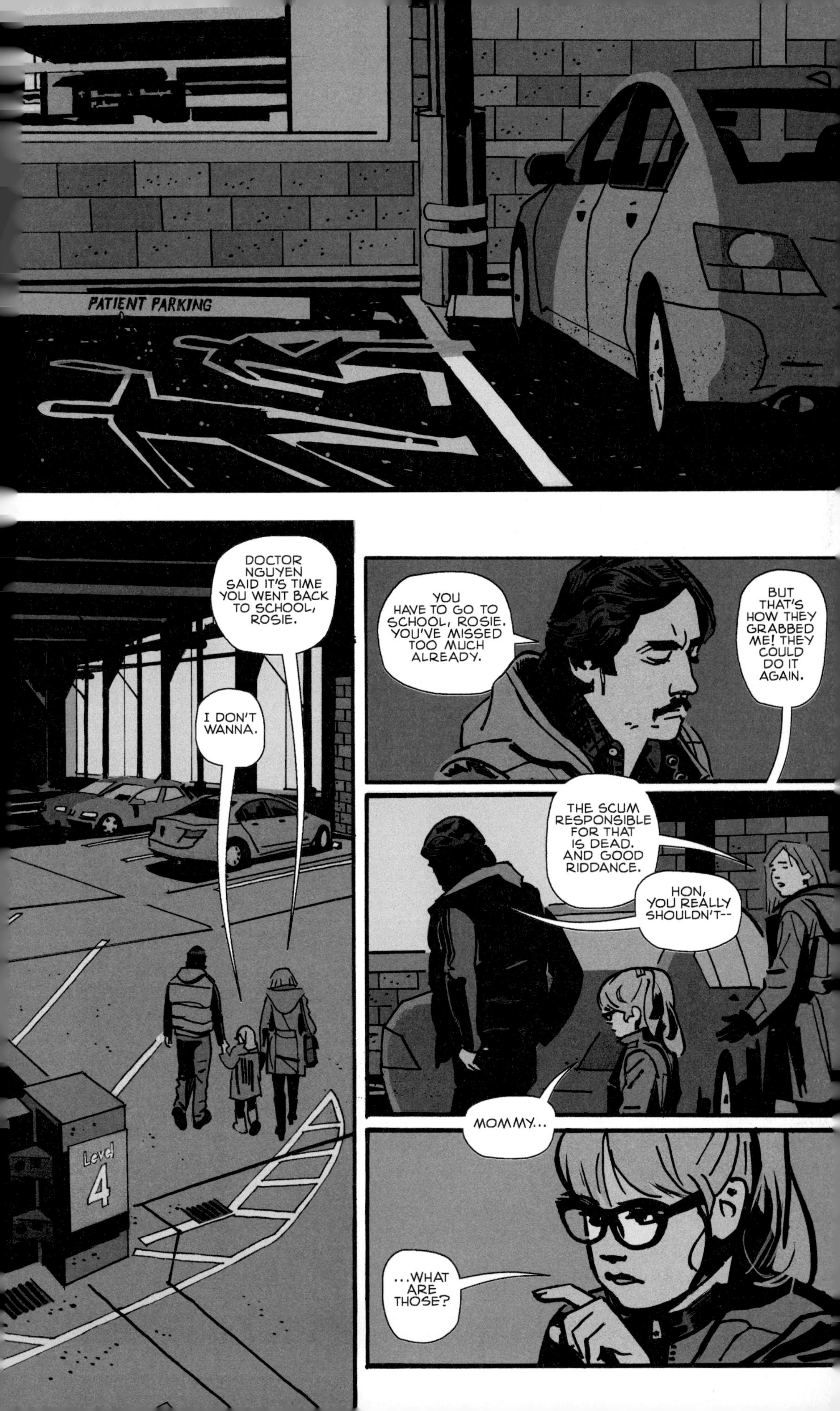
PATIENT PARKING
DOCTOR NGUYEN SAID IT'S TIME YOU WENT BACK TO SCHOOL, ROSIE.
I DON'T WANNA.
Level 4
YOU HAVE TO GO TO SCHOOL, ROSIE. YOU'VE MISSED TOO MUCH ALREADY.
BUT THAT'S HOW THEY GRABBED ME! THEY COULD DO IT AGAIN.
THE SCUM RESPONSIBLE FOR THAT IS DEAD. AND GOOD RIDDANCE.
HON, YOU REALLY SHOULDN'T--
MOMMY...
...WHAT ARE THOSE?

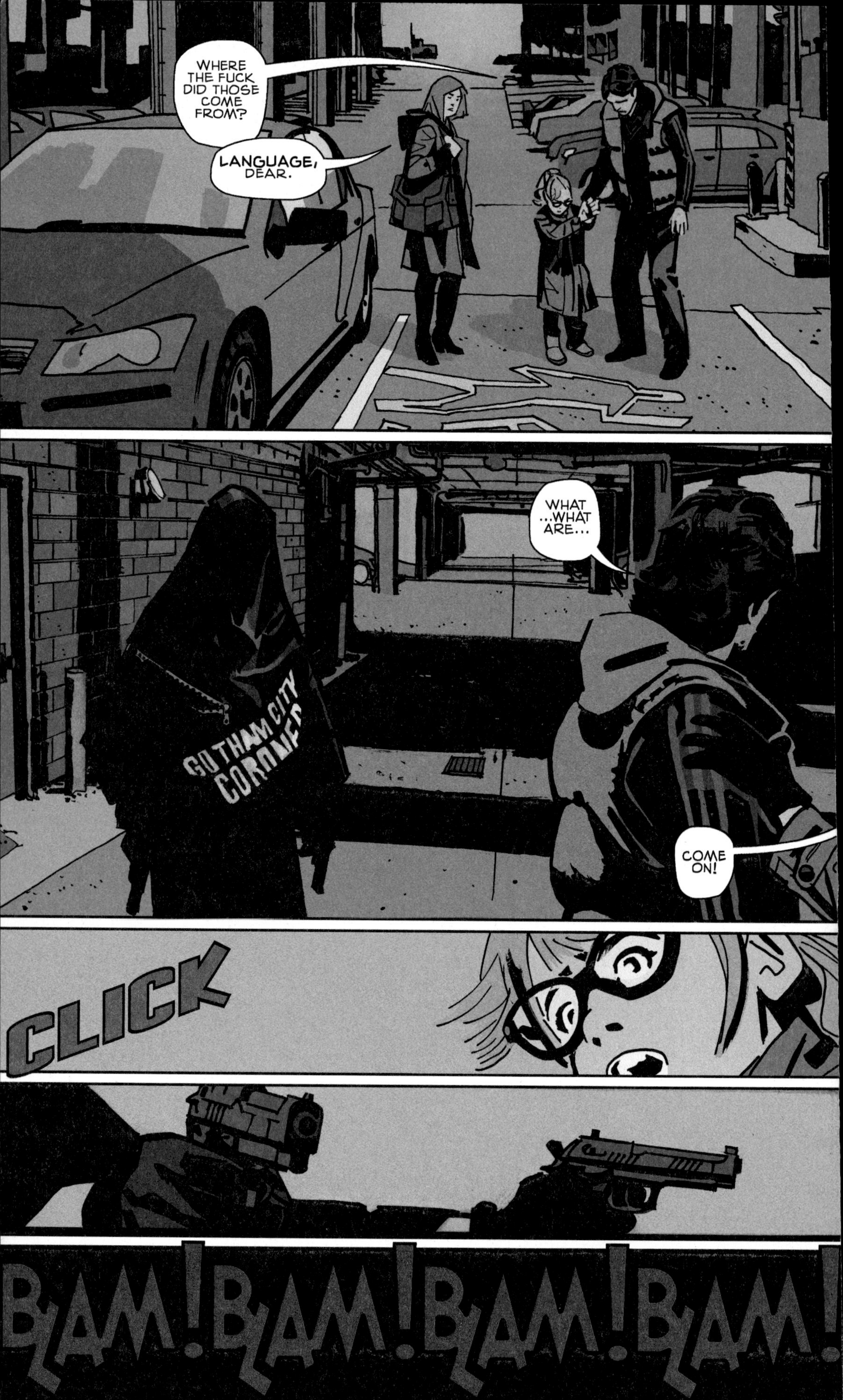
WHERE THE FUCK DID THOSE COME FROM?
LANGUAGE, DEAR.
WHAT ...WHAT ARE...
GOTHAM CITY CORONER
COME ON!
CLICK
BAM! BAM! BAM! BAM!

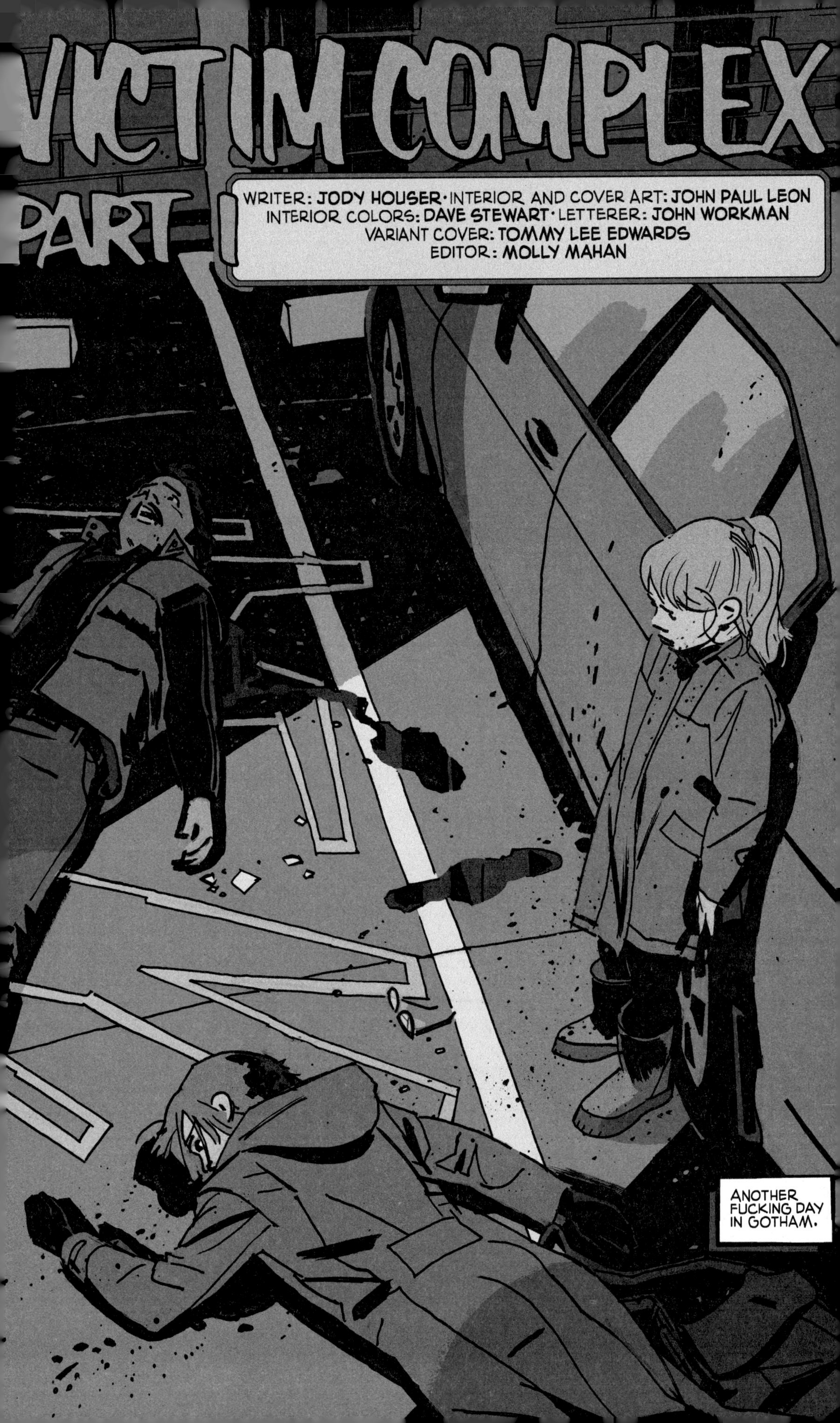
VICTIM COMPLEX
PART
WRITER: JODY HOUSER • INTERIOR AND COVER ART: JOHN PAUL LEON
INTERIOR COLORS: DAVE STEWART • LETTERER: JOHN WORKMAN
VARIANT COVER: TOMMY LEE EDWARDS
EDITOR: MOLLY MAHAN
ANOTHER FUCKING DAY IN GOTHAM.

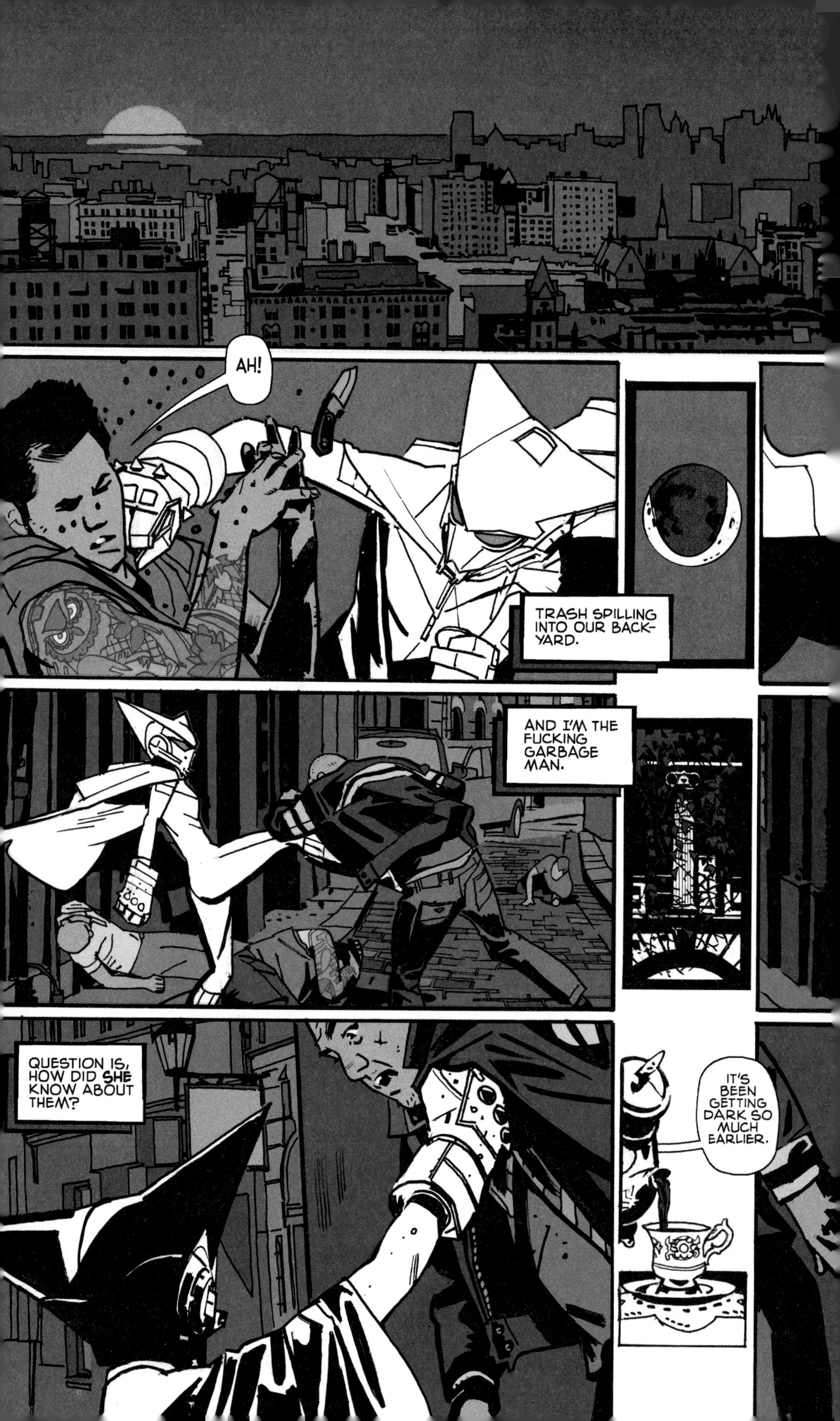
AH!
TRASH SPILLING INTO OUR BACK-YARD.
AND I'M THE FUCKING GARBAGE MAN.
QUESTION IS, HOW DID SHE KNOW ABOUT THEM?
IT'S BEEN GETTING DARK SO MUCH EARLIER.

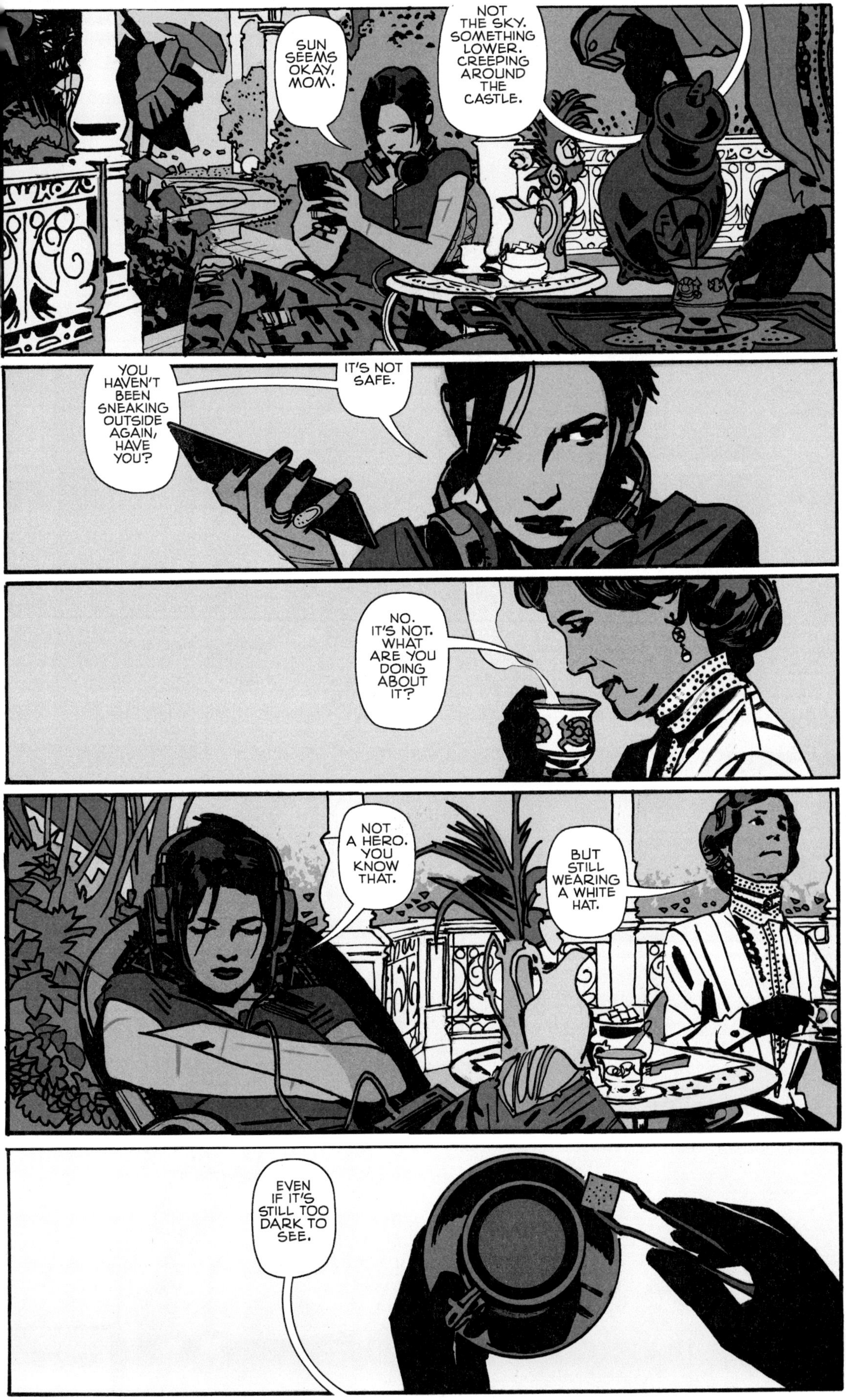
SUN SEEMS OKAY, MOM.
NOT THE SKY. SOMETHING LOWER. CREEPING AROUND THE CASTLE.
YOU HAVEN'T BEEN SNEAKING OUTSIDE AGAIN, HAVE YOU?
IT'S NOT SAFE.
NO. IT'S NOT. WHAT ARE YOU DOING ABOUT IT?
NOT A HERO. YOU KNOW THAT.
BUT STILL WEARING A WHITE HAT.
EVEN IF IT'S STILL TOO DARK TO SEE.

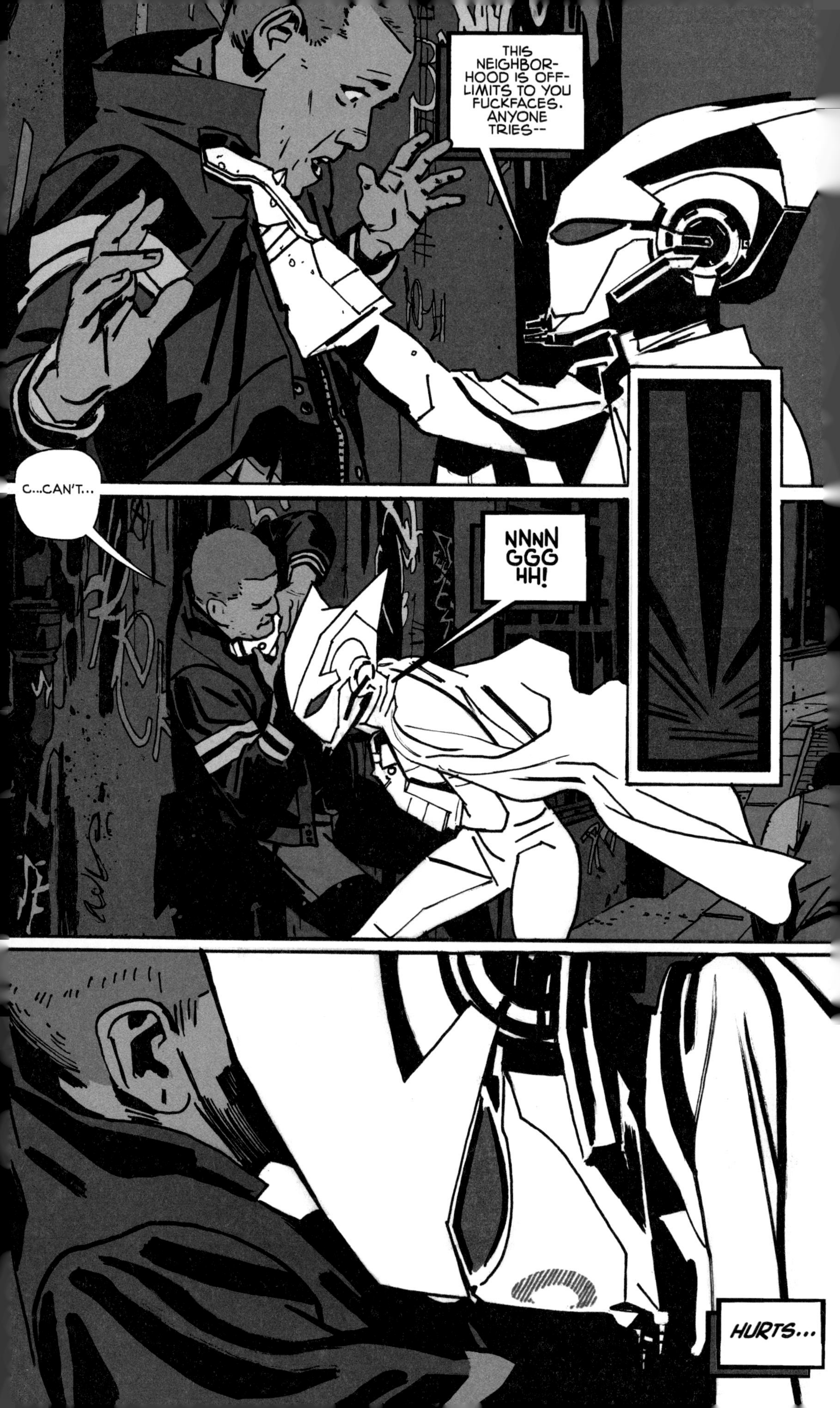
THIS NEIGHBOR-HOOD IS OFF-LIMITS TO YOU FUCKFACES. ANYONE TRIES--
C...CAN'T...
NNNN GGG HH!
HURTS...

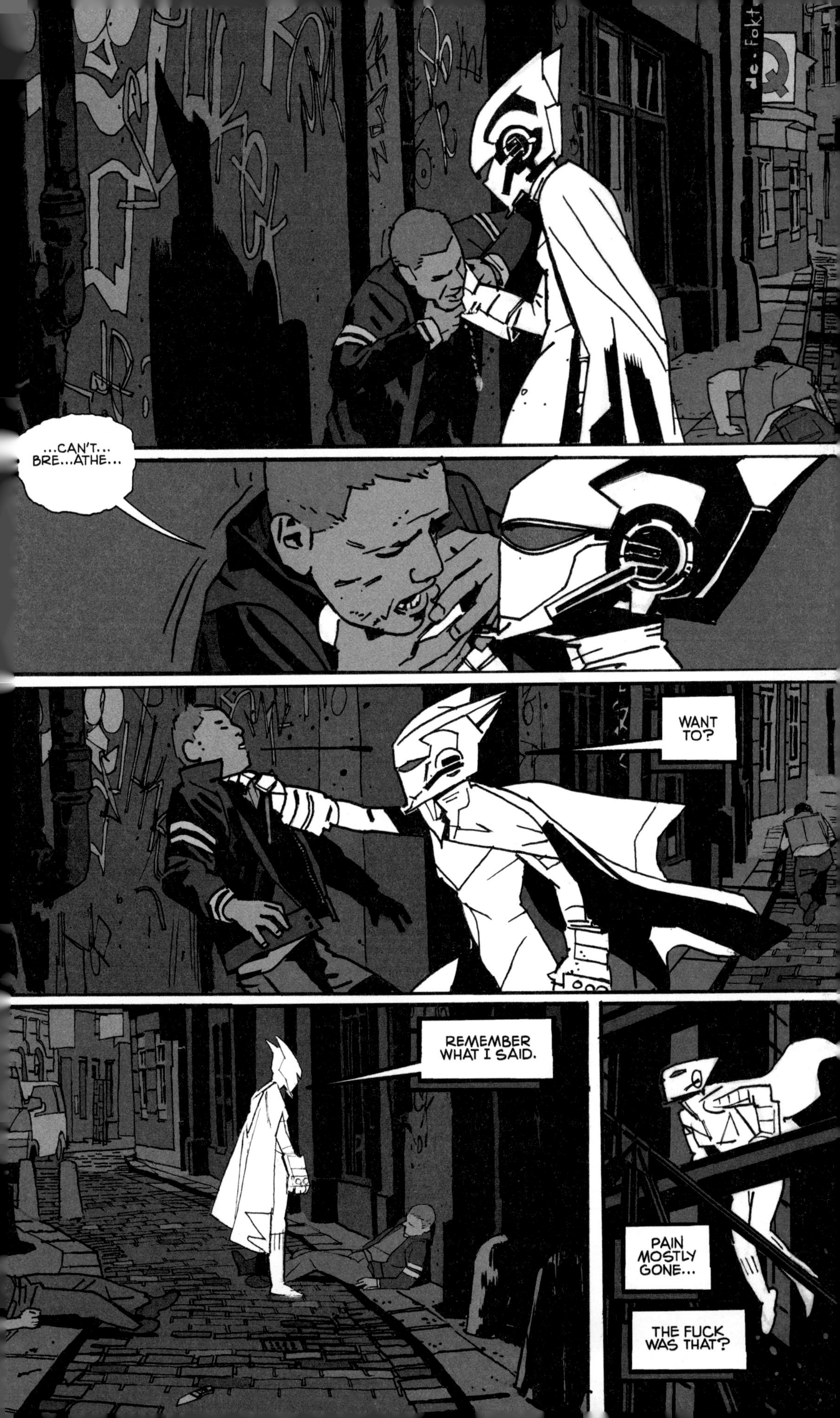
de.Fokt
...CAN'T... BRE...ATHE...
WANT TO?
REMEMBER WHAT I SAID.
PAIN MOSTLY GONE...
THE FUCK WAS THAT?

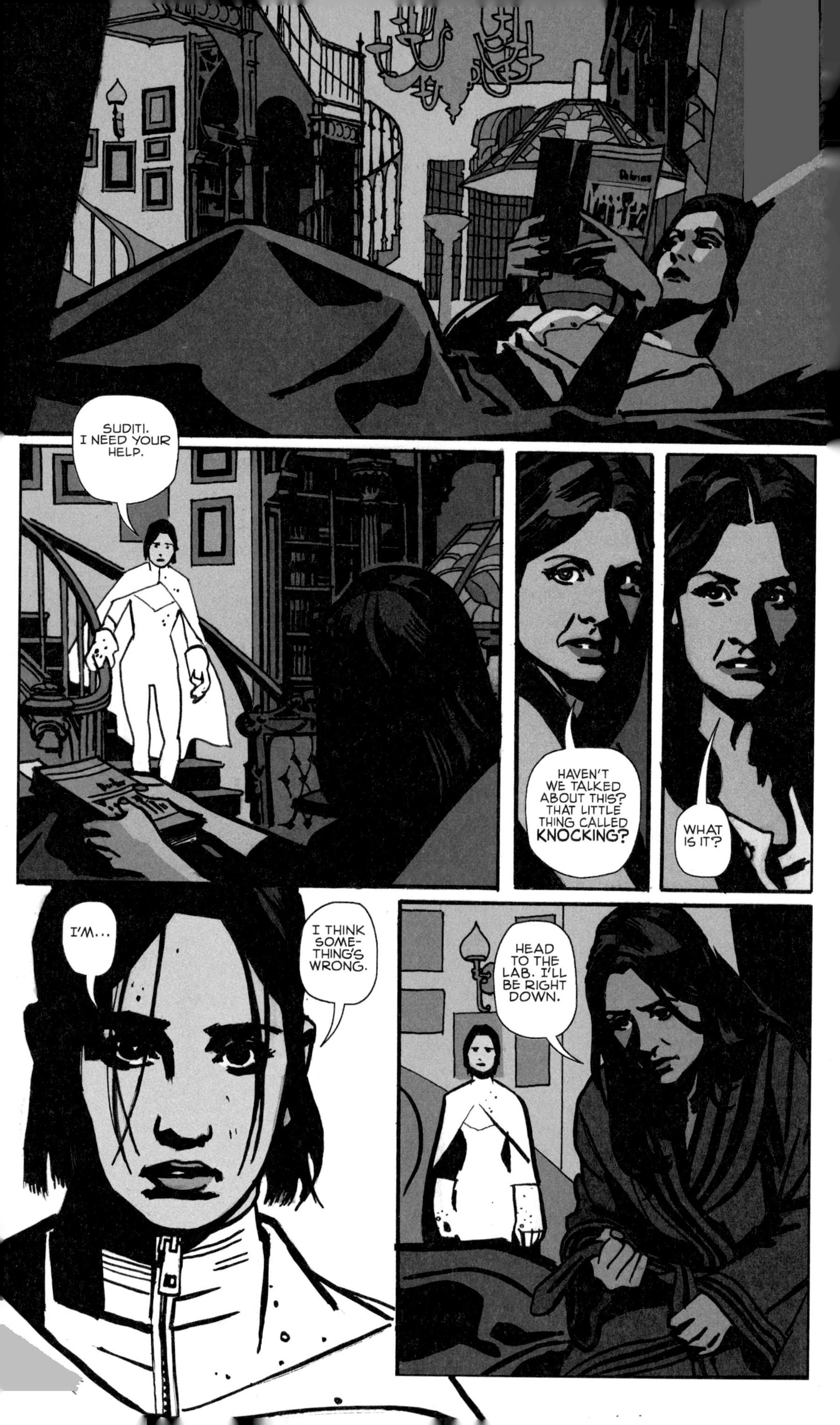
SUDITI. I NEED YOUR HELP.
HAVEN'T WE TALKED ABOUT THIS? THAT LITTLE THING CALLED KNOCKING?
WHAT IS IT?
I'M...
I THINK SOME-THING'S WRONG.
HEAD TO THE LAB. I'LL BE RIGHT DOWN.

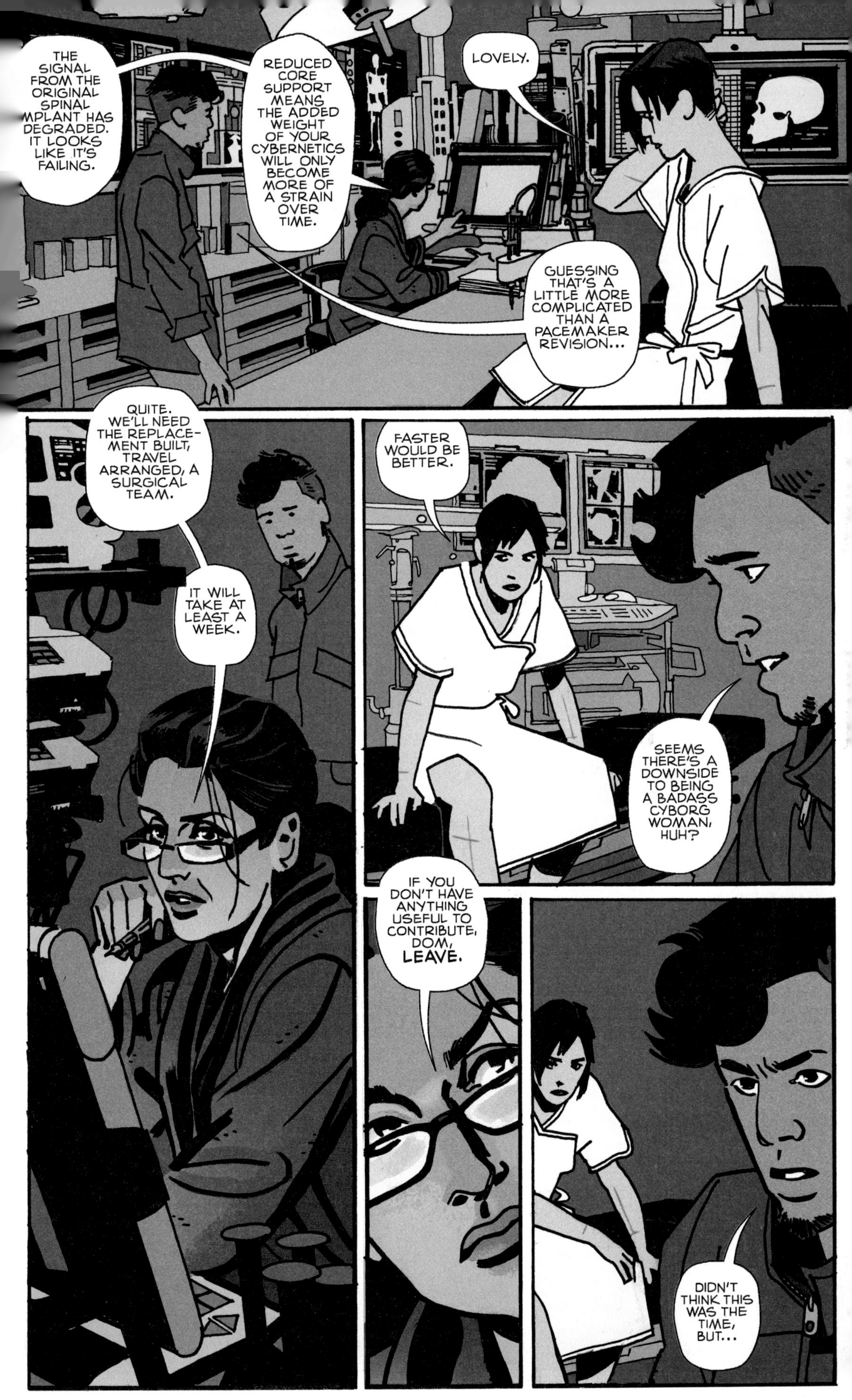
THE SIGNAL FROM THE ORIGINAL SPINAL IMPLANT HAS DEGRADED. IT LOOKS LIKE IT'S FAILING.
REDUCED CORE SUPPORT MEANS THE ADDED WEIGHT OF YOUR CYBERNETICS WILL ONLY BECOME MORE OF A STRAIN OVER TIME.
LOVELY.
GUESSING THAT'S A LITTLE MORE COMPLICATED THAN A PACEMAKER REVISION...
QUITE. WE'LL NEED THE REPLACEMENT BUILT, TRAVEL ARRANGED, A SURGICAL TEAM.
IT WILL TAKE AT LEAST A WEEK.
FASTER WOULD BE BETTER.
SEEMS THERE'S A DOWNSIDE TO BEING A BADASS CYBORG WOMAN, HUH?
IF YOU DON'T HAVE ANYTHING USEFUL TO CONTRIBUTE, DOM, **LEAVE.**
DIDN'T THINK THIS WAS THE TIME, BUT...

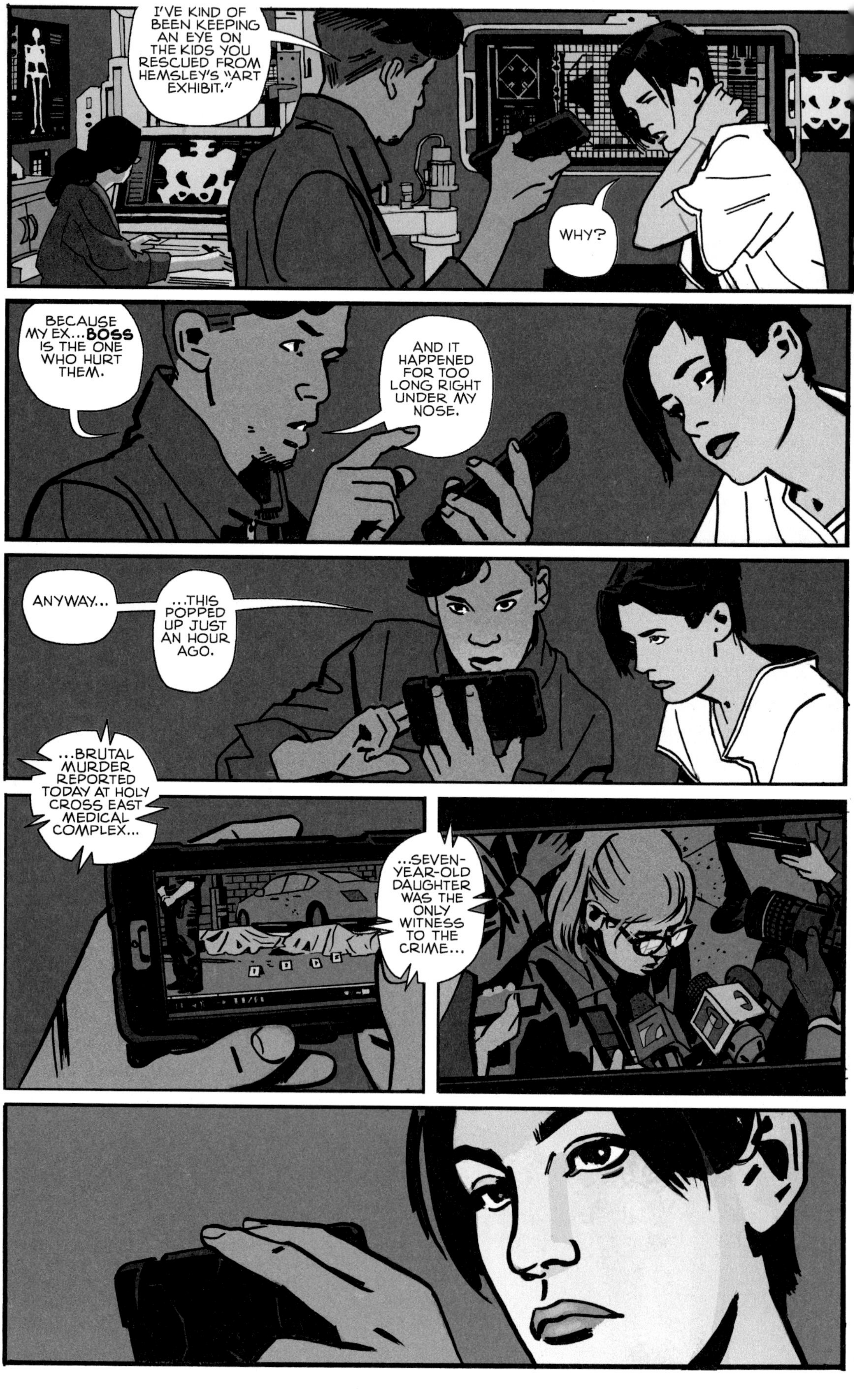
I'VE KIND OF BEEN KEEPING AN EYE ON THE KIDS YOU RESCUED FROM HEMSLEY'S "ART EXHIBIT."
WHY?
BECAUSE MY EX... **BOSS** IS THE ONE WHO HURT THEM.
AND IT HAPPENED FOR TOO LONG RIGHT UNDER MY NOSE.
ANYWAY...
...THIS POPPED UP JUST AN HOUR AGO.
...BRUTAL MURDER REPORTED TODAY AT HOLY CROSS EAST MEDICAL COMPLEX...
...SEVEN-YEAR-OLD DAUGHTER WAS THE ONLY WITNESS TO THE CRIME...

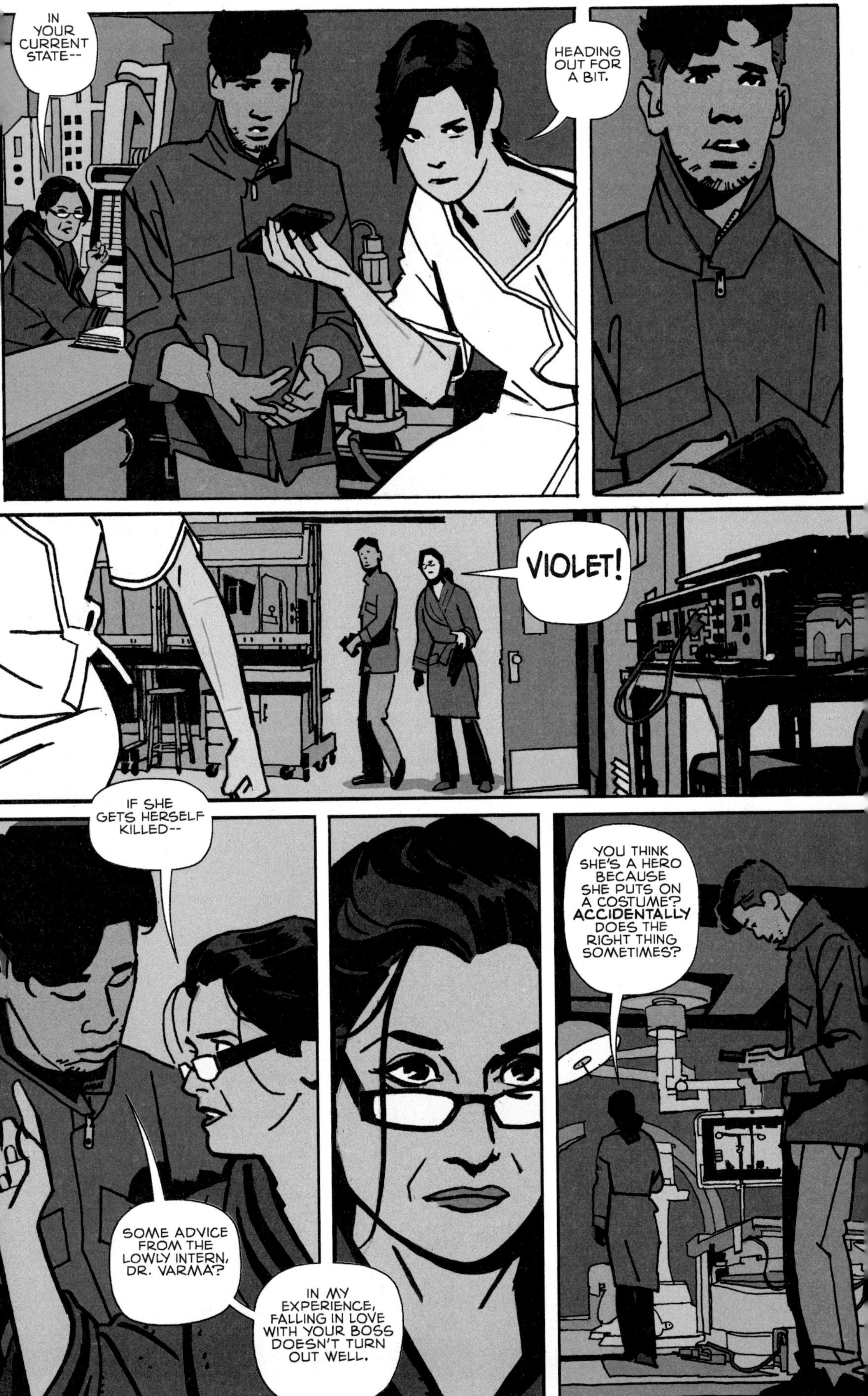
IN YOUR CURRENT STATE--
HEADING OUT FOR A BIT.
VIOLET!
IF SHE GETS HERSELF KILLED--
SOME ADVICE FROM THE LOWLY INTERN, DR. VARMA?
IN MY EXPERIENCE, FALLING IN LOVE WITH YOUR BOSS DOESN'T TURN OUT WELL.
YOU THINK SHE'S A HERO BECAUSE SHE PUTS ON A COSTUME? ACCIDENTALLY DOES THE RIGHT THING SOMETIMES?

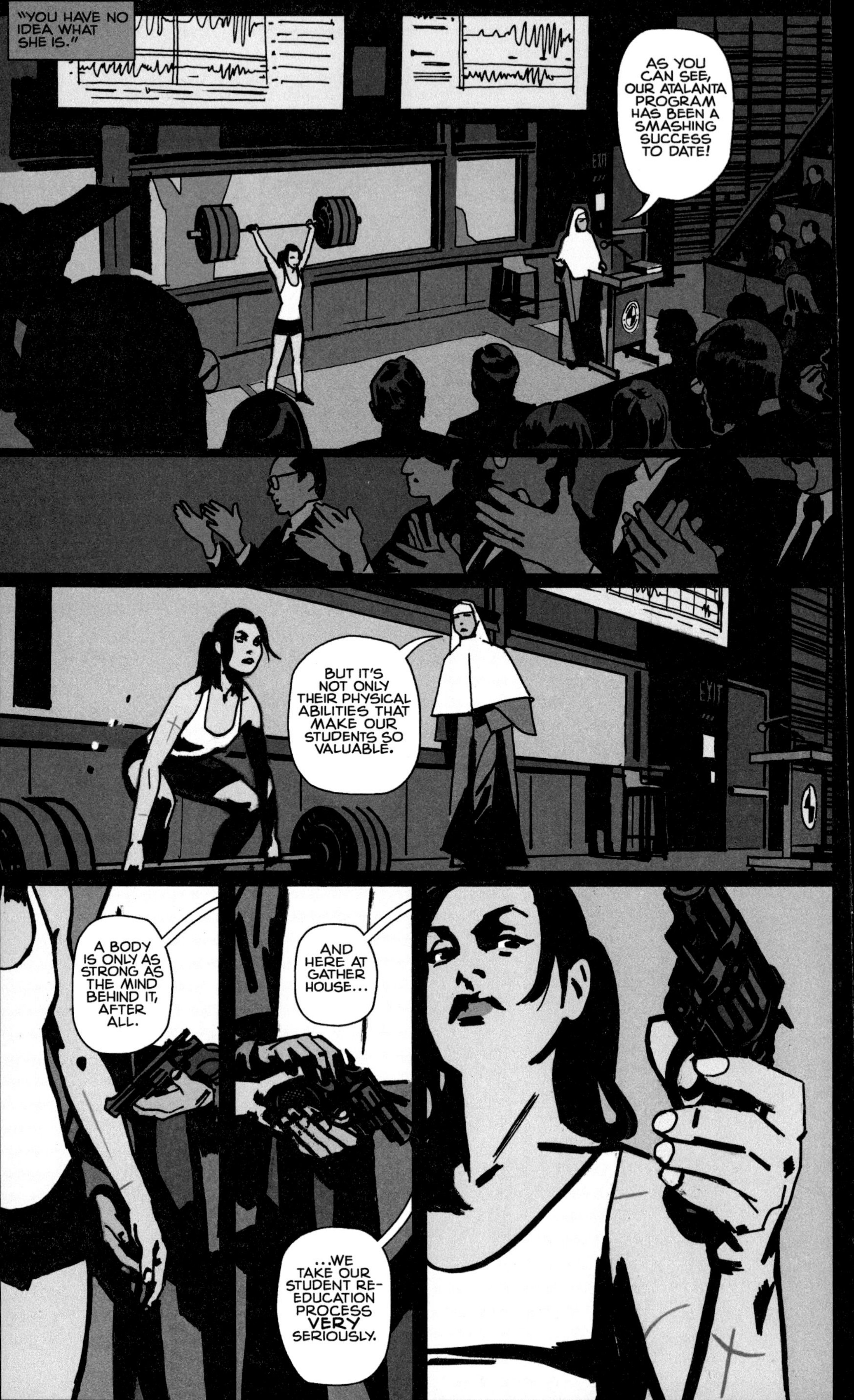
"YOU HAVE NO IDEA WHAT SHE IS."
AS YOU CAN SEE, OUR ATALANTA PROGRAM HAS BEEN A SMASHING SUCCESS TO DATE!
EXIT
BUT IT'S NOT ONLY THEIR PHYSICAL ABILITIES THAT MAKE OUR STUDENTS SO VALUABLE.
A BODY IS ONLY AS STRONG AS THE MIND BEHIND IT, AFTER ALL.
AND HERE AT GATHER HOUSE...
...WE TAKE OUR STUDENT RE-EDUCATION PROCESS VERY SERIOUSLY.

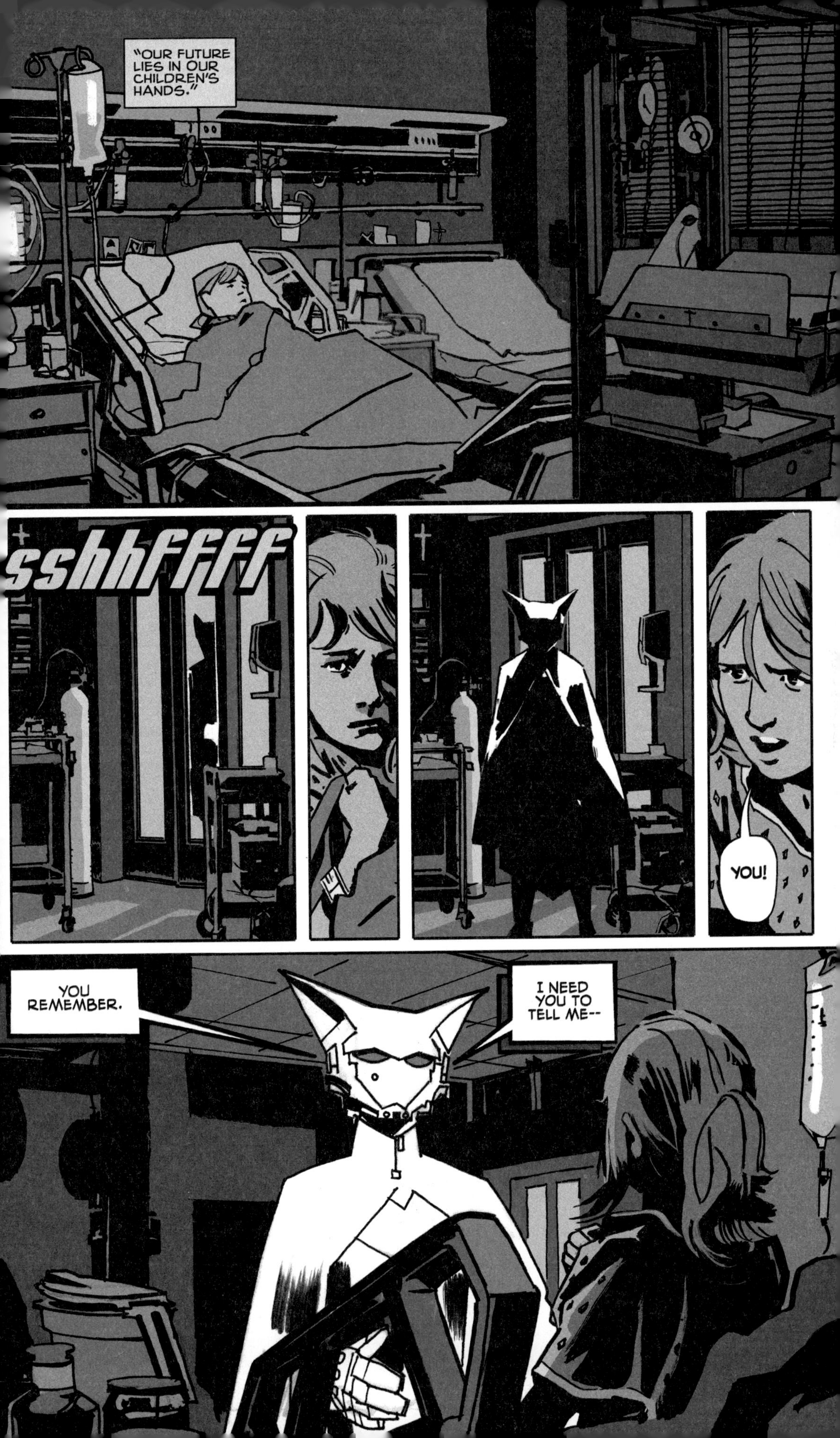
"OUR FUTURE LIES IN OUR CHILDREN'S HANDS."
sshhffff
YOU!
YOU REMEMBER.
I NEED YOU TO TELL ME--

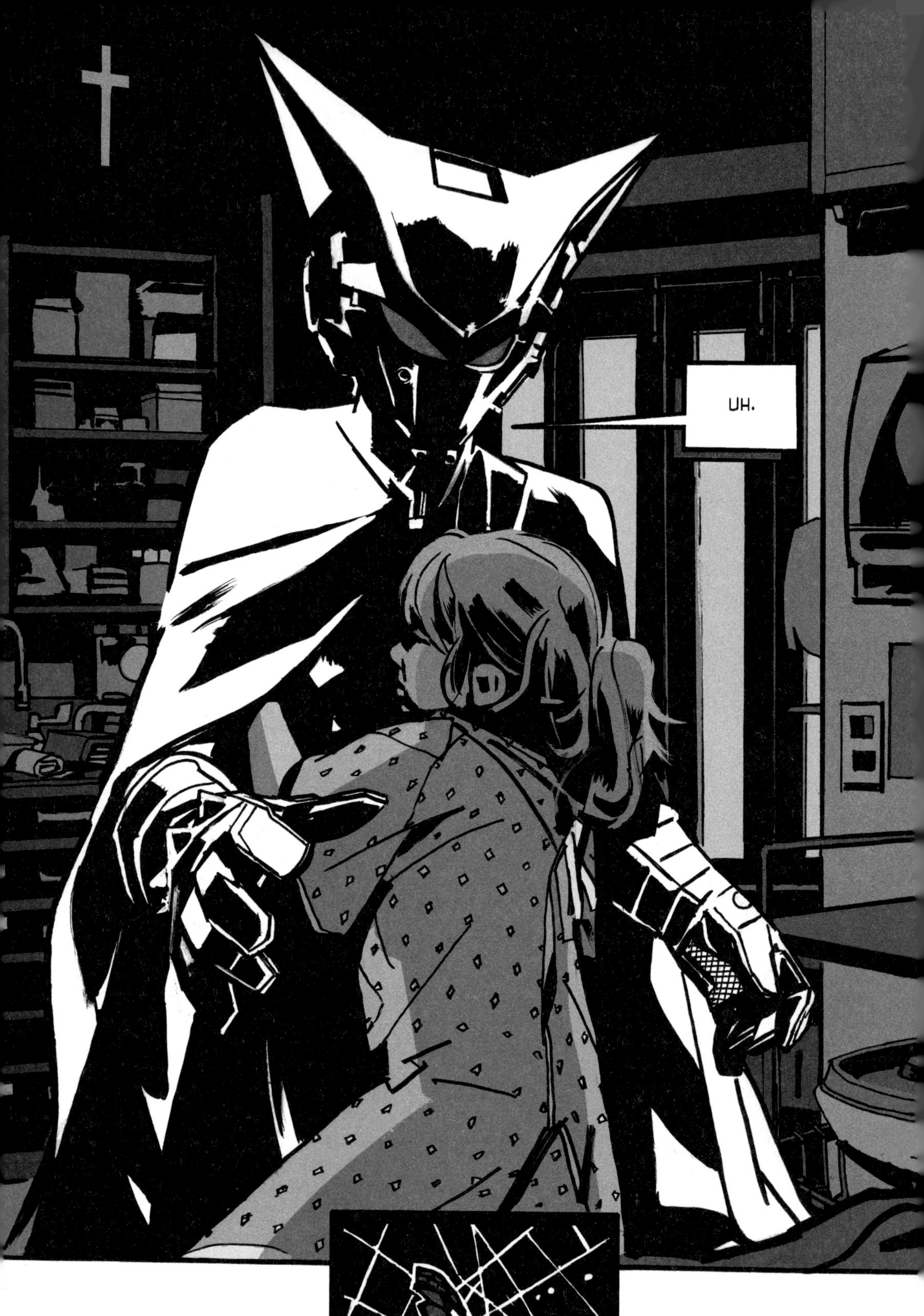
UH.

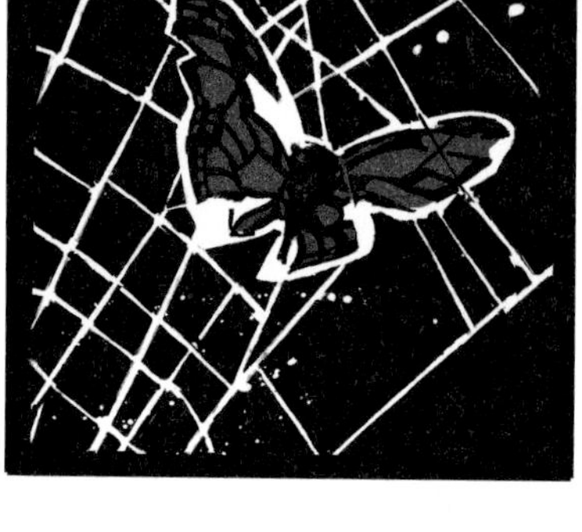

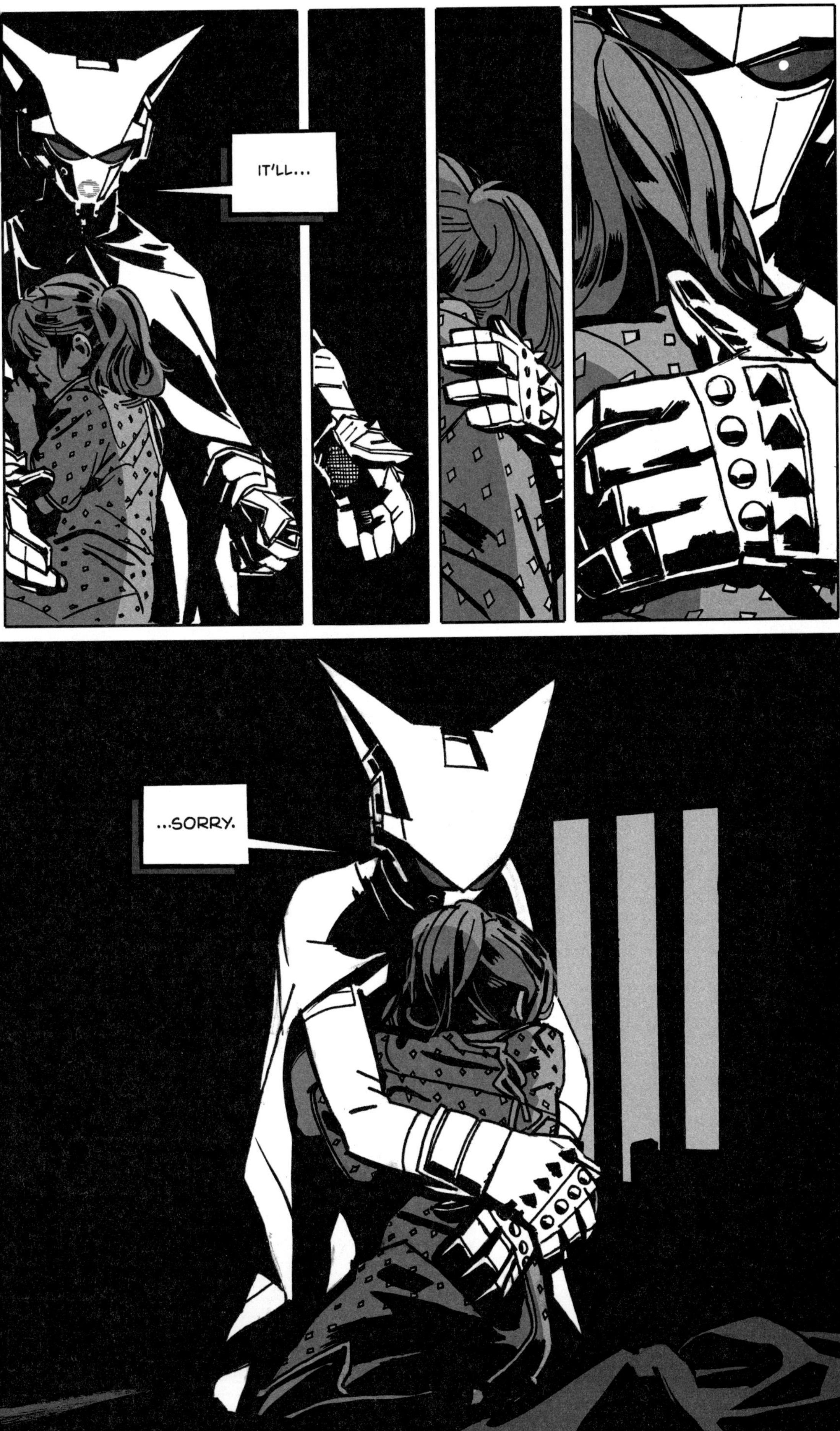
IT'LL...
...SORRY.

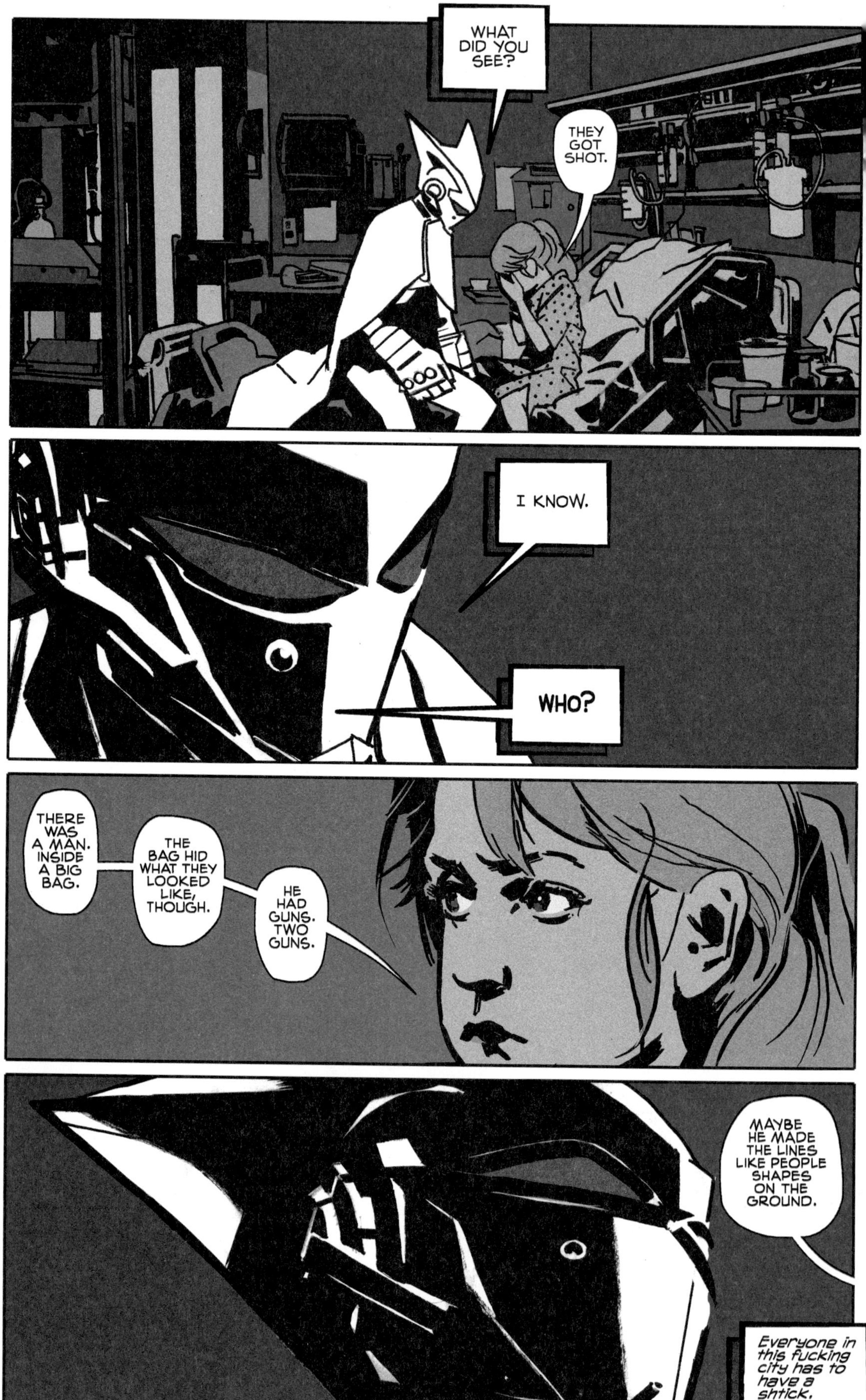
WHAT DID YOU SEE?
THEY GOT SHOT.
I KNOW.
WHO?
THERE WAS A MAN. INSIDE A BIG BAG.
THE BAG HID WHAT THEY LOOKED LIKE, THOUGH.
HE HAD GUNS. TWO GUNS.
MAYBE HE MADE THE LINES LIKE PEOPLE SHAPES ON THE GROUND.
Everyone in this fucking city has to have a shtick.

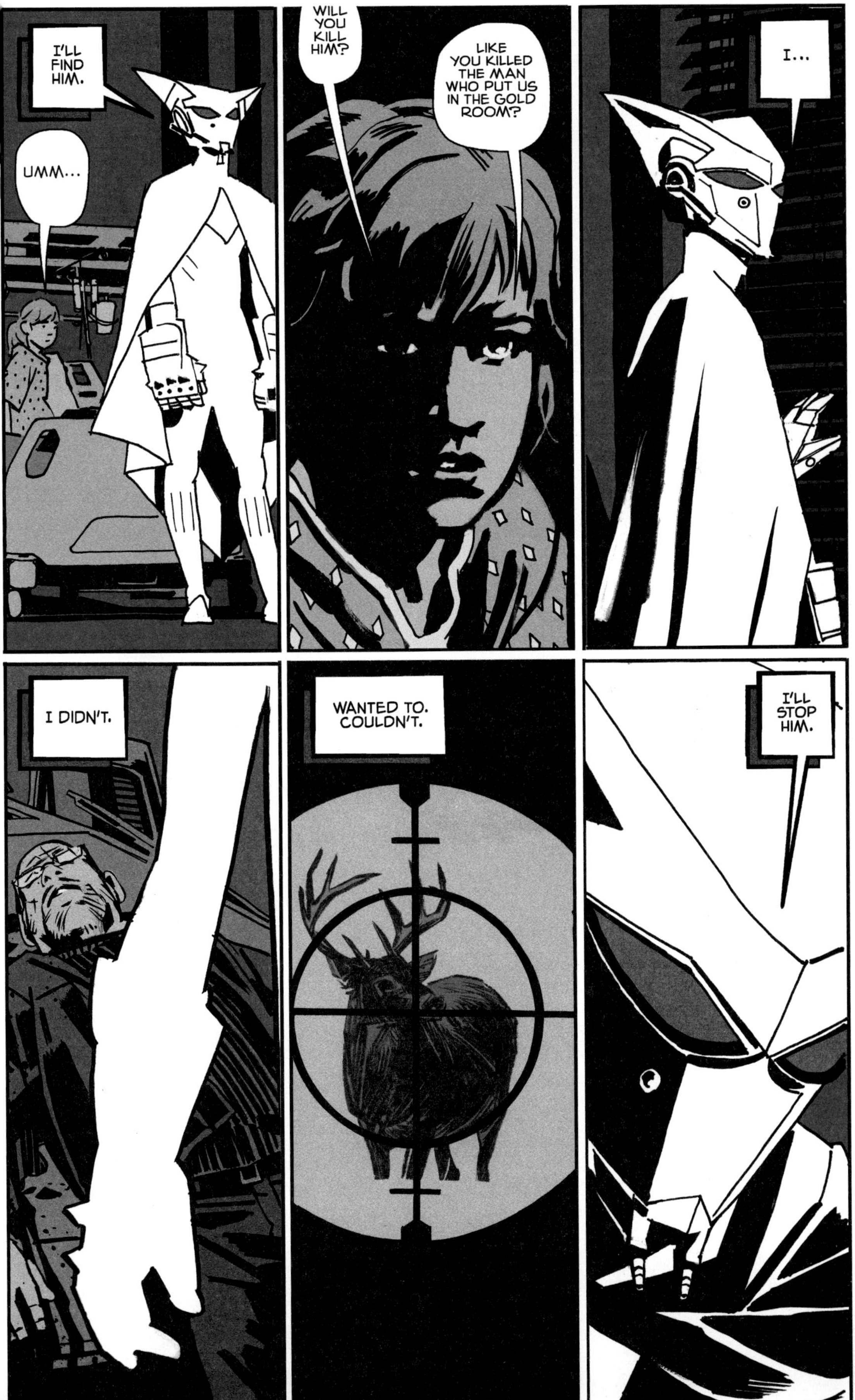
I'LL FIND HIM.
UMM...
WILL YOU KILL HIM?
LIKE YOU KILLED THE MAN WHO PUT US IN THE GOLD ROOM?
I...
I DIDN'T.
WANTED TO. COULDN'T.
I'LL STOP HIM.

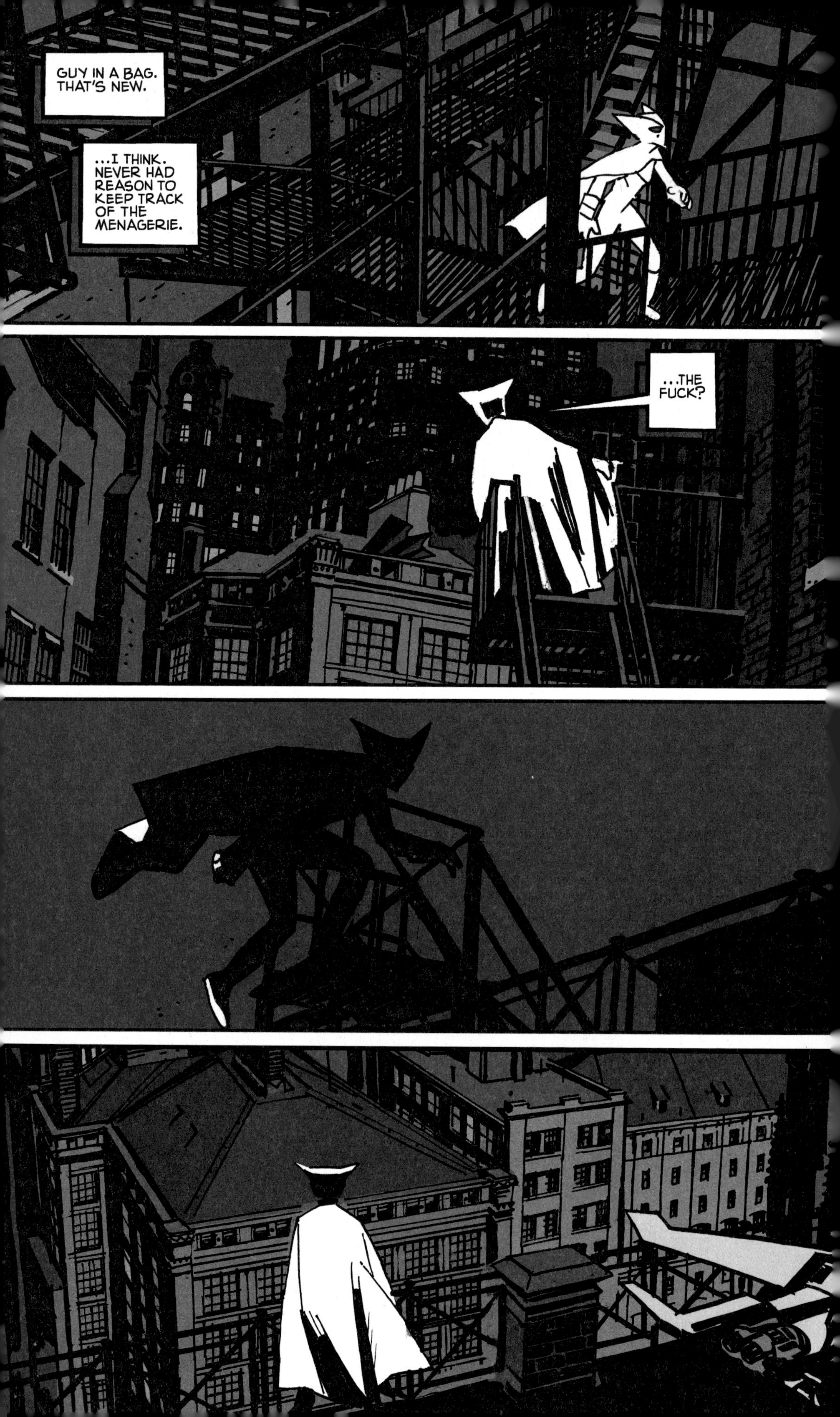
GUY IN A BAG. THAT'S NEW.
...I THINK. NEVER HAD REASON TO KEEP TRACK OF THE MENAGERIE.
...THE FUCK?

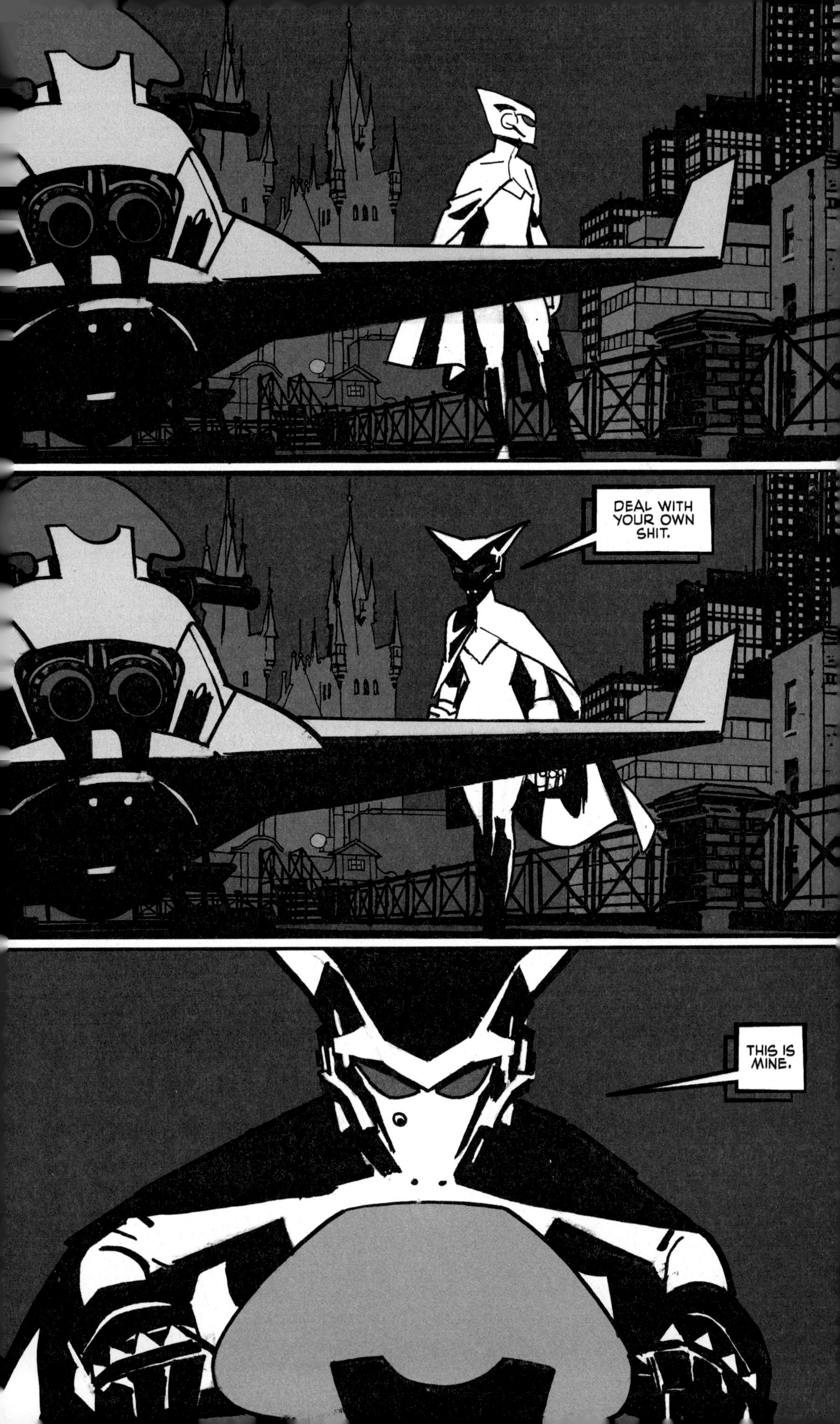
DEAL WITH YOUR OWN SHIT.
THIS IS MINE.

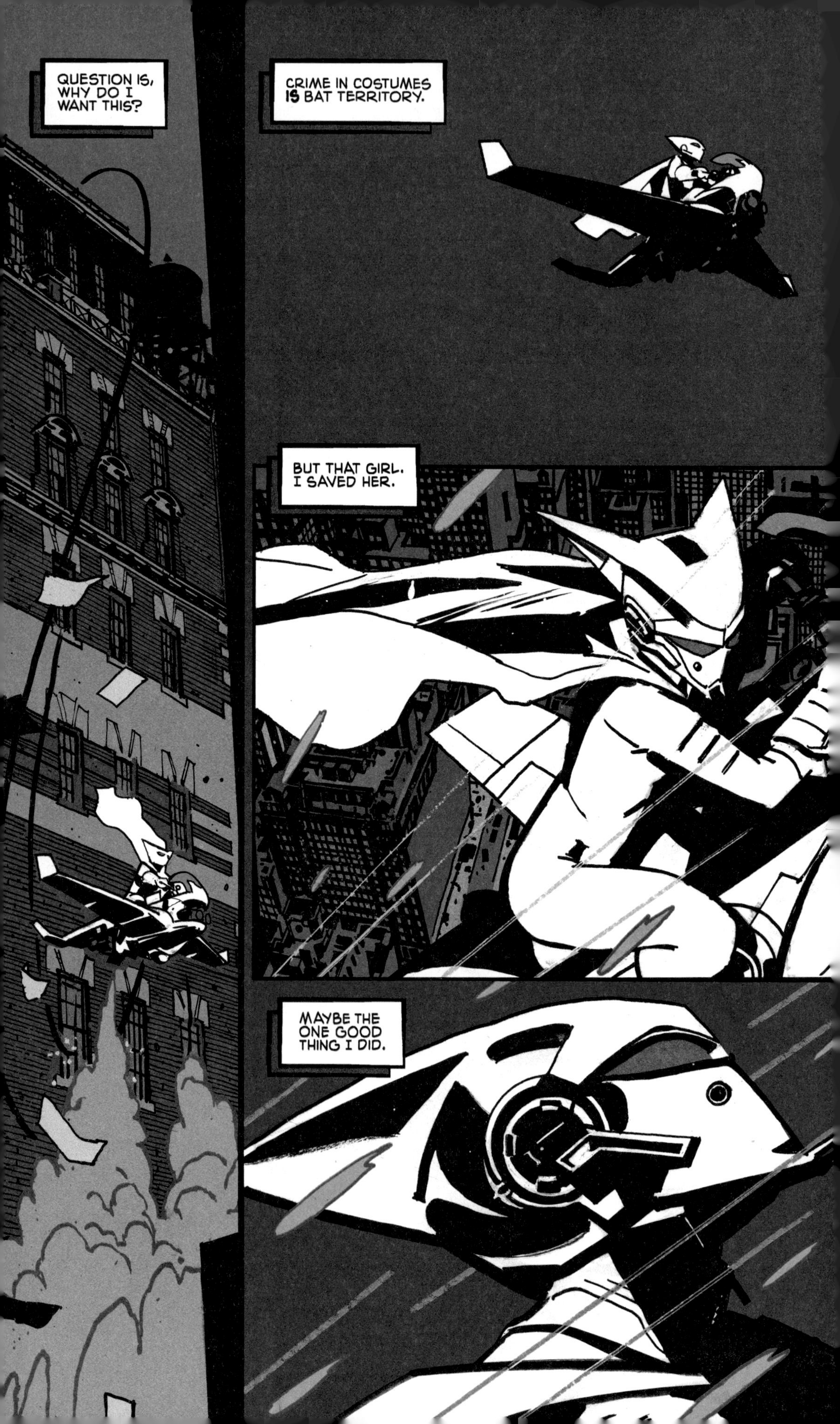
QUESTION IS, WHY DO I WANT THIS?
CRIME IN COSTUMES IS BAT TERRITORY.
BUT THAT GIRL. I SAVED HER.
MAYBE THE ONE GOOD THING I DID.

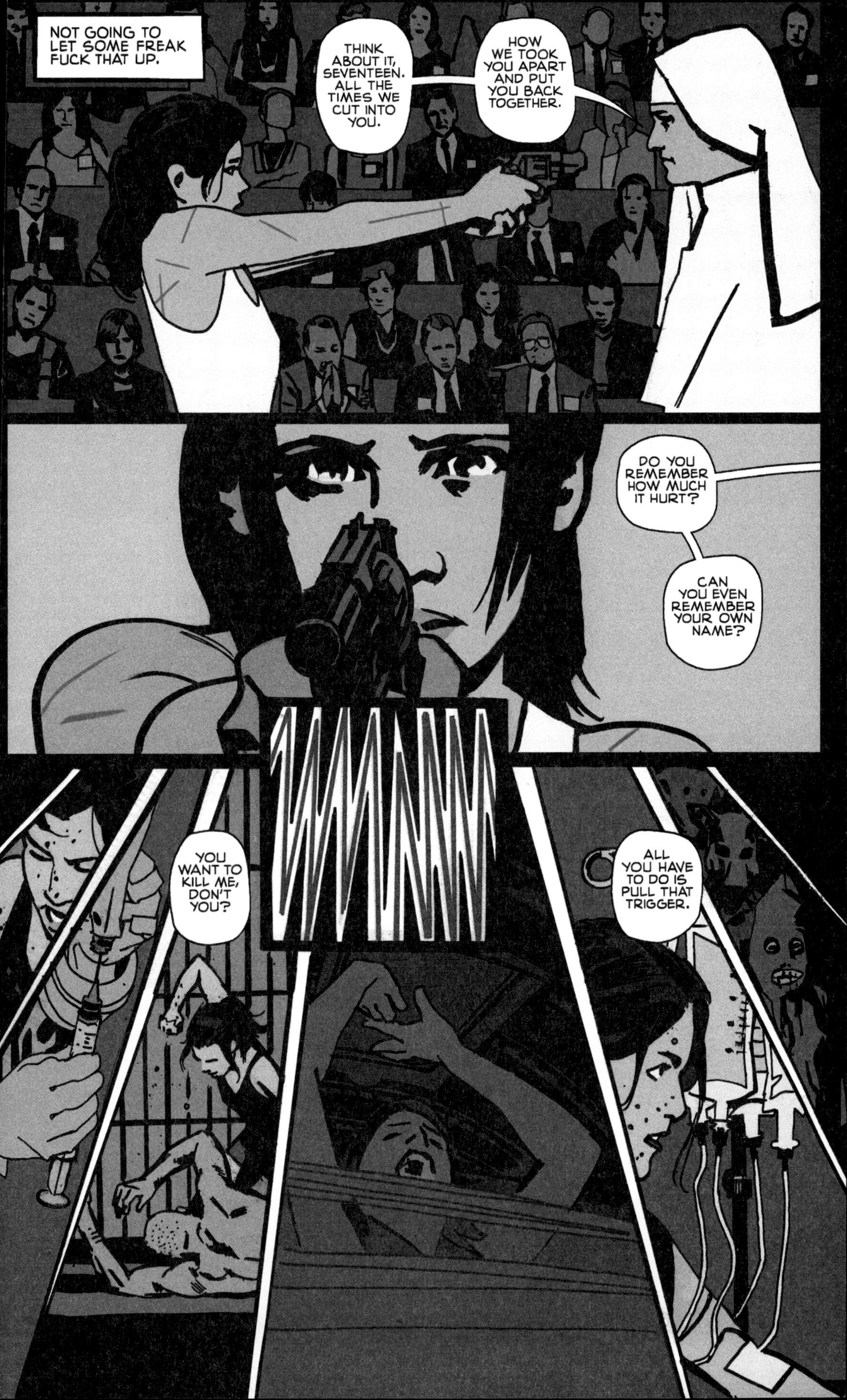
NOT GOING TO LET SOME FREAK FUCK THAT UP.
THINK ABOUT IT, SEVENTEEN. ALL THE TIMES WE CUT INTO YOU.
HOW WE TOOK YOU APART AND PUT YOU BACK TOGETHER.
DO YOU REMEMBER HOW MUCH IT HURT?
CAN YOU EVEN REMEMBER YOUR OWN NAME?
WNNN
YOU WANT TO KILL ME, DON'T YOU?
ALL YOU HAVE TO DO IS PULL THAT TRIGGER.

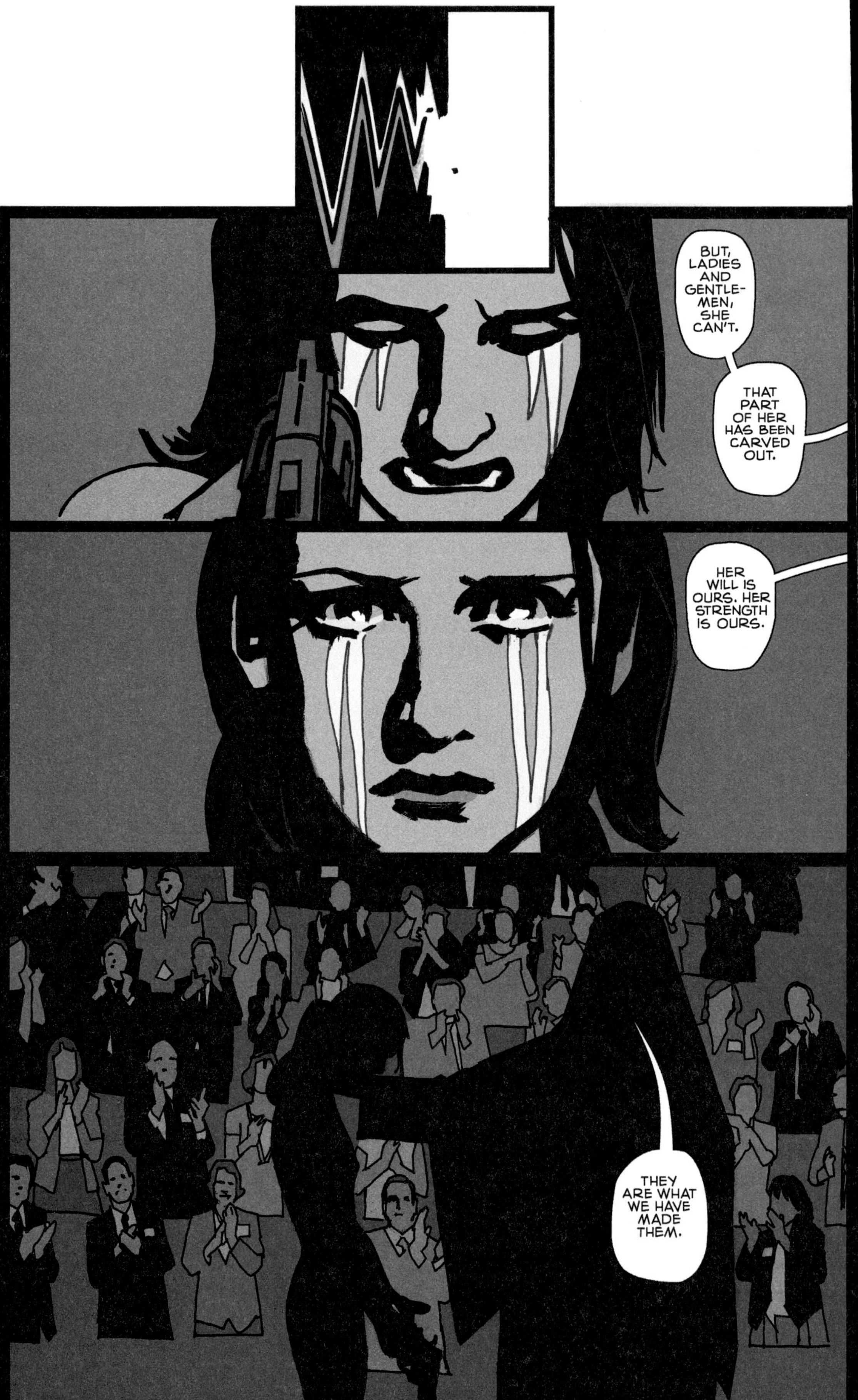
BUT, LADIES AND GENTLE-MEN, SHE CAN'T.
THAT PART OF HER HAS BEEN CARVED OUT.
HER WILL IS OURS. HER STRENGTH IS OURS.
THEY ARE WHAT WE HAVE MADE THEM.

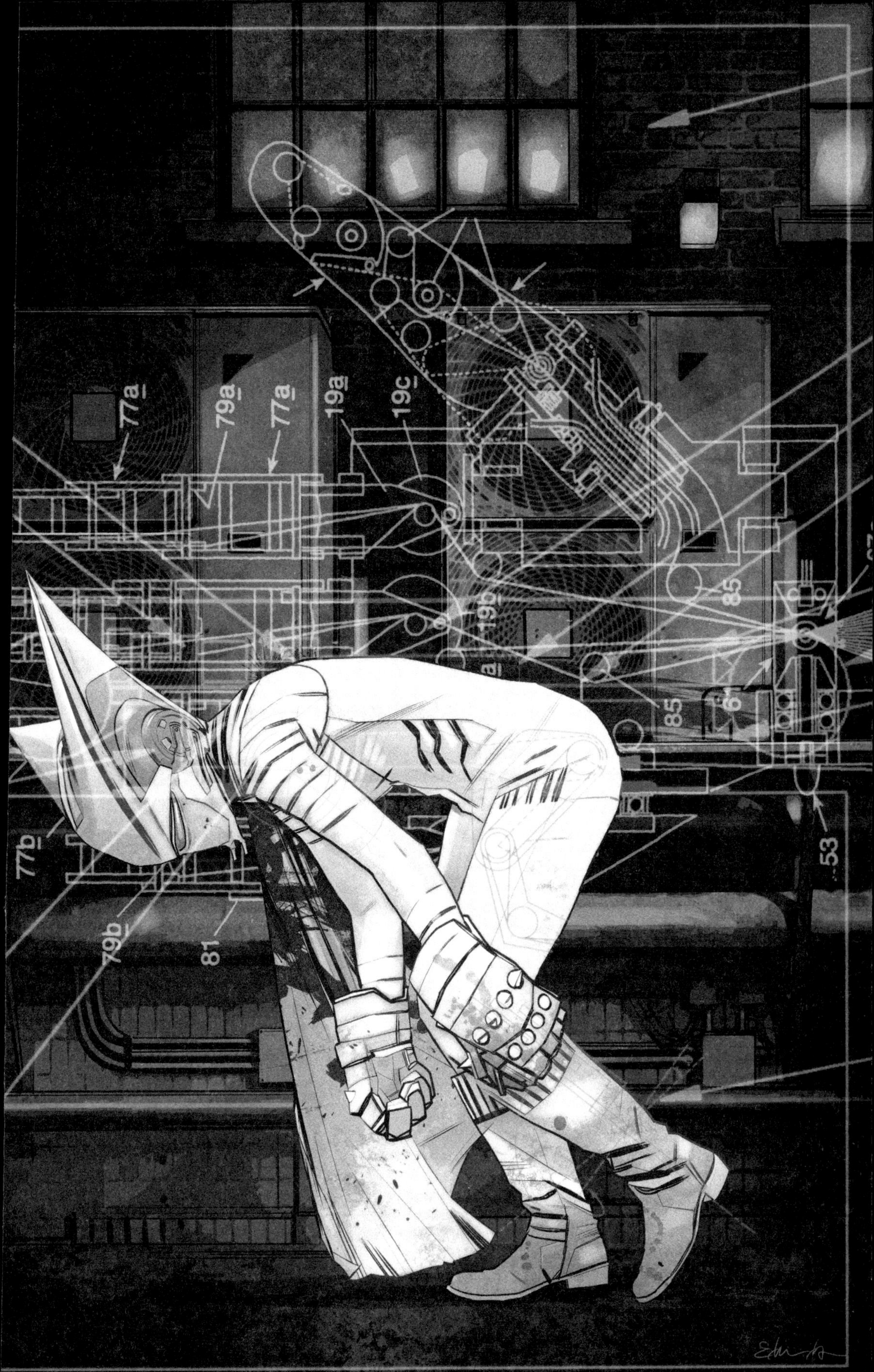
77a
79a
77a
19a
19c
19b
85
85
53
77b
79b
81

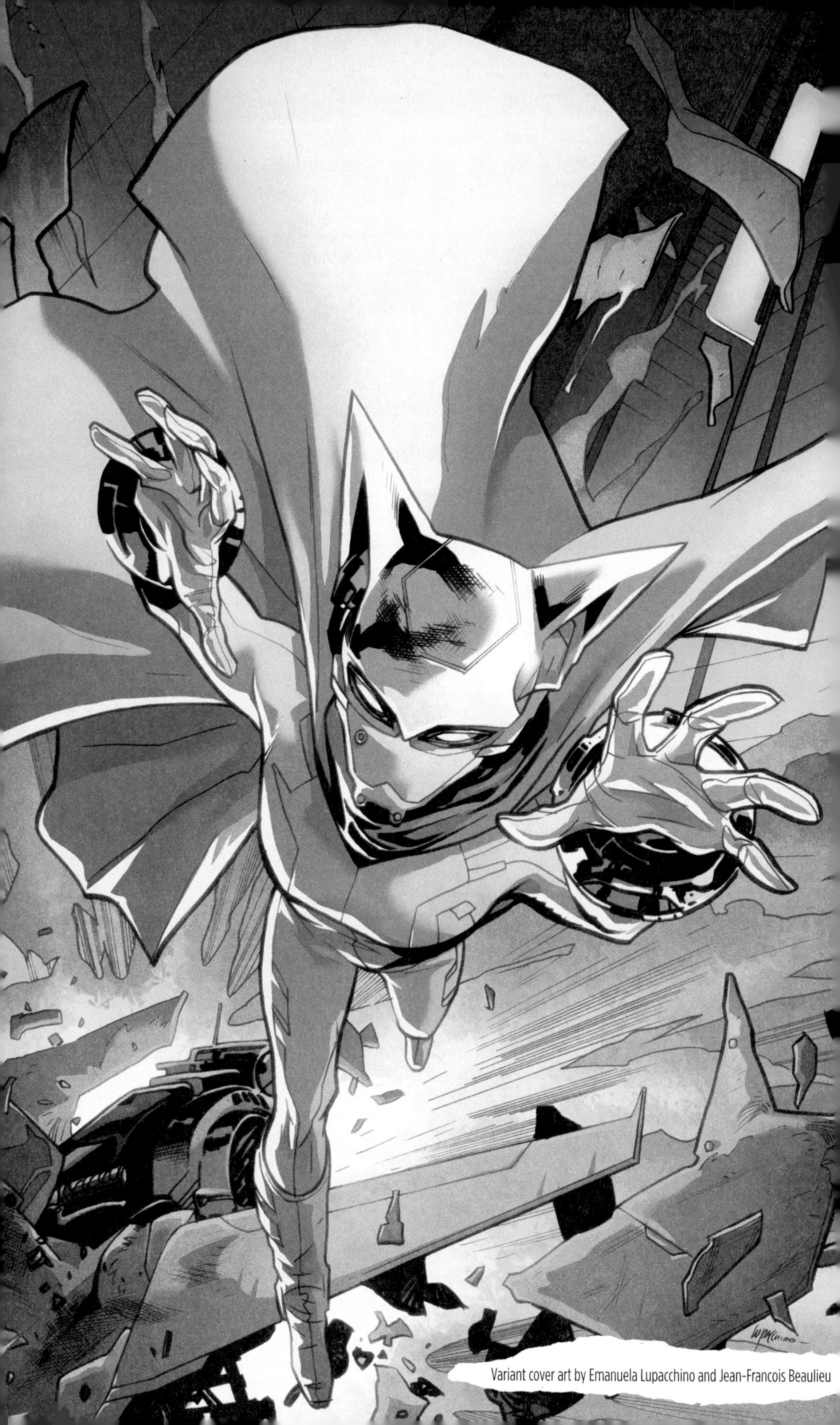

Variant cover art by Emanuela Lupacchino and Jean-Francois Beaulieu

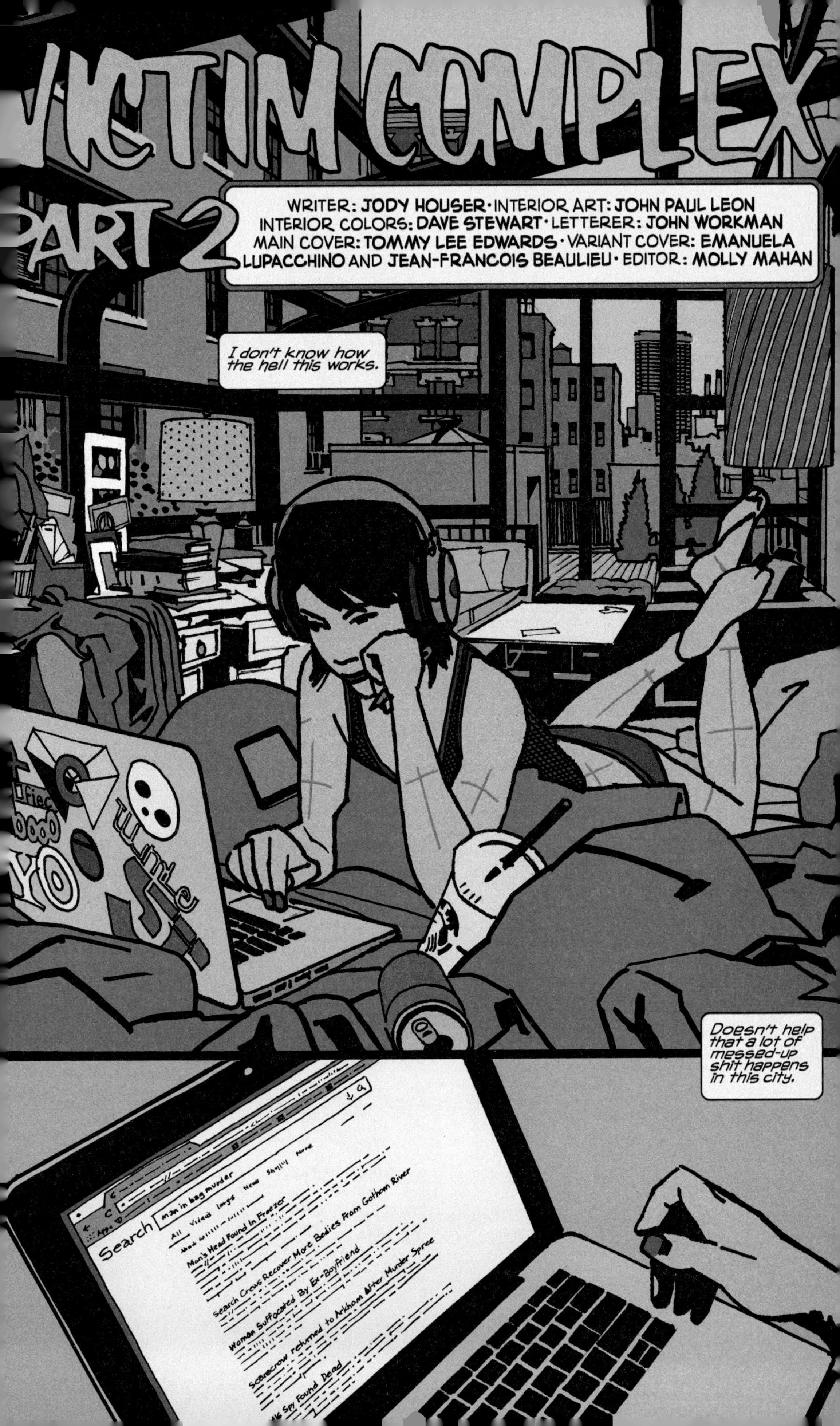
VICTIM COMPLEX
PART 2
WRITER: JODY HOUSER · INTERIOR ART: JOHN PAUL LEON
INTERIOR COLORS: DAVE STEWART · LETTERER: JOHN WORKMAN
MAIN COVER: TOMMY LEE EDWARDS · VARIANT COVER: EMANUELA LUPACCHINO AND JEAN-FRANCOIS BEAULIEU · EDITOR: MOLLY MAHAN
I don't know how the hell this works.
Doesn't help that a lot of messed-up shit happens in this city.
Search
man in bag murder
Man's Head Found In Freezer
Search Crews Recover More Bodies From Gotham River
Woman Suffocated By Ex-Boyfriend
Scarecrow returned to Arkham After Murder Spree

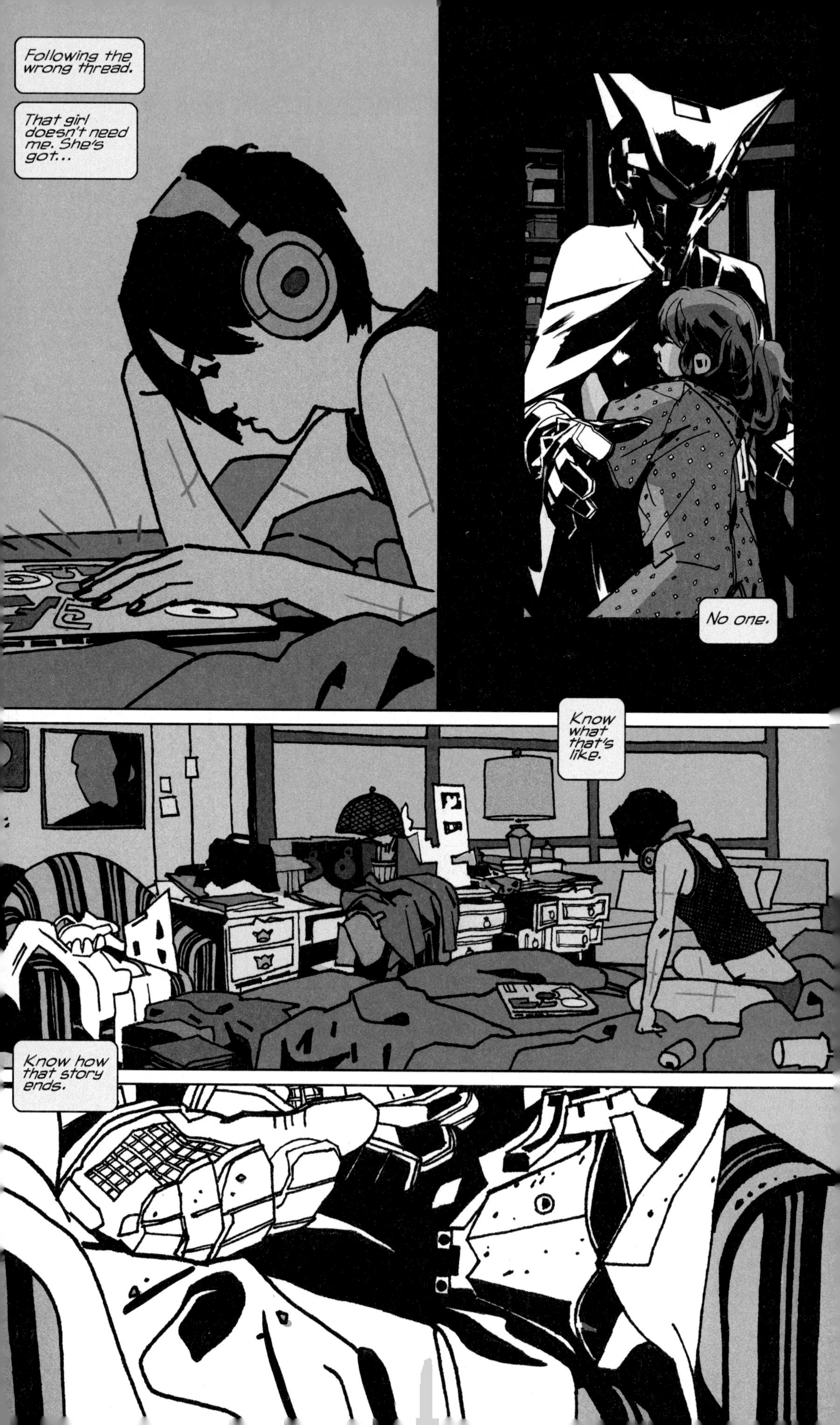
Following the wrong thread.
That girl doesn't need me. She's got...
No one.
Know what that's like.
Know how that story ends.

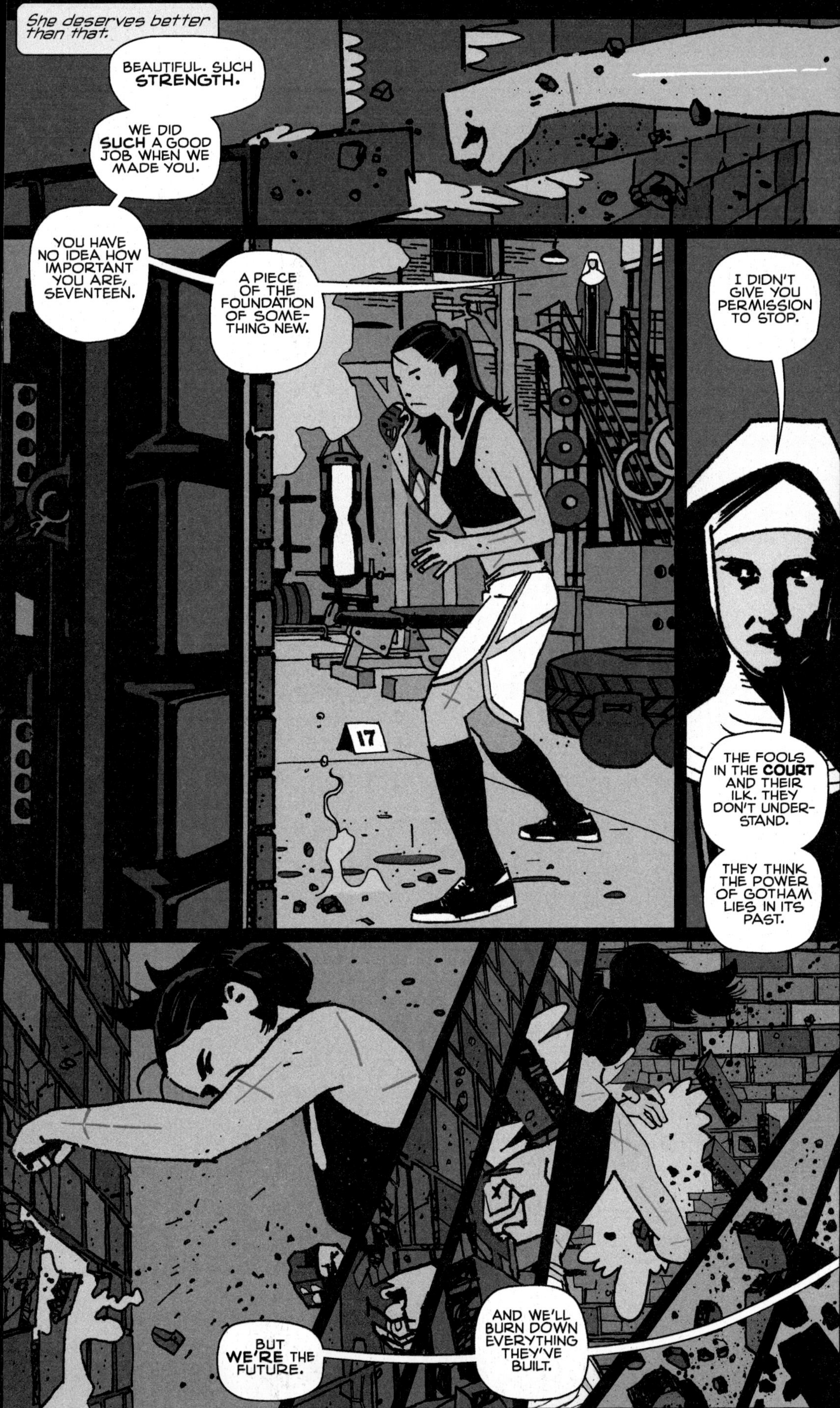
She deserves better than that.
BEAUTIFUL. SUCH STRENGTH.
WE DID SUCH A GOOD JOB WHEN WE MADE YOU.
YOU HAVE NO IDEA HOW IMPORTANT YOU ARE, SEVENTEEN.
A PIECE OF THE FOUNDATION OF SOME-THING NEW.
I DIDN'T GIVE YOU PERMISSION TO STOP.
17
THE FOOLS IN THE COURT AND THEIR ILK. THEY DON'T UNDER-STAND.
THEY THINK THE POWER OF GOTHAM LIES IN ITS PAST.
BUT WE'RE THE FUTURE.
AND WE'LL BURN DOWN EVERYTHING THEY'VE BUILT.

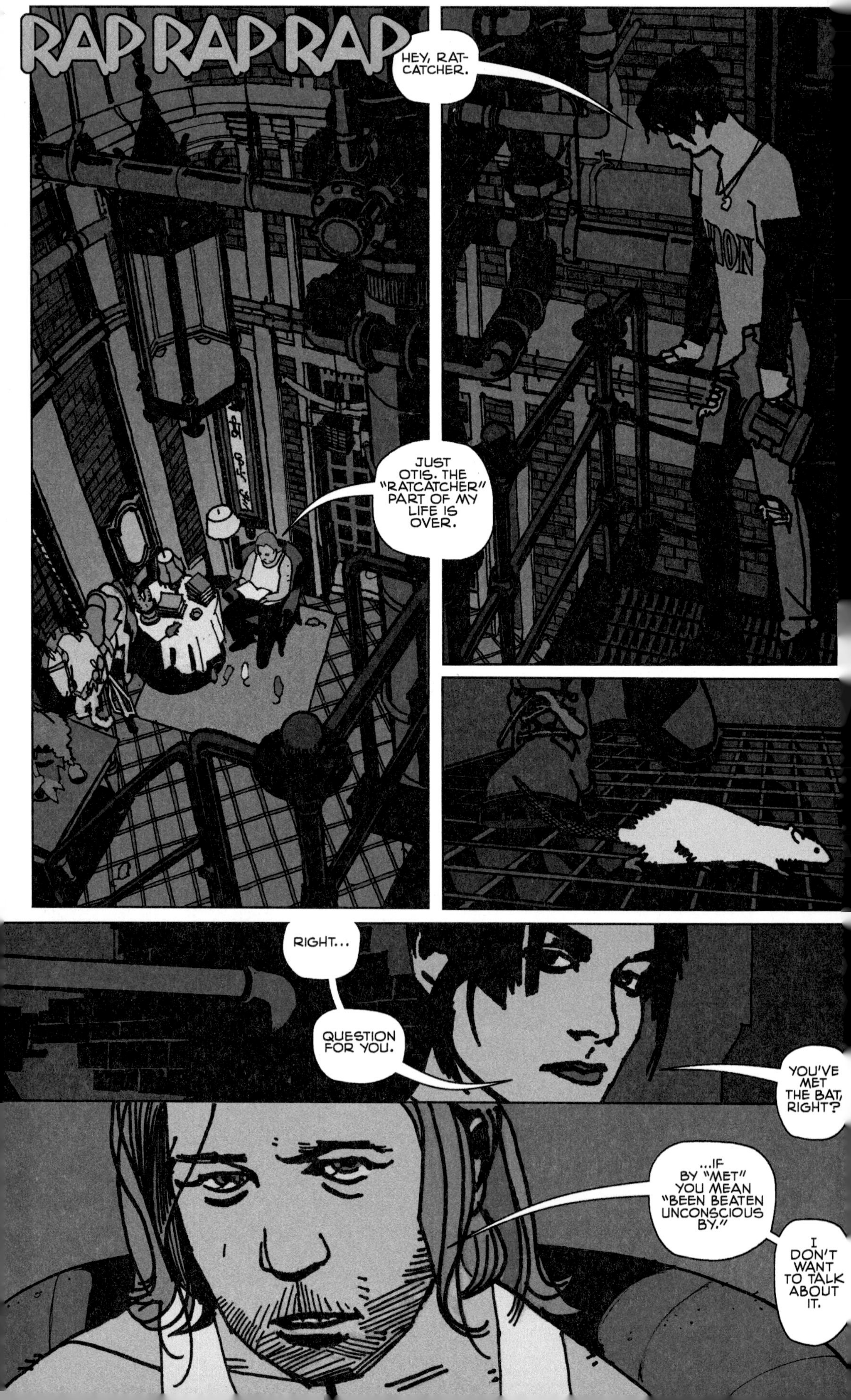
RAP RAP RAP
HEY, RAT-CATCHER.
JUST OTIS. THE "RATCATCHER" PART OF MY LIFE IS OVER.
RIGHT...
QUESTION FOR YOU.
YOU'VE MET THE BAT, RIGHT?
...IF BY "MET" YOU MEAN "BEEN BEATEN UNCONSCIOUS BY."
I DON'T WANT TO TALK ABOUT IT.

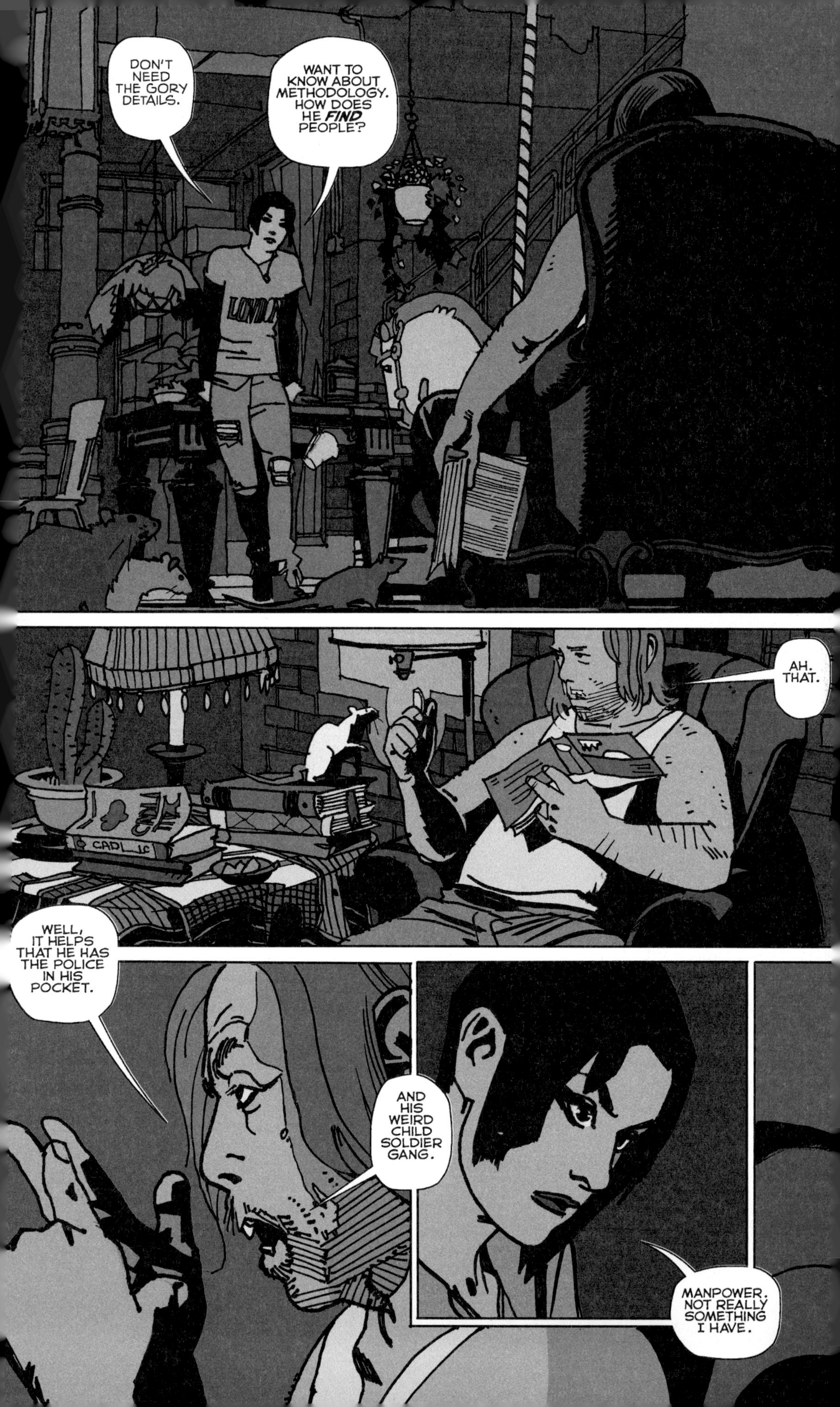
DON'T NEED THE GORY DETAILS.
WANT TO KNOW ABOUT METHODOLOGY. HOW DOES HE *FIND* PEOPLE?
AH. THAT.
WELL, IT HELPS THAT HE HAS THE POLICE IN HIS POCKET.
AND HIS WEIRD CHILD SOLDIER GANG.
MANPOWER. NOT REALLY SOMETHING I HAVE.

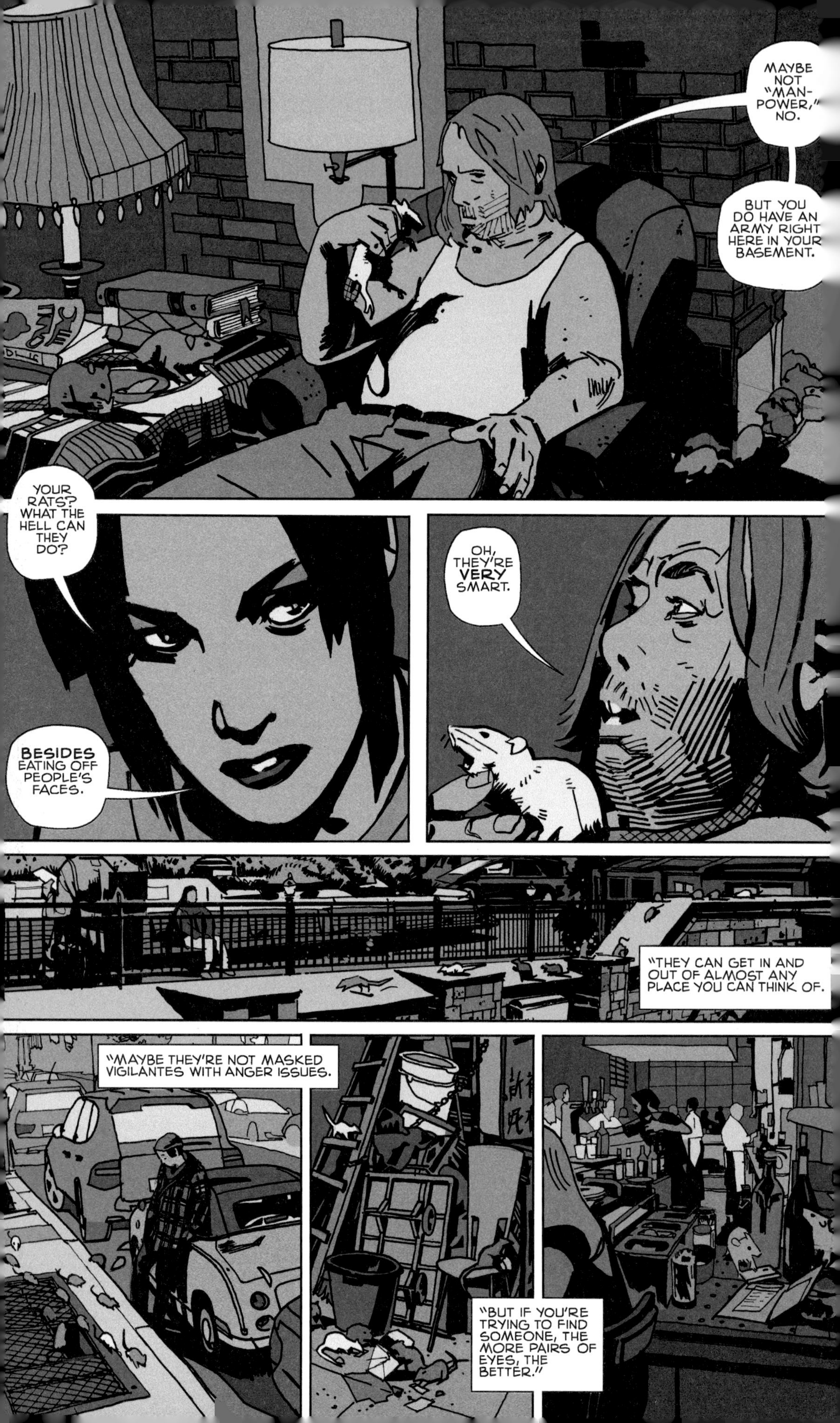
MAYBE NOT "MAN-POWER," NO.
BUT YOU DO HAVE AN ARMY RIGHT HERE IN YOUR BASEMENT.
YOUR RATS? WHAT THE HELL CAN THEY DO?
BESIDES EATING OFF PEOPLE'S FACES.
OH, THEY'RE VERY SMART.
"THEY CAN GET IN AND OUT OF ALMOST ANY PLACE YOU CAN THINK OF.
"MAYBE THEY'RE NOT MASKED VIGILANTES WITH ANGER ISSUES.
"BUT IF YOU'RE TRYING TO FIND SOMEONE, THE MORE PAIRS OF EYES, THE BETTER."

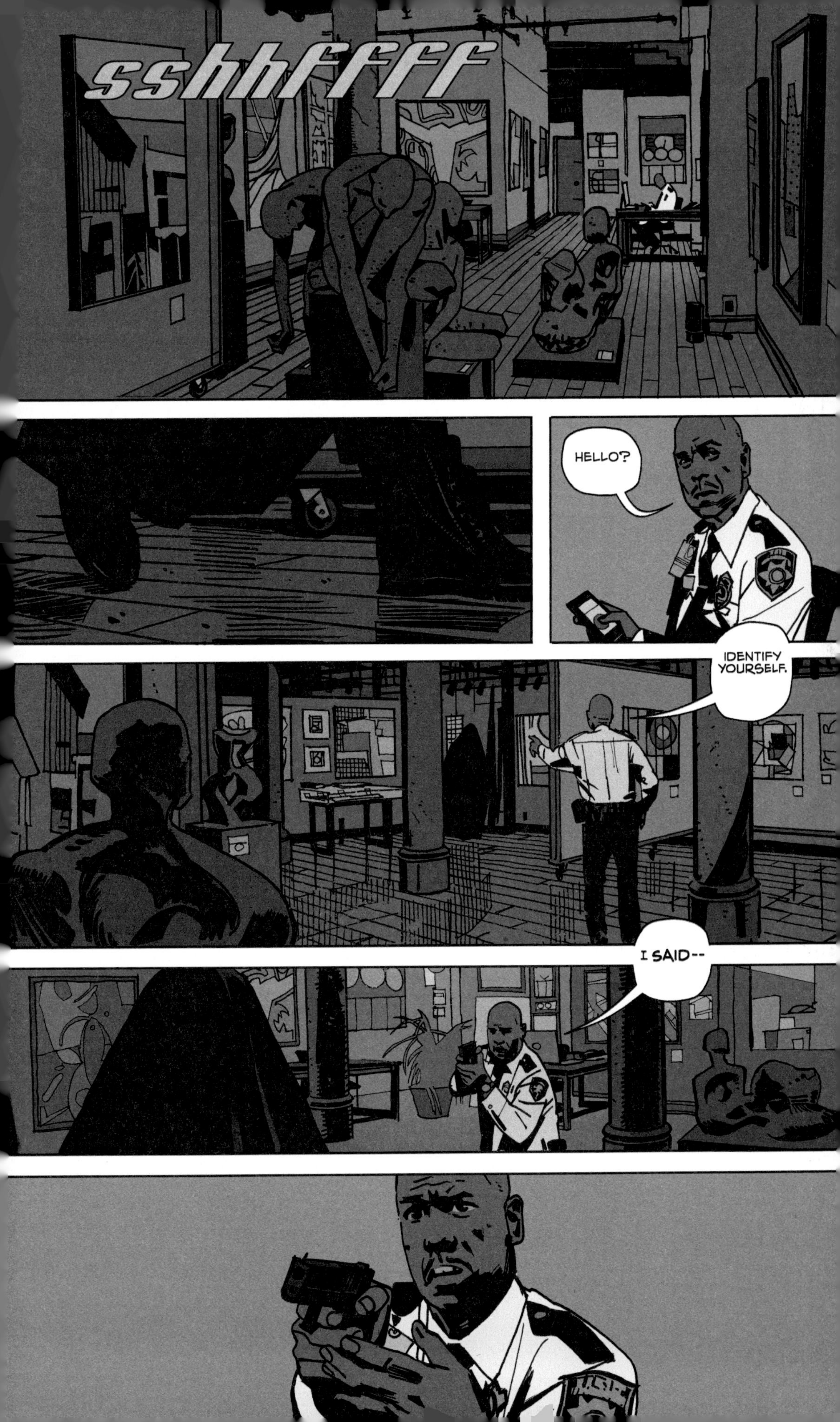
sshhffff
HELLO?
IDENTIFY YOURSELF.
I SAID--

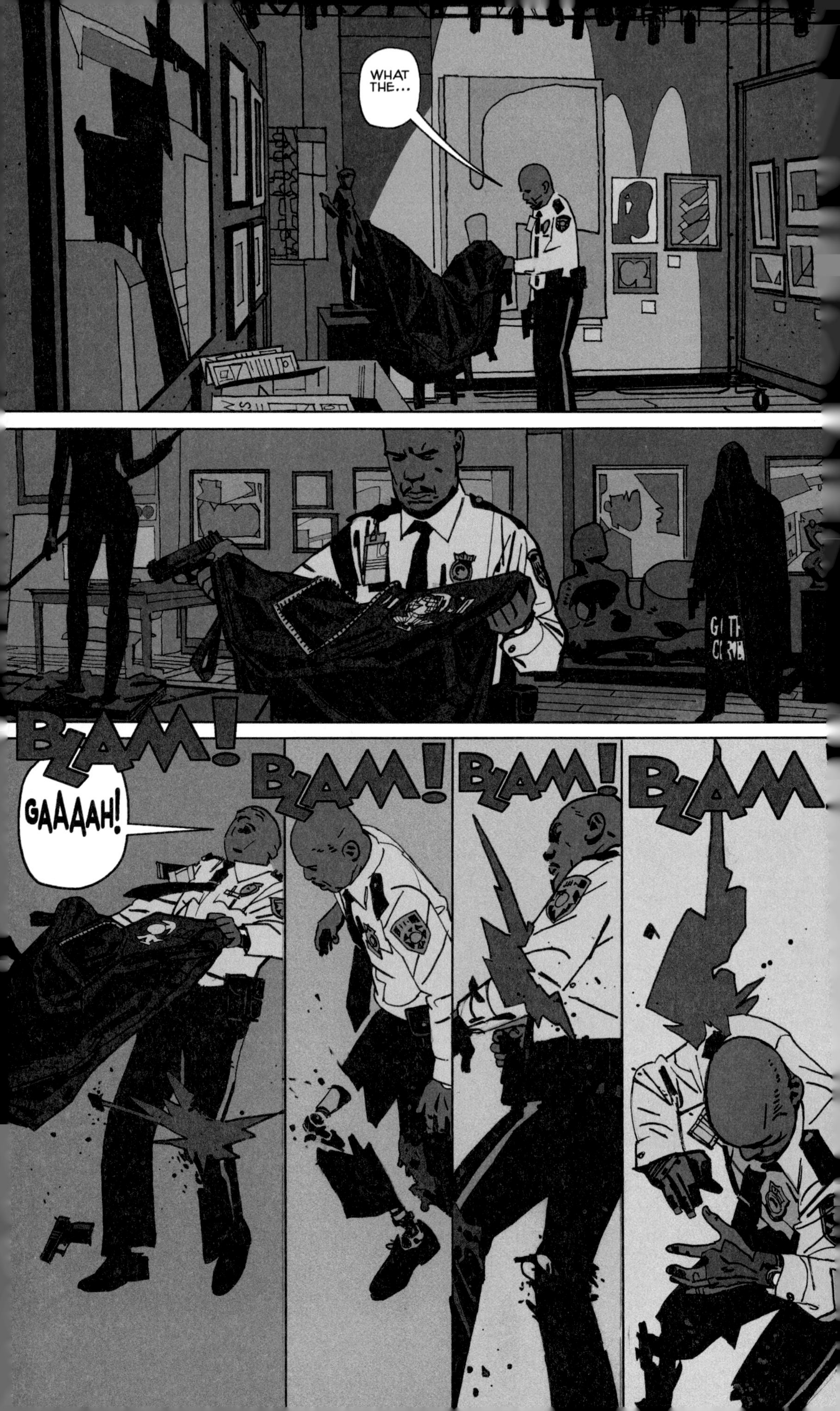
WHAT THE...
BLAM!
GAAAAH!
BLAM!
BLAM!
BLAM

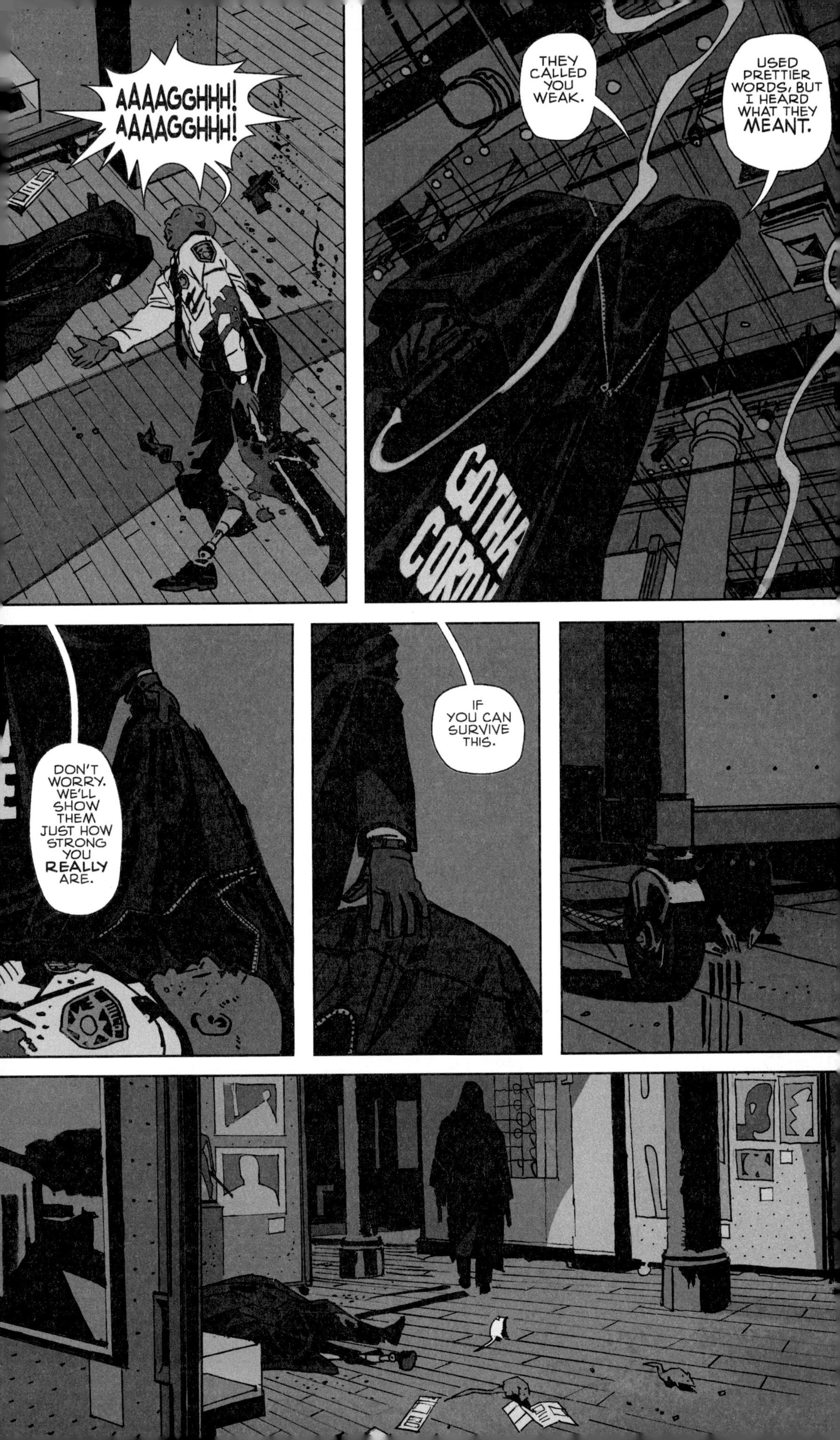
AAAAGGHHH! AAAAGGHHH!
THEY CALLED YOU WEAK.
USED PRETTIER WORDS, BUT I HEARD WHAT THEY MEANT.
DON'T WORRY. WE'LL SHOW THEM JUST HOW STRONG YOU REALLY ARE.
IF YOU CAN SURVIVE THIS.

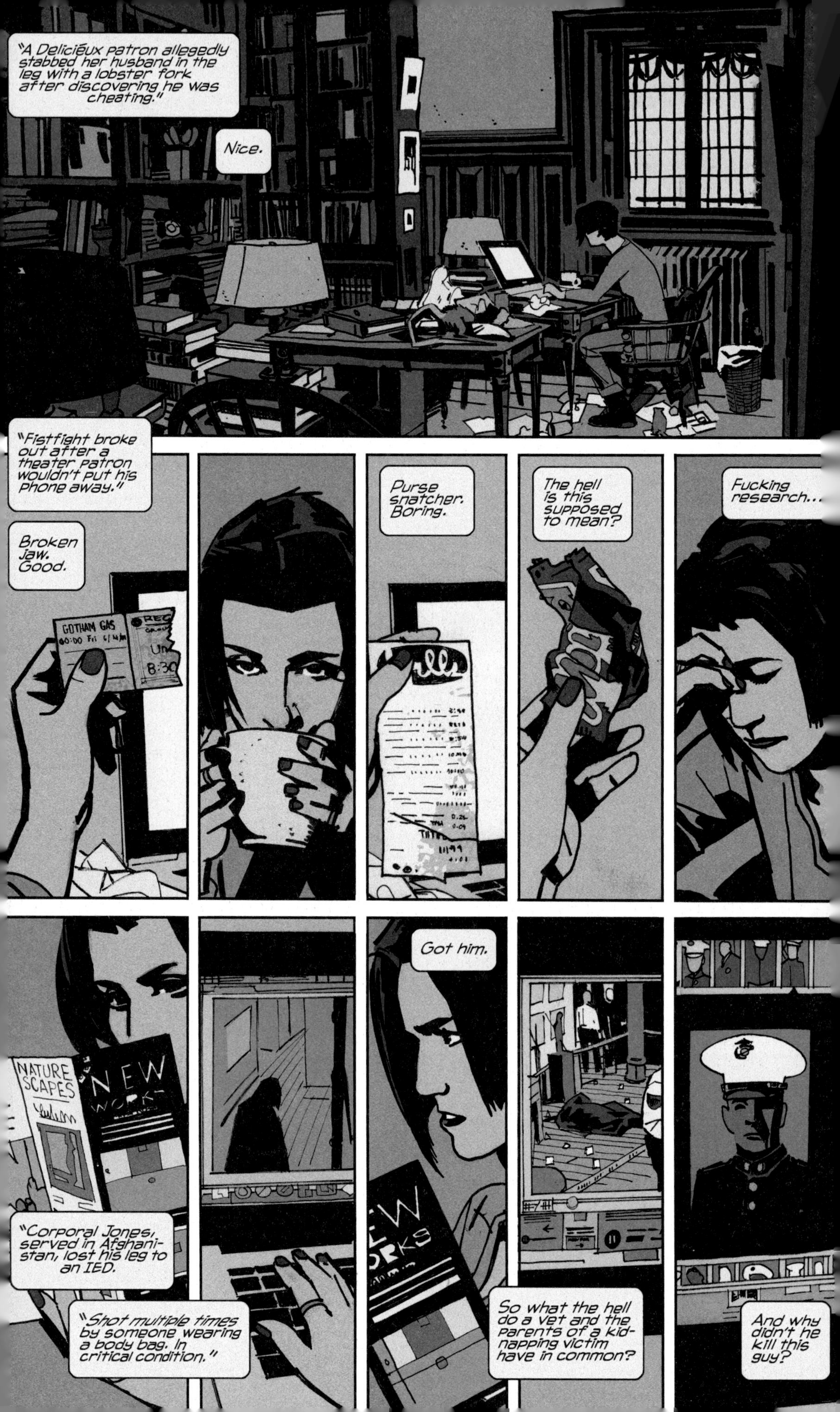
"A Deliciéux patron allegedly stabbed her husband in the leg with a lobster fork after discovering he was cheating."
Nice.
"Fistfight broke out after a theater patron wouldn't put his phone away."
Broken jaw. Good.
GOTHAM GAS
Purse snatcher. Boring.
The hell is this supposed to mean?
Fucking research...
NATURE SCAPES
NEW WORKS
"Corporal Jones, served in Afghanistan, lost his leg to an IED.
"Shot multiple times by someone wearing a body bag. In critical condition."
Got him.
So what the hell do a vet and the parents of a kidnapping victim have in common?
And why didn't he kill this guy?

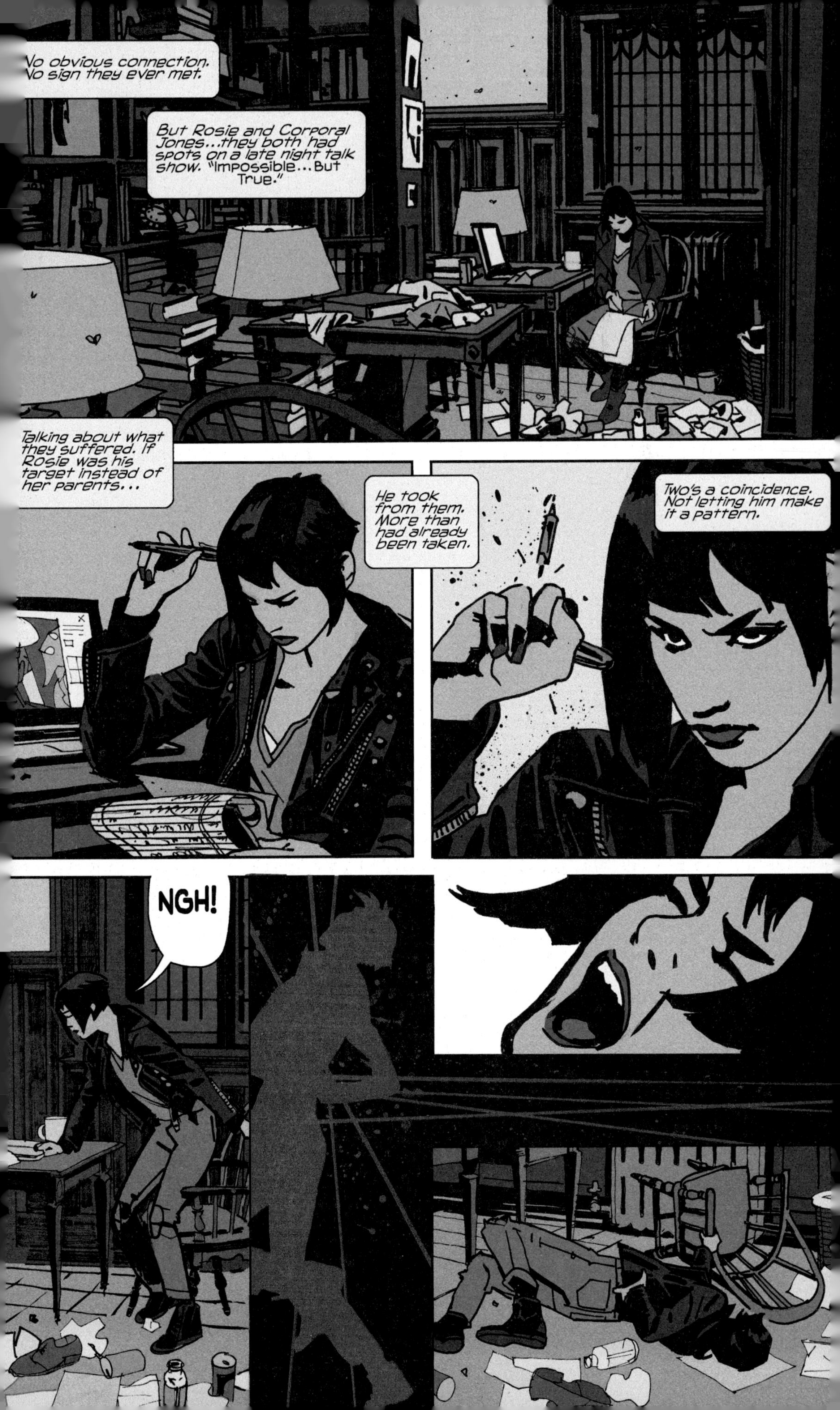
No obvious connection. No sign they ever met.
But Rosie and Corporal Jones...they both had spots on a late night talk show. "Impossible...But True."
Talking about what they suffered. If Rosie was his target instead of her parents...
He took from them. More than had already been taken.
Two's a coincidence. Not letting him make it a pattern.
NGH!

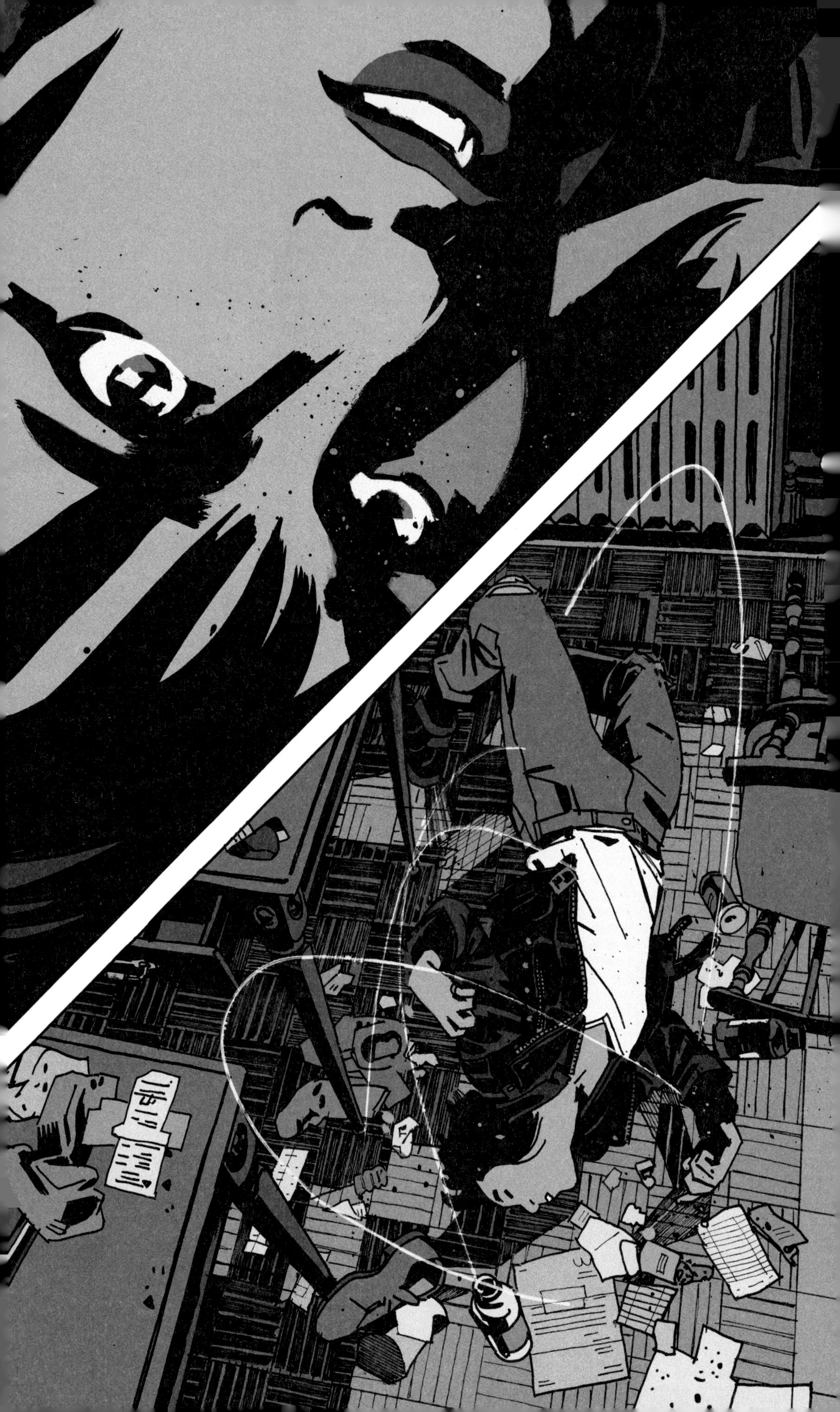

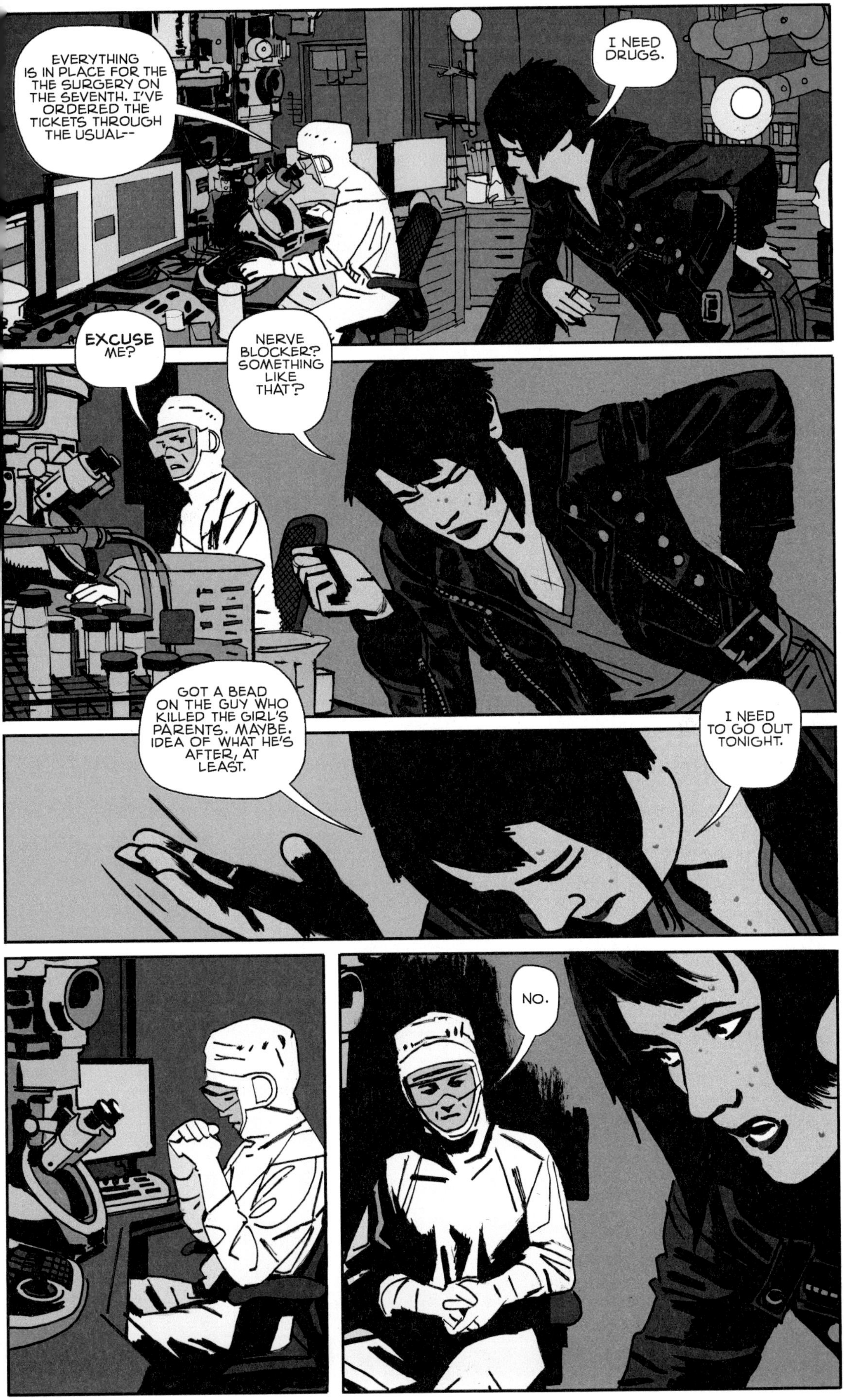
EVERYTHING IS IN PLACE FOR THE THE SURGERY ON THE SEVENTH. I'VE ORDERED THE TICKETS THROUGH THE USUAL--
I NEED DRUGS.
EXCUSE ME?
NERVE BLOCKER? SOMETHING LIKE THAT?
GOT A BEAD ON THE GUY WHO KILLED THE GIRL'S PARENTS. MAYBE. IDEA OF WHAT HE'S AFTER, AT LEAST.
I NEED TO GO OUT TONIGHT.
NO.

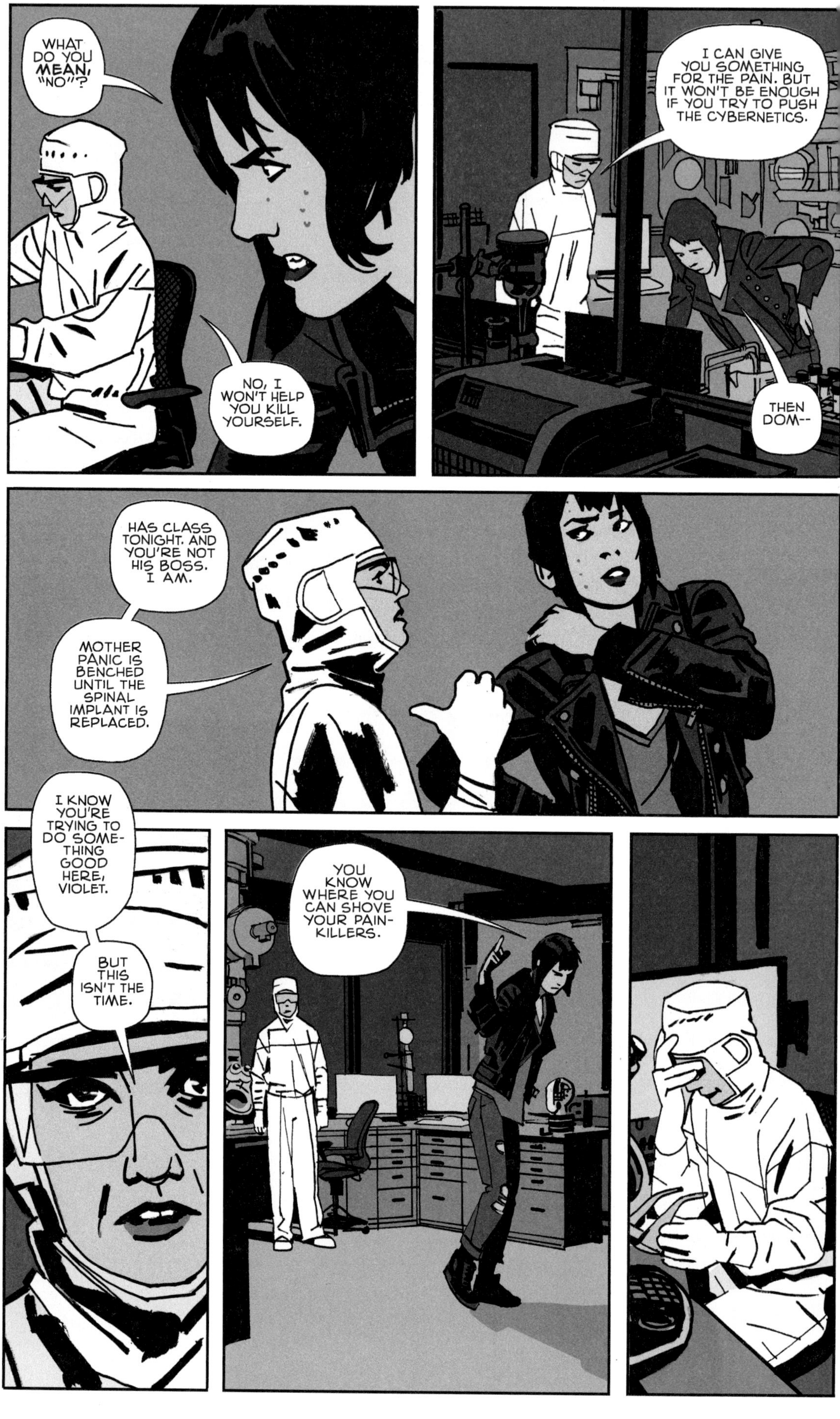
WHAT DO YOU MEAN, "NO"?
NO, I WON'T HELP YOU KILL YOURSELF.
I CAN GIVE YOU SOMETHING FOR THE PAIN. BUT IT WON'T BE ENOUGH IF YOU TRY TO PUSH THE CYBERNETICS.
THEN DOM--
HAS CLASS TONIGHT. AND YOU'RE NOT HIS BOSS. I AM.
MOTHER PANIC IS BENCHED UNTIL THE SPINAL IMPLANT IS REPLACED.
I KNOW YOU'RE TRYING TO DO SOME-THING GOOD HERE, VIOLET.
BUT THIS ISN'T THE TIME.
YOU KNOW WHERE YOU CAN SHOVE YOUR PAIN-KILLERS.

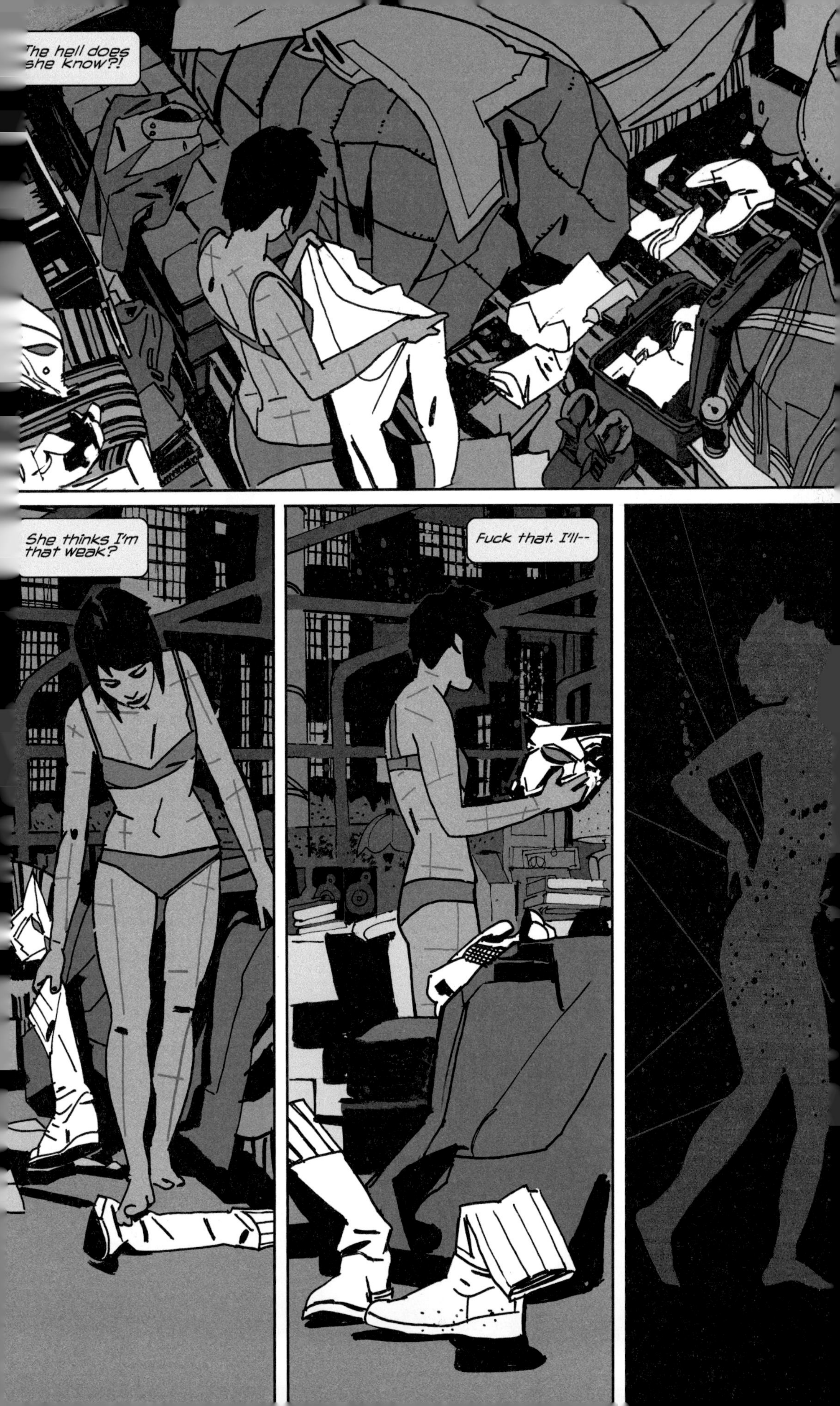
The hell does she know?!
She thinks I'm that weak?
Fuck that. I'll--

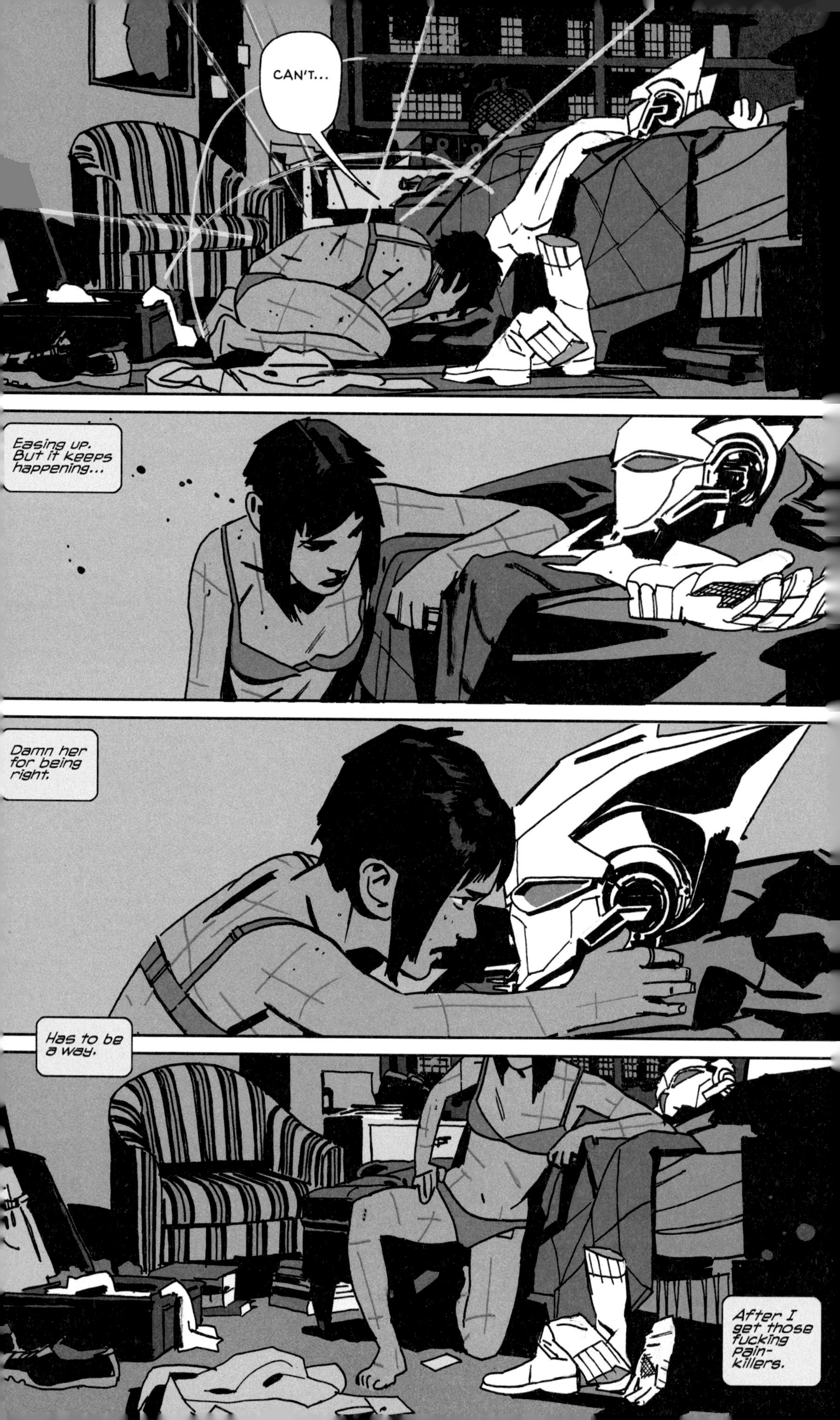
CAN'T...
Easing up. But it keeps happening...
Damn her for being right.
Has to be a way.
After I get those fucking pain-killers.

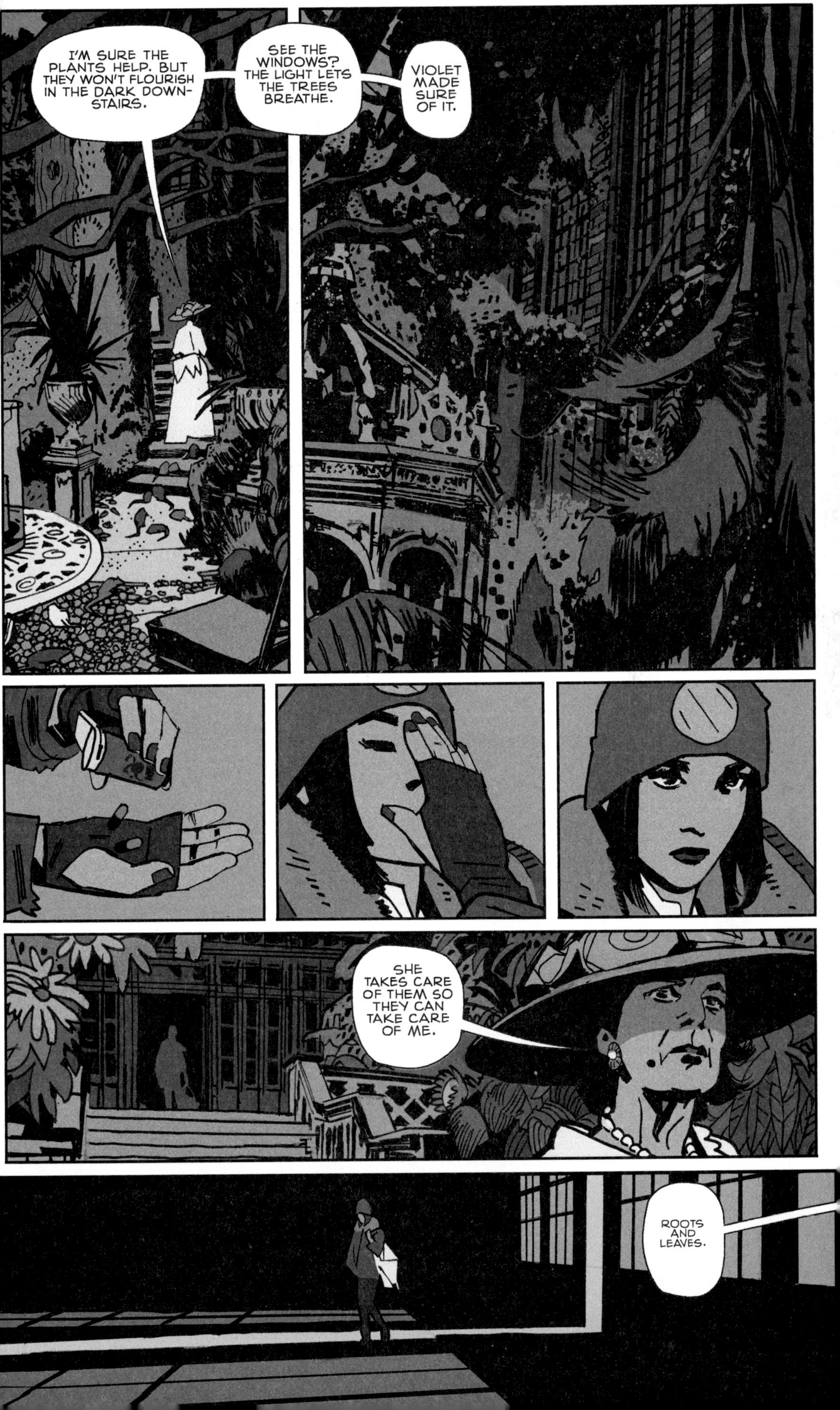
I'M SURE THE PLANTS HELP. BUT THEY WON'T FLOURISH IN THE DARK DOWN-STAIRS.
SEE THE WINDOWS? THE LIGHT LETS THE TREES BREATHE.
VIOLET MADE SURE OF IT.
SHE TAKES CARE OF THEM SO THEY CAN TAKE CARE OF ME.
ROOTS AND LEAVES.

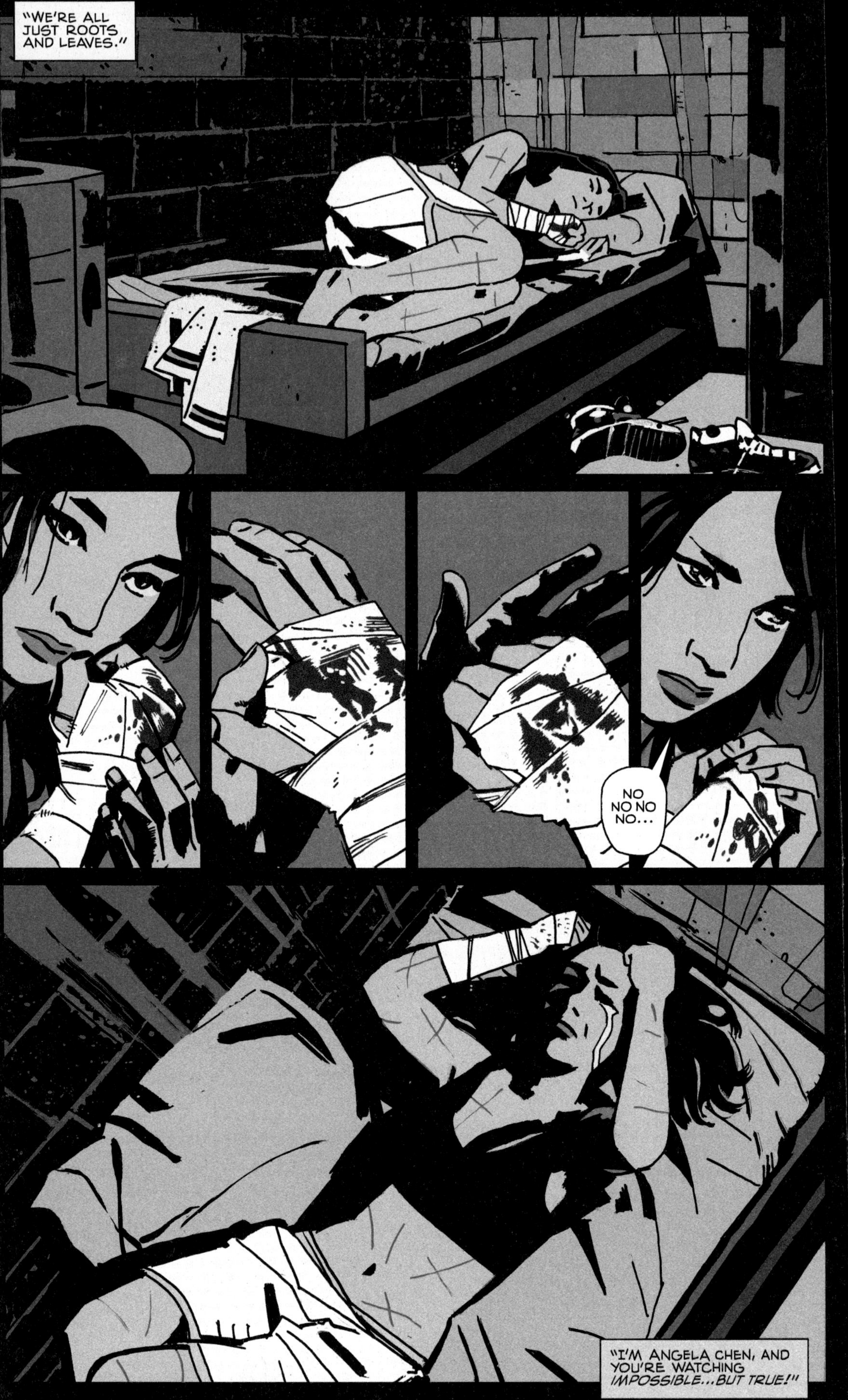
"WE'RE ALL JUST ROOTS AND LEAVES."
NO NO NO NO...
"I'M ANGELA CHEN, AND YOU'RE WATCHING *IMPOSSIBLE...BUT TRUE!*"

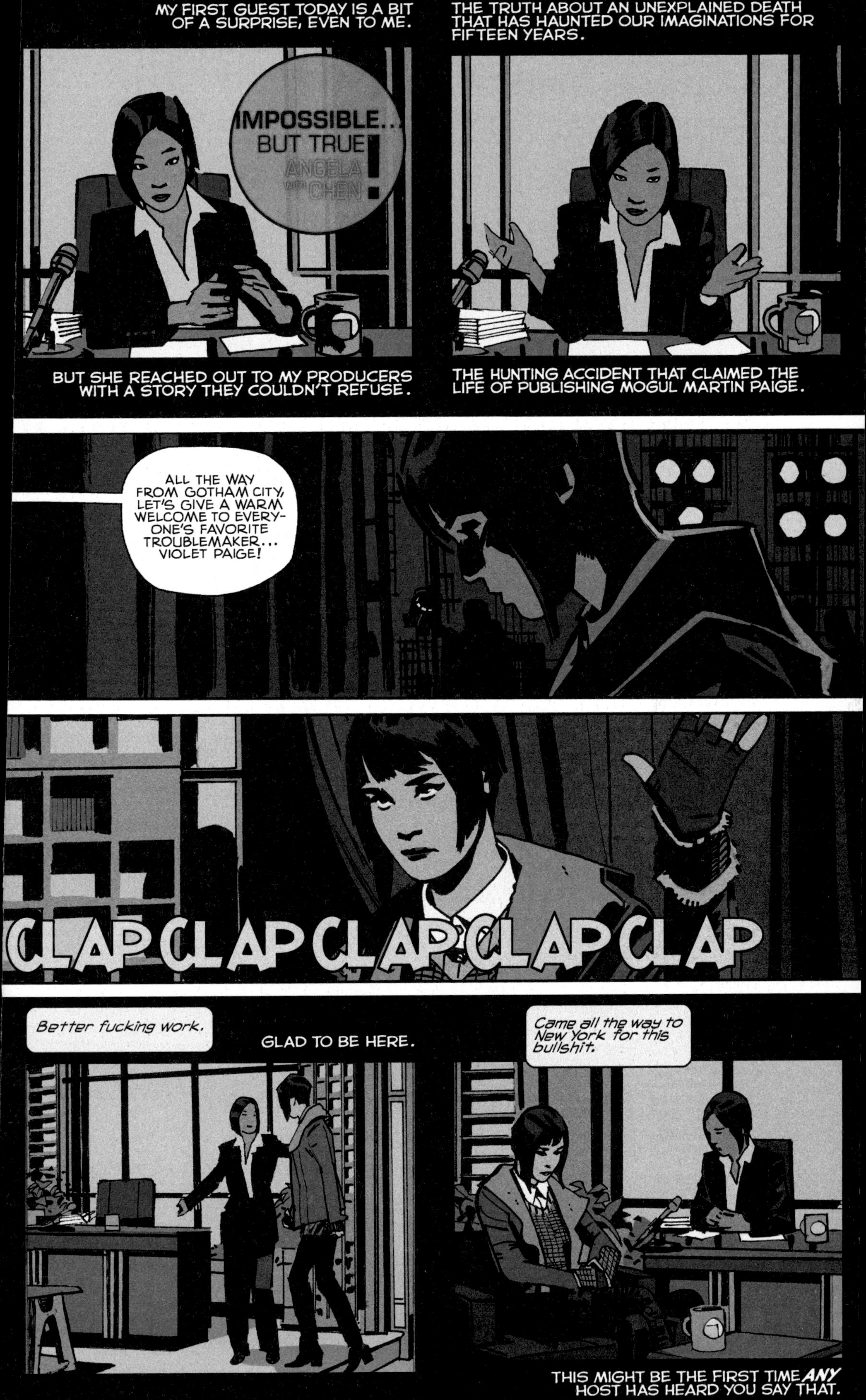
MY FIRST GUEST TODAY IS A BIT OF A SURPRISE, EVEN TO ME.
IMPOSSIBLE... BUT TRUE! ANGELA WITH CHEN
BUT SHE REACHED OUT TO MY PRODUCERS WITH A STORY THEY COULDN'T REFUSE.
THE TRUTH ABOUT AN UNEXPLAINED DEATH THAT HAS HAUNTED OUR IMAGINATIONS FOR FIFTEEN YEARS.
THE HUNTING ACCIDENT THAT CLAIMED THE LIFE OF PUBLISHING MOGUL MARTIN PAIGE.
ALL THE WAY FROM GOTHAM CITY, LET'S GIVE A WARM WELCOME TO EVERY-ONE'S FAVORITE TROUBLEMAKER... VIOLET PAIGE!
CLAP CLAP CLAP CLAP CLAP
Better fucking work.
GLAD TO BE HERE.
Came all the way to New York for this bullshit.
THIS MIGHT BE THE FIRST TIME *ANY* HOST HAS HEARD YOU SAY THAT.

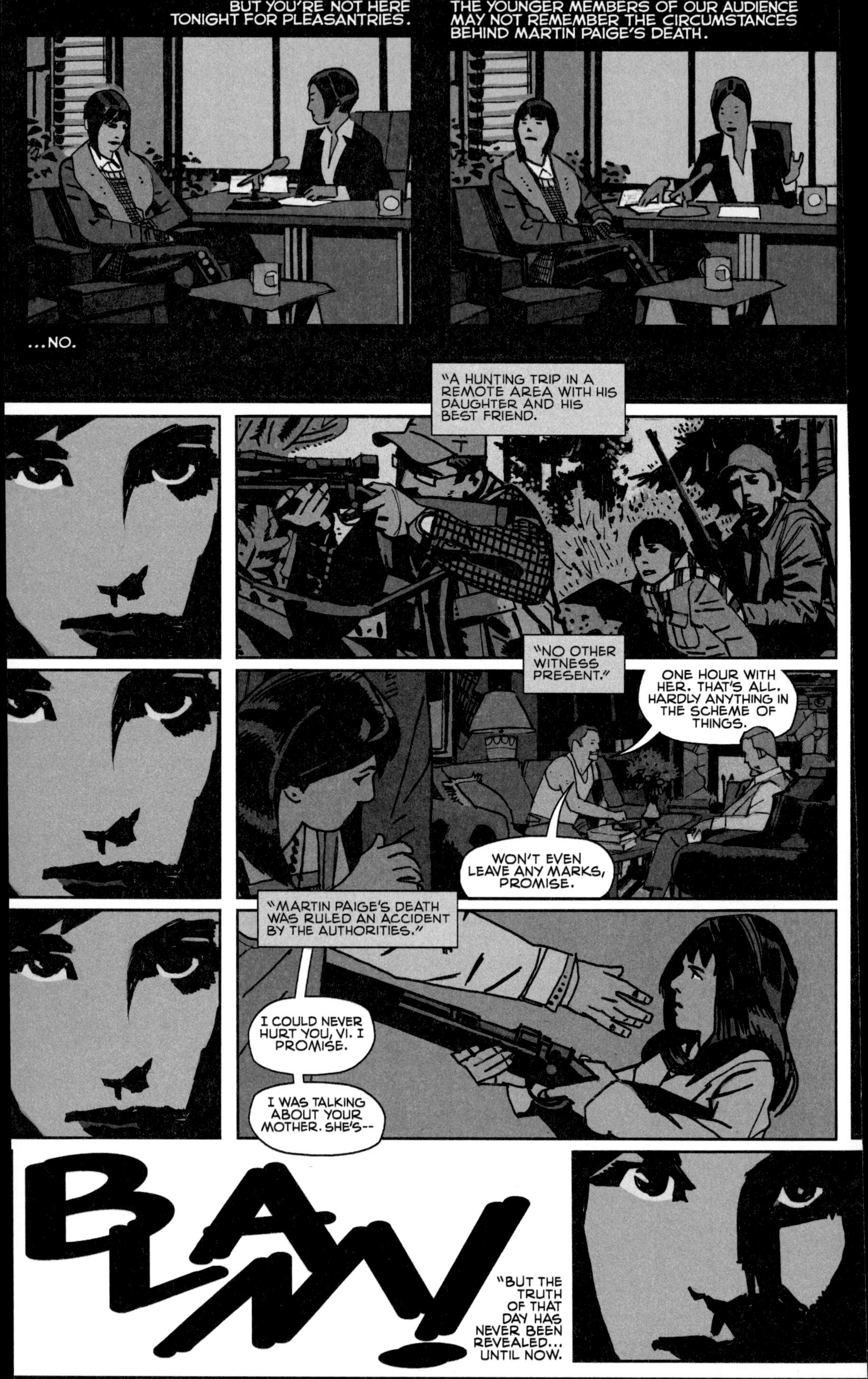
BUT YOU'RE NOT HERE TONIGHT FOR PLEASANTRIES.
THE YOUNGER MEMBERS OF OUR AUDIENCE MAY NOT REMEMBER THE CIRCUMSTANCES BEHIND MARTIN PAIGE'S DEATH.
...NO.
"A HUNTING TRIP IN A REMOTE AREA WITH HIS DAUGHTER AND HIS BEST FRIEND.
"NO OTHER WITNESS PRESENT."
ONE HOUR WITH HER. THAT'S ALL. HARDLY ANYTHING IN THE SCHEME OF THINGS.
WON'T EVEN LEAVE ANY MARKS, PROMISE.
"MARTIN PAIGE'S DEATH WAS RULED AN ACCIDENT BY THE AUTHORITIES."
I COULD NEVER HURT YOU, VI. I PROMISE.
I WAS TALKING ABOUT YOUR MOTHER. SHE'S--
BLAM!
"BUT THE TRUTH OF THAT DAY HAS NEVER BEEN REVEALED... UNTIL NOW.

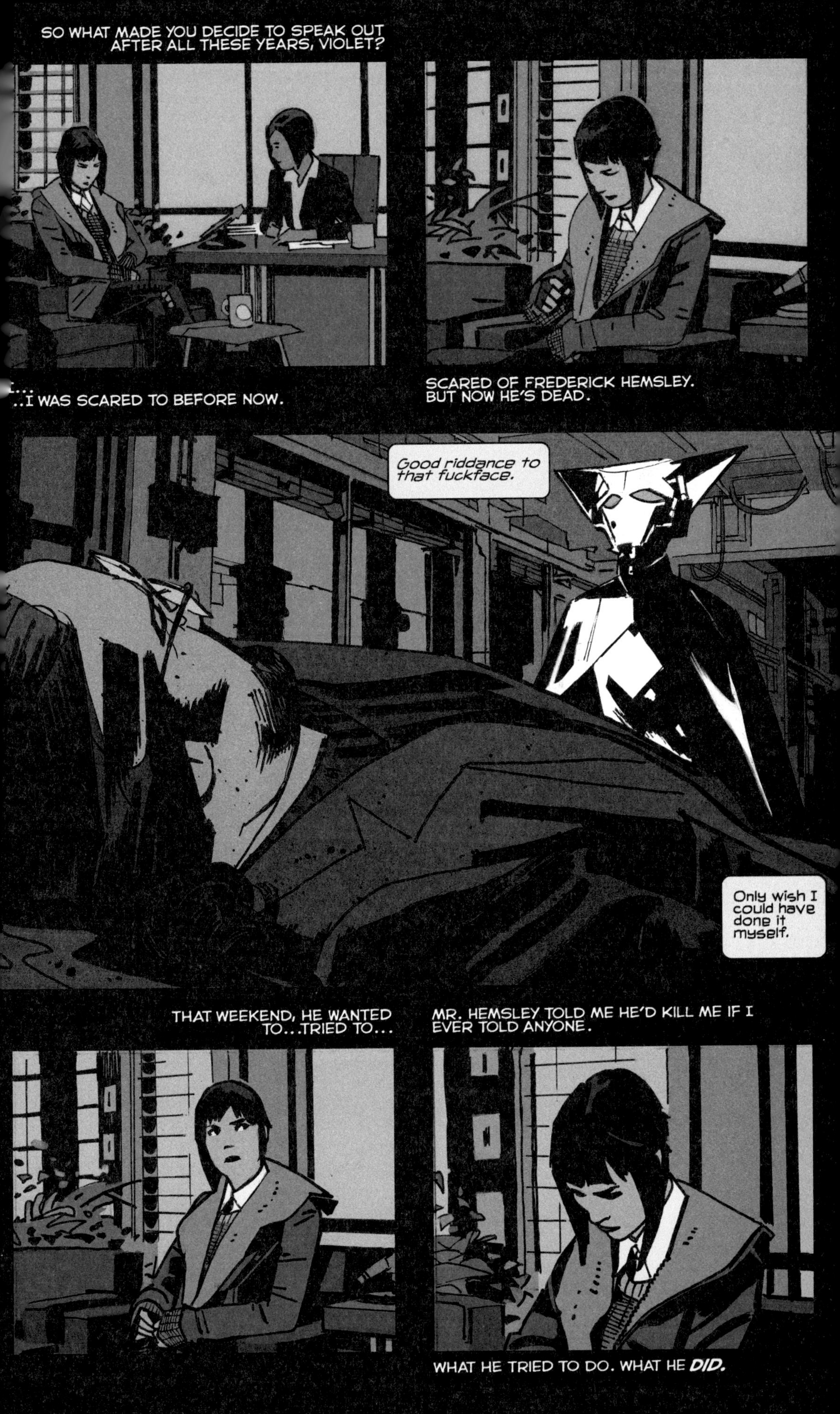
SO WHAT MADE YOU DECIDE TO SPEAK OUT AFTER ALL THESE YEARS, VIOLET?
...
..I WAS SCARED TO BEFORE NOW.
SCARED OF FREDERICK HEMSLEY. BUT NOW HE'S DEAD.
Good riddance to that fuckface.
Only wish I could have done it myself.
THAT WEEKEND, HE WANTED TO...TRIED TO...
MR. HEMSLEY TOLD ME HE'D KILL ME IF I EVER TOLD ANYONE.
WHAT HE TRIED TO DO. WHAT HE *DID.*

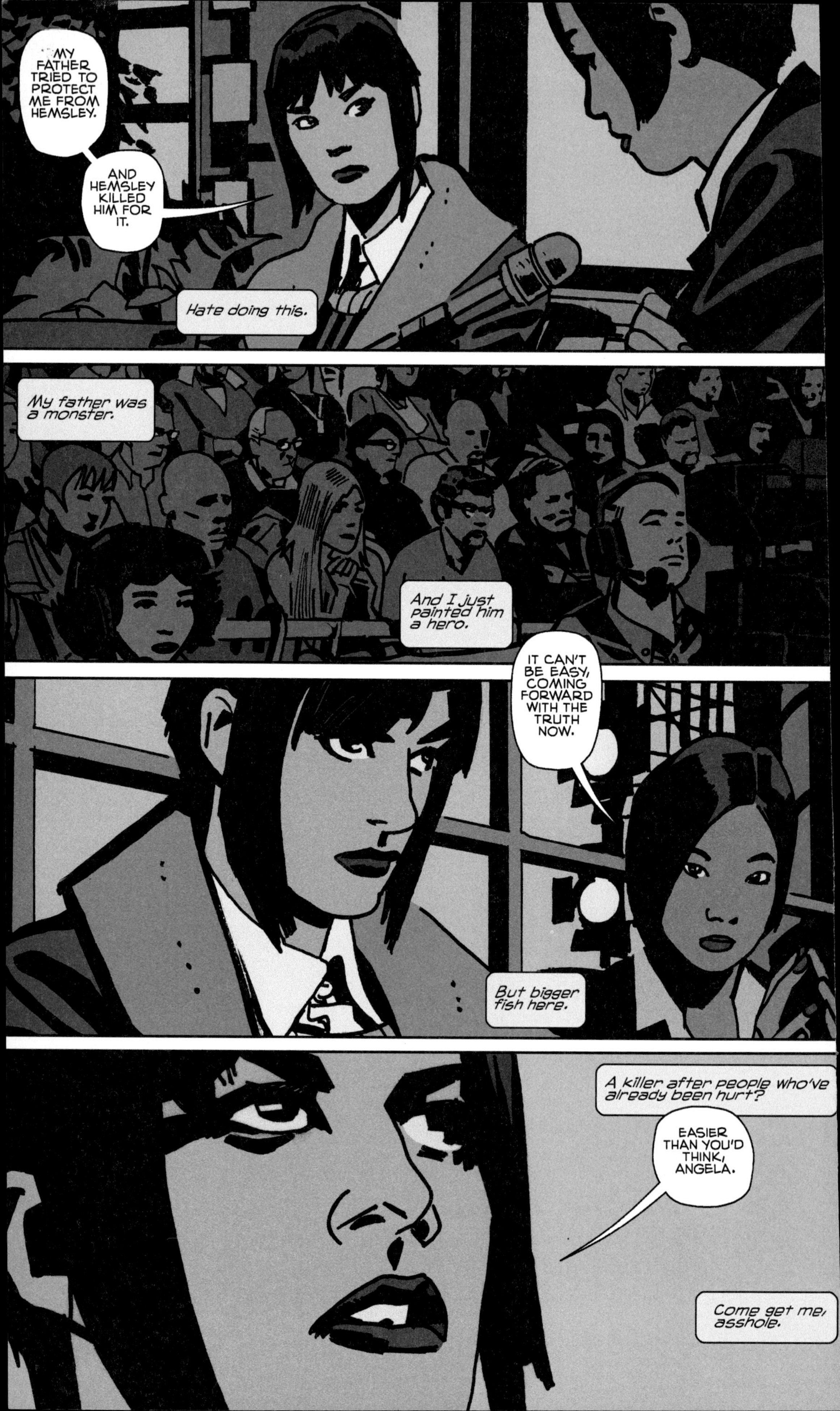
MY FATHER TRIED TO PROTECT ME FROM HEMSLEY.
AND HEMSLEY KILLED HIM FOR IT.
Hate doing this.
My father was a monster.
And I just painted him a hero.
IT CAN'T BE EASY, COMING FORWARD WITH THE TRUTH NOW.
But bigger fish here.
A killer after people who've already been hurt?
EASIER THAN YOU'D THINK, ANGELA.
Come get me, asshole.

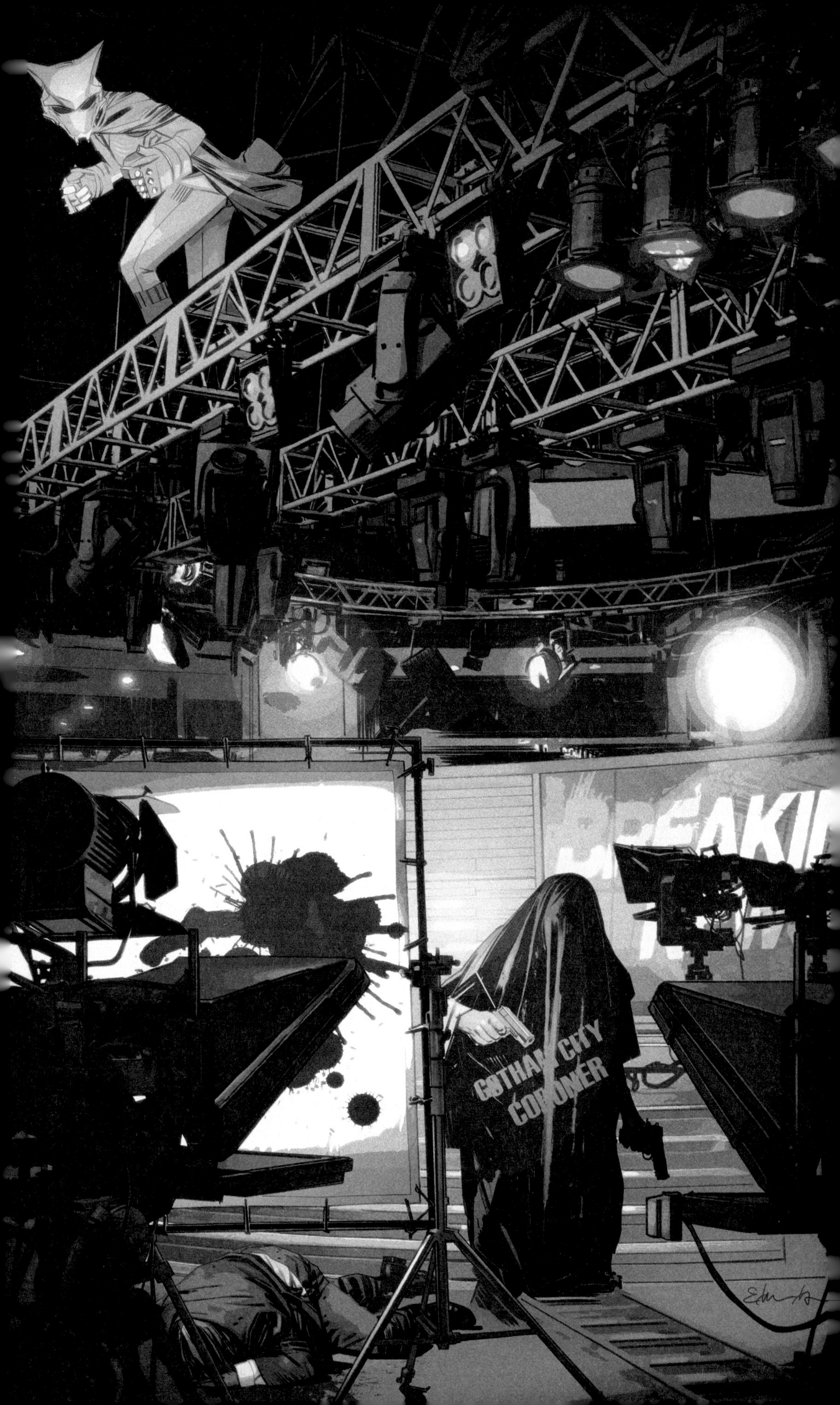
GOTHAM CITY CORONER

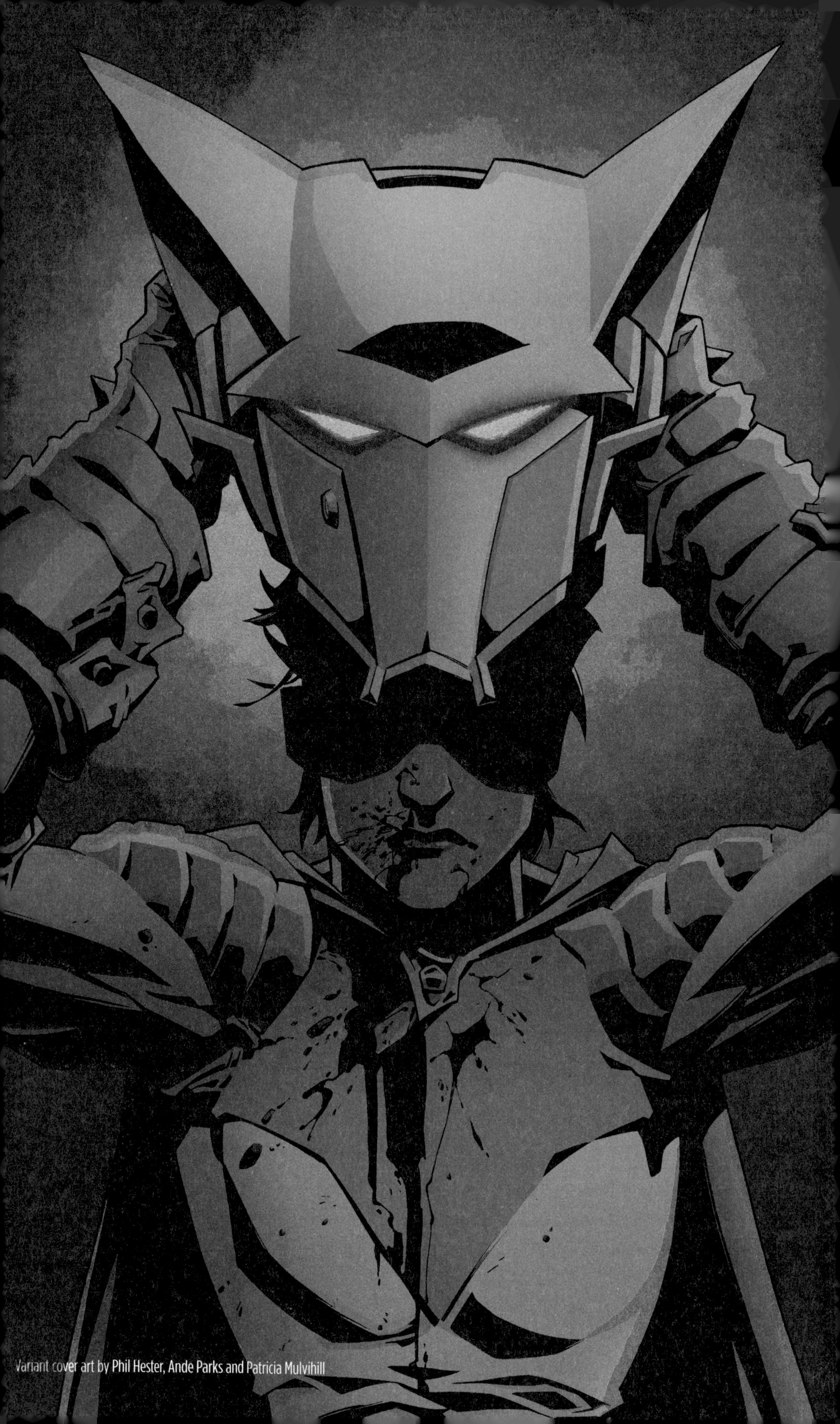
Variant cover art by Phil Hester, Ande Parks and Patricia Mulvihill

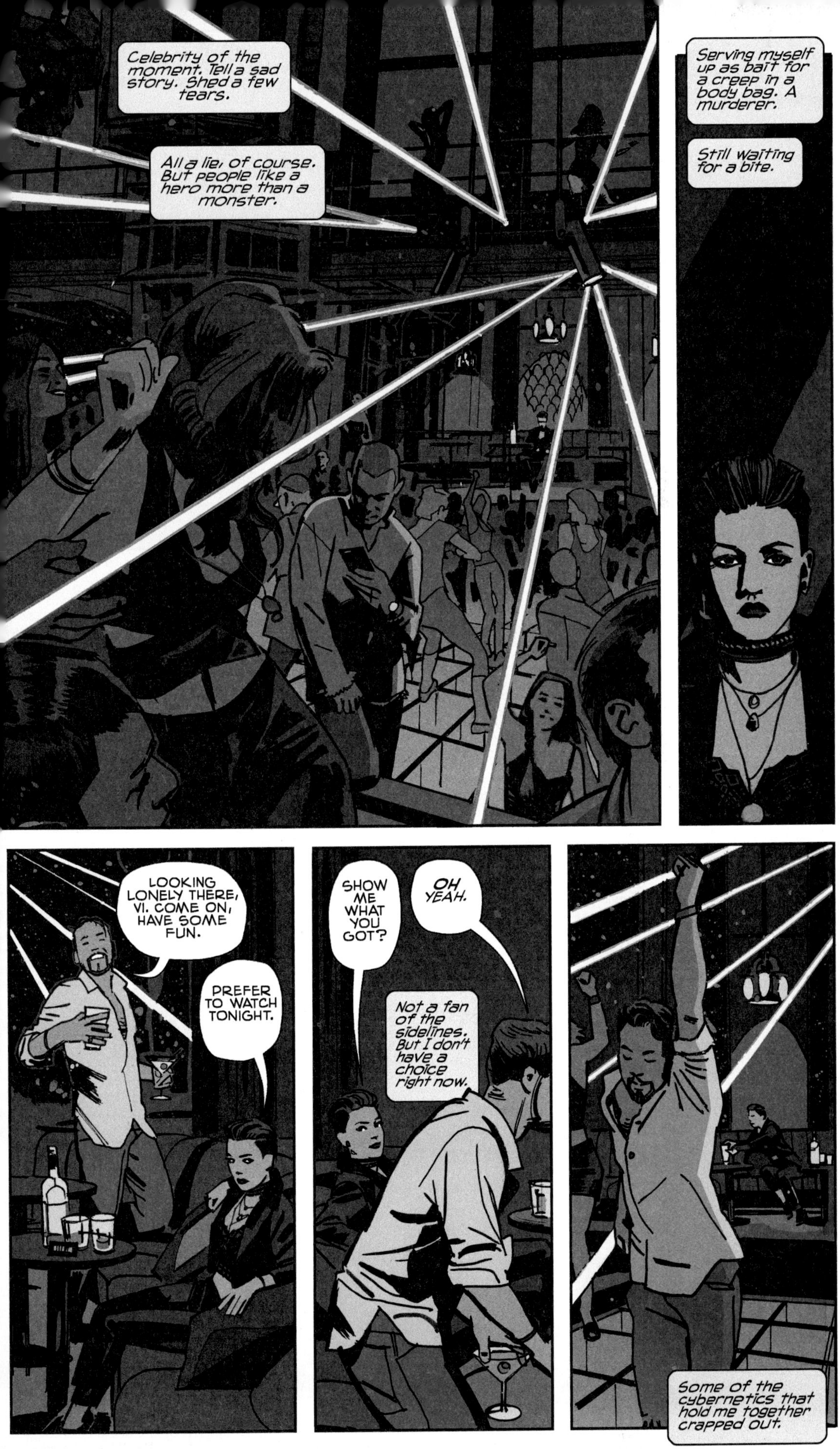
Celebrity of the moment. Tell a sad story. Shed a few tears.
All a lie, of course. But people like a hero more than a monster.
Serving myself up as bait for a creep in a body bag. A murderer.
Still waiting for a bite.
LOOKING LONELY THERE, VI. COME ON, HAVE SOME FUN.
PREFER TO WATCH TONIGHT.
SHOW ME WHAT YOU GOT?
OH YEAH.
Not a fan of the sidelines. But I don't have a choice right now.
Some of the cybernetics that hold me together crapped out.

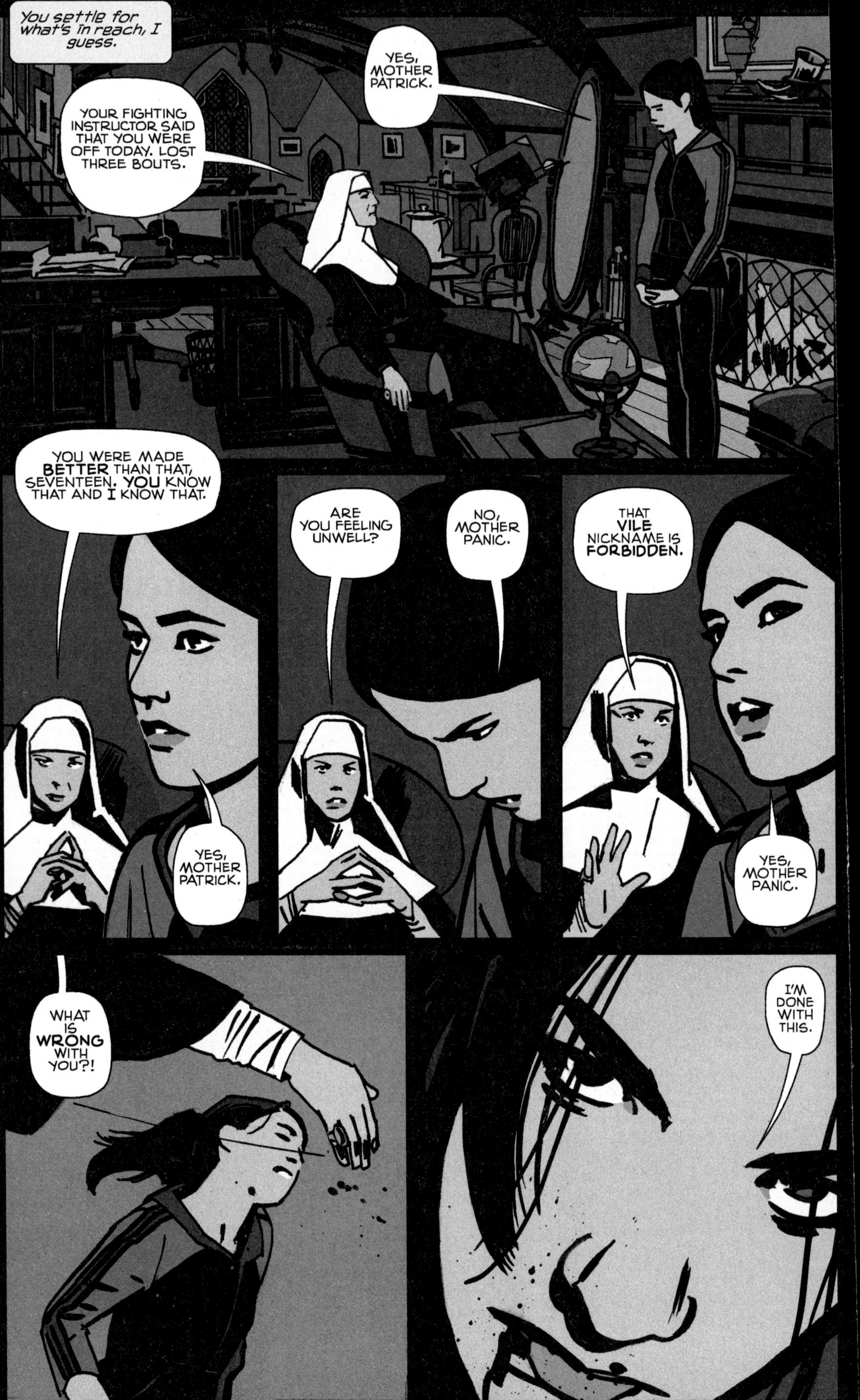

You settle for what's in reach, I guess.
YOUR FIGHTING INSTRUCTOR SAID THAT YOU WERE OFF TODAY. LOST THREE BOUTS.
YES, MOTHER PATRICK.
YOU WERE MADE **BETTER** THAN THAT, SEVENTEEN. **YOU** KNOW THAT AND **I** KNOW THAT.
YES, MOTHER PATRICK.
ARE YOU FEELING UNWELL?
NO, MOTHER PANIC.
THAT **VILE** NICKNAME IS **FORBIDDEN.**
YES, MOTHER PANIC.
WHAT IS **WRONG** WITH YOU?!
I'M DONE WITH THIS.

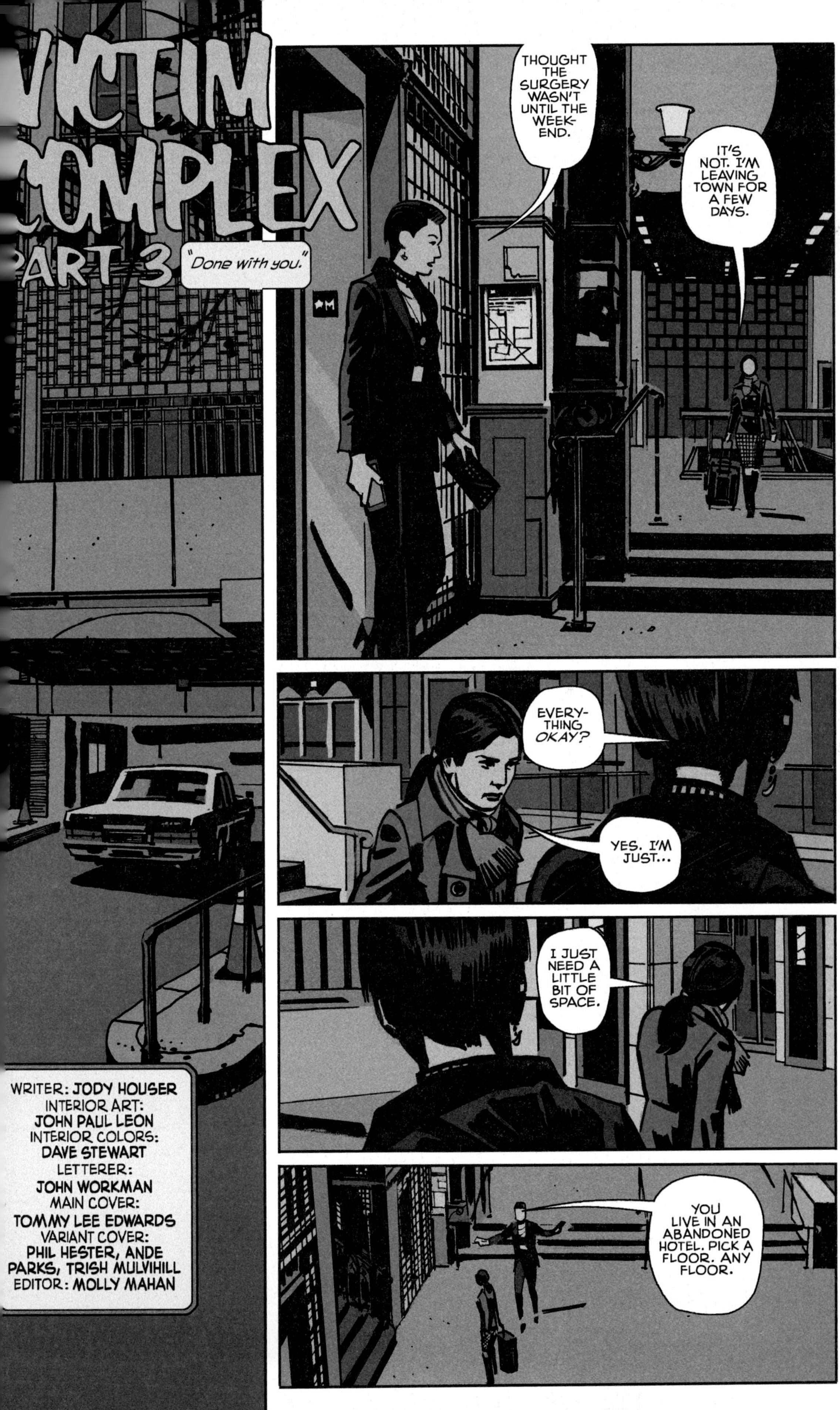

VICTIM COMPLEX
PART 3
"Done with you."
THOUGHT THE SURGERY WASN'T UNTIL THE WEEKEND.
IT'S NOT. I'M LEAVING TOWN FOR A FEW DAYS.
EVERYTHING *OKAY?*
YES. I'M JUST...
I JUST NEED A LITTLE BIT OF SPACE.
YOU LIVE IN AN ABANDONED HOTEL. PICK A FLOOR. ANY FLOOR.
WRITER: JODY HOUSER
INTERIOR ART: JOHN PAUL LEON
INTERIOR COLORS: DAVE STEWART
LETTERER: JOHN WORKMAN
MAIN COVER: TOMMY LEE EDWARDS
VARIANT COVER: PHIL HESTER, ANDE PARKS, TRISH MULVIHILL
EDITOR: MOLLY MAHAN

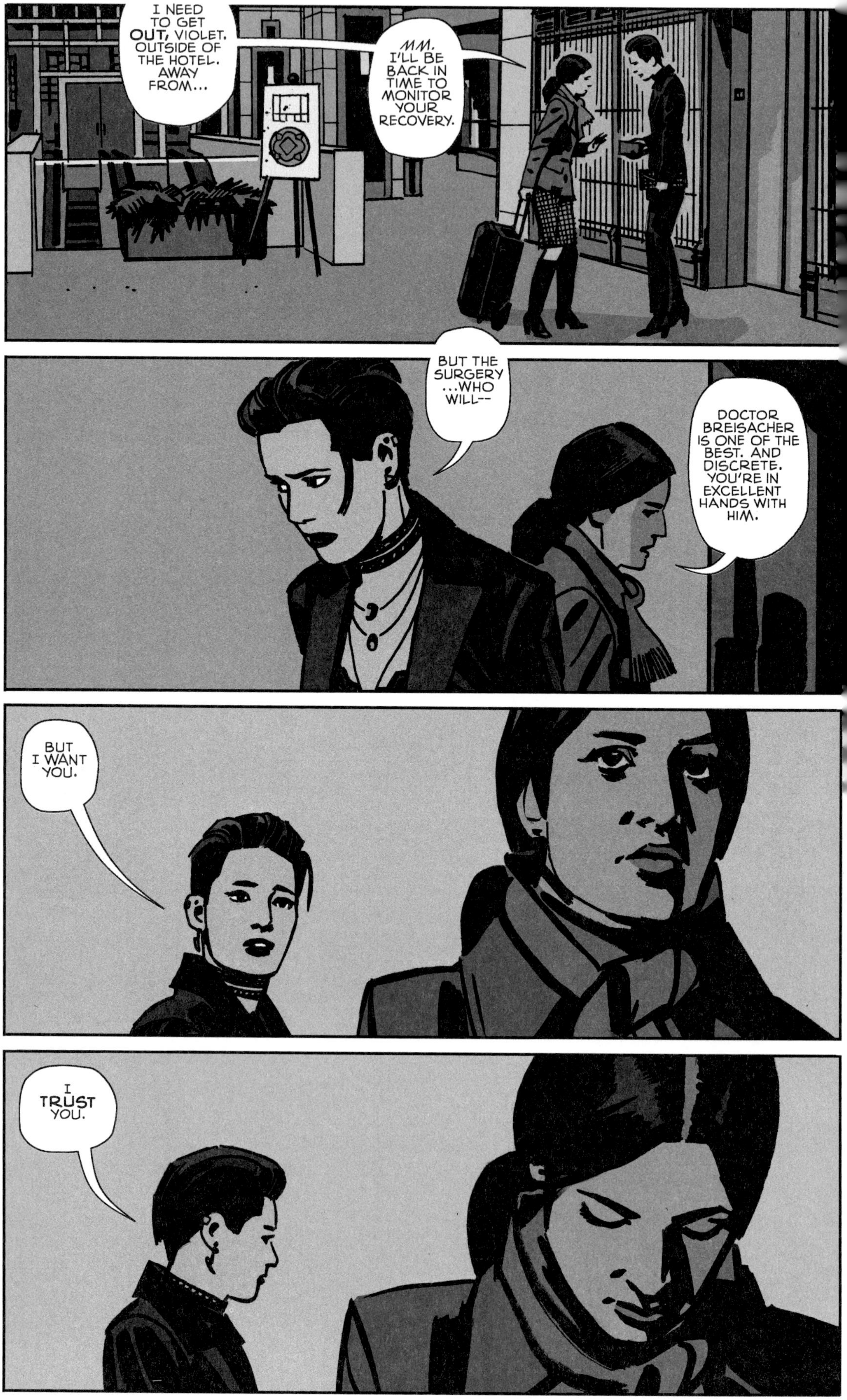
I NEED TO GET OUT, VIOLET. OUTSIDE OF THE HOTEL. AWAY FROM...
MM. I'LL BE BACK IN TIME TO MONITOR YOUR RECOVERY.
BUT THE SURGERY ...WHO WILL--
DOCTOR BREISACHER IS ONE OF THE BEST. AND DISCRETE. YOU'RE IN EXCELLENT HANDS WITH HIM.
BUT I WANT YOU.
I TRUST YOU.

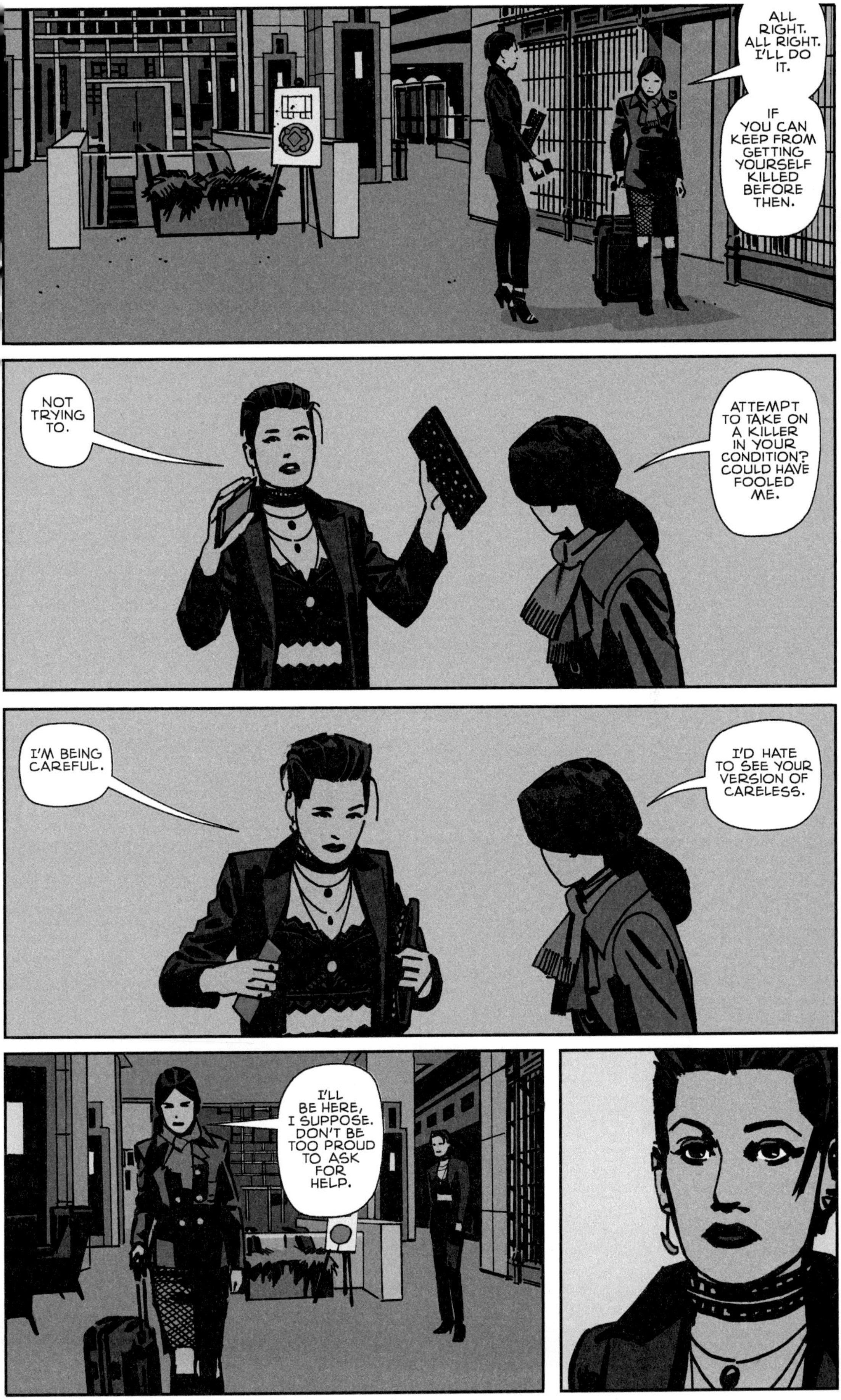
ALL RIGHT. ALL RIGHT. I'LL DO IT.
IF YOU CAN KEEP FROM GETTING YOURSELF KILLED BEFORE THEN.
NOT TRYING TO.
ATTEMPT TO TAKE ON A KILLER IN YOUR CONDITION? COULD HAVE FOOLED ME.
I'M BEING CAREFUL.
I'D HATE TO SEE YOUR VERSION OF CARELESS.
I'LL BE HERE, I SUPPOSE. DON'T BE TOO PROUD TO ASK FOR HELP.

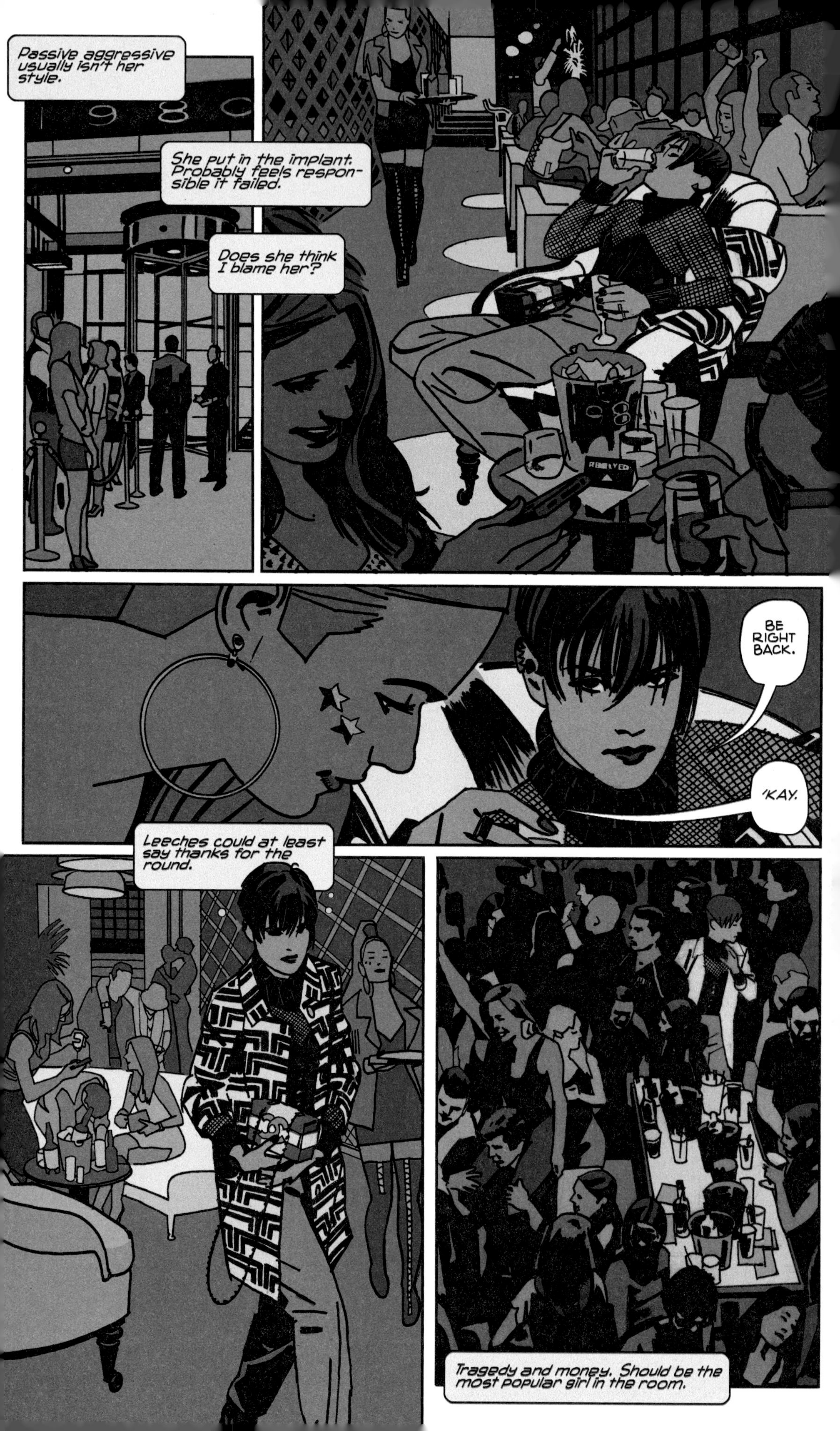

Passive aggressive usually isn't her style.
She put in the implant. Probably feels responsible it failed.
Does she think I blame her?
BE RIGHT BACK.
'KAY.
Leeches could at least say thanks for the round.
Tragedy and money. Should be the most popular girl in the room.

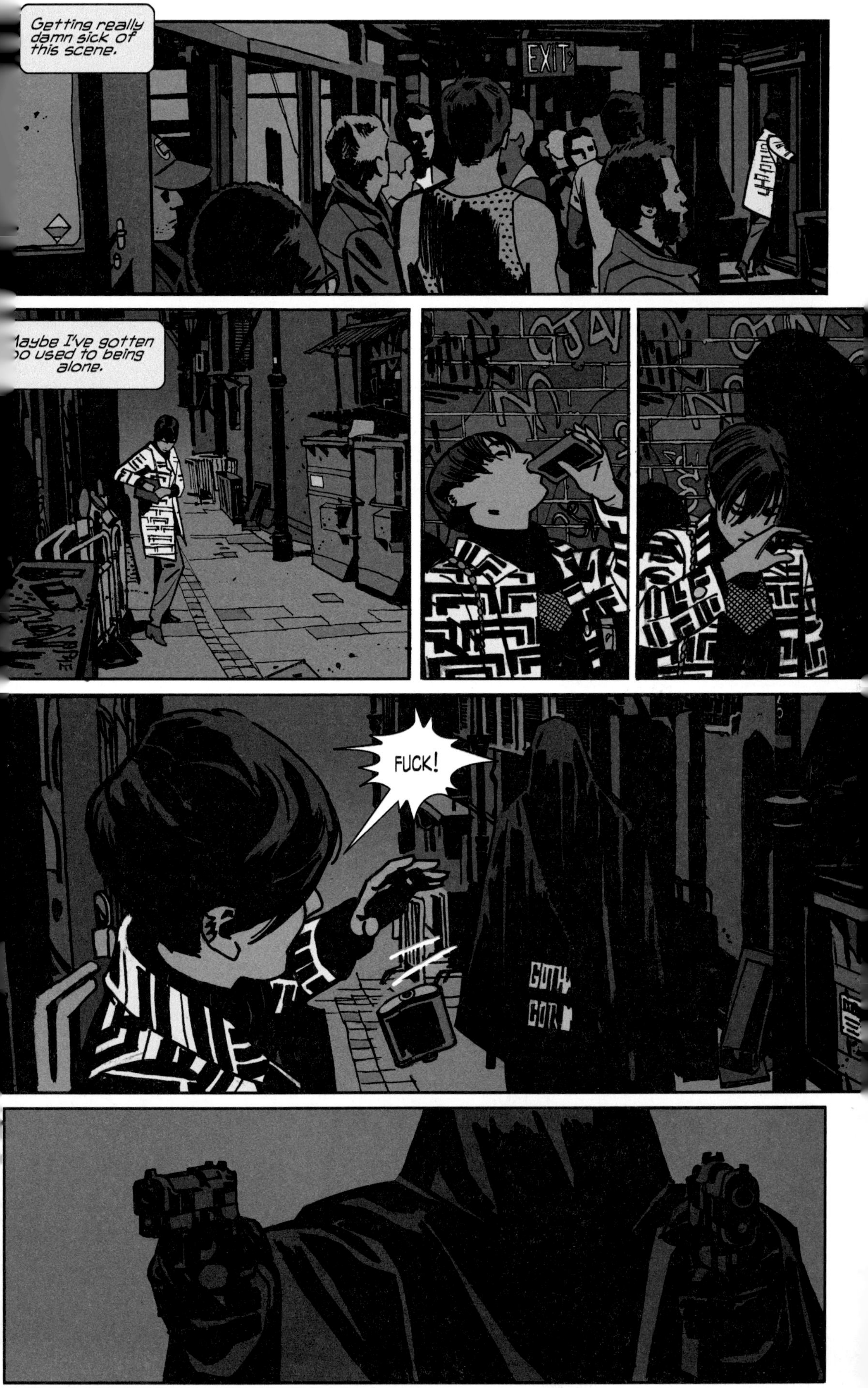
Getting really damn sick of this scene.
EXIT
Maybe I've gotten so used to being alone.
FUCK!

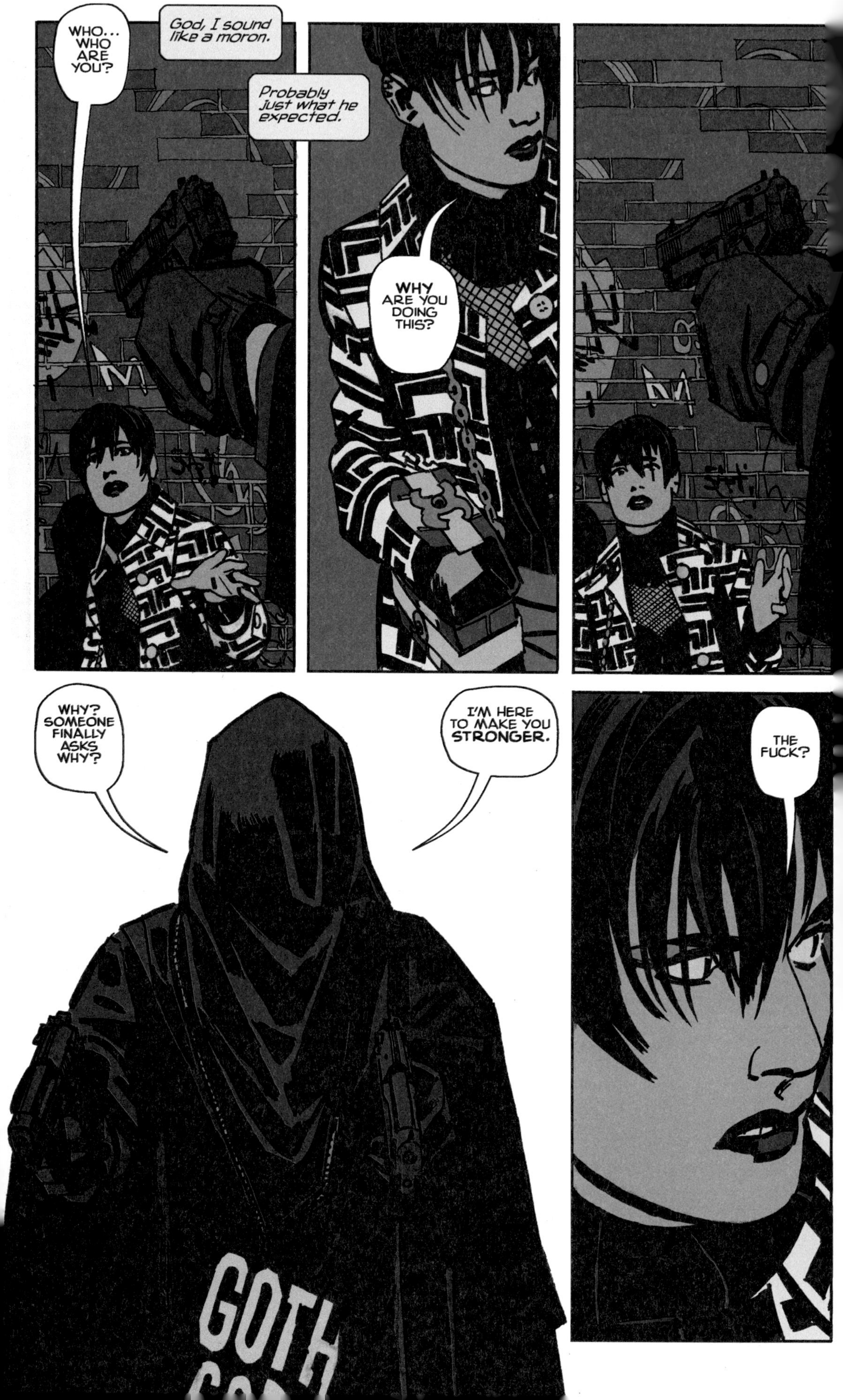
WHO... WHO ARE YOU?
God, I sound like a moron.
Probably just what he expected.
WHY ARE YOU DOING THIS?
WHY? SOMEONE FINALLY ASKS WHY?
I'M HERE TO MAKE YOU STRONGER.
THE FUCK?
GOTH

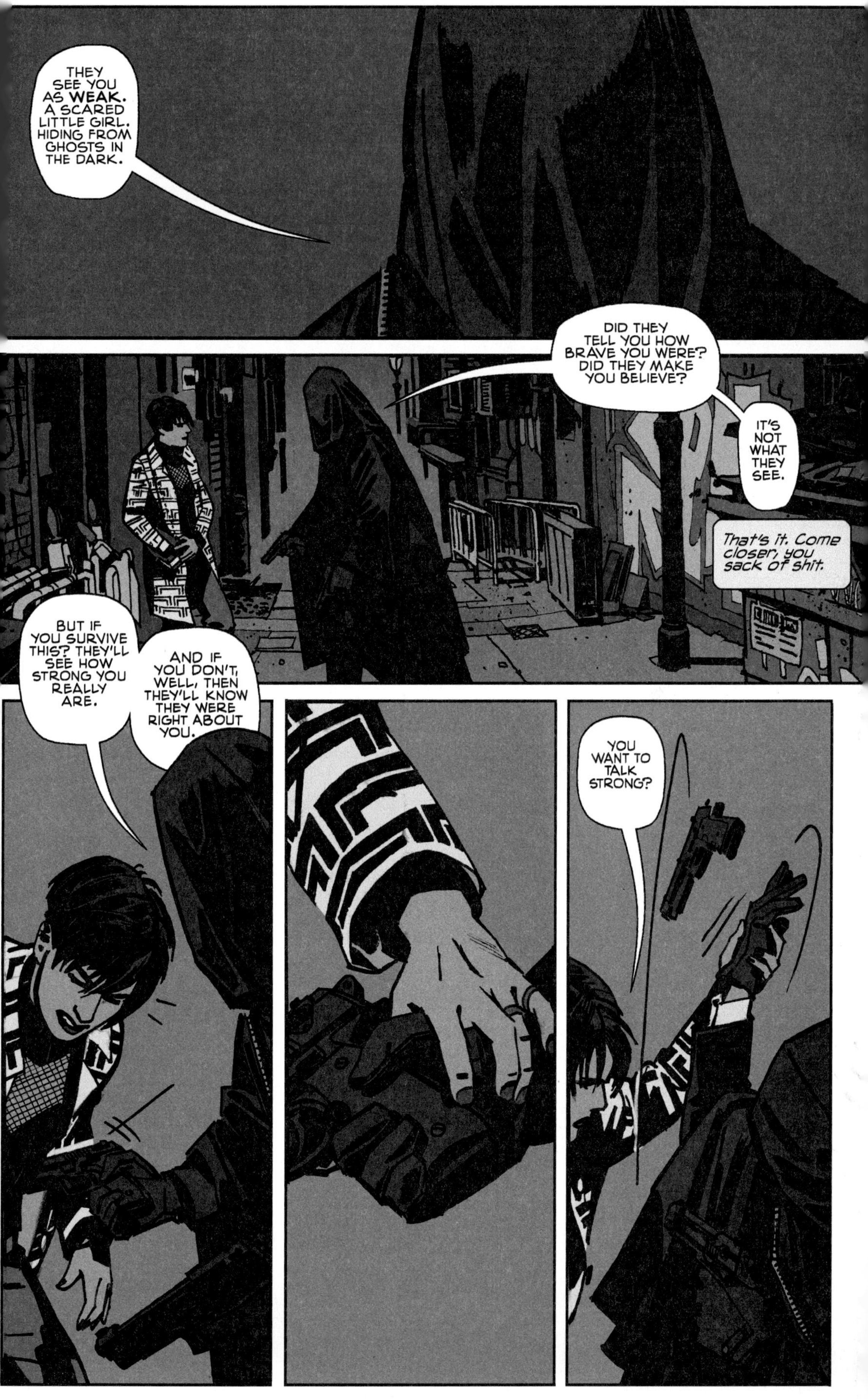
THEY SEE YOU AS **WEAK.** A SCARED LITTLE GIRL. HIDING FROM GHOSTS IN THE DARK.
DID THEY TELL YOU HOW BRAVE YOU WERE? DID THEY MAKE YOU BELIEVE?
IT'S NOT WHAT THEY SEE.
That's it. Come closer, you sack of shit.
BUT IF YOU SURVIVE THIS? THEY'LL SEE HOW STRONG YOU REALLY ARE.
AND IF YOU DON'T, WELL, THEN THEY'LL KNOW THEY WERE RIGHT ABOUT YOU.
YOU WANT TO TALK STRONG?

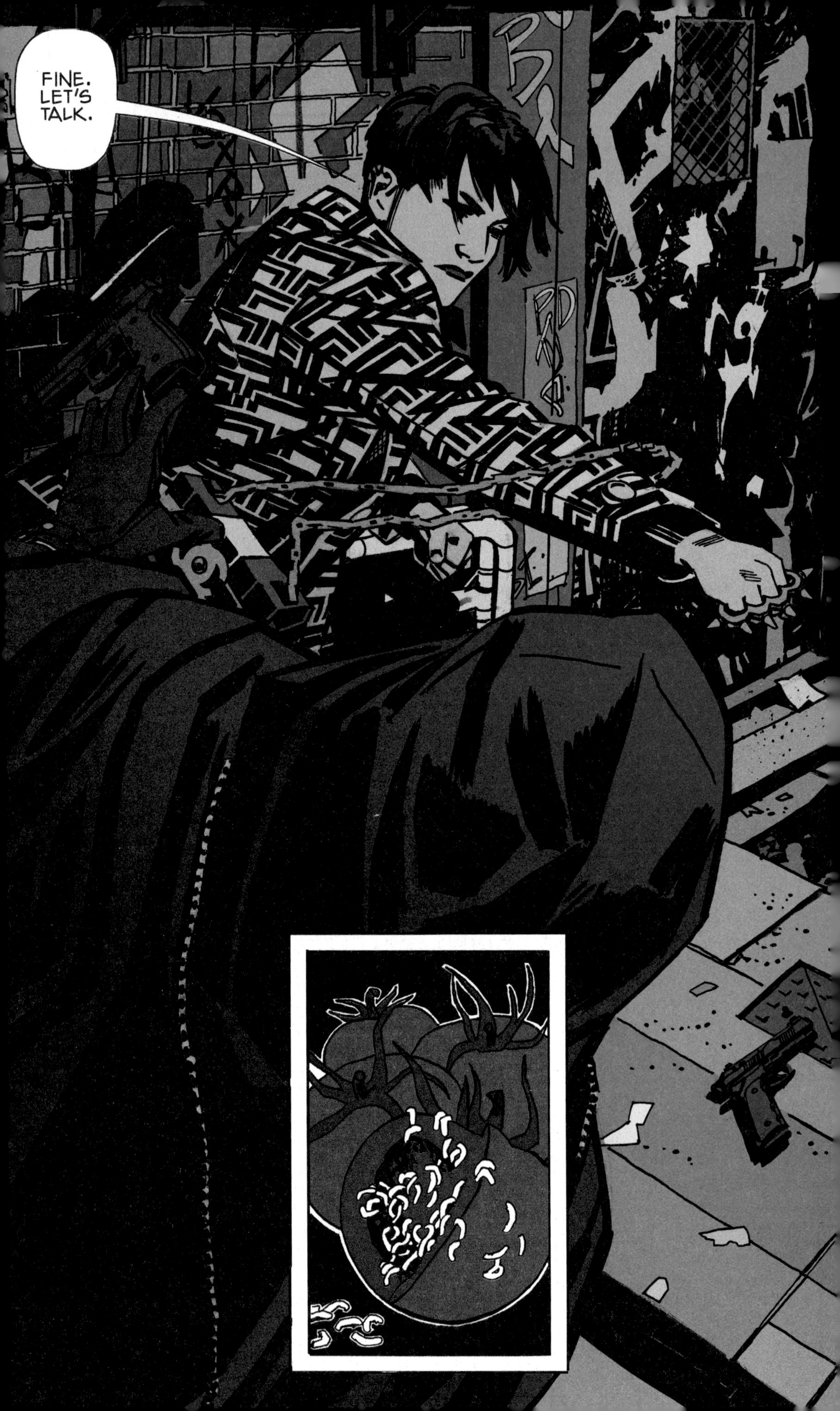
FINE. LET'S TALK.

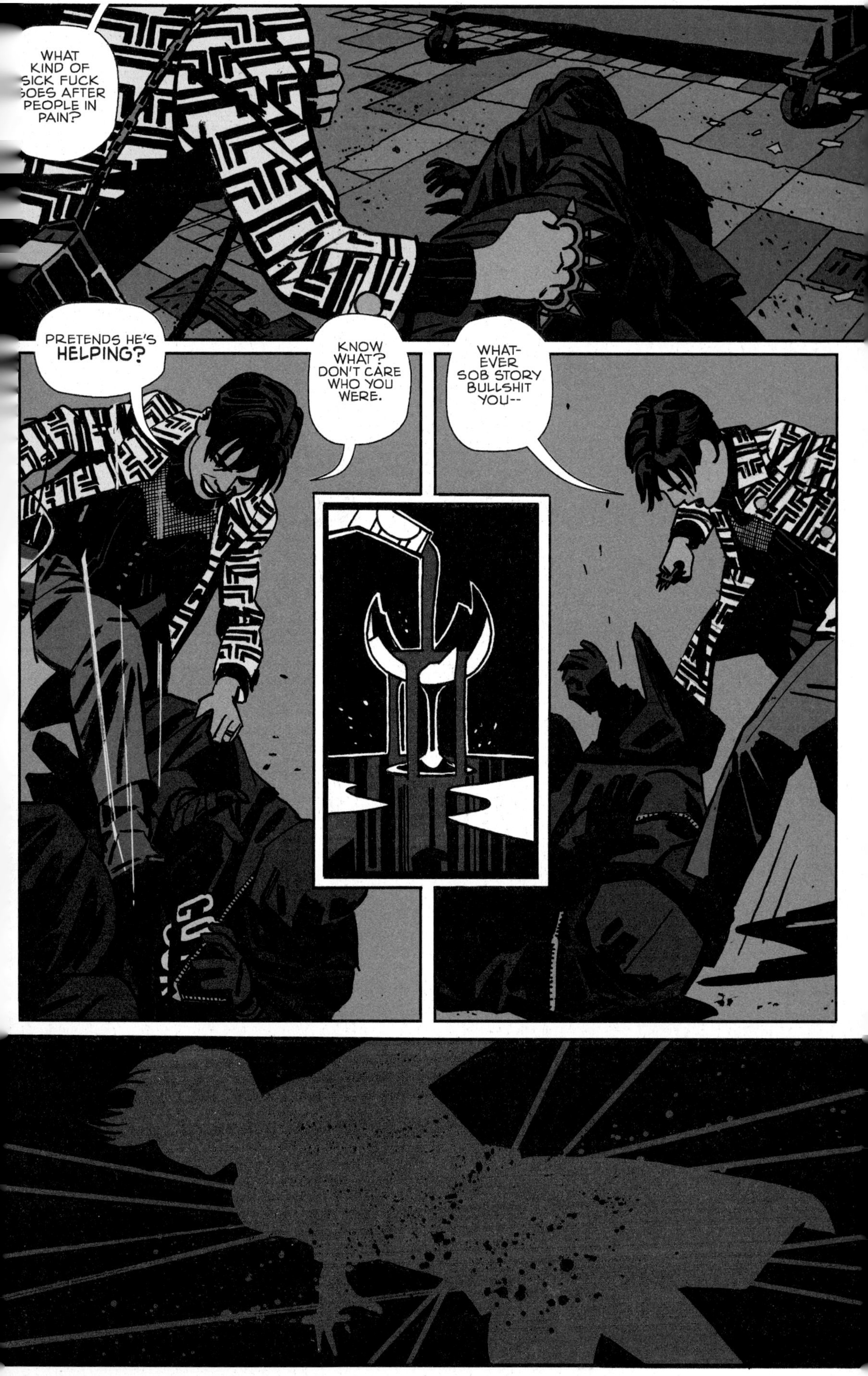
WHAT KIND OF SICK FUCK GOES AFTER PEOPLE IN PAIN?
PRETENDS HE'S **HELPING?**
KNOW WHAT? DON'T CARE WHO YOU WERE.
WHAT-EVER SOB STORY BULLSHIT YOU--

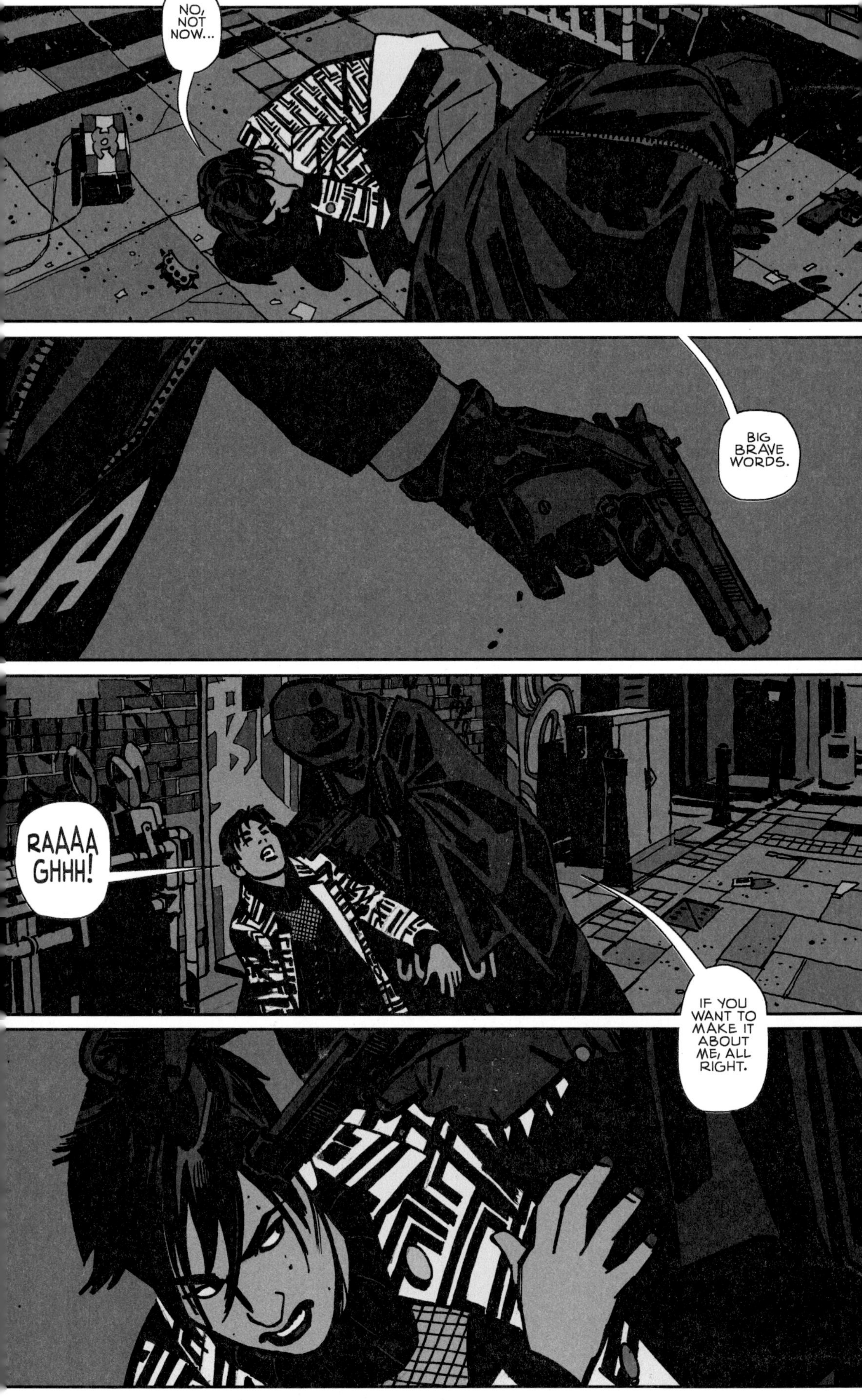

NO, NOT NOW...
BIG BRAVE WORDS.
RAAAA GHHH!
IF YOU WANT TO MAKE IT ABOUT ME, ALL RIGHT.

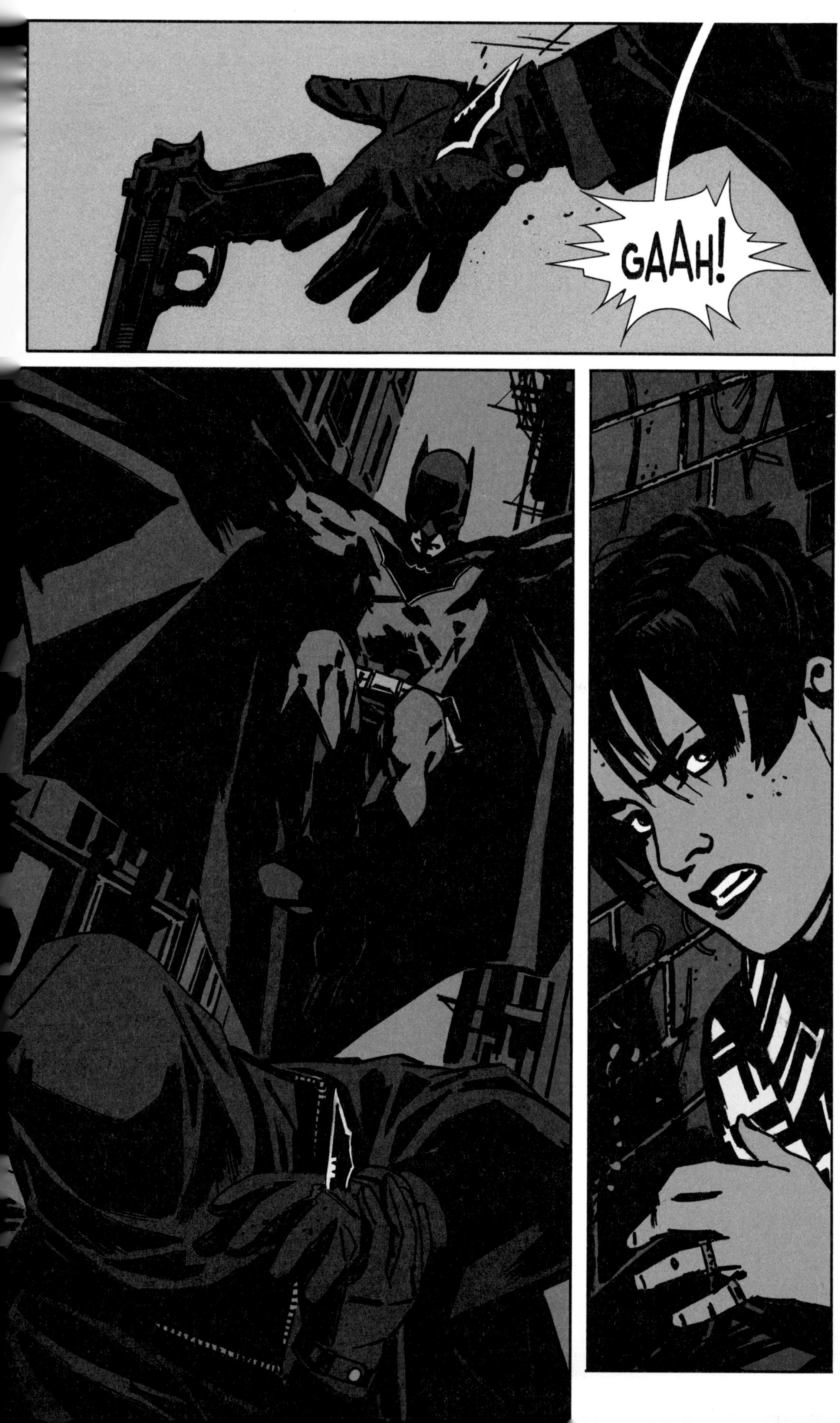
GAAH!

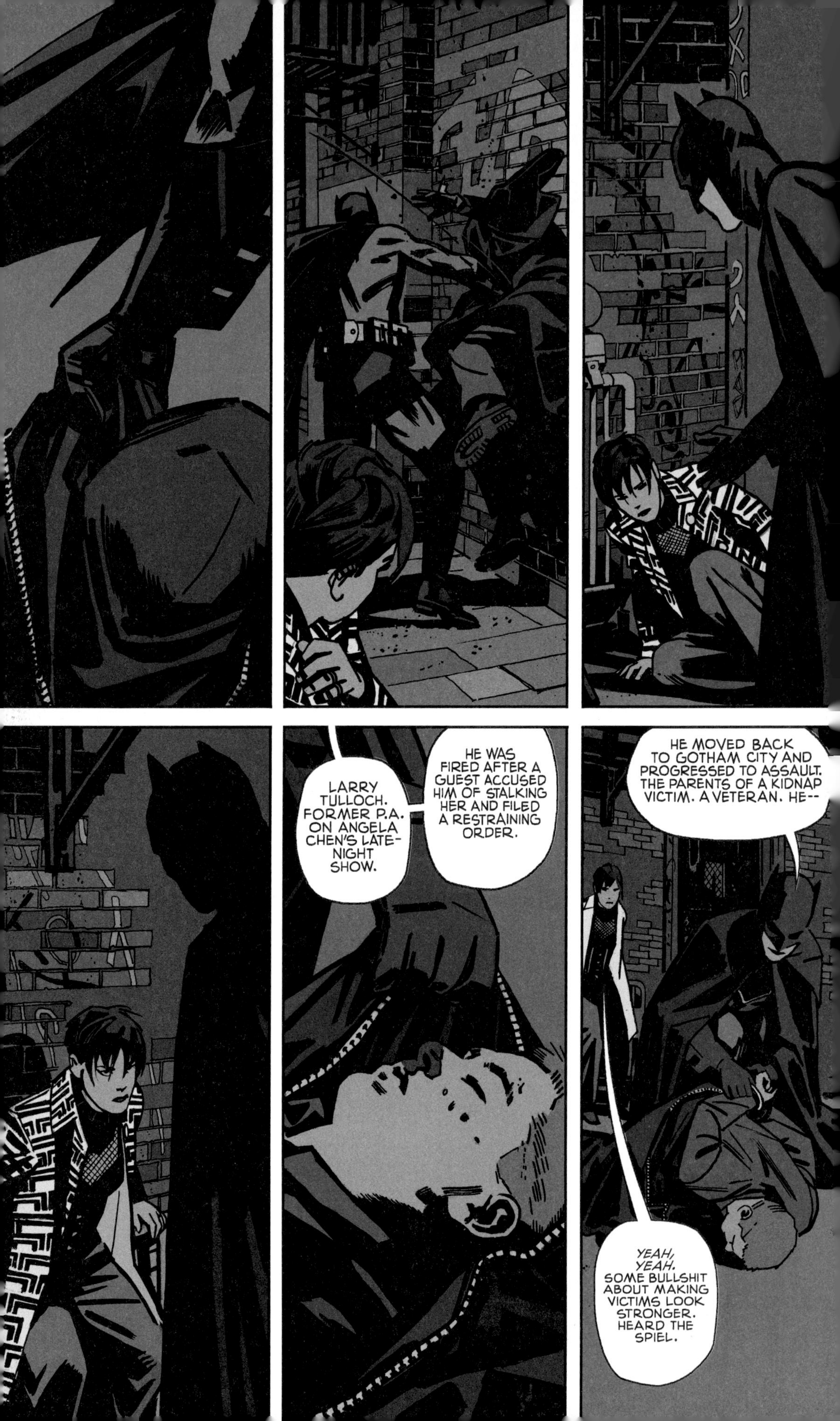
LARRY TULLOCH. FORMER P.A. ON ANGELA CHEN'S LATE-NIGHT SHOW.
HE WAS FIRED AFTER A GUEST ACCUSED HIM OF STALKING HER AND FILED A RESTRAINING ORDER.
HE MOVED BACK TO GOTHAM CITY AND PROGRESSED TO ASSAULT. THE PARENTS OF A KIDNAP VICTIM. A VETERAN. HE--
YEAH, YEAH. SOME BULLSHIT ABOUT MAKING VICTIMS LOOK STRONGER. HEARD THE SPIEL.

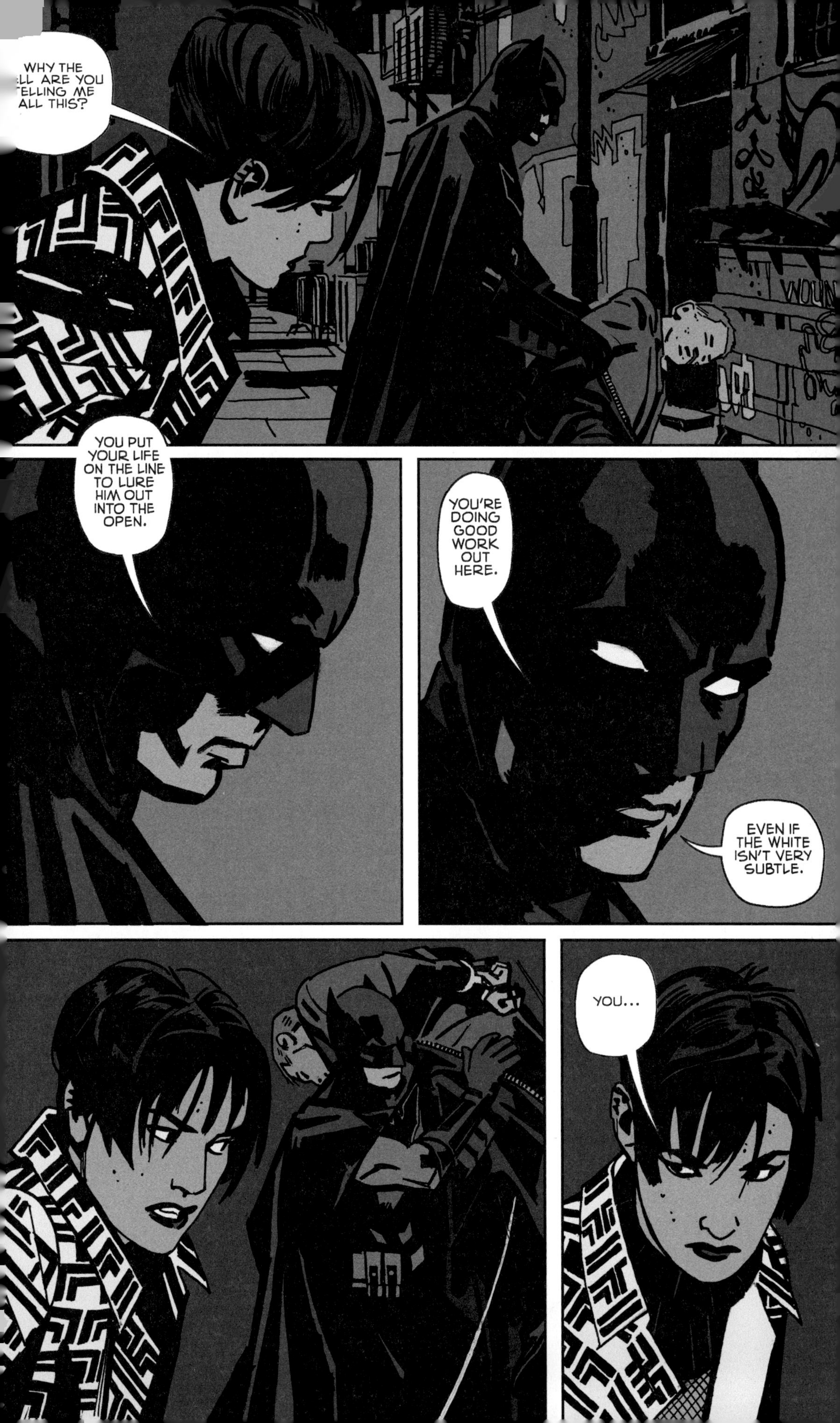
WHY THE LL ARE YOU TELLING ME ALL THIS?
YOU PUT YOUR LIFE ON THE LINE TO LURE HIM OUT INTO THE OPEN.
YOU'RE DOING GOOD WORK OUT HERE.
EVEN IF THE WHITE ISN'T VERY SUBTLE.
YOU...

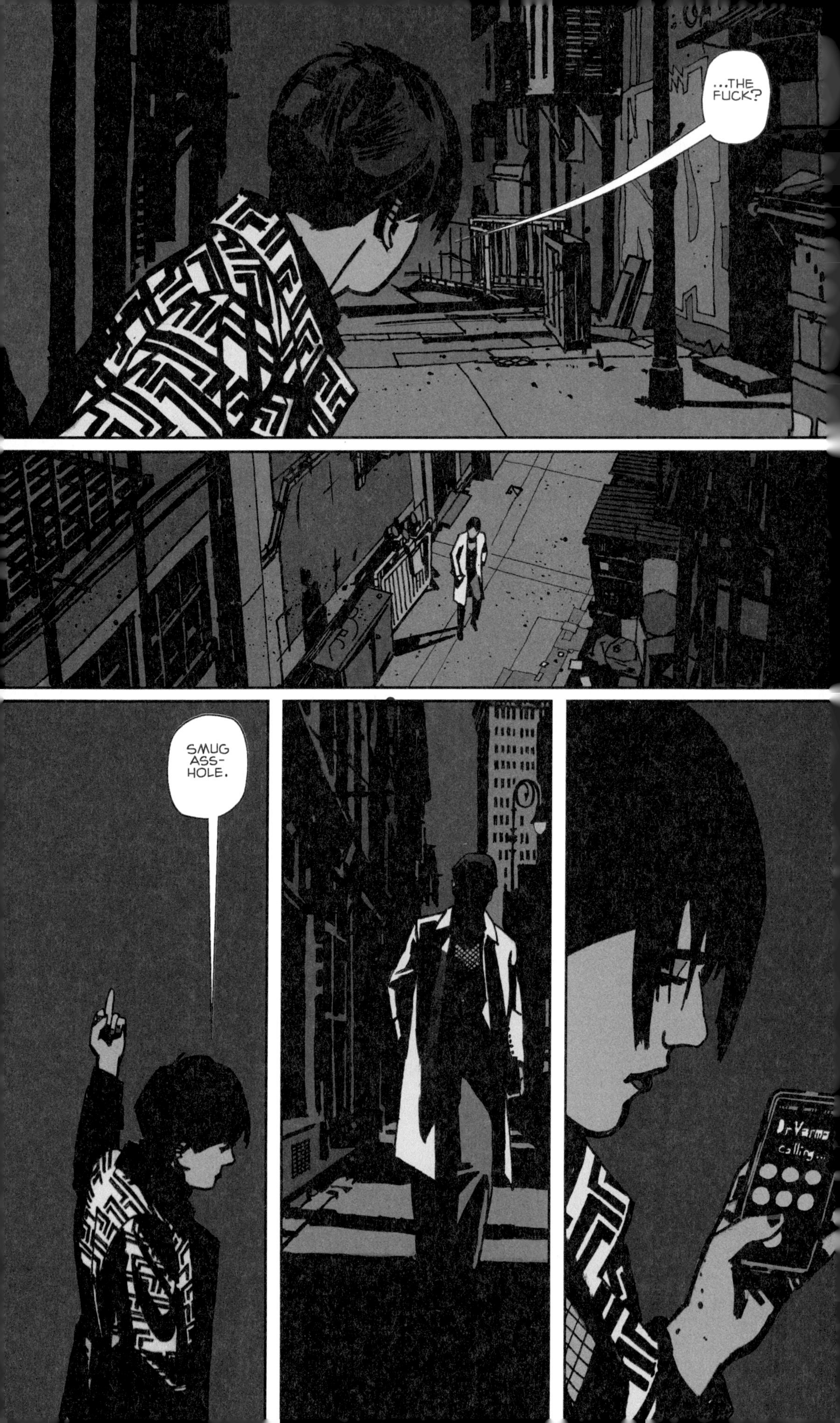
...THE FUCK?
SMUG ASS-HOLE.
Dr Varma calling...

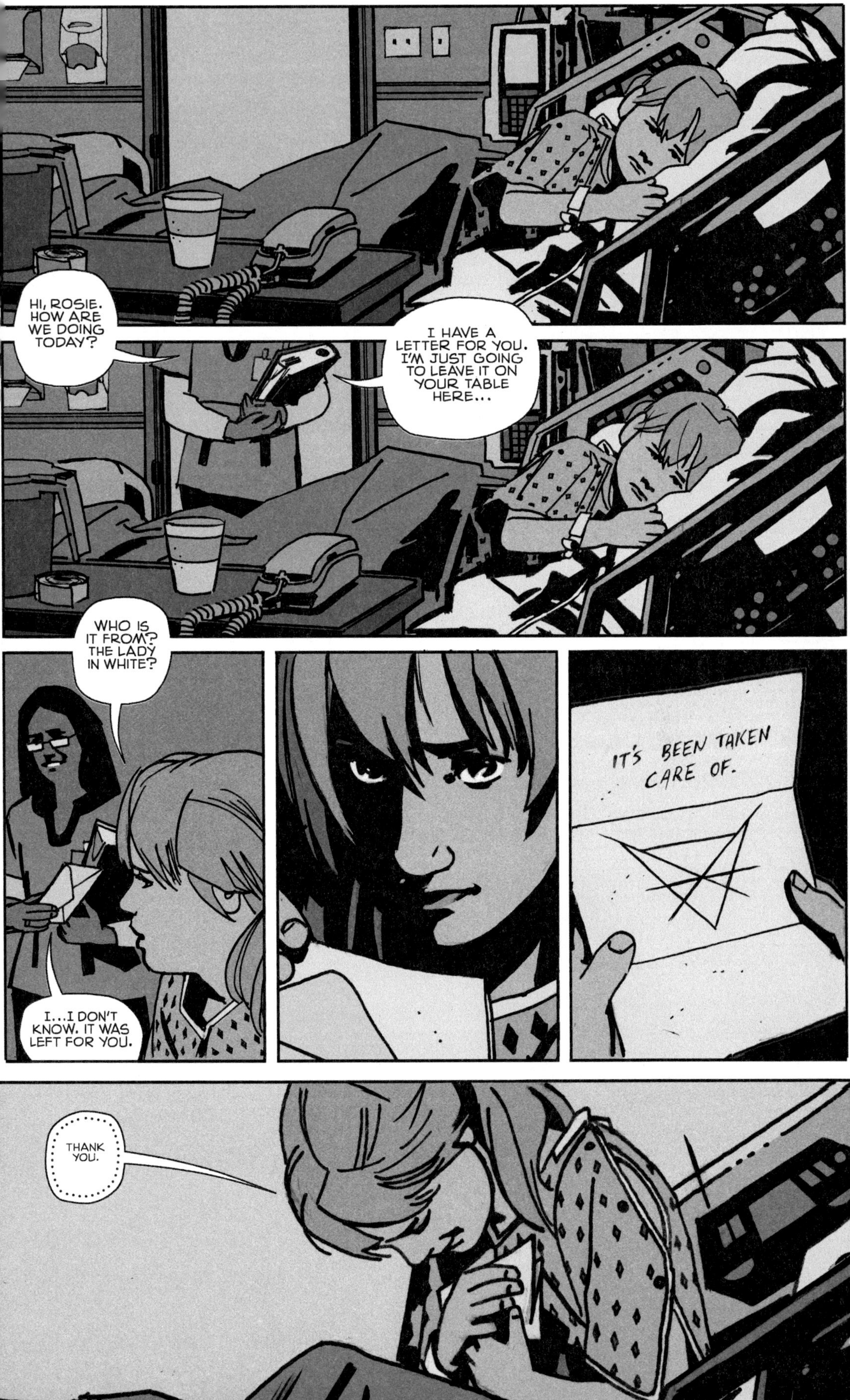
HI, ROSIE. HOW ARE WE DOING TODAY?
I HAVE A LETTER FOR YOU. I'M JUST GOING TO LEAVE IT ON YOUR TABLE HERE...
WHO IS IT FROM? THE LADY IN WHITE?
I...I DON'T KNOW. IT WAS LEFT FOR YOU.
IT'S BEEN TAKEN CARE OF.
THANK YOU.

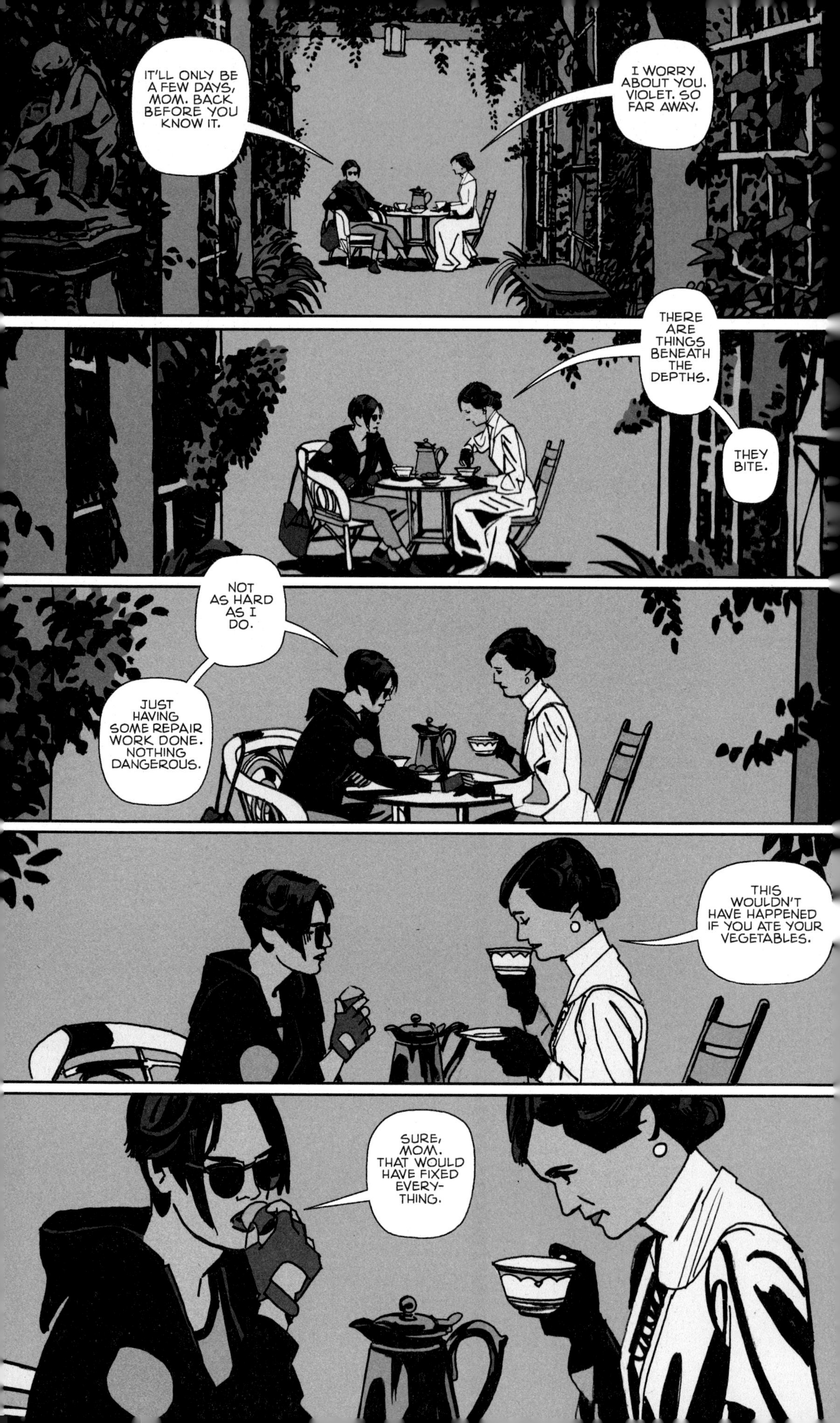
IT'LL ONLY BE A FEW DAYS, MOM. BACK BEFORE YOU KNOW IT.
I WORRY ABOUT YOU, VIOLET. SO FAR AWAY.
THERE ARE THINGS BENEATH THE DEPTHS.
THEY BITE.
NOT AS HARD AS I DO.
JUST HAVING SOME REPAIR WORK DONE. NOTHING DANGEROUS.
THIS WOULDN'T HAVE HAPPENED IF YOU ATE YOUR VEGETABLES.
SURE, MOM. THAT WOULD HAVE FIXED EVERY-THING.

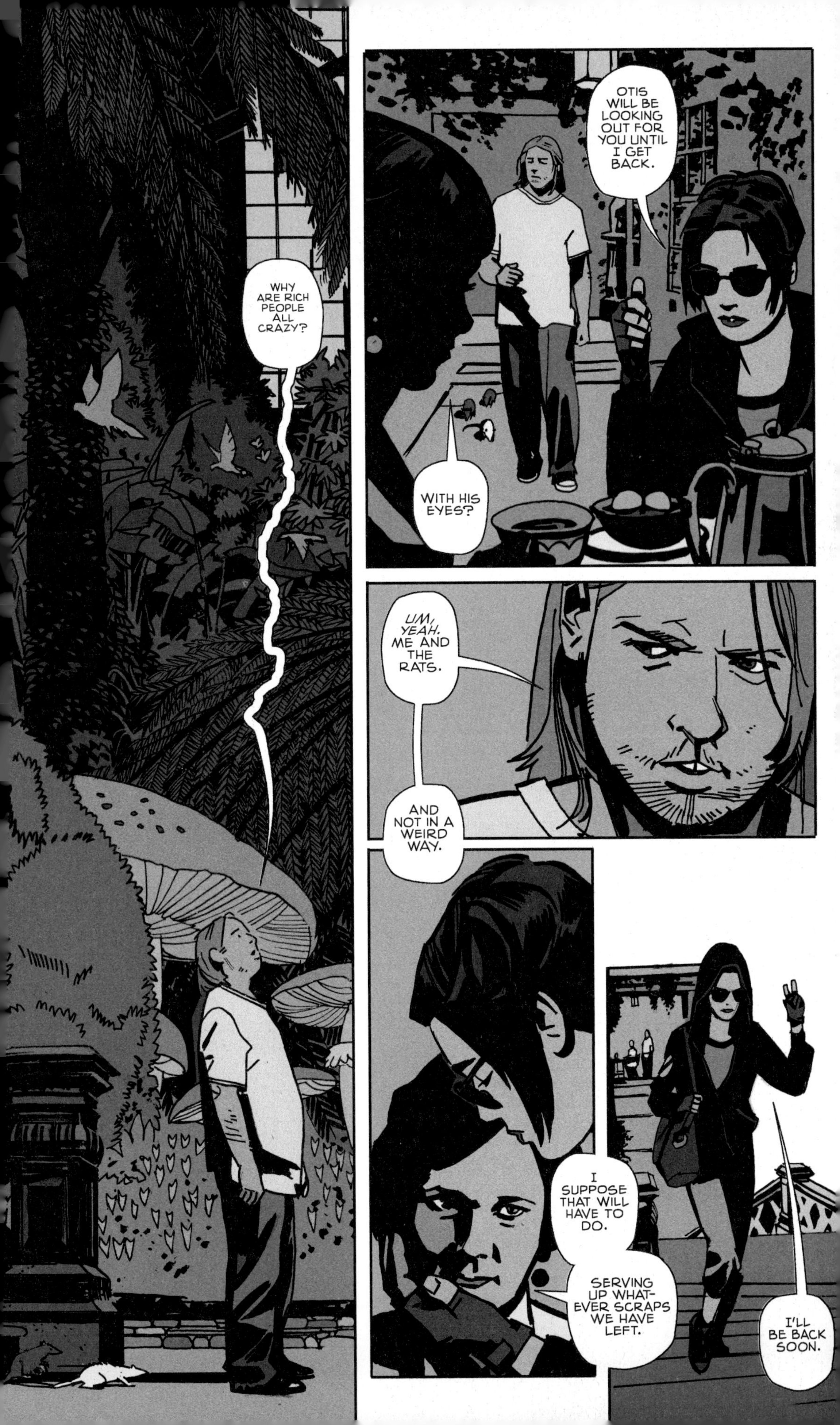
WHY ARE RICH PEOPLE ALL CRAZY?
OTIS WILL BE LOOKING OUT FOR YOU UNTIL I GET BACK.
WITH HIS EYES?
UM, YEAH. ME AND THE RATS.
AND NOT IN A WEIRD WAY.
I SUPPOSE THAT WILL HAVE TO DO.
SERVING UP WHAT-EVER SCRAPS WE HAVE LEFT.
I'LL BE BACK SOON.

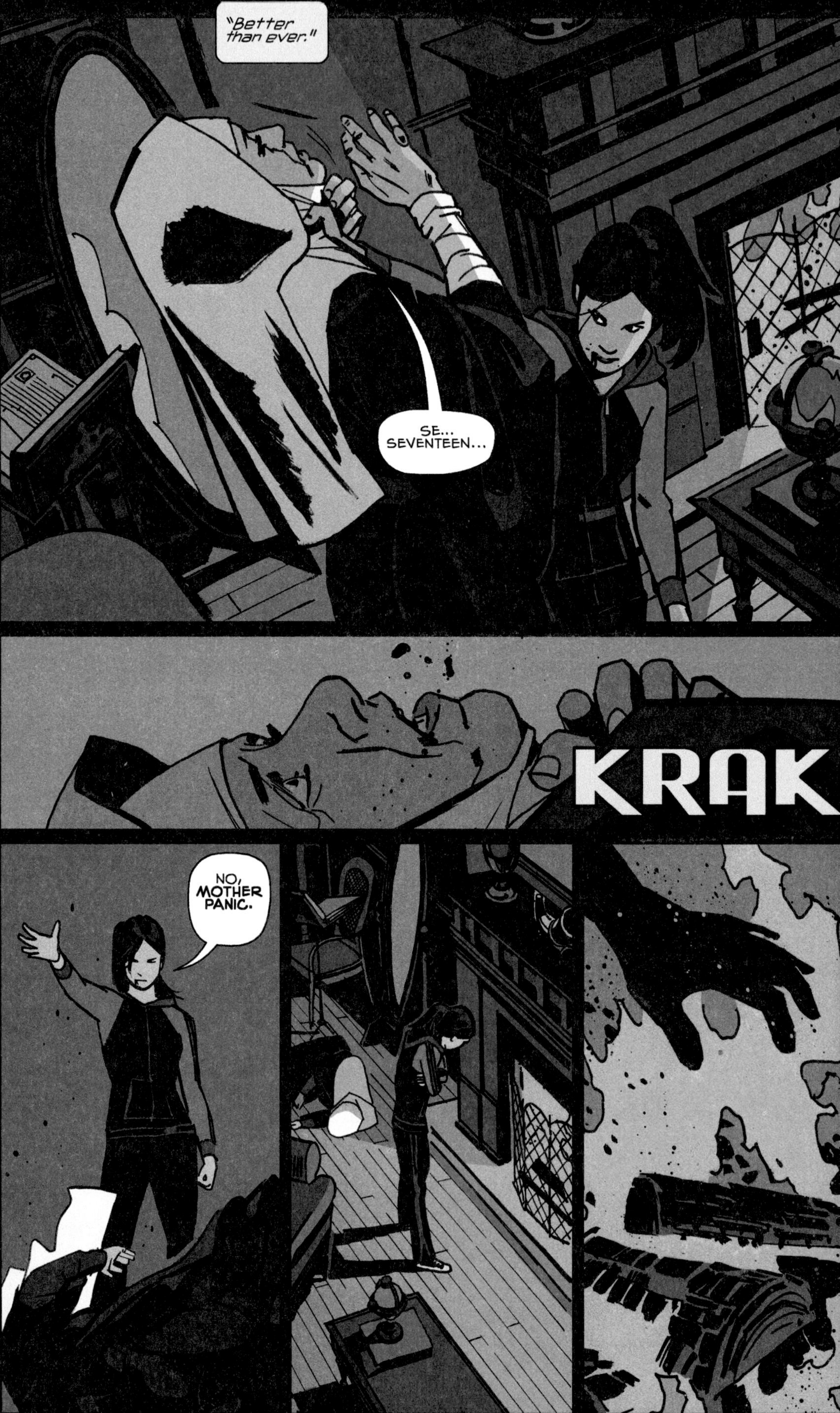
"Better than ever."
SE... SEVENTEEN...
KRAK
NO, MOTHER PANIC.

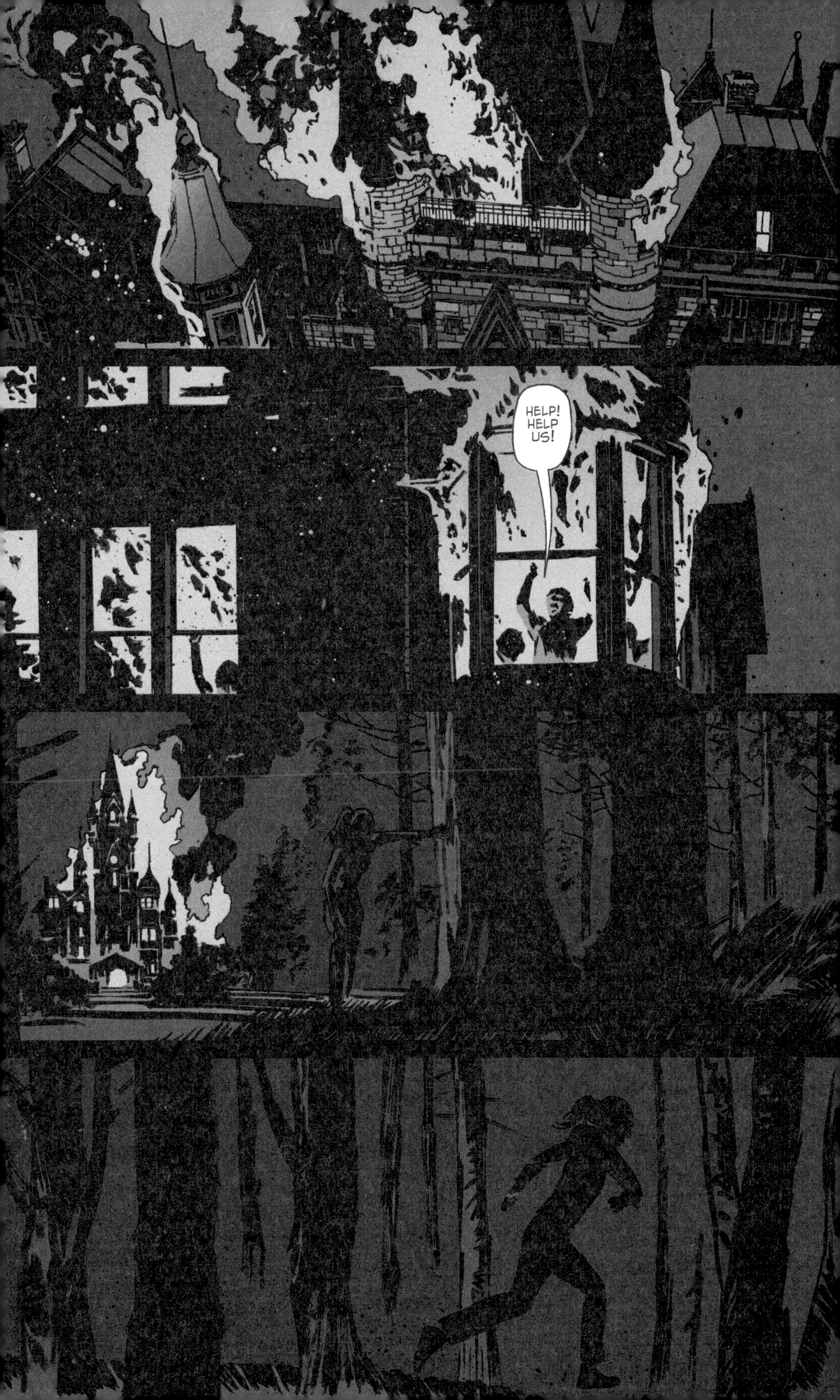
HELP! HELP US!

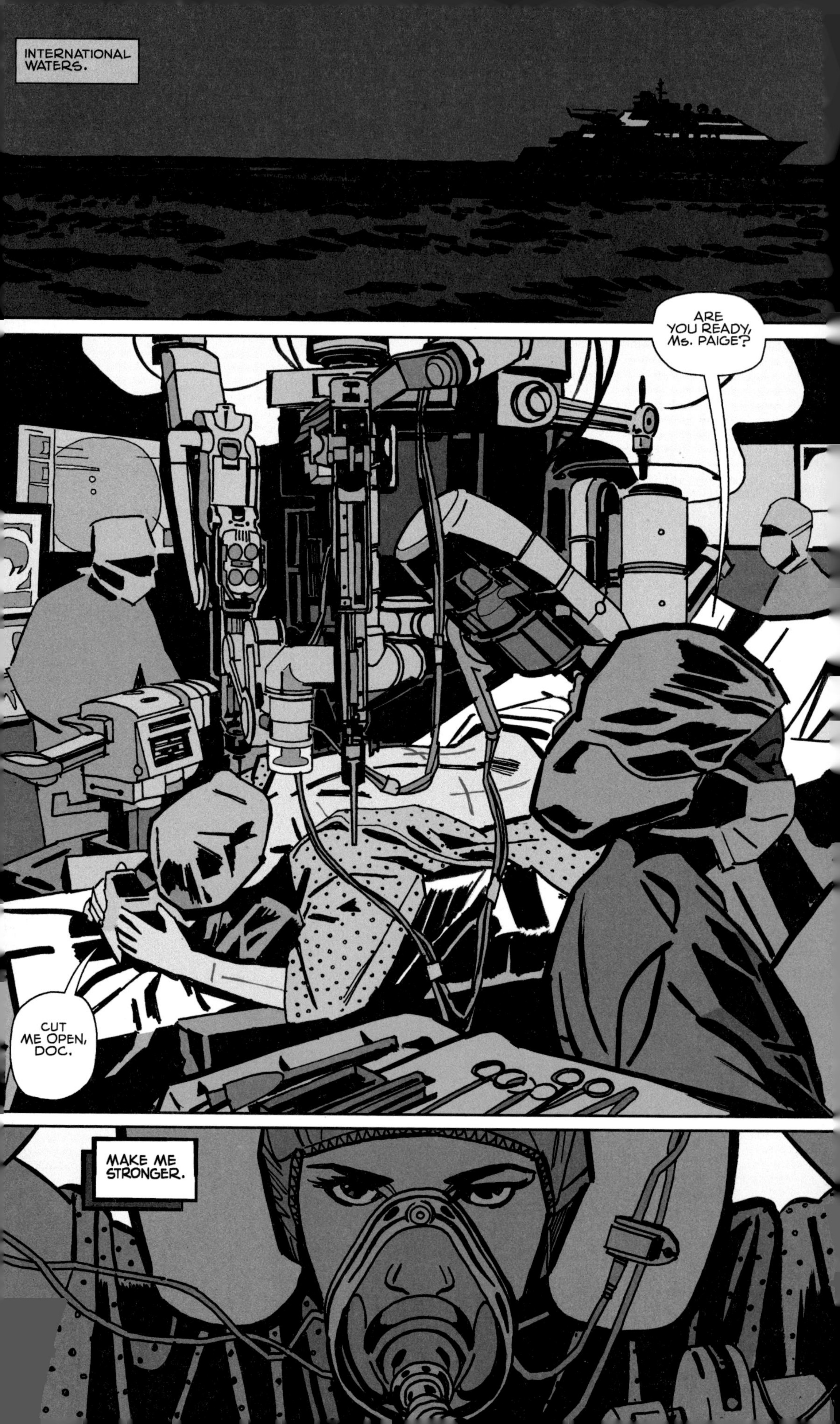
INTERNATIONAL WATERS.
ARE YOU READY, Ms. PAIGE?
CUT ME OPEN, DOC.
MAKE ME STRONGER.

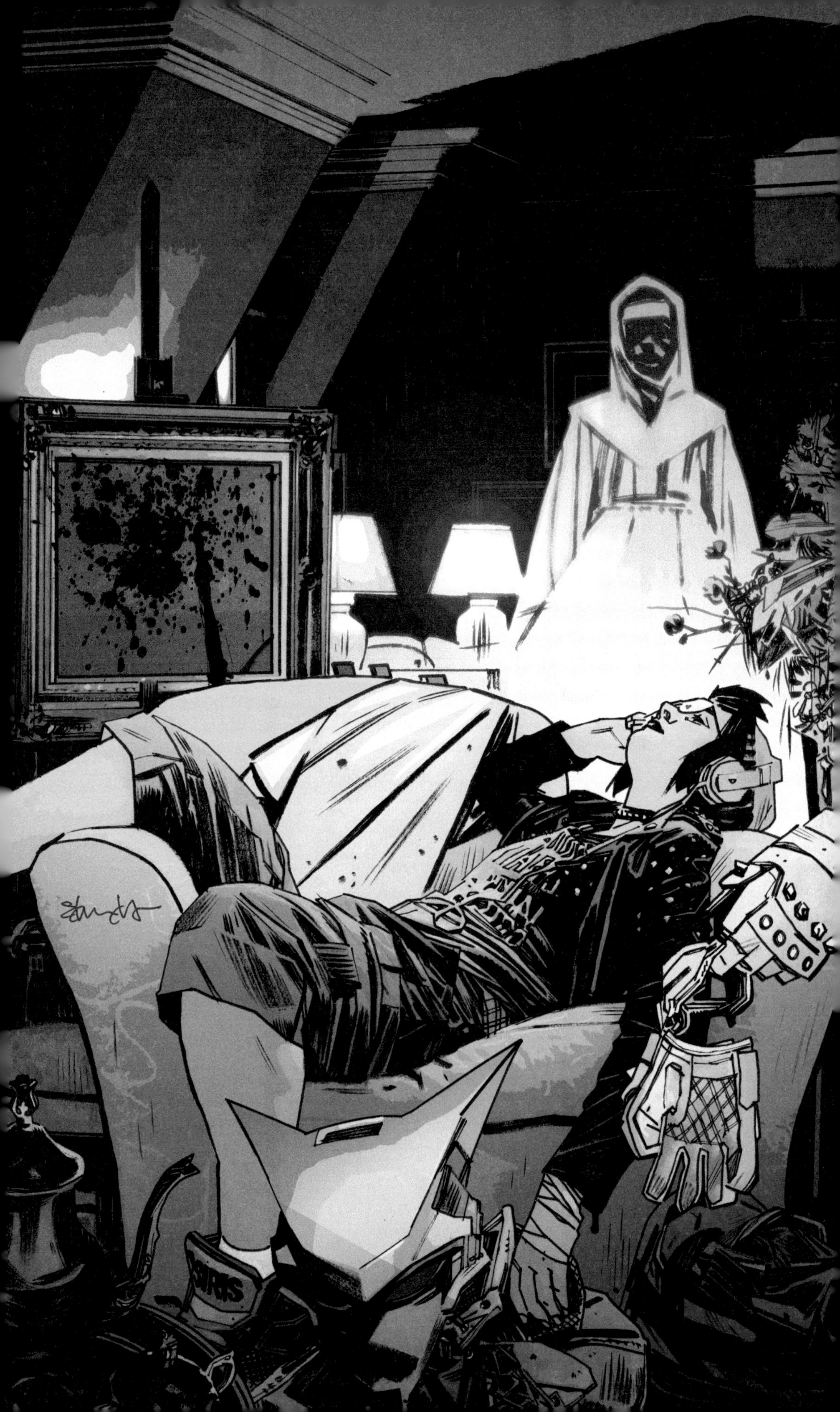

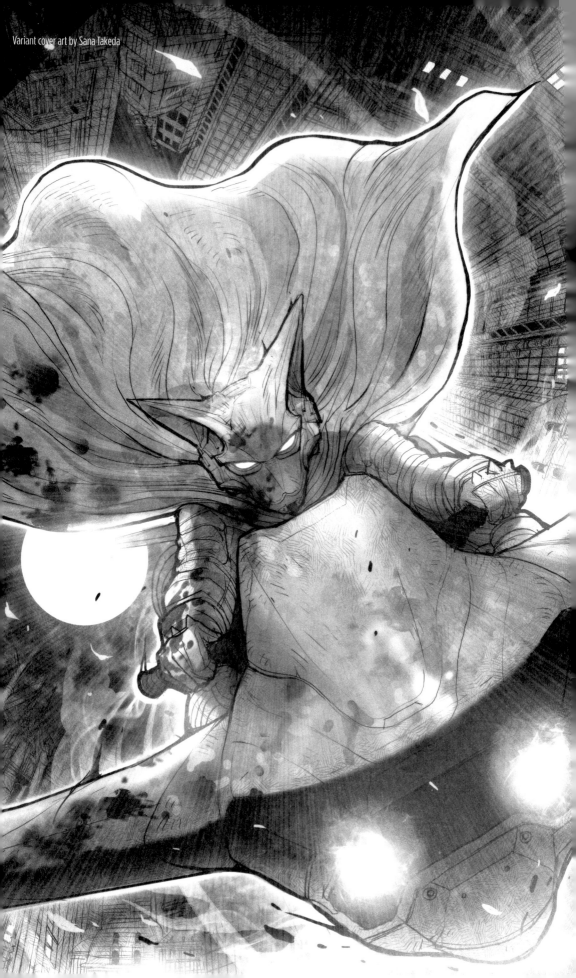
Variant cover art by Sana Takeda

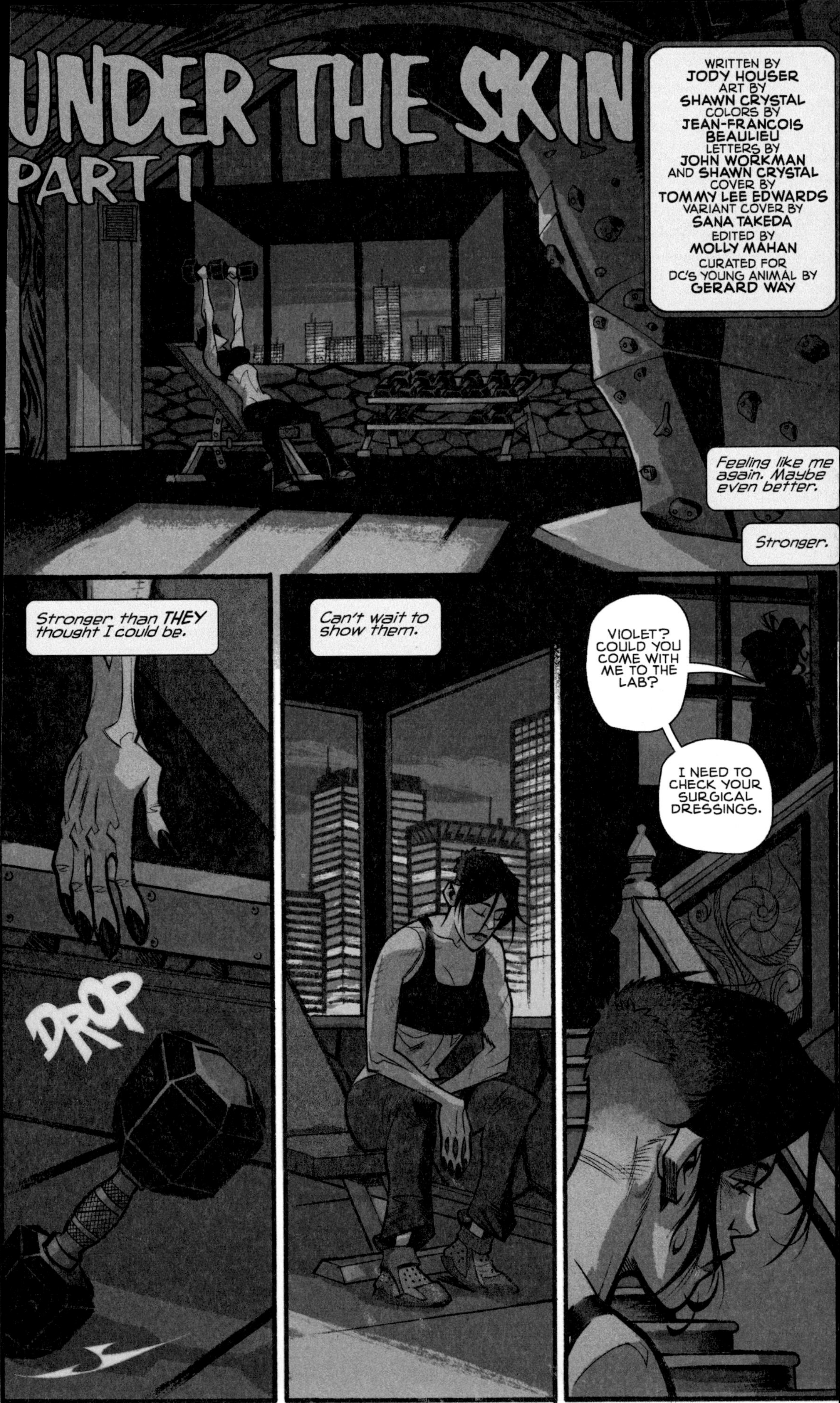
UNDER THE SKIN
PART 1
WRITTEN BY JODY HOUSER ART BY SHAWN CRYSTAL COLORS BY JEAN-FRANCOIS BEAULIEU LETTERS BY JOHN WORKMAN AND SHAWN CRYSTAL COVER BY TOMMY LEE EDWARDS VARIANT COVER BY SANA TAKEDA EDITED BY MOLLY MAHAN CURATED FOR DC'S YOUNG ANIMAL BY GERARD WAY
Feeling like me again. Maybe even better.
Stronger.
Stronger than THEY thought I could be.
DROP
Can't wait to show them.
VIOLET? COULD YOU COME WITH ME TO THE LAB?
I NEED TO CHECK YOUR SURGICAL DRESSINGS.

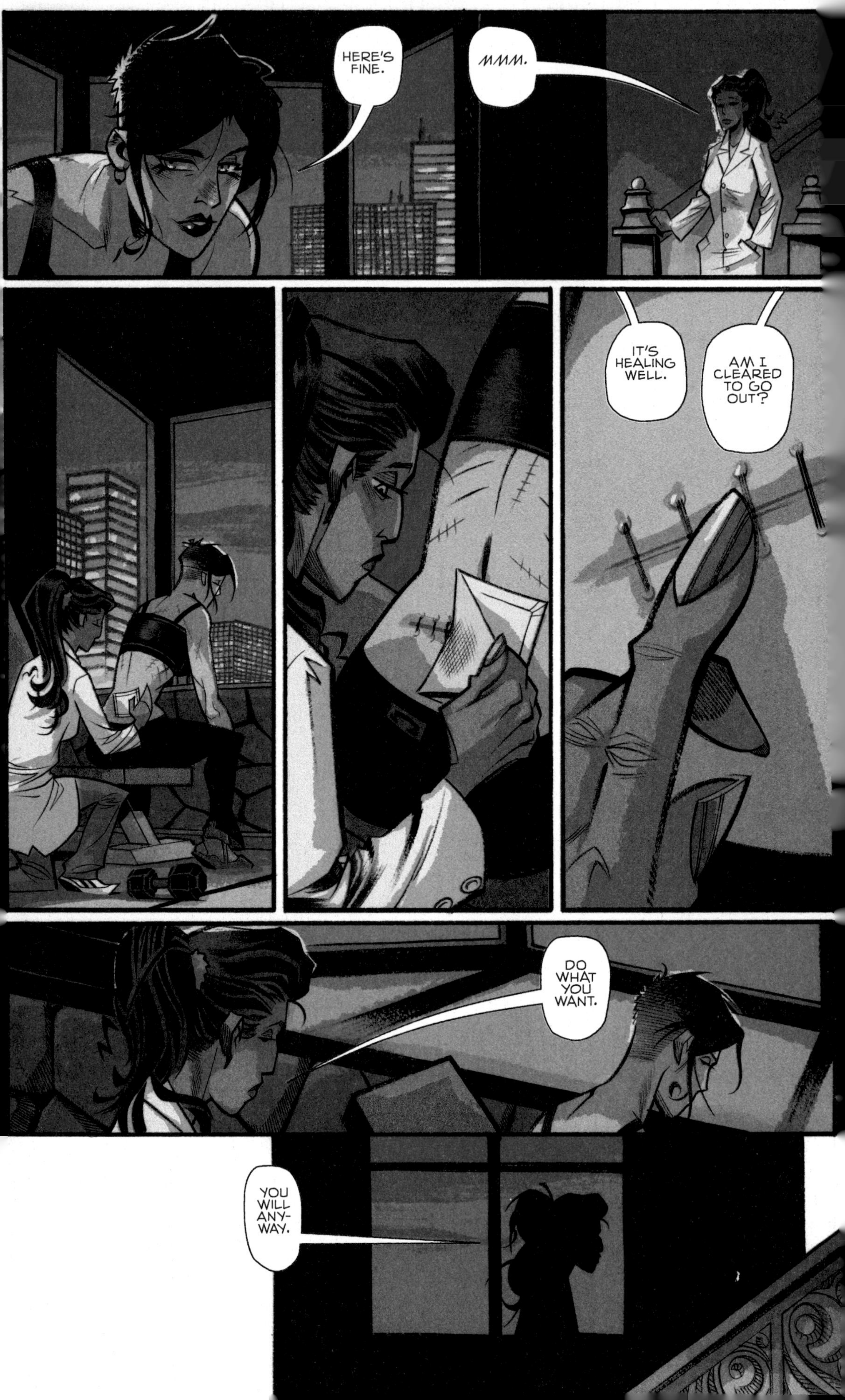
HERE'S FINE.
MMM.
IT'S HEALING WELL.
AM I CLEARED TO GO OUT?
DO WHAT YOU WANT.
YOU WILL ANY-WAY.

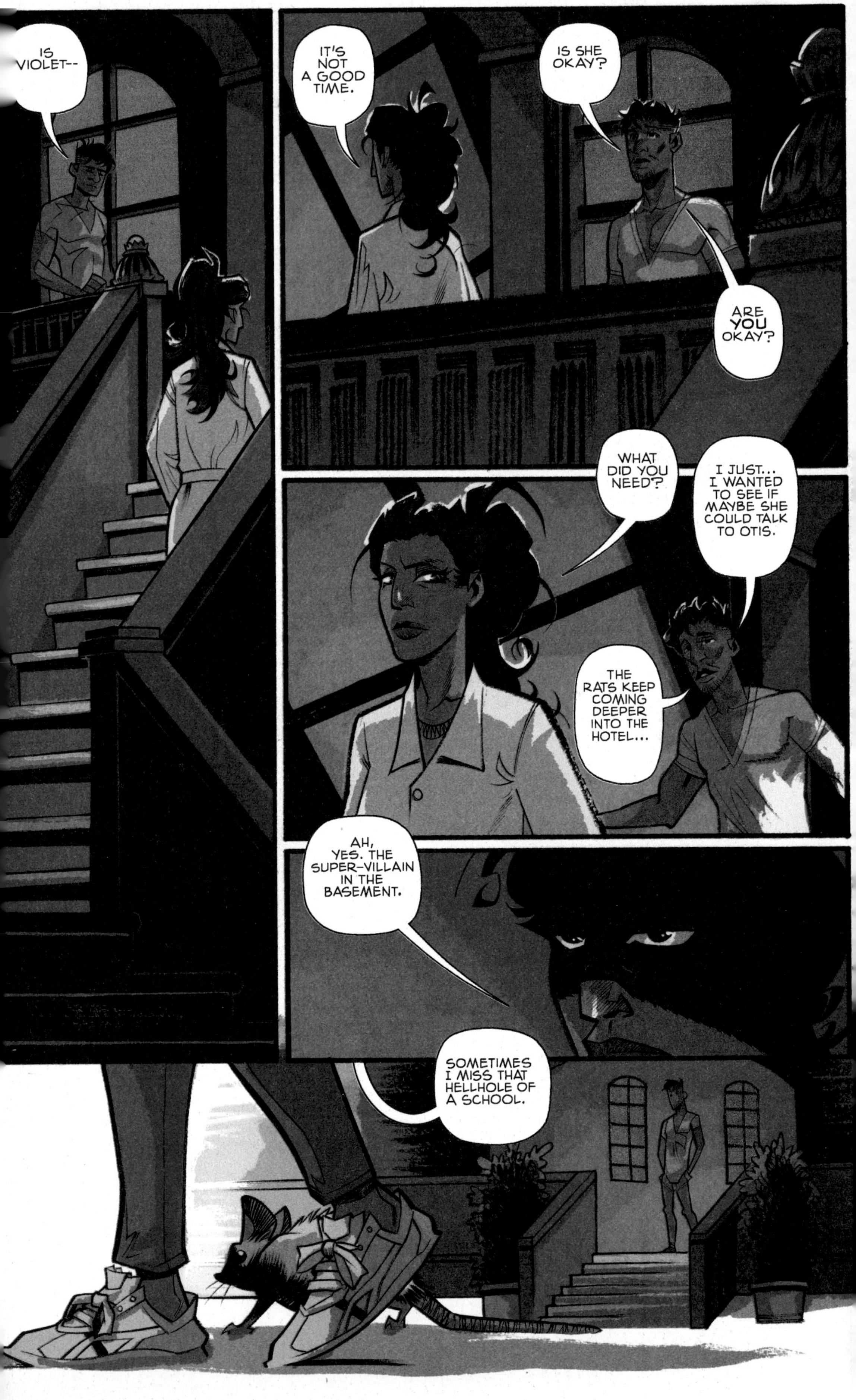
IS VIOLET--
IT'S NOT A GOOD TIME.
IS SHE OKAY?
ARE YOU OKAY?
WHAT DID YOU NEED?
I JUST... I WANTED TO SEE IF MAYBE SHE COULD TALK TO OTIS.
THE RATS KEEP COMING DEEPER INTO THE HOTEL...
AH, YES. THE SUPER-VILLAIN IN THE BASEMENT.
SOMETIMES I MISS THAT HELLHOLE OF A SCHOOL.

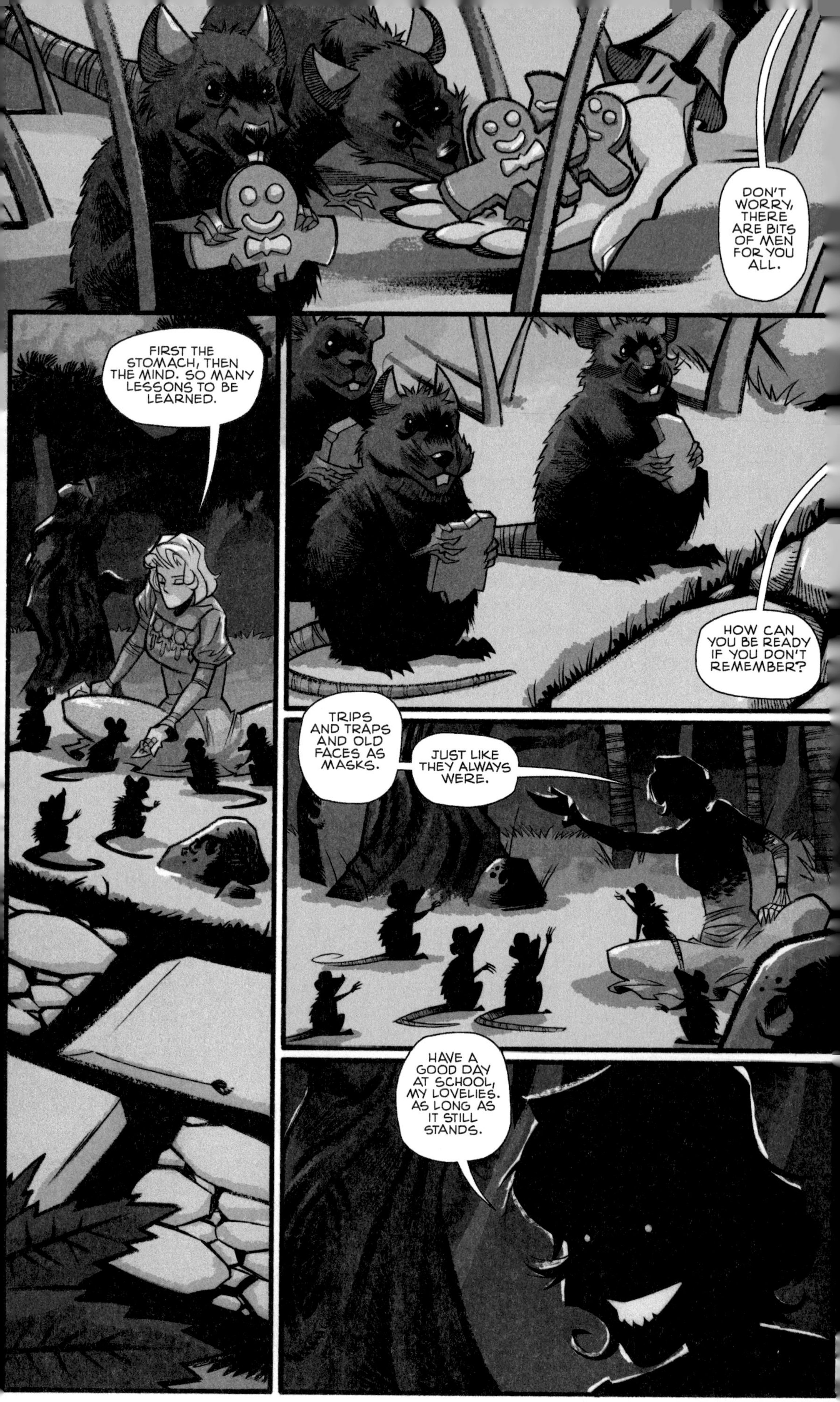
DON'T WORRY, THERE ARE BITS OF MEN FOR YOU ALL.
FIRST THE STOMACH, THEN THE MIND. SO MANY LESSONS TO BE LEARNED.
HOW CAN YOU BE READY IF YOU DON'T REMEMBER?
TRIPS AND TRAPS AND OLD FACES AS MASKS.
JUST LIKE THEY ALWAYS WERE.
HAVE A GOOD DAY AT SCHOOL, MY LOVELIES. AS LONG AS IT STILL STANDS.

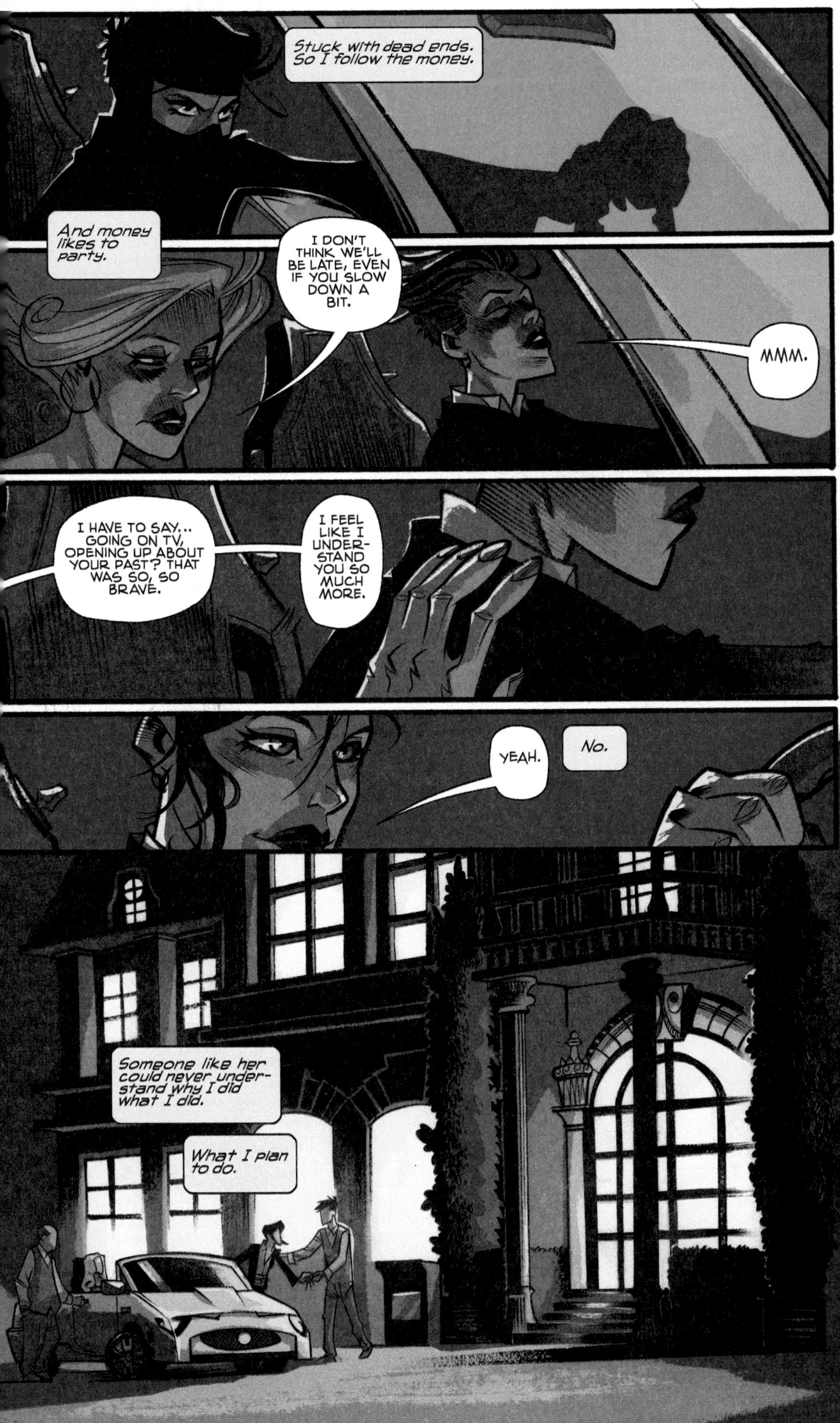
Stuck with dead ends. So I follow the money.
And money likes to party.
I DON'T THINK WE'LL BE LATE, EVEN IF YOU SLOW DOWN A BIT.
MMM.
I HAVE TO SAY... GOING ON TV, OPENING UP ABOUT YOUR PAST? THAT WAS SO, SO BRAVE.
I FEEL LIKE I UNDERSTAND YOU SO MUCH MORE.
YEAH.
No.
Someone like her could never understand why I did what I did.
What I plan to do.

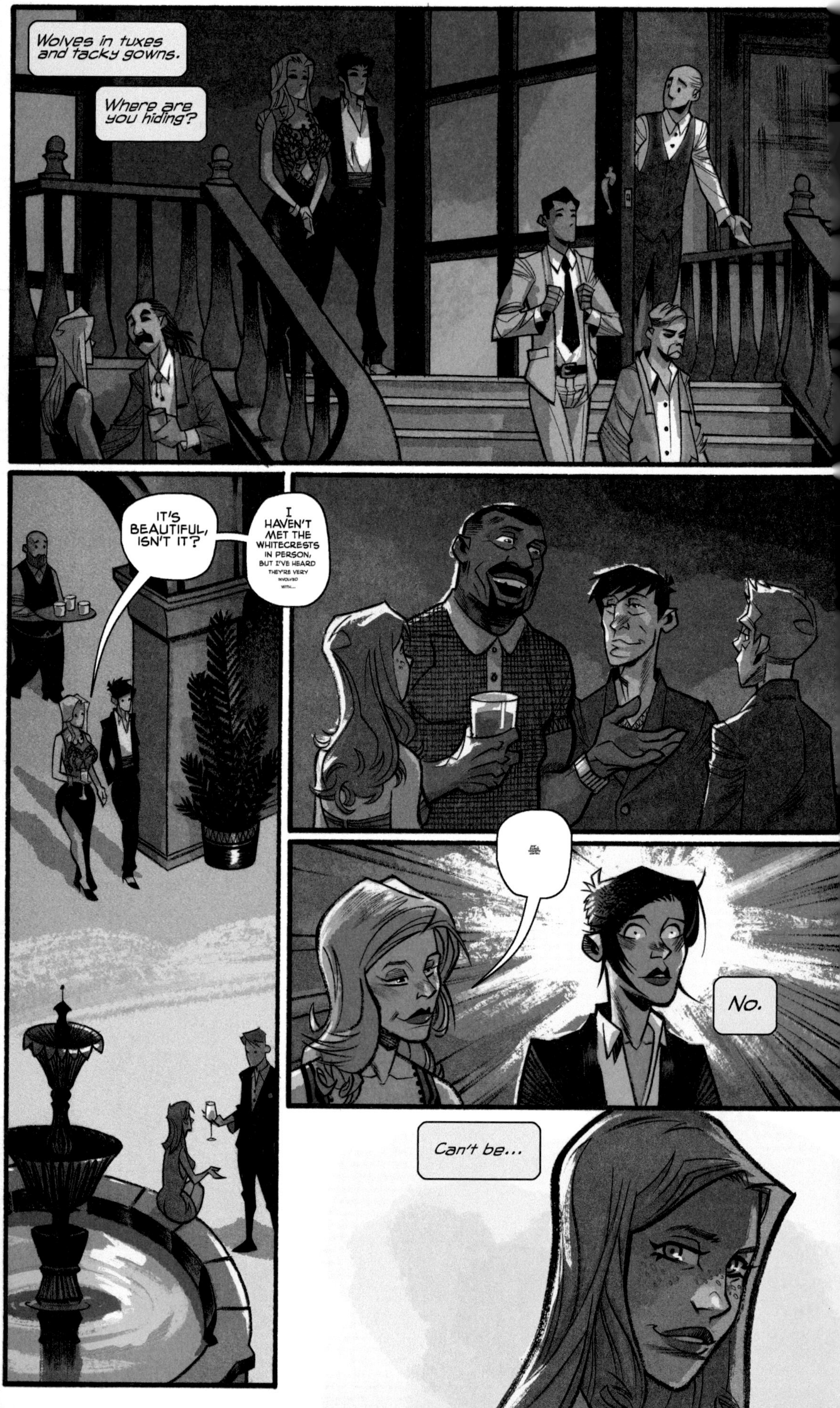
Wolves in tuxes and tacky gowns.
Where are you hiding?
IT'S BEAUTIFUL, ISN'T IT?
I HAVEN'T MET THE WHITECRESTS IN PERSON, BUT I'VE HEARD THEY'RE VERY INVOLVED WITH...
No.
Can't be...

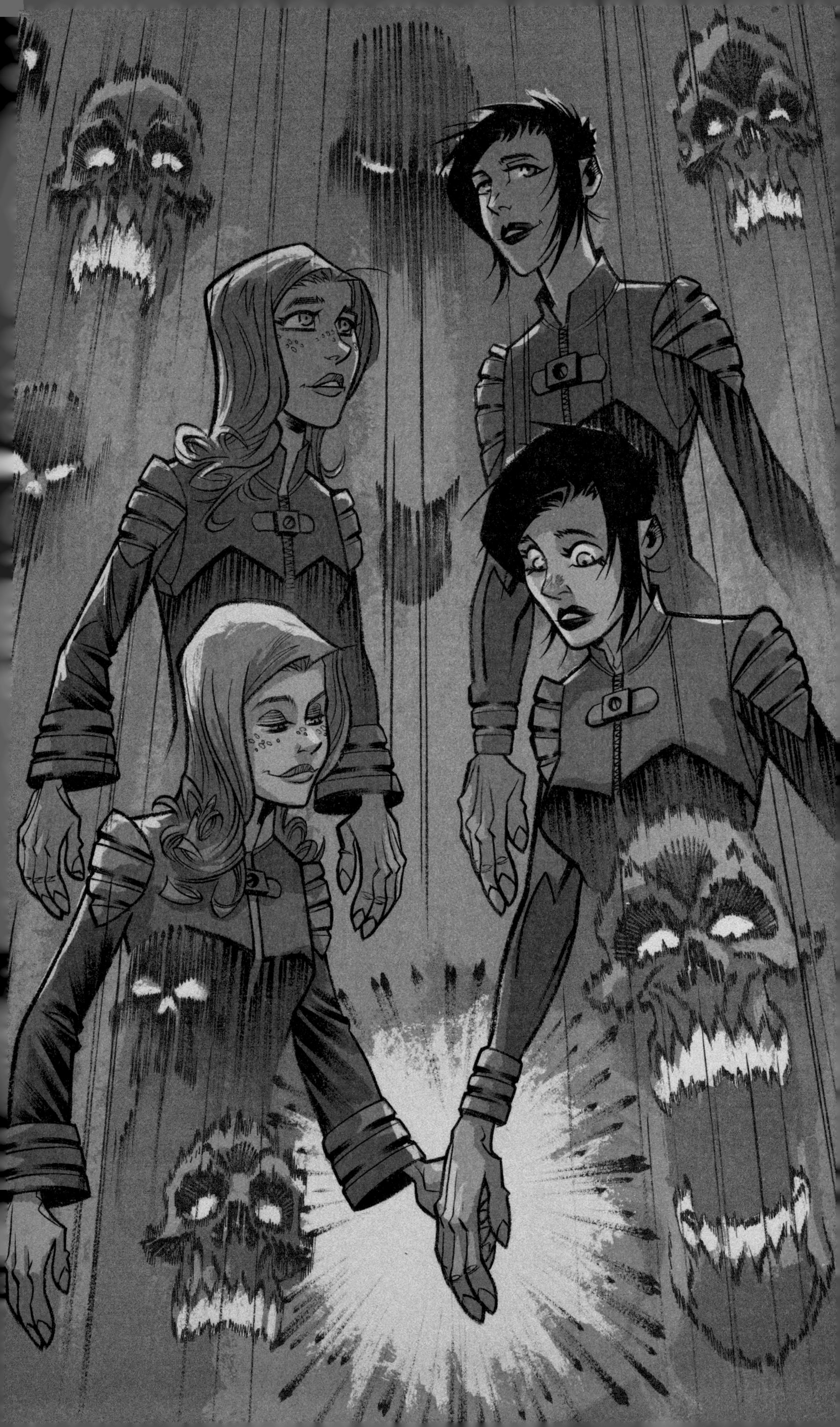

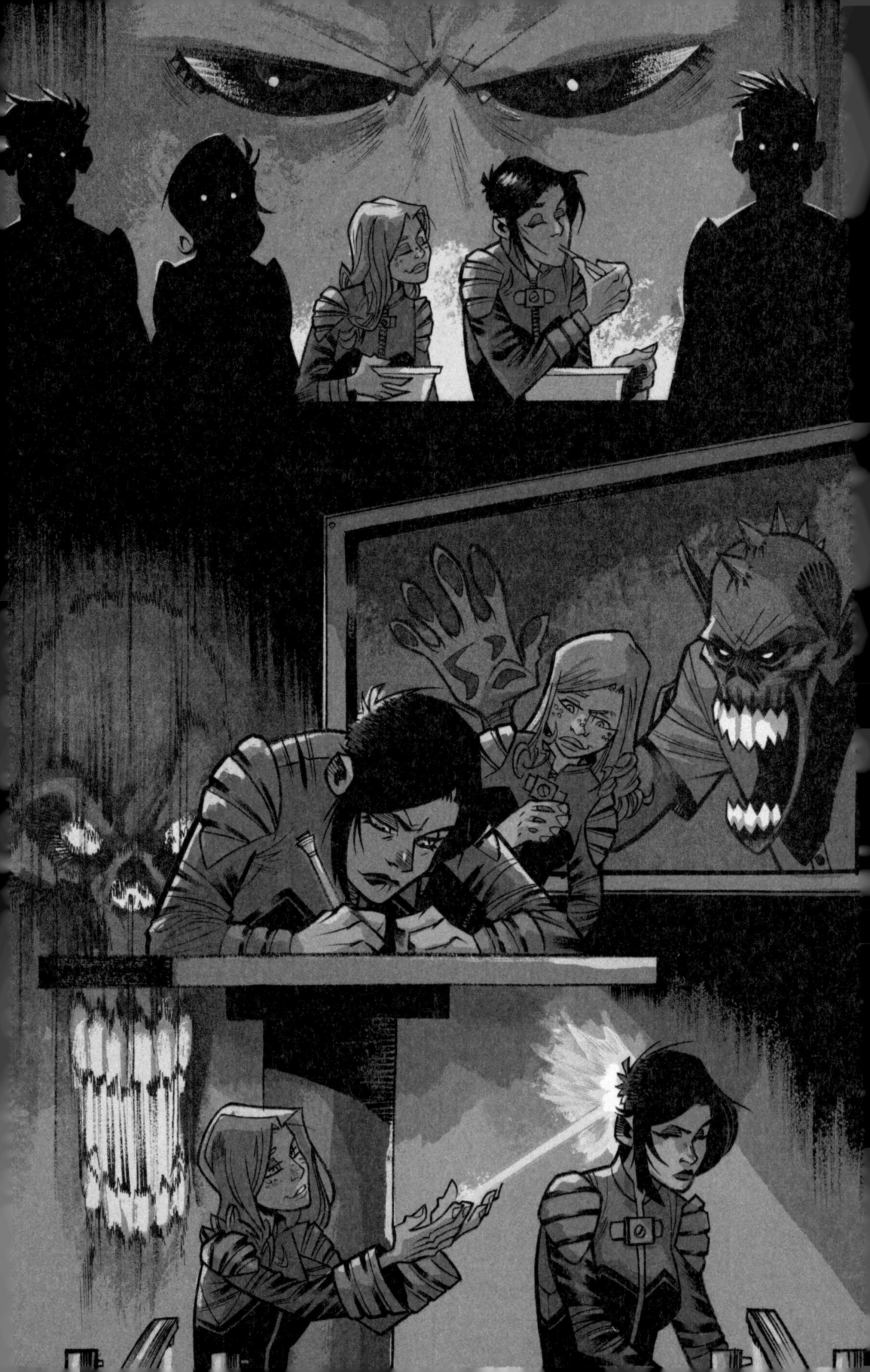

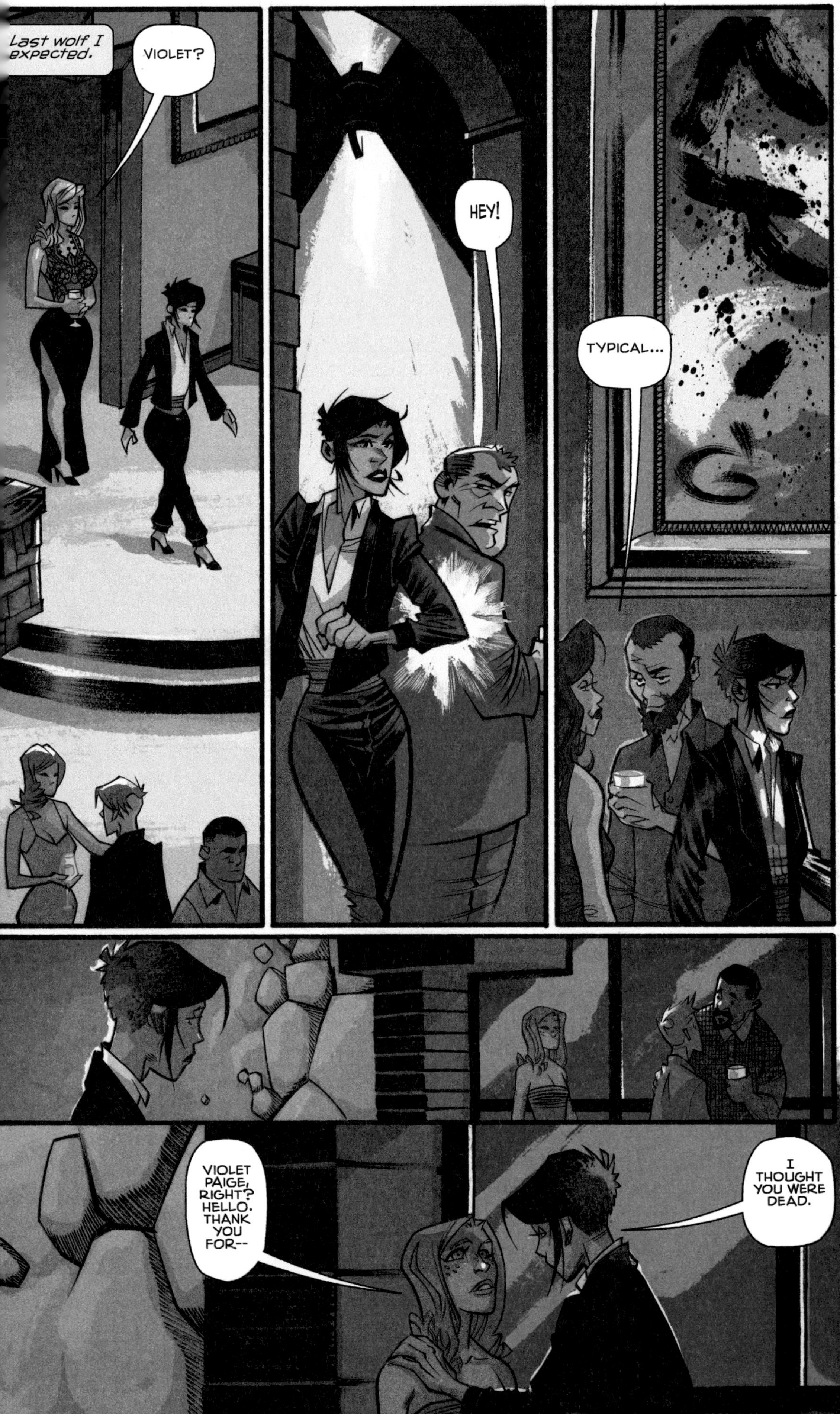
Last wolf I expected.
VIOLET?
HEY!
TYPICAL...
VIOLET PAIGE, RIGHT? HELLO. THANK YOU FOR--
I THOUGHT YOU WERE DEAD.

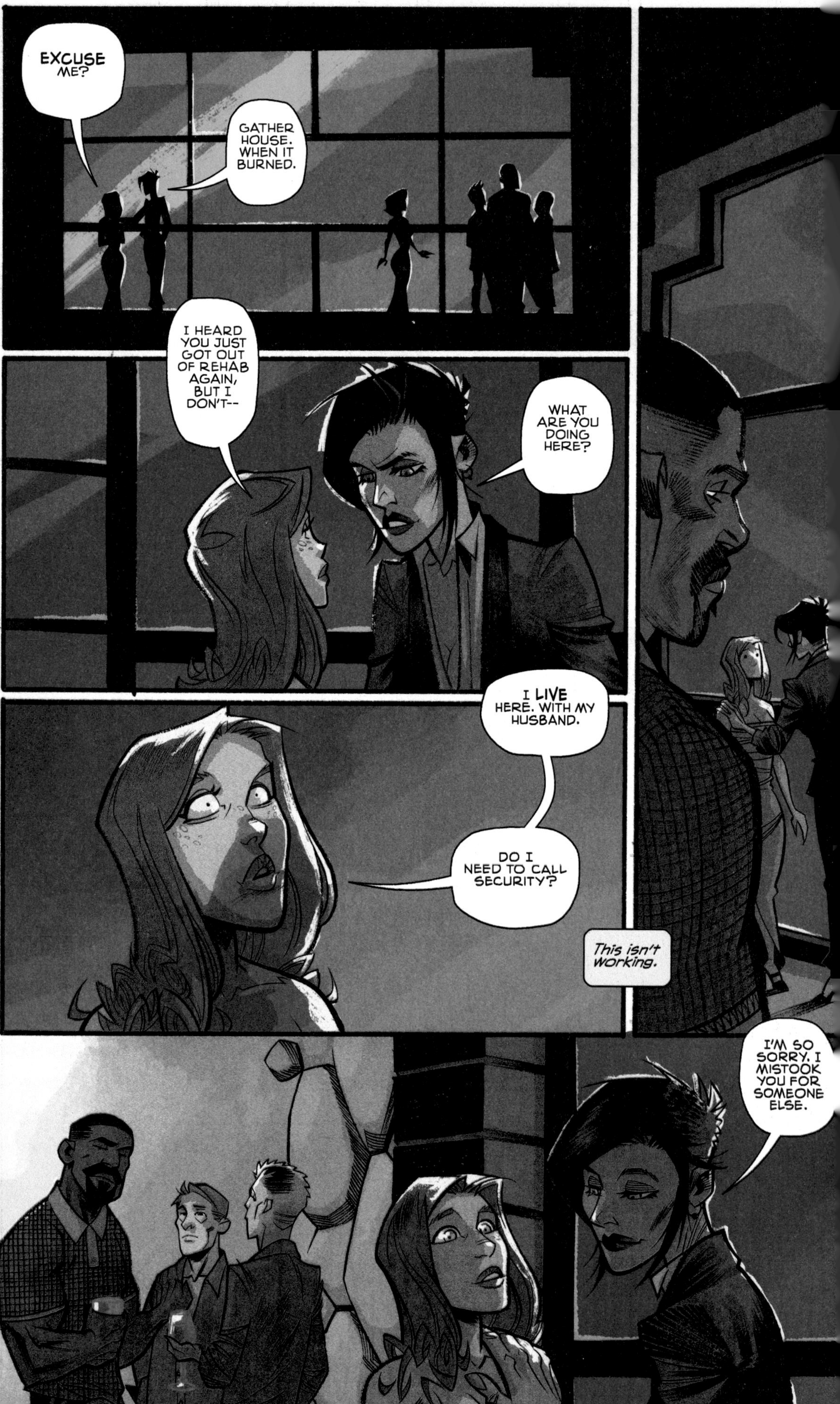
EXCUSE ME?
GATHER HOUSE. WHEN IT BURNED.
I HEARD YOU JUST GOT OUT OF REHAB AGAIN, BUT I DON'T--
WHAT ARE YOU DOING HERE?
I LIVE HERE. WITH MY HUSBAND.
DO I NEED TO CALL SECURITY?
This isn't working.
I'M SO SORRY. I MISTOOK YOU FOR SOMEONE ELSE.

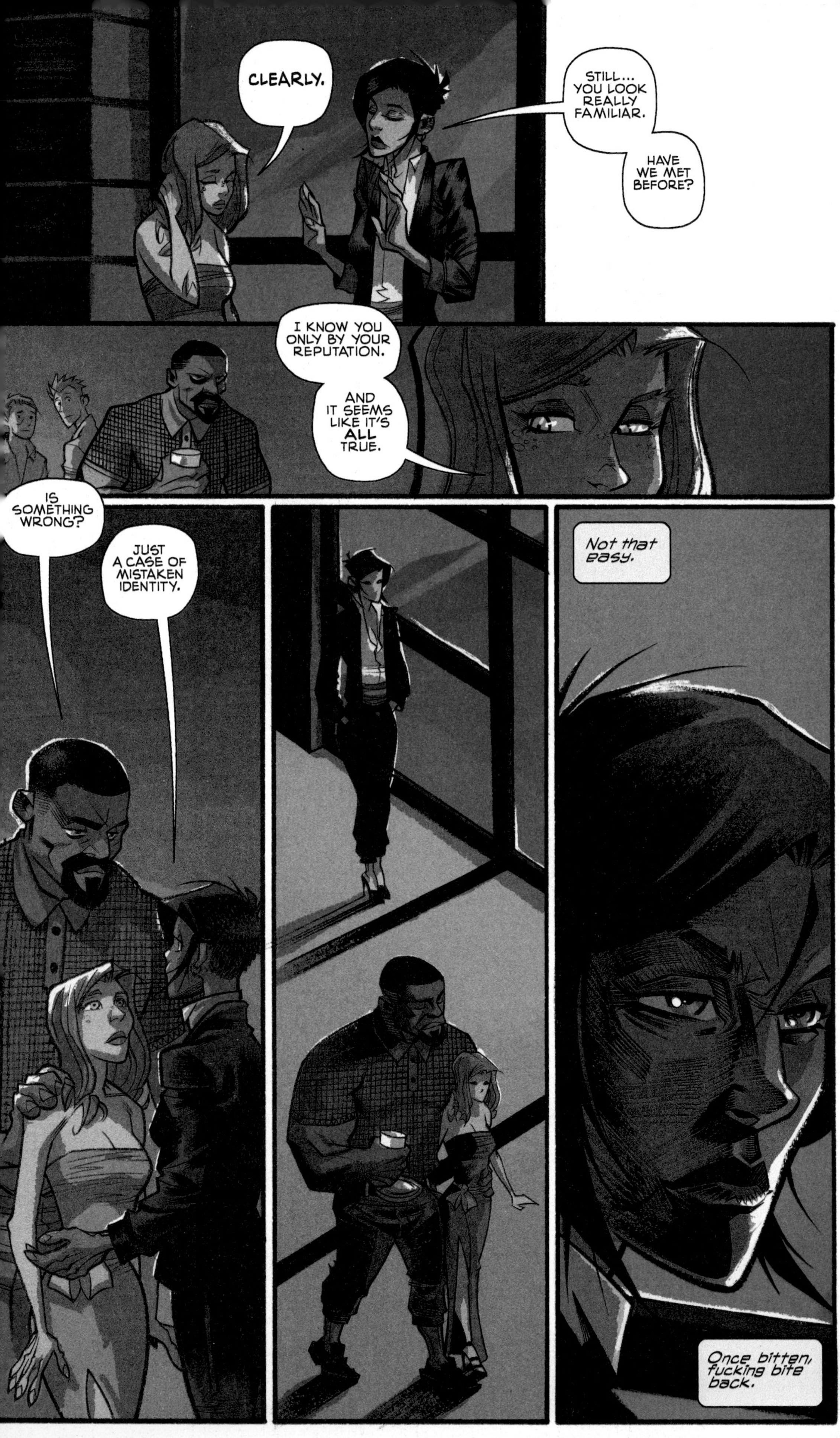
CLEARLY.
STILL... YOU LOOK REALLY FAMILIAR.
HAVE WE MET BEFORE?
I KNOW YOU ONLY BY YOUR REPUTATION.
AND IT SEEMS LIKE IT'S ALL TRUE.
IS SOMETHING WRONG?
JUST A CASE OF MISTAKEN IDENTITY.
Not that easy.
Once bitten, fucking bite back.

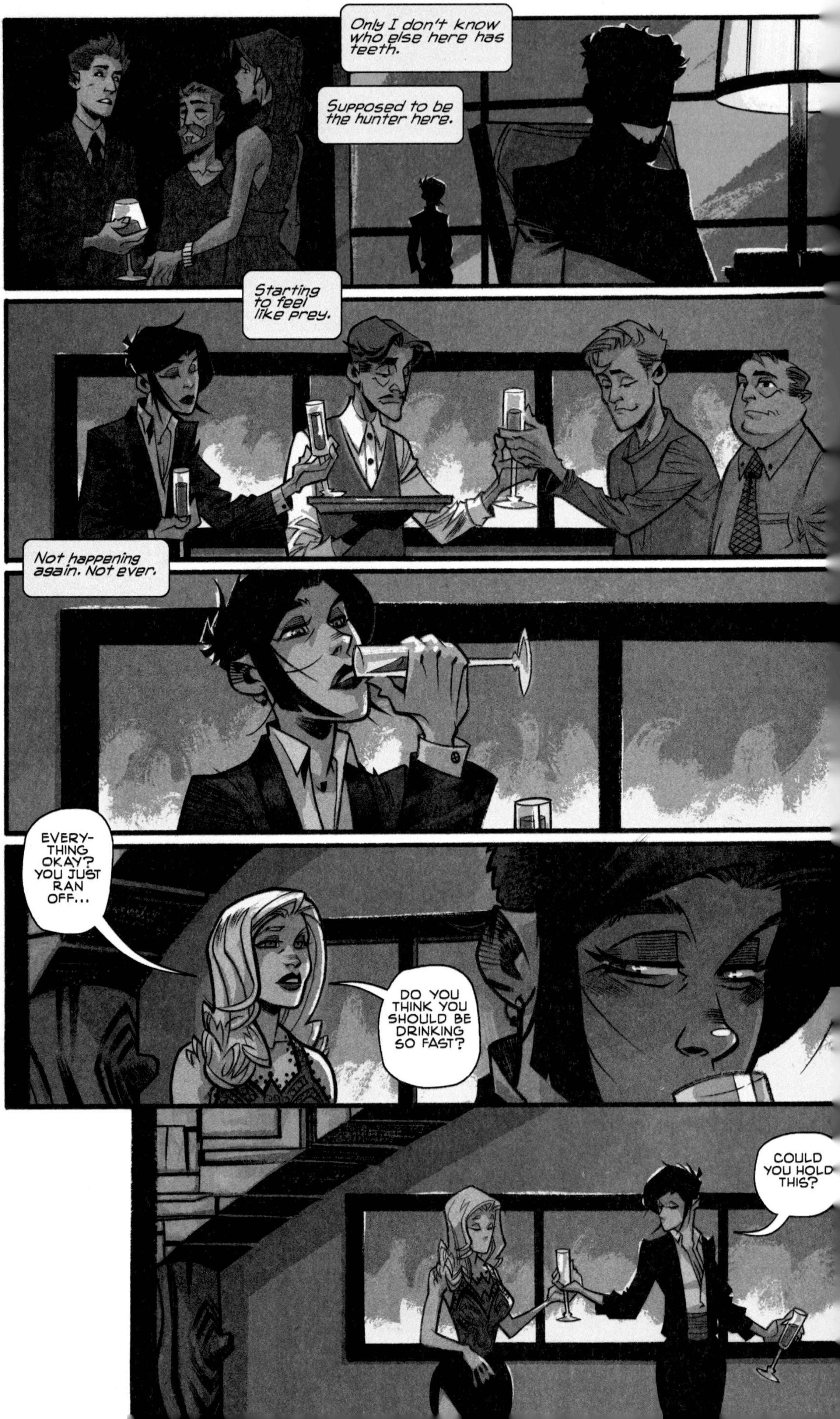

Only I don't know who else here has teeth.
Supposed to be the hunter here.
Starting to feel like prey.
Not happening again. Not ever.
EVERY-THING OKAY? YOU JUST RAN OFF...
DO YOU THINK YOU SHOULD BE DRINKING SO FAST?
COULD YOU HOLD THIS?

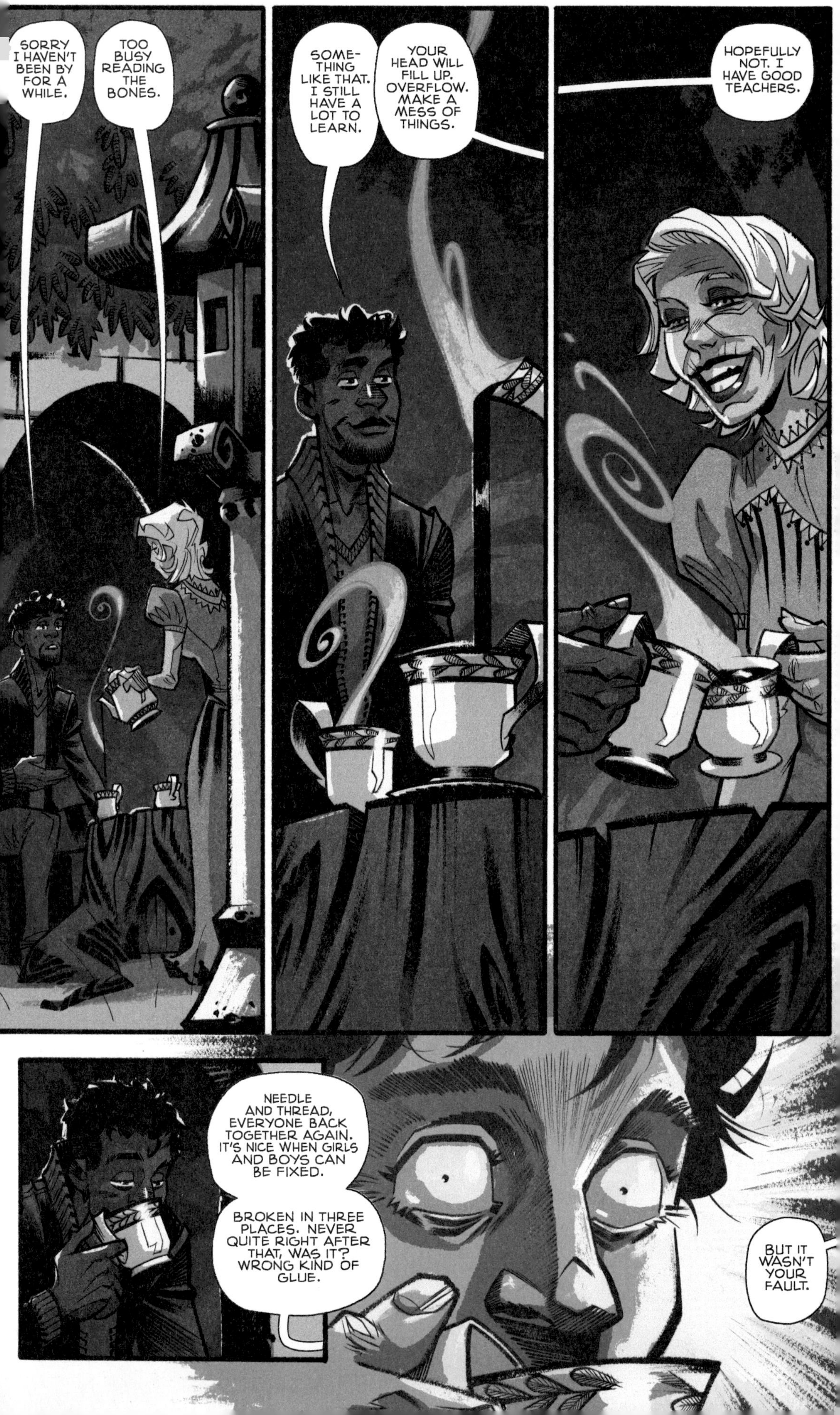

SORRY I HAVEN'T BEEN BY FOR A WHILE.
TOO BUSY READING THE BONES.
SOME-THING LIKE THAT. I STILL HAVE A LOT TO LEARN.
YOUR HEAD WILL FILL UP. OVERFLOW. MAKE A MESS OF THINGS.
HOPEFULLY NOT. I HAVE GOOD TEACHERS.
NEEDLE AND THREAD, EVERYONE BACK TOGETHER AGAIN. IT'S NICE WHEN GIRLS AND BOYS CAN BE FIXED.
BROKEN IN THREE PLACES. NEVER QUITE RIGHT AFTER THAT, WAS IT? WRONG KIND OF GLUE.
BUT IT WASN'T YOUR FAULT.

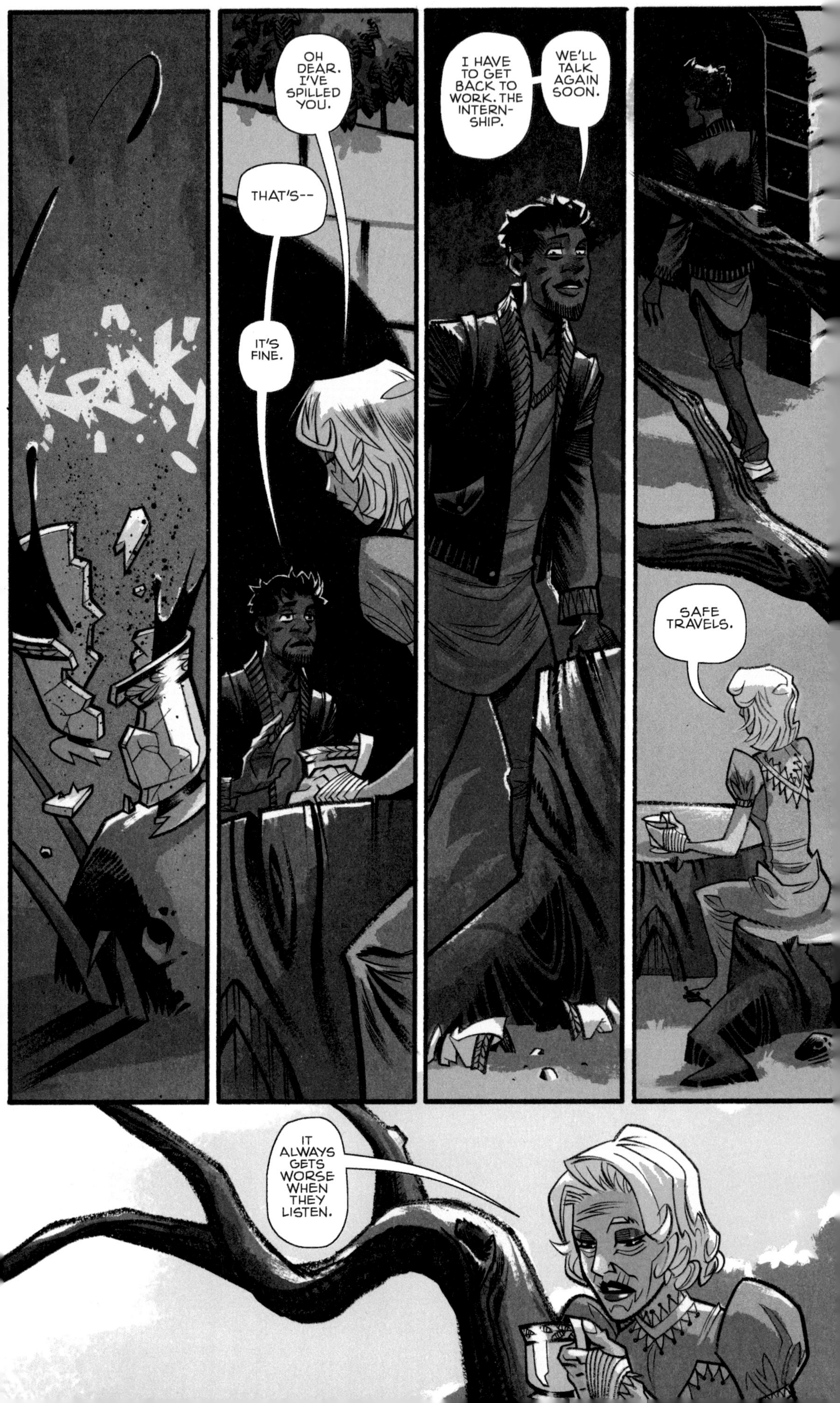
KRAK!
OH DEAR. I'VE SPILLED YOU.
THAT'S--
IT'S FINE.
I HAVE TO GET BACK TO WORK. THE INTERN-SHIP.
WE'LL TALK AGAIN SOON.
SAFE TRAVELS.
IT ALWAYS GETS WORSE WHEN THEY LISTEN.

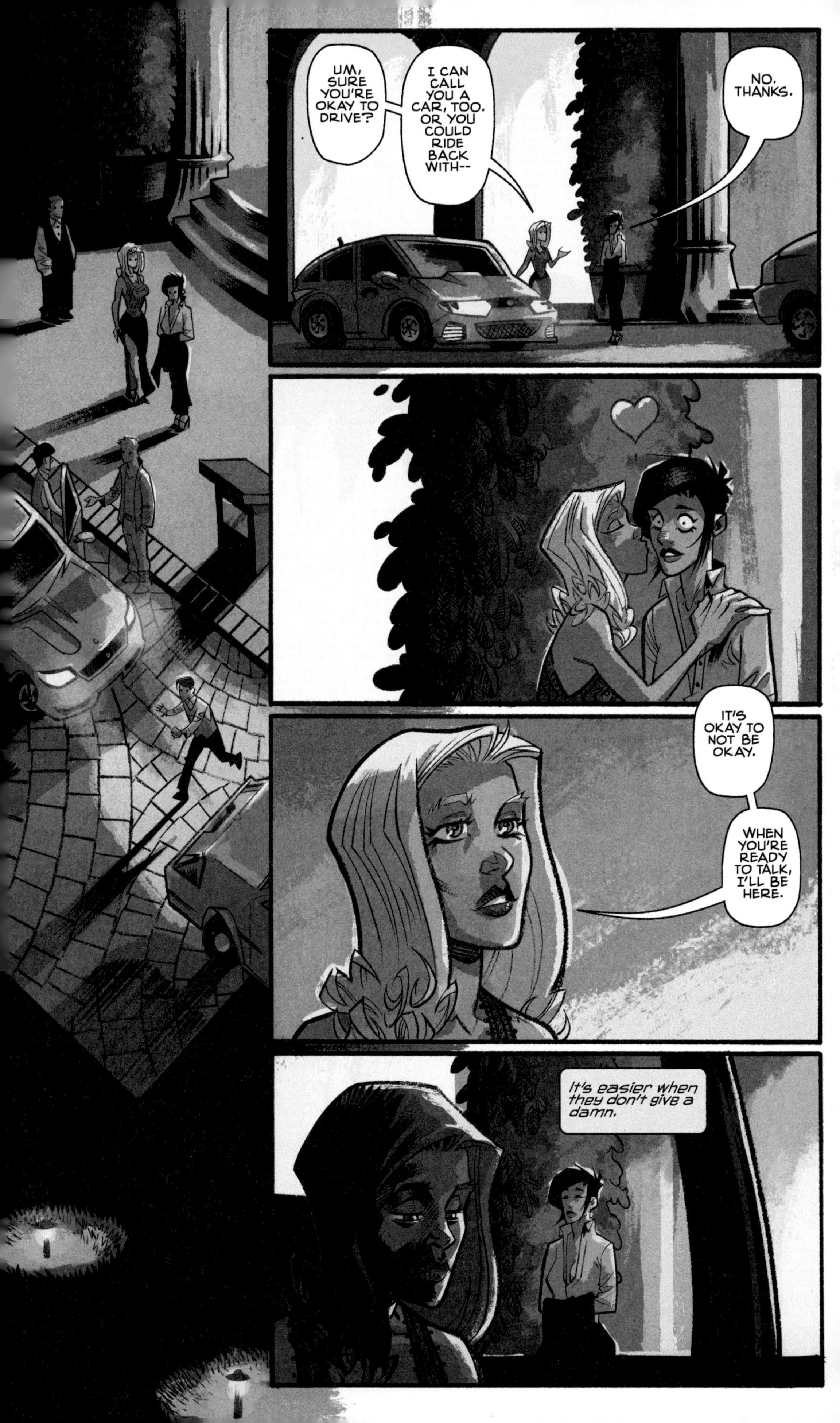
UM, SURE YOU'RE OKAY TO DRIVE?
I CAN CALL YOU A CAR, TOO. OR YOU COULD RIDE BACK WITH--
NO. THANKS.
IT'S OKAY TO NOT BE OKAY.
WHEN YOU'RE READY TO TALK, I'LL BE HERE.
It's easier when they don't give a damn.

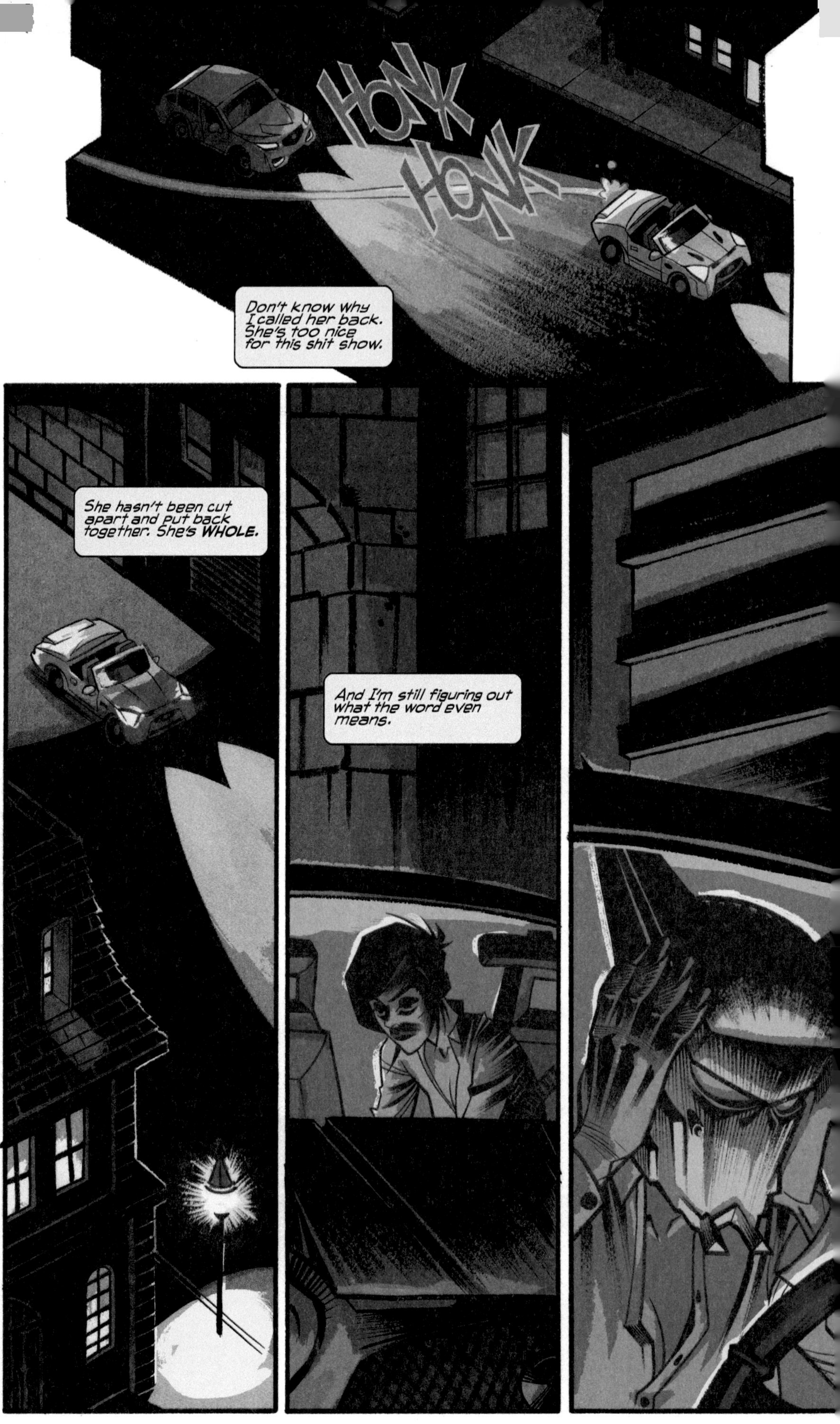
HONK HONK
Don't know why I called her back. She's too nice for this shit show.
She hasn't been cut apart and put back together. She's WHOLE.
And I'm still figuring out what the word even means.

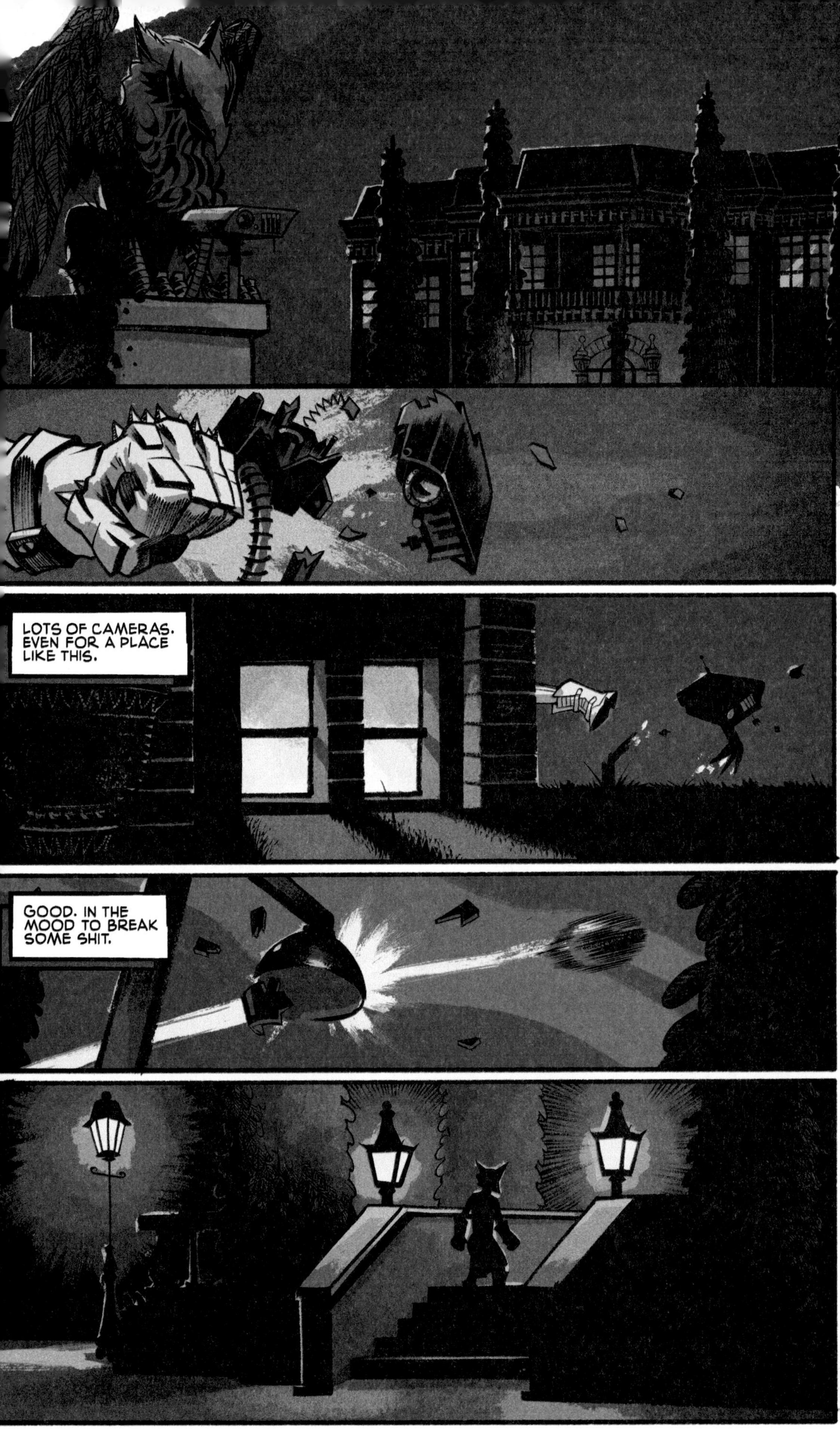
LOTS OF CAMERAS. EVEN FOR A PLACE LIKE THIS.
GOOD. IN THE MOOD TO BREAK SOME SHIT.

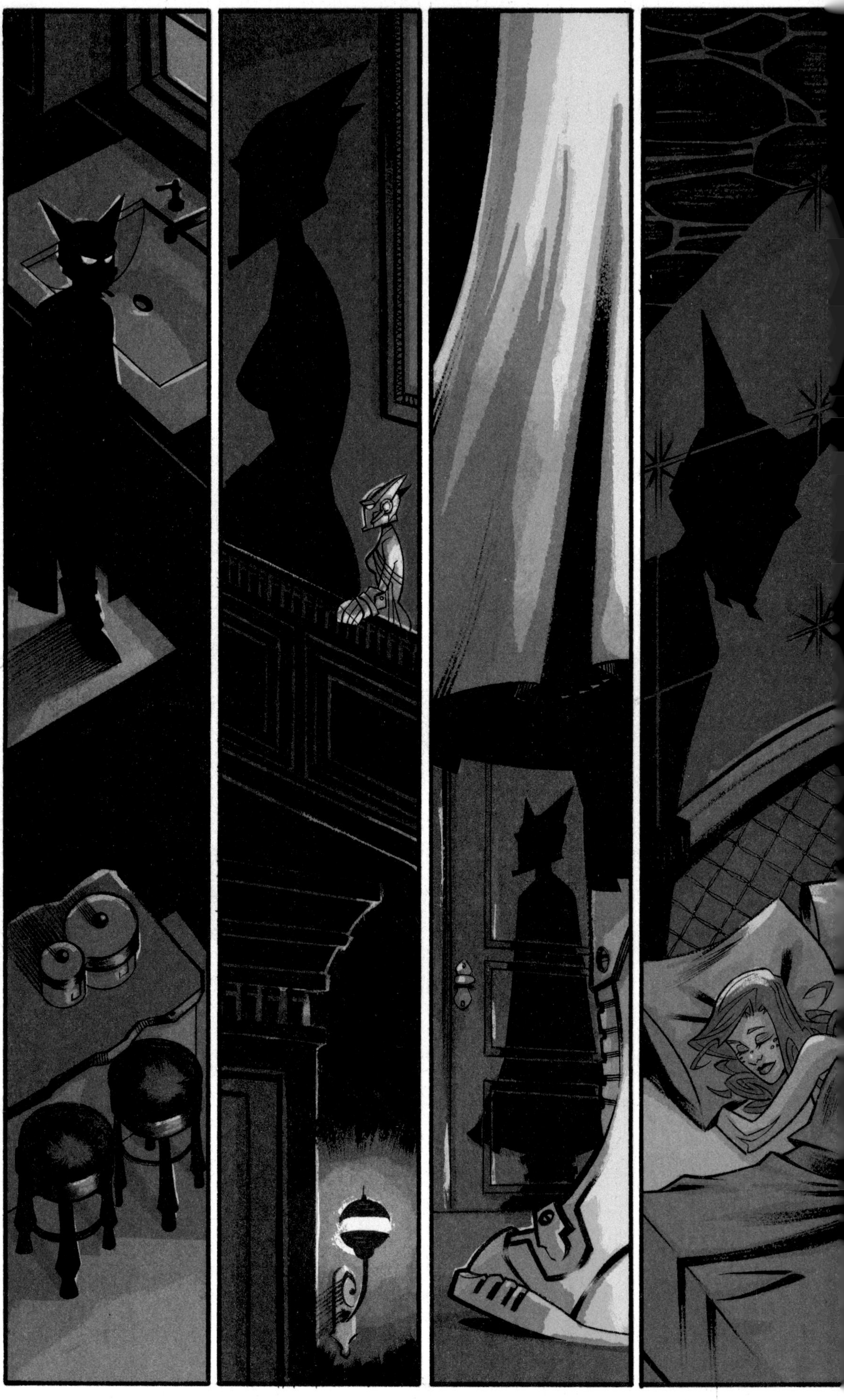

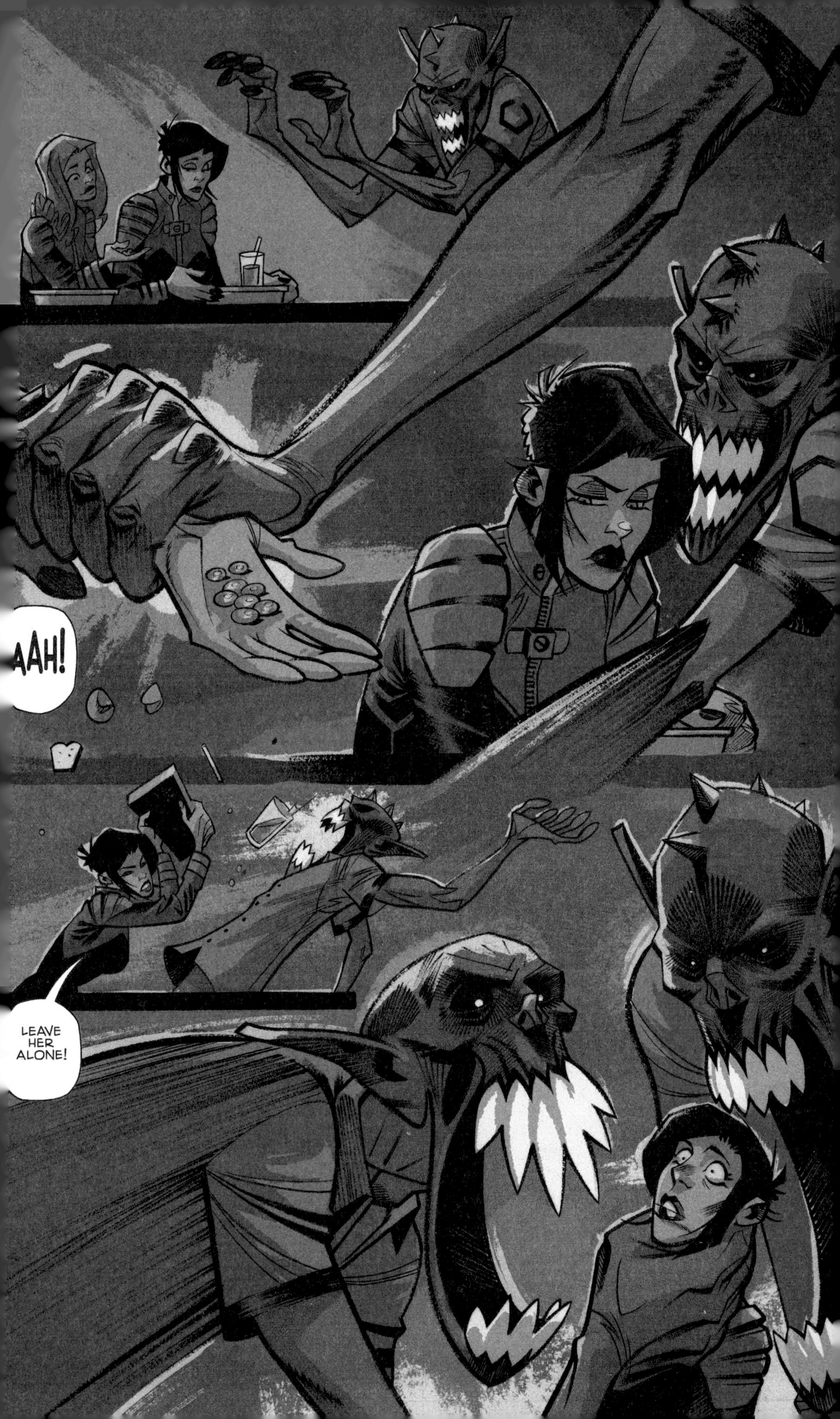
AAH!
LEAVE HER ALONE!

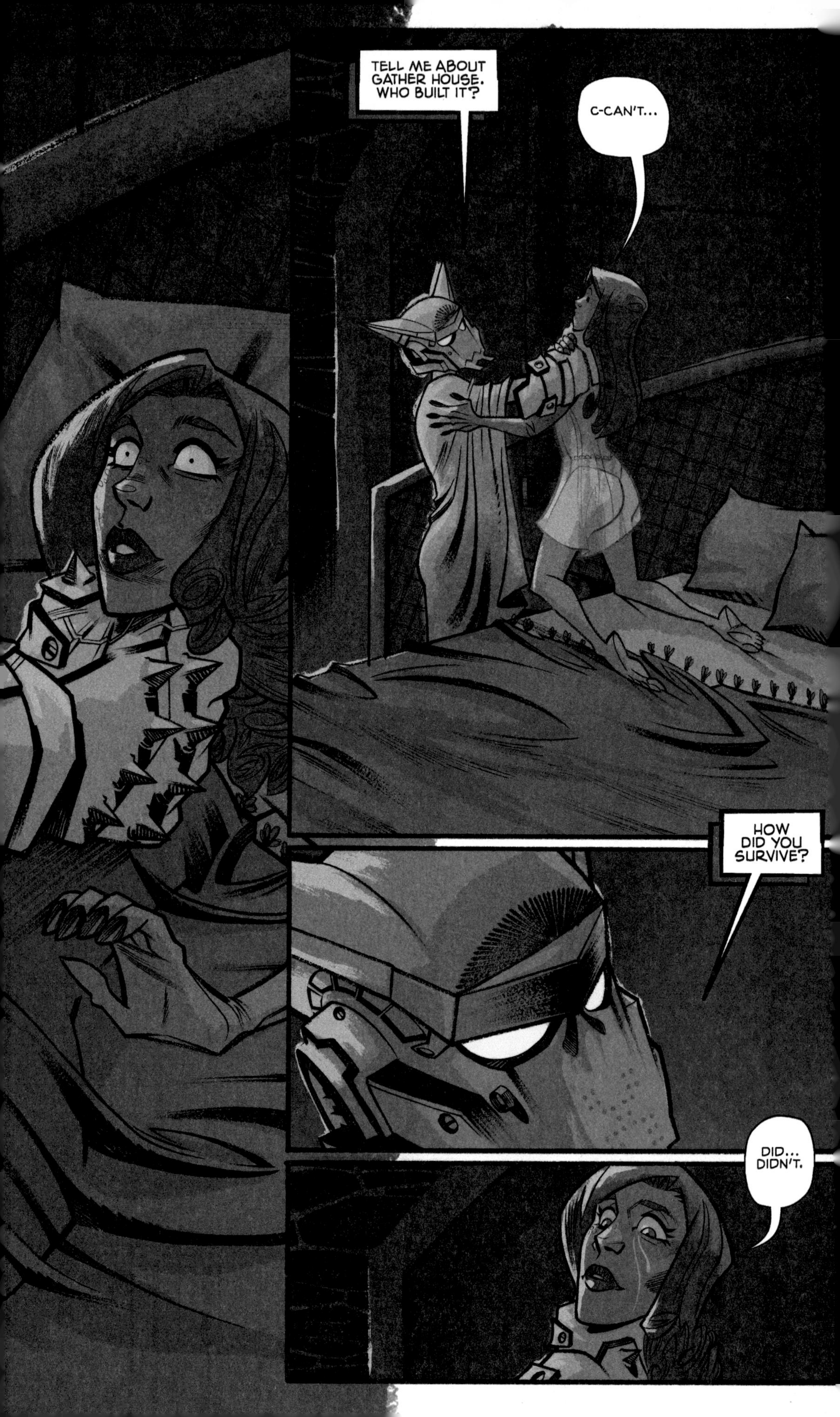
TELL ME ABOUT GATHER HOUSE. WHO BUILT IT?
C-CAN'T...
HOW DID YOU SURVIVE?
DID... DIDN'T.

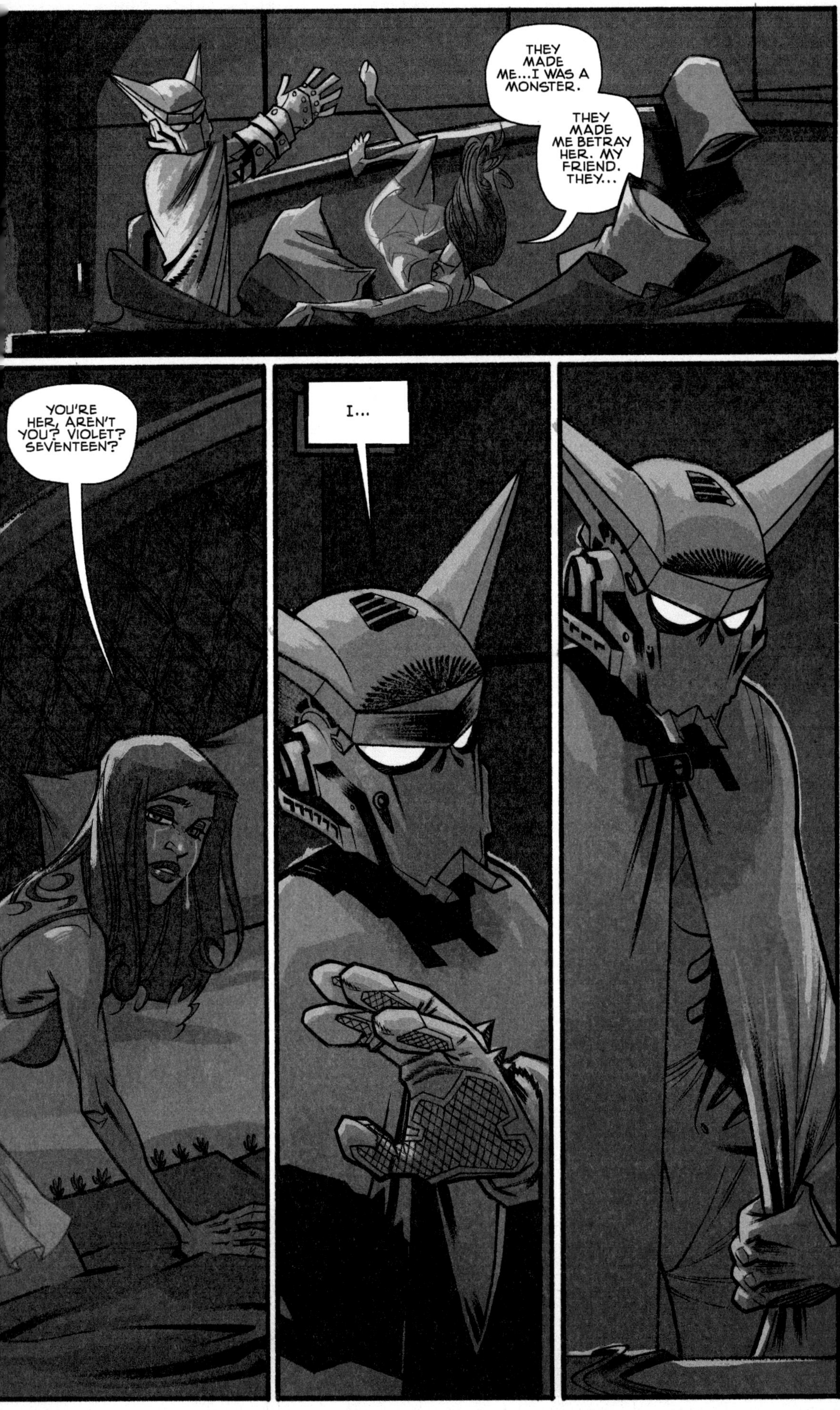
THEY MADE ME...I WAS A MONSTER.
THEY MADE ME BETRAY HER. MY FRIEND. THEY...
YOU'RE HER, AREN'T YOU? VIOLET? SEVENTEEN?
I...

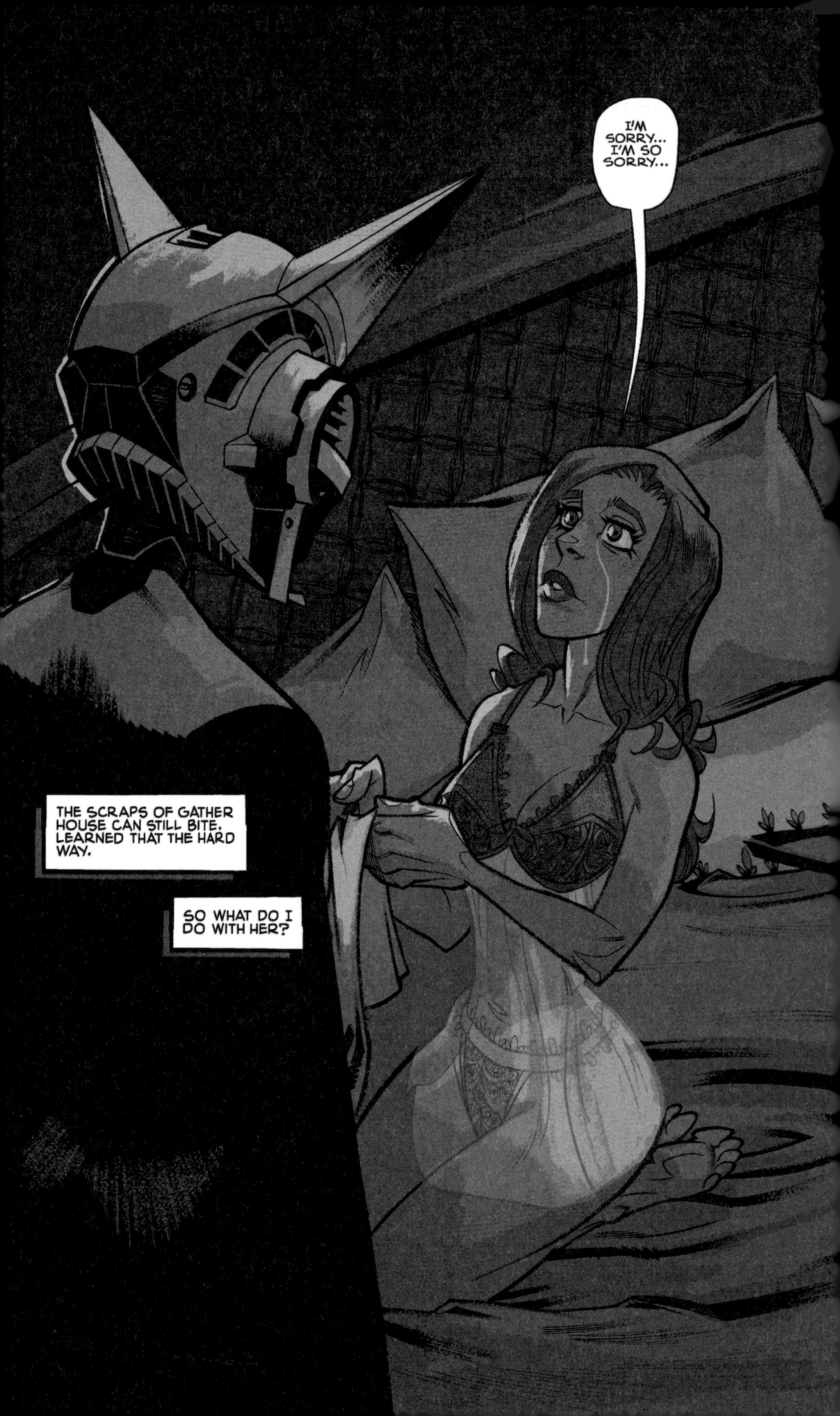
I'M SORRY... I'M SO SORRY...
THE SCRAPS OF GATHER HOUSE CAN STILL BITE. LEARNED THAT THE HARD WAY.
SO WHAT DO I DO WITH HER?

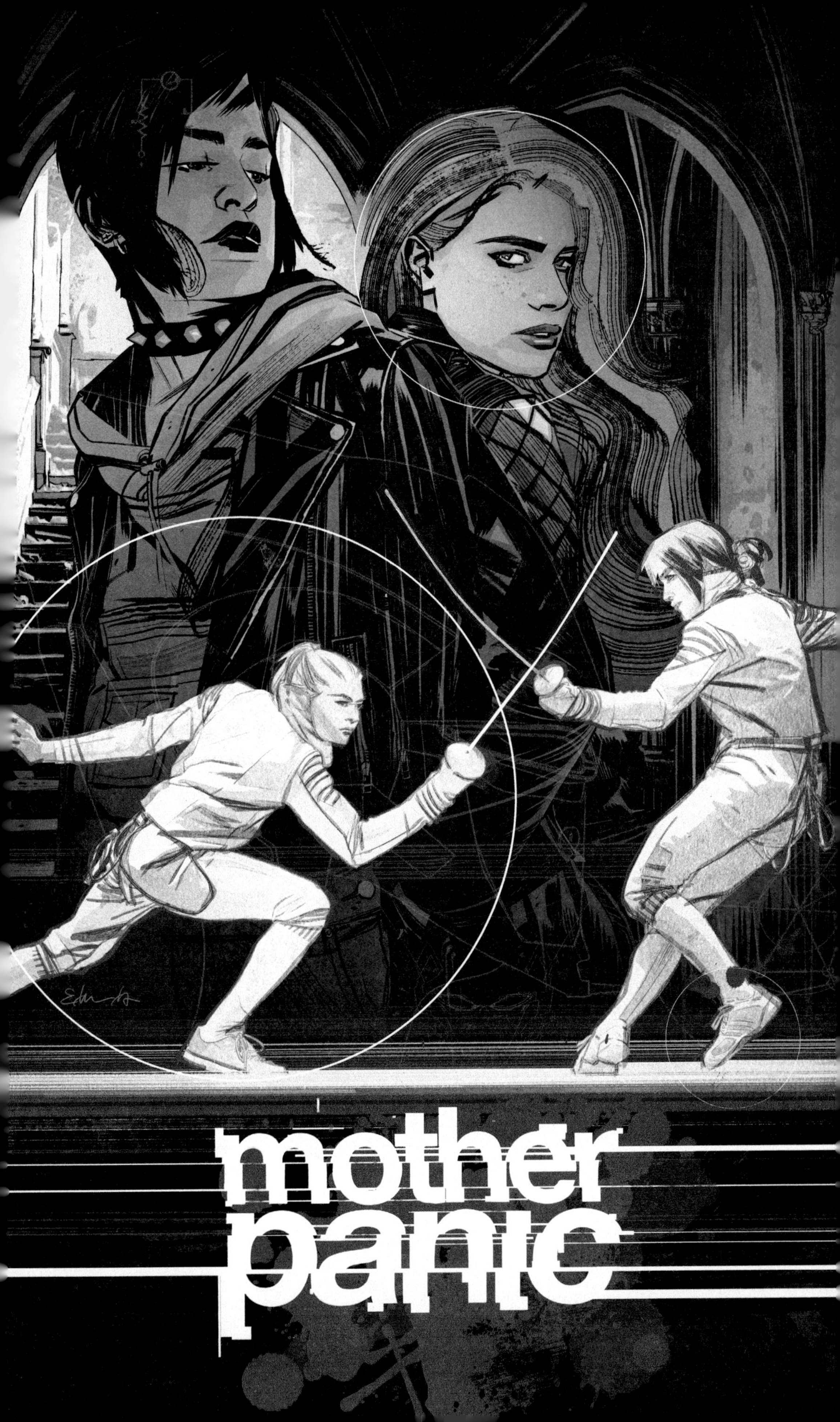
mother
panic

Mondo variant cover art by Jay Shaw

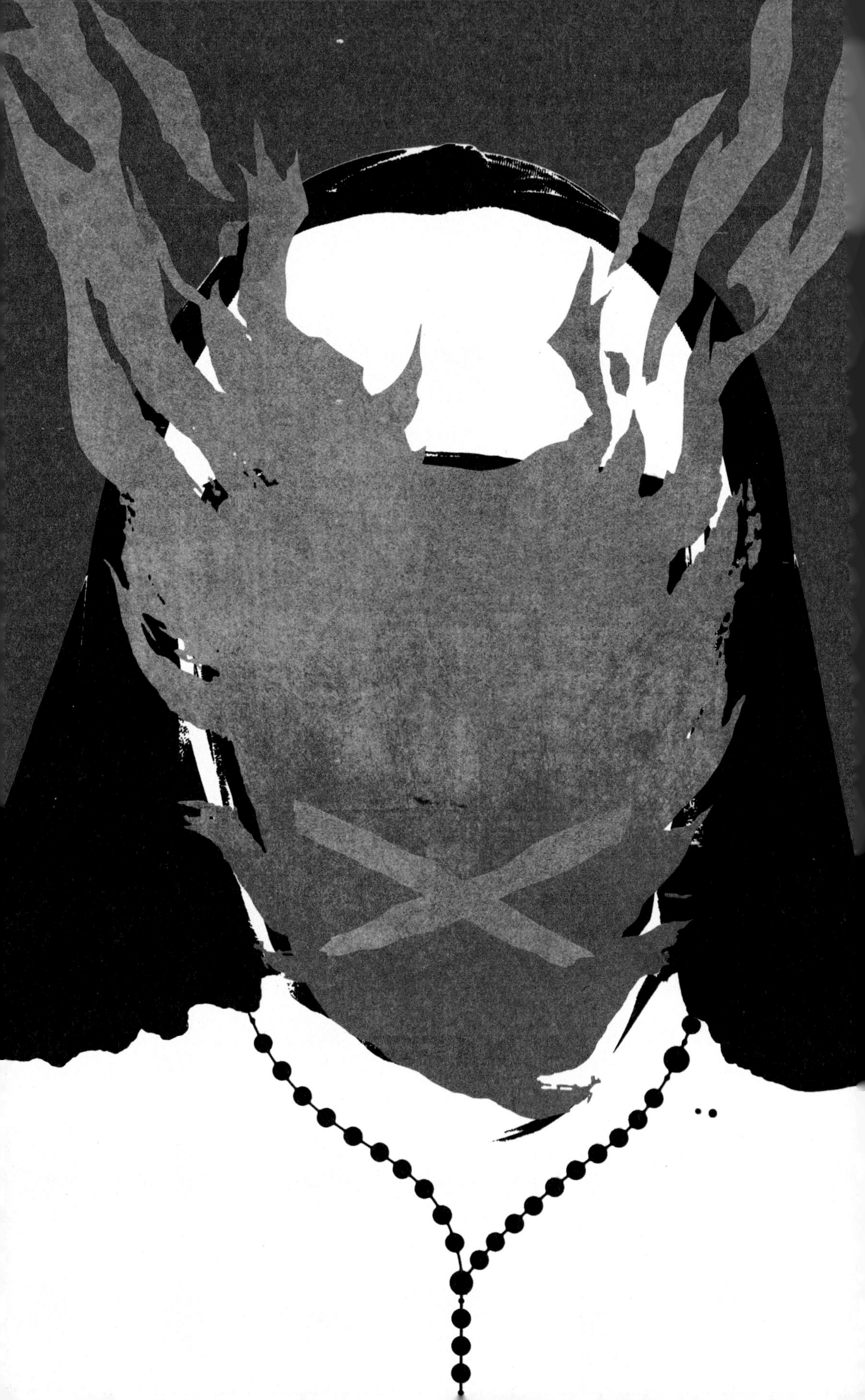

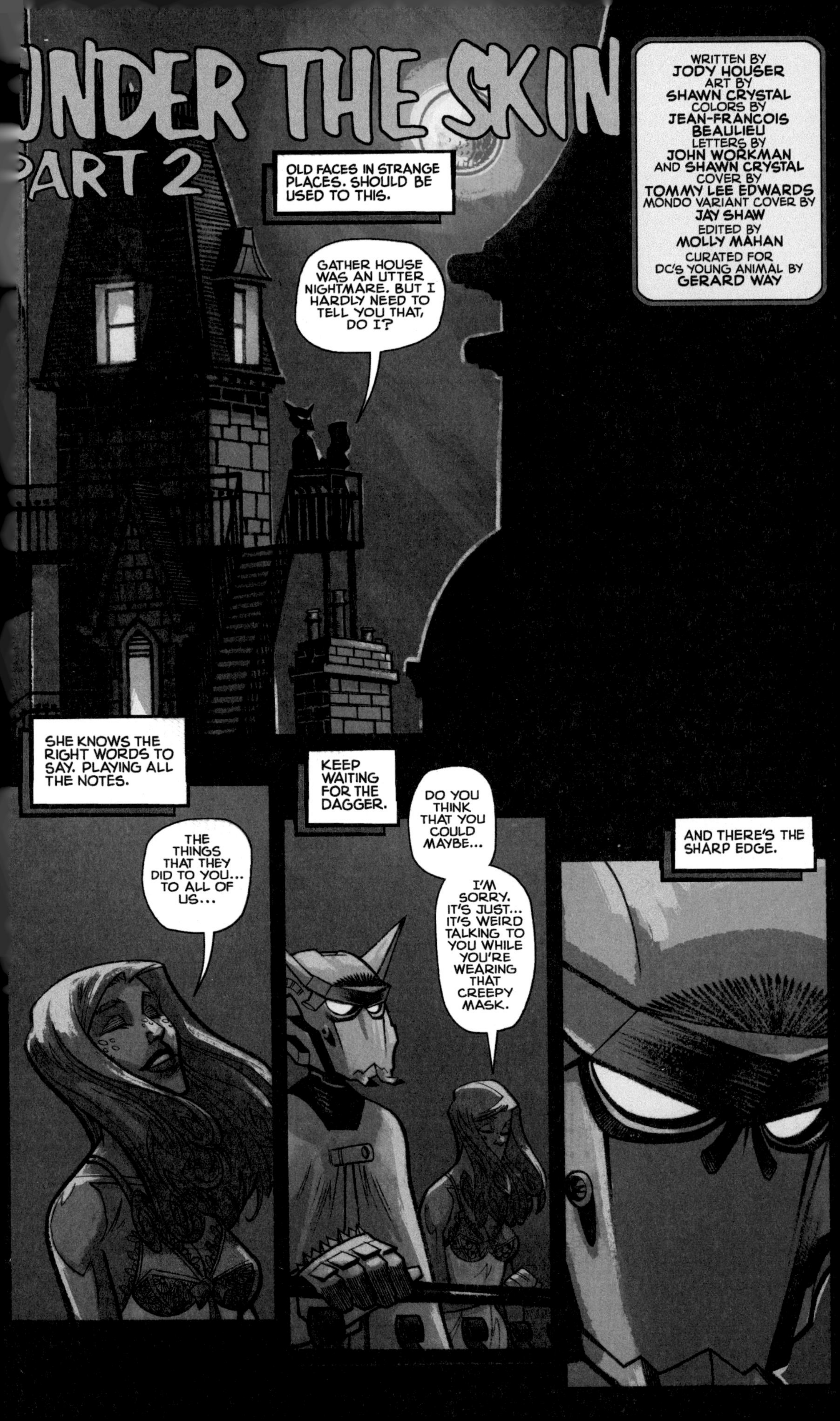
UNDER THE SKIN
PART 2
WRITTEN BY JODY HOUSER
ART BY SHAWN CRYSTAL
COLORS BY JEAN-FRANCOIS BEAULIEU
LETTERS BY JOHN WORKMAN AND SHAWN CRYSTAL
COVER BY TOMMY LEE EDWARDS
MONDO VARIANT COVER BY JAY SHAW
EDITED BY MOLLY MAHAN
CURATED FOR DC'S YOUNG ANIMAL BY GERARD WAY
OLD FACES IN STRANGE PLACES. SHOULD BE USED TO THIS.
GATHER HOUSE WAS AN UTTER NIGHTMARE. BUT I HARDLY NEED TO TELL YOU THAT, DO I?
SHE KNOWS THE RIGHT WORDS TO SAY. PLAYING ALL THE NOTES.
THE THINGS THAT THEY DID TO YOU... TO ALL OF US...
KEEP WAITING FOR THE DAGGER.
DO YOU THINK THAT YOU COULD MAYBE...
I'M SORRY. IT'S JUST... IT'S WEIRD TALKING TO YOU WHILE YOU'RE WEARING THAT CREEPY MASK.
AND THERE'S THE SHARP EDGE.

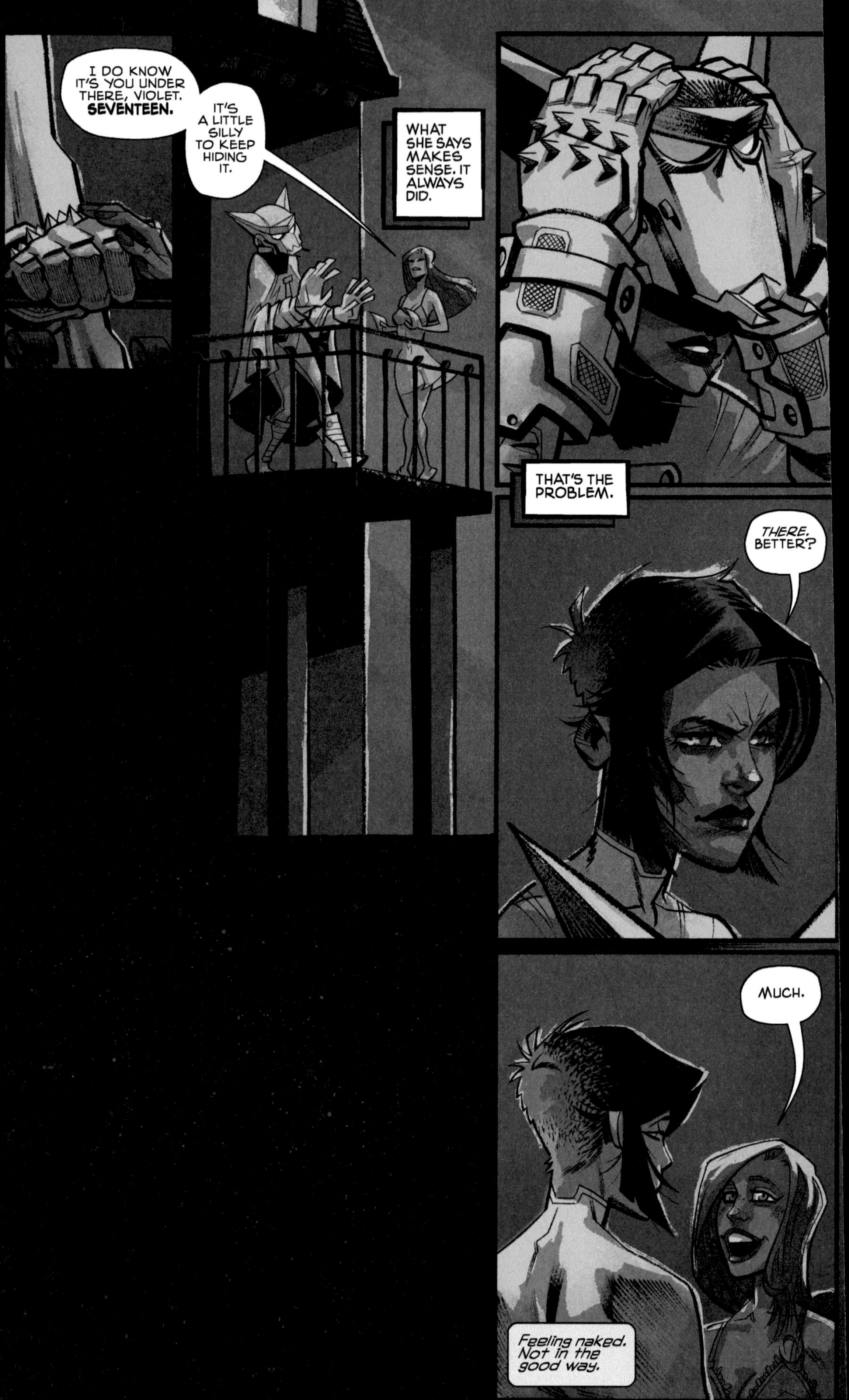
I DO KNOW IT'S YOU UNDER THERE, VIOLET. **SEVENTEEN.**
IT'S A LITTLE SILLY TO KEEP HIDING IT.
WHAT SHE SAYS MAKES SENSE. IT ALWAYS DID.
THAT'S THE PROBLEM.
THERE. BETTER?
MUCH.
Feeling naked. Not in the good way.

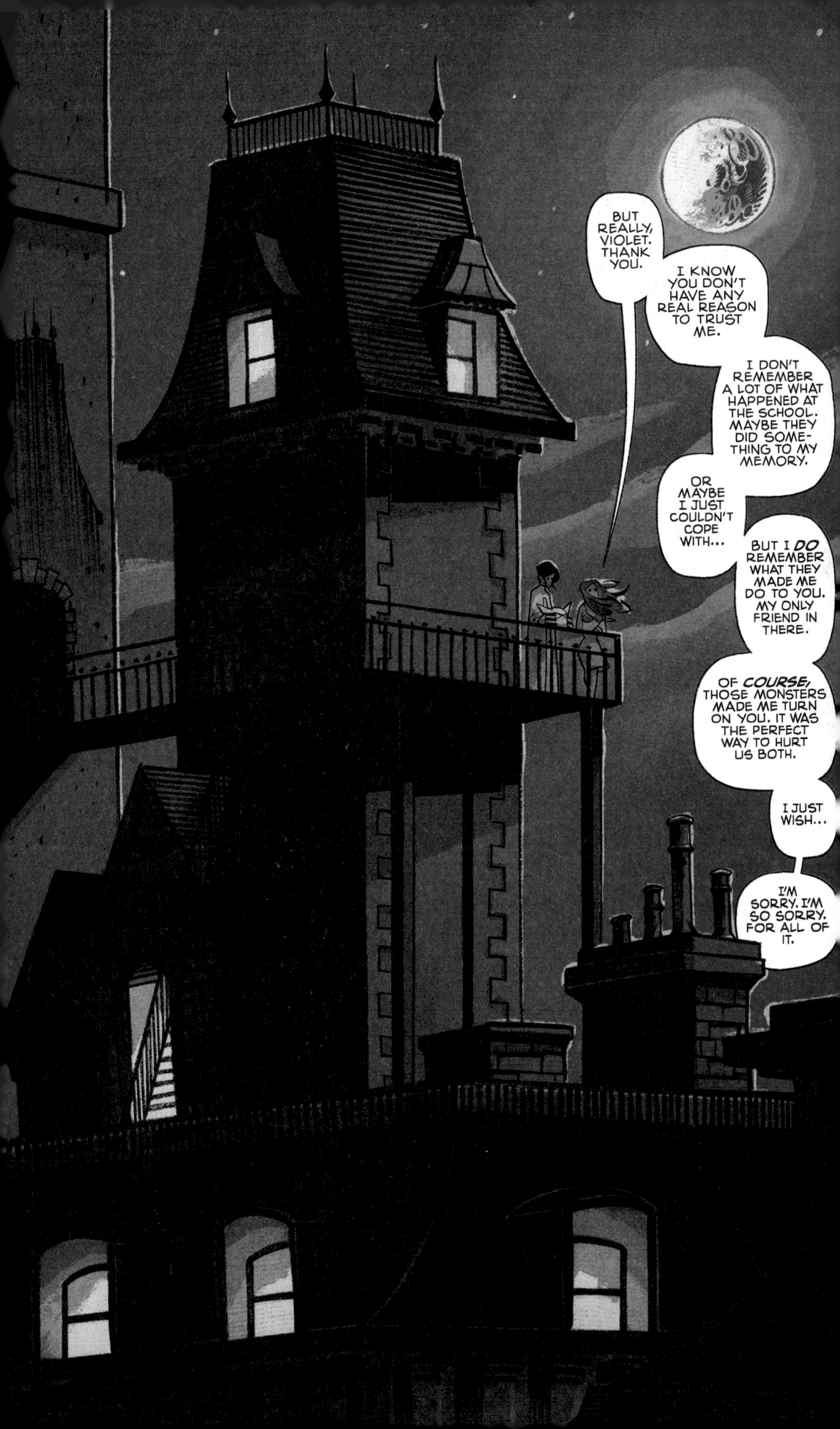
BUT REALLY, VIOLET. THANK YOU.
I KNOW YOU DON'T HAVE ANY REAL REASON TO TRUST ME.
I DON'T REMEMBER A LOT OF WHAT HAPPENED AT THE SCHOOL. MAYBE THEY DID SOME-THING TO MY MEMORY.
OR MAYBE I JUST COULDN'T COPE WITH...
BUT I *DO* REMEMBER WHAT THEY MADE ME DO TO YOU. MY ONLY FRIEND IN THERE.
OF ***COURSE,*** THOSE MONSTERS MADE ME TURN ON YOU. IT WAS THE PERFECT WAY TO HURT US BOTH.
I JUST WISH...
I'M SORRY. I'M SO SORRY. FOR ALL OF IT.

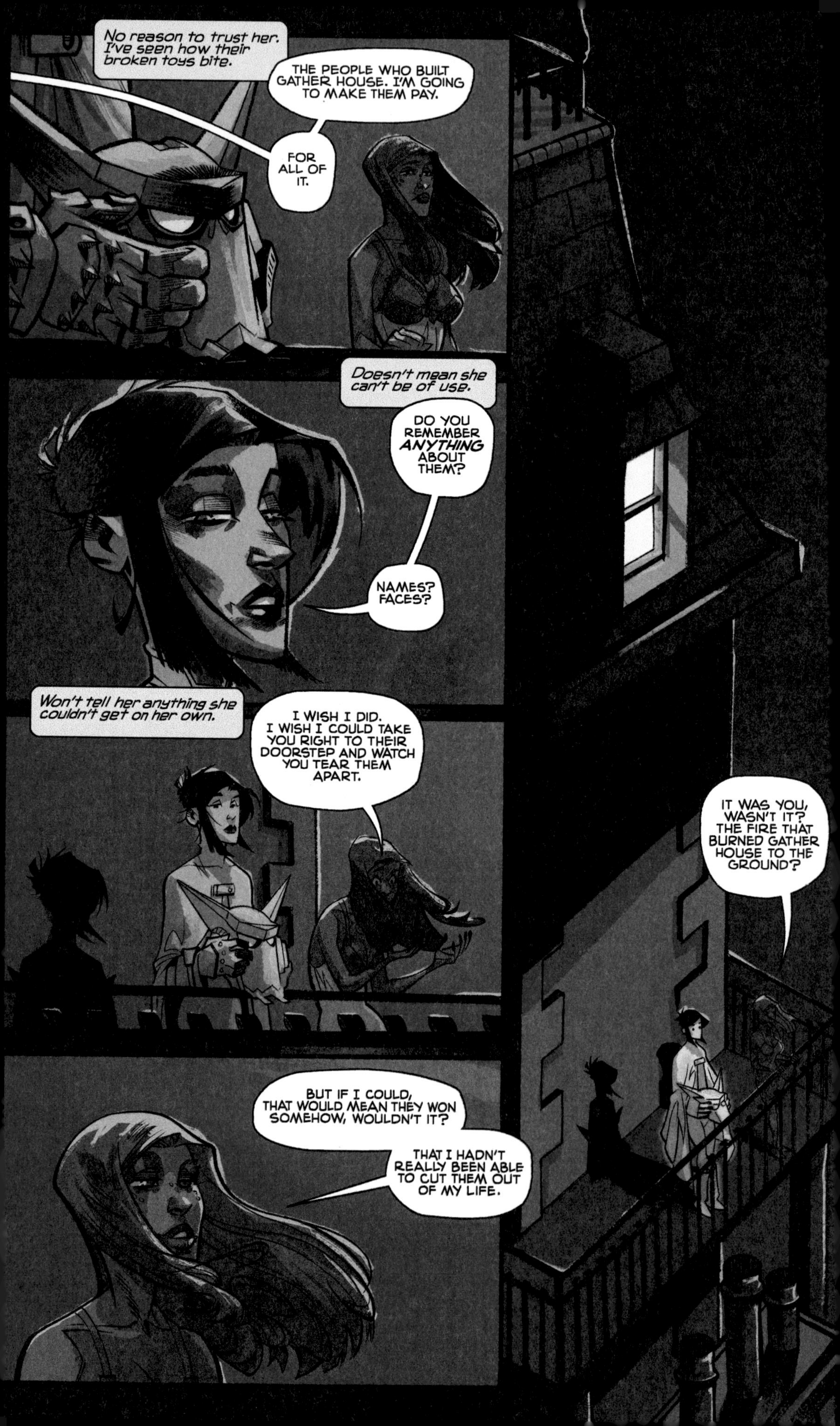

No reason to trust her. I've seen how their broken toys bite.
THE PEOPLE WHO BUILT GATHER HOUSE. I'M GOING TO MAKE THEM PAY.
FOR ALL OF IT.
Doesn't mean she can't be of use.
DO YOU REMEMBER *ANYTHING* ABOUT THEM?
NAMES? FACES?
Won't tell her anything she couldn't get on her own.
I WISH I DID. I WISH I COULD TAKE YOU RIGHT TO THEIR DOORSTEP AND WATCH YOU TEAR THEM APART.
BUT IF I COULD, THAT WOULD MEAN THEY WON SOMEHOW, WOULDN'T IT?
THAT I HADN'T REALLY BEEN ABLE TO CUT THEM OUT OF MY LIFE.
IT WAS YOU, WASN'T IT? THE FIRE THAT BURNED GATHER HOUSE TO THE GROUND?

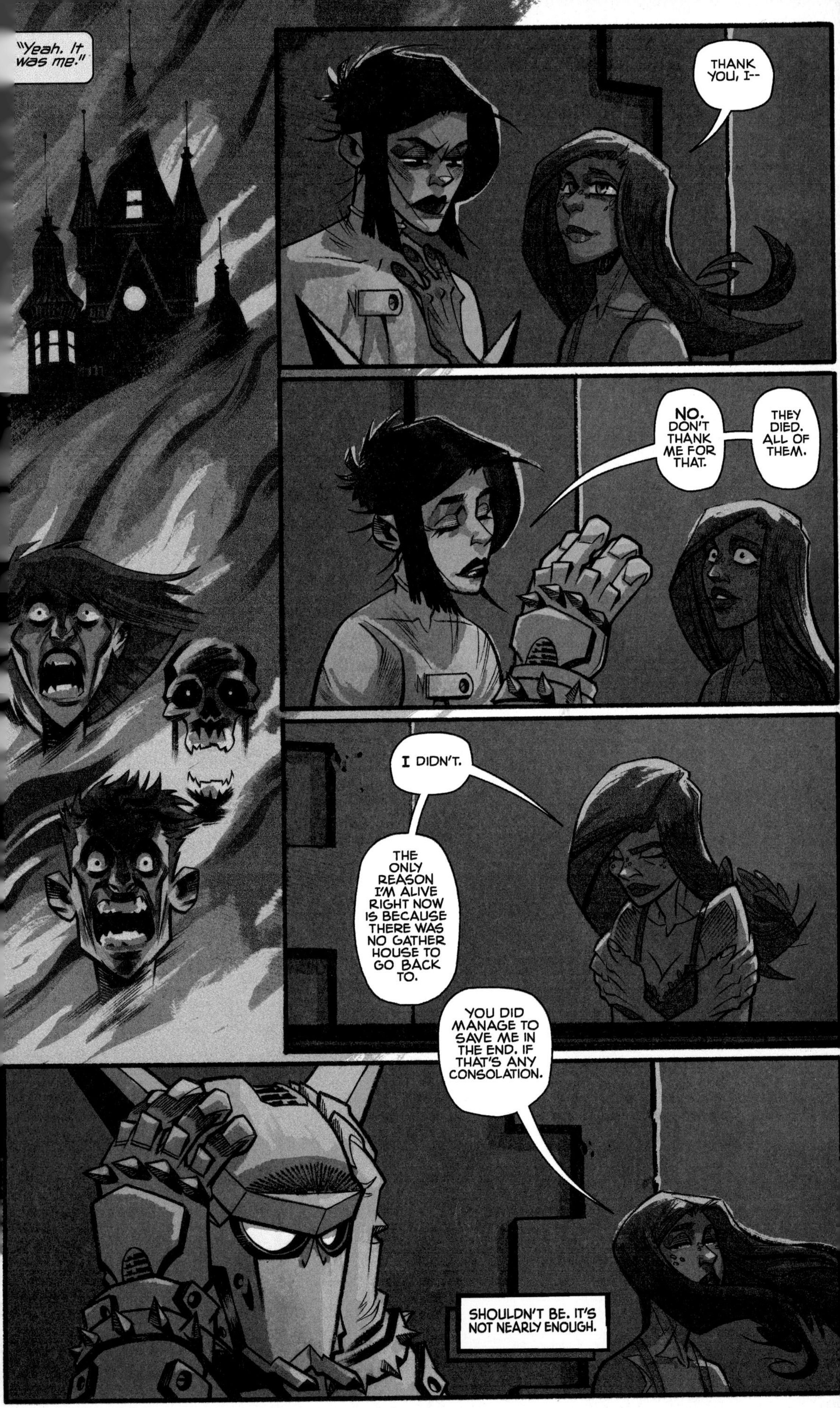
"Yeah. It was me."
THANK YOU, I--
NO. DON'T THANK ME FOR THAT.
THEY DIED. ALL OF THEM.
I DIDN'T.
THE ONLY REASON I'M ALIVE RIGHT NOW IS BECAUSE THERE WAS NO GATHER HOUSE TO GO BACK TO.
YOU DID MANAGE TO SAVE ME IN THE END. IF THAT'S ANY CONSOLATION.
SHOULDN'T BE. IT'S NOT NEARLY ENOUGH.

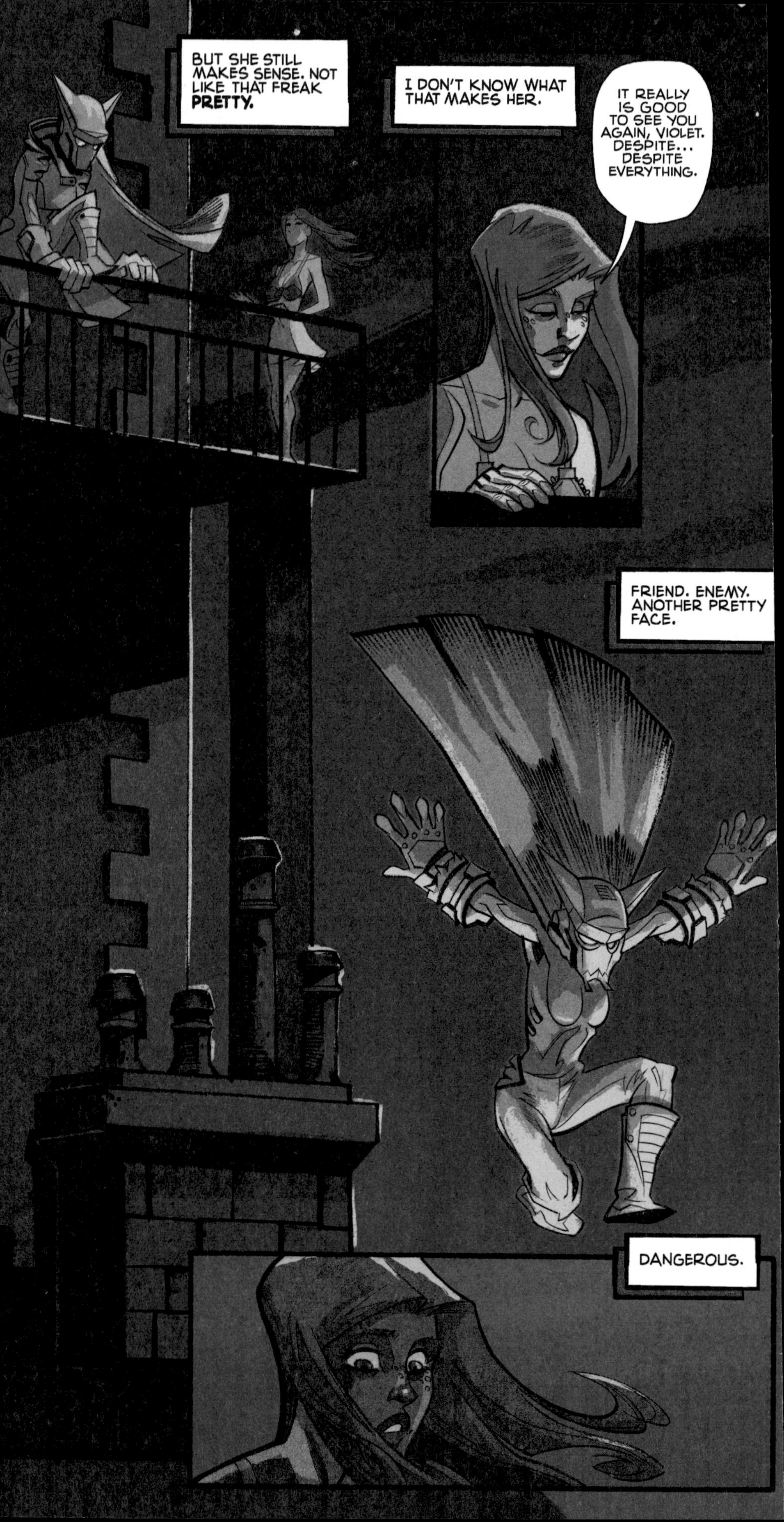
BUT SHE STILL MAKES SENSE. NOT LIKE THAT FREAK **PRETTY.**
I DON'T KNOW WHAT THAT MAKES HER.
IT REALLY IS GOOD TO SEE YOU AGAIN, VIOLET. DESPITE... DESPITE EVERYTHING.
FRIEND. ENEMY. ANOTHER PRETTY FACE.
DANGEROUS.

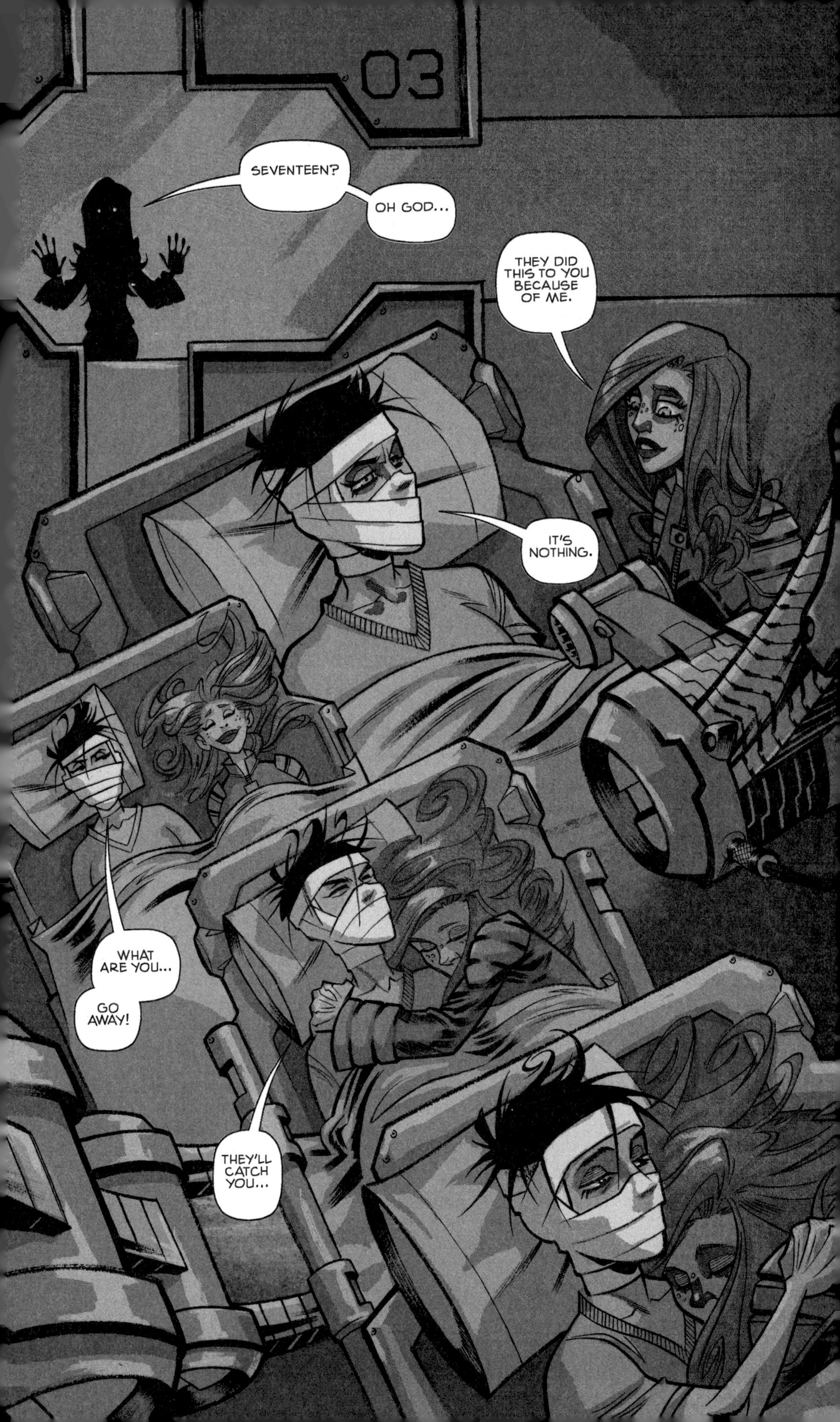
03
SEVENTEEN?
OH GOD...
THEY DID THIS TO YOU BECAUSE OF ME.
IT'S NOTHING.
WHAT ARE YOU...
GO AWAY!
THEY'LL CATCH YOU...

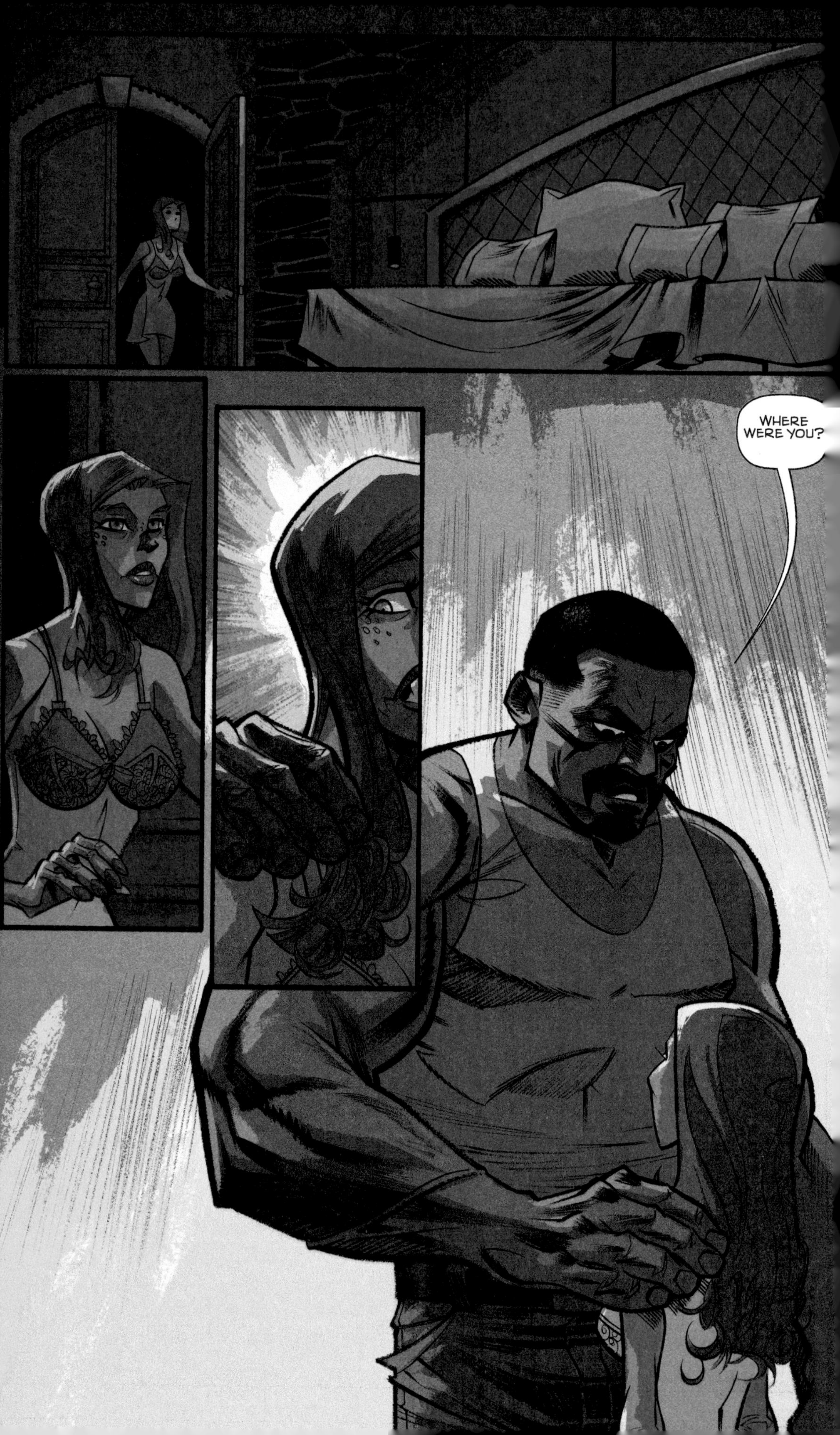
WHERE WERE YOU?

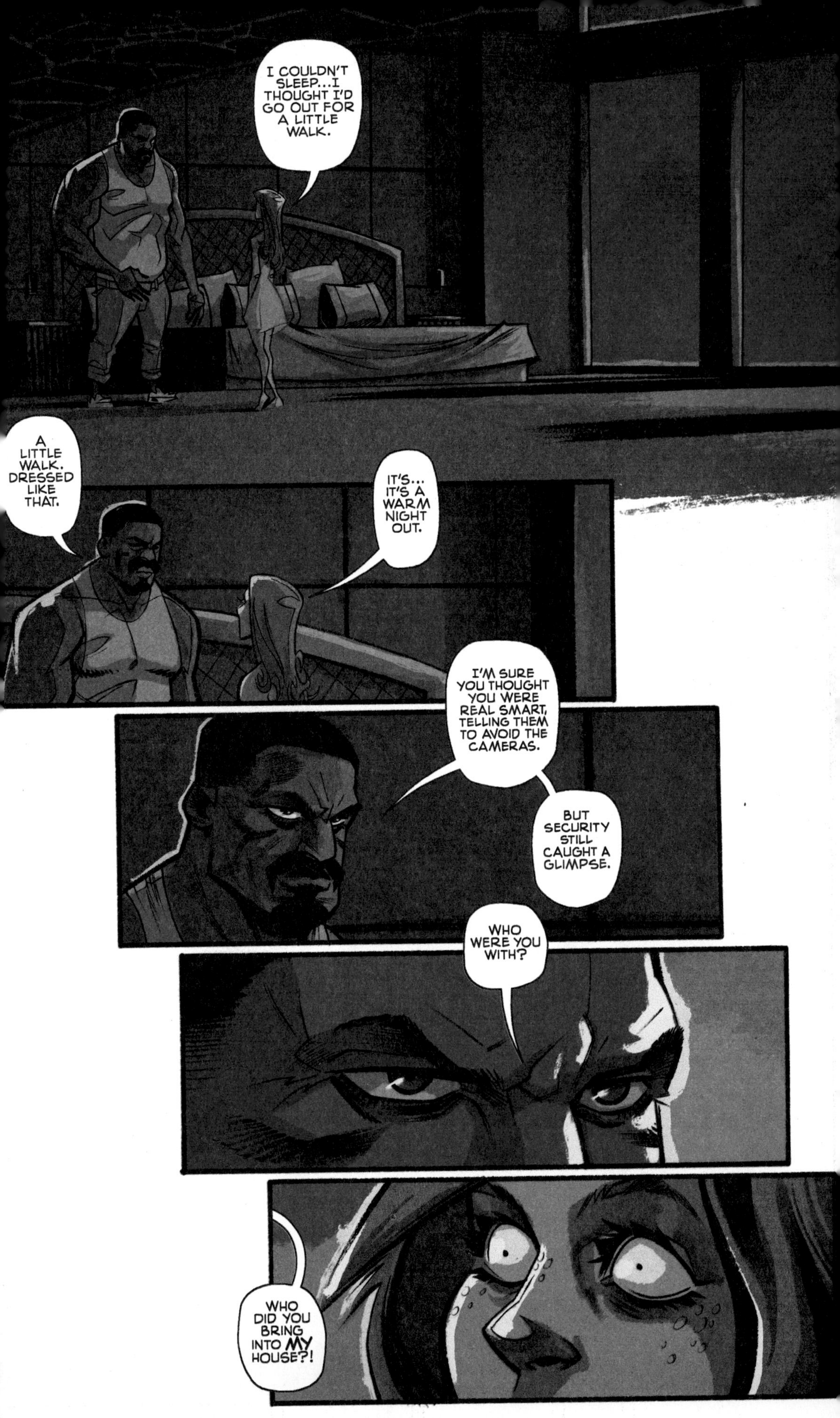
I COULDN'T SLEEP...I THOUGHT I'D GO OUT FOR A LITTLE WALK.
A LITTLE WALK. DRESSED LIKE THAT.
IT'S... IT'S A WARM NIGHT OUT.
I'M SURE YOU THOUGHT YOU WERE REAL SMART, TELLING THEM TO AVOID THE CAMERAS.
BUT SECURITY STILL CAUGHT A GLIMPSE.
WHO WERE YOU WITH?
WHO DID YOU BRING INTO MY HOUSE?!

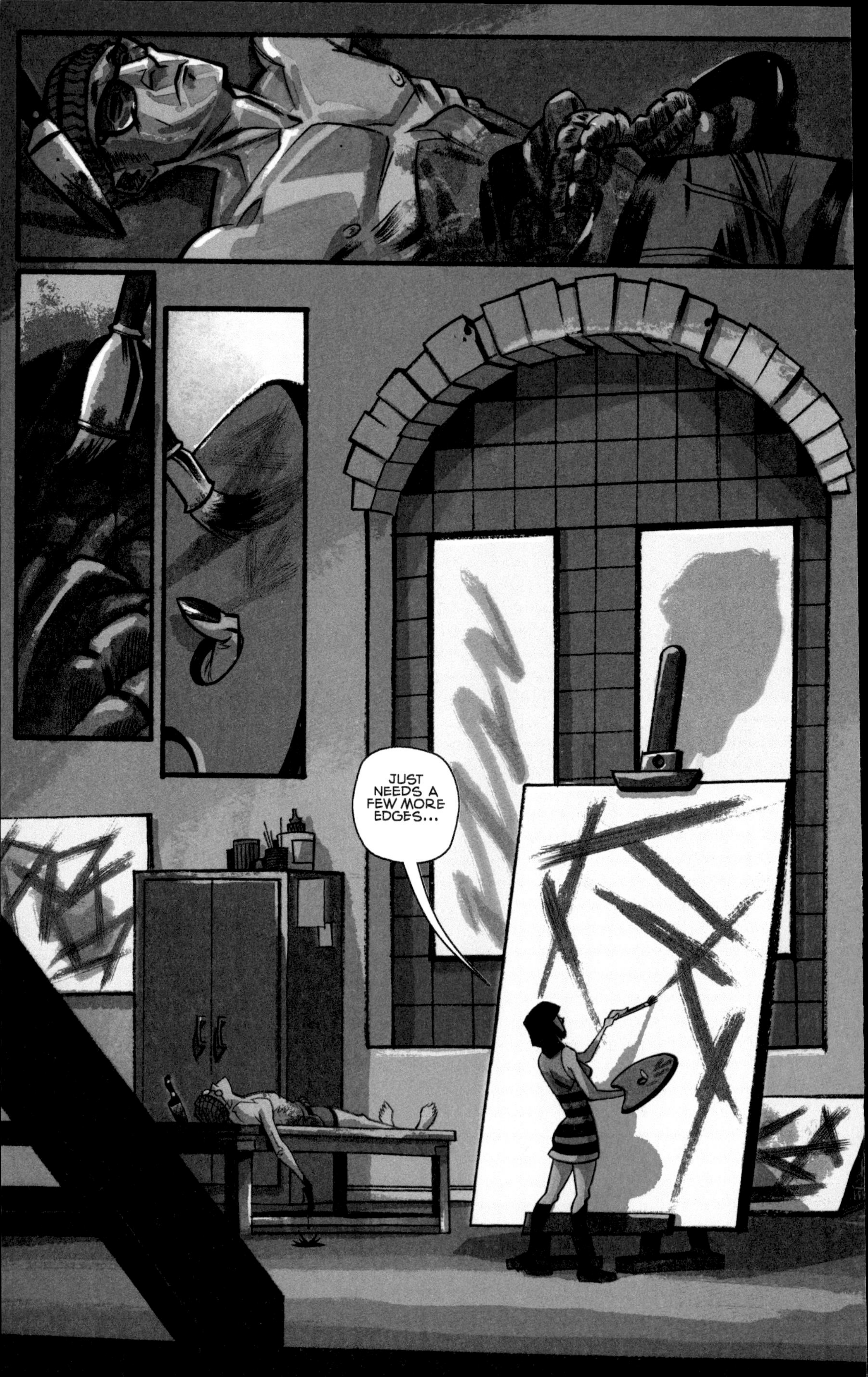
JUST NEEDS A FEW MORE EDGES...

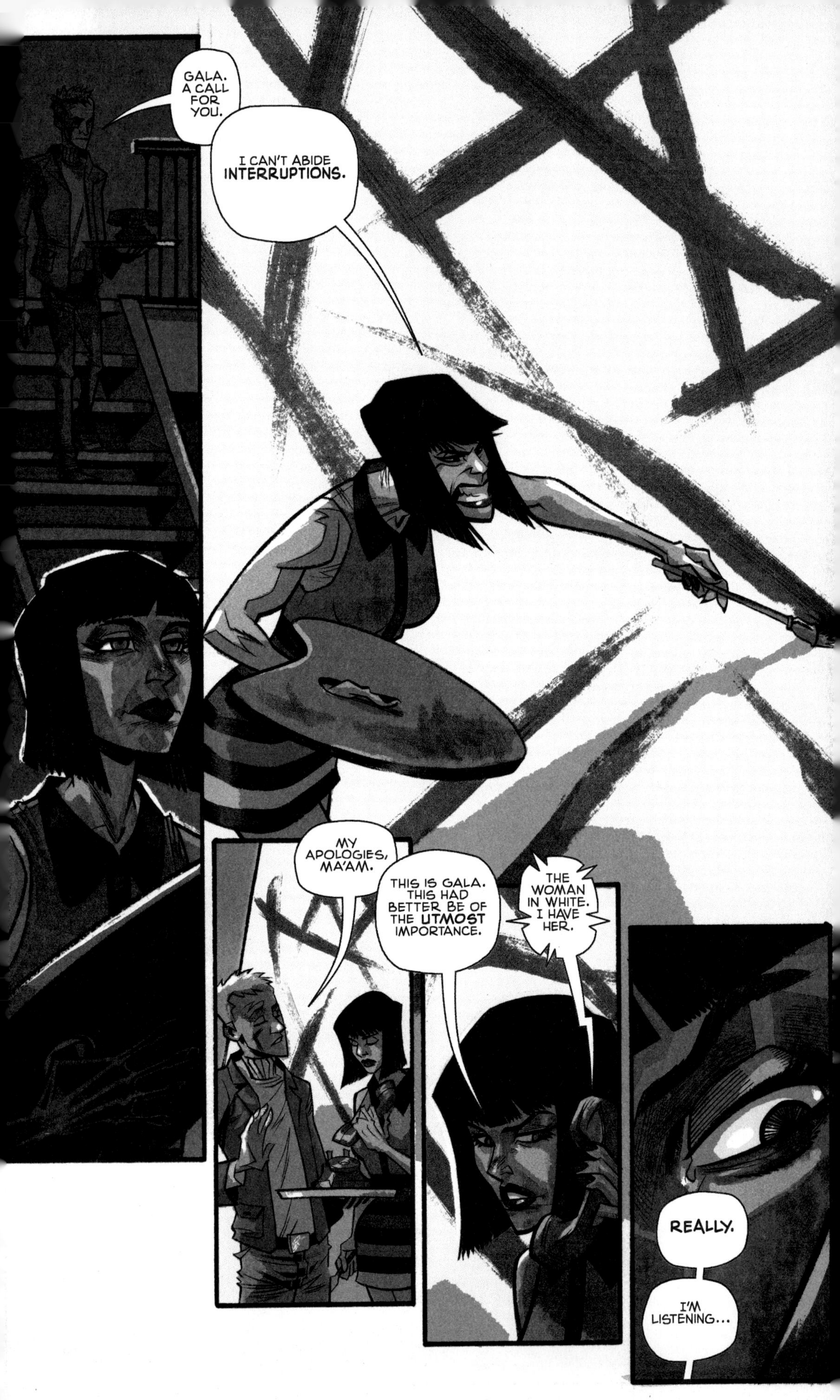
GALA. A CALL FOR YOU.
I CAN'T ABIDE INTERRUPTIONS.
MY APOLOGIES, MA'AM.
THIS IS GALA. THIS HAD BETTER BE OF THE UTMOST IMPORTANCE.
THE WOMAN IN WHITE. I HAVE HER.
REALLY.
I'M LISTENING...

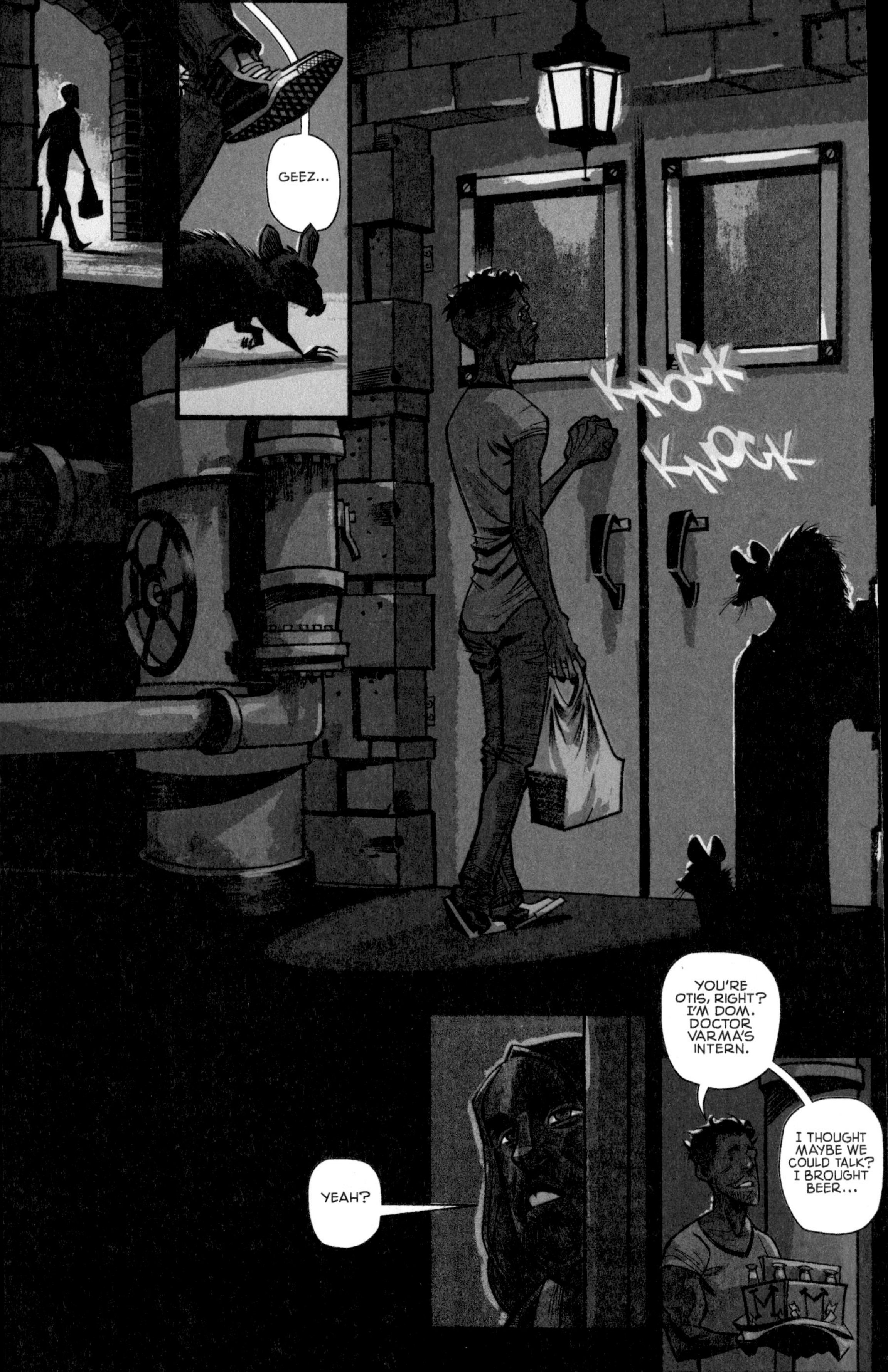
GEEZ...
KNOCK KNOCK
YOU'RE OTIS, RIGHT? I'M DOM. DOCTOR VARMA'S INTERN.
I THOUGHT MAYBE WE COULD TALK? I BROUGHT BEER...
YEAH?

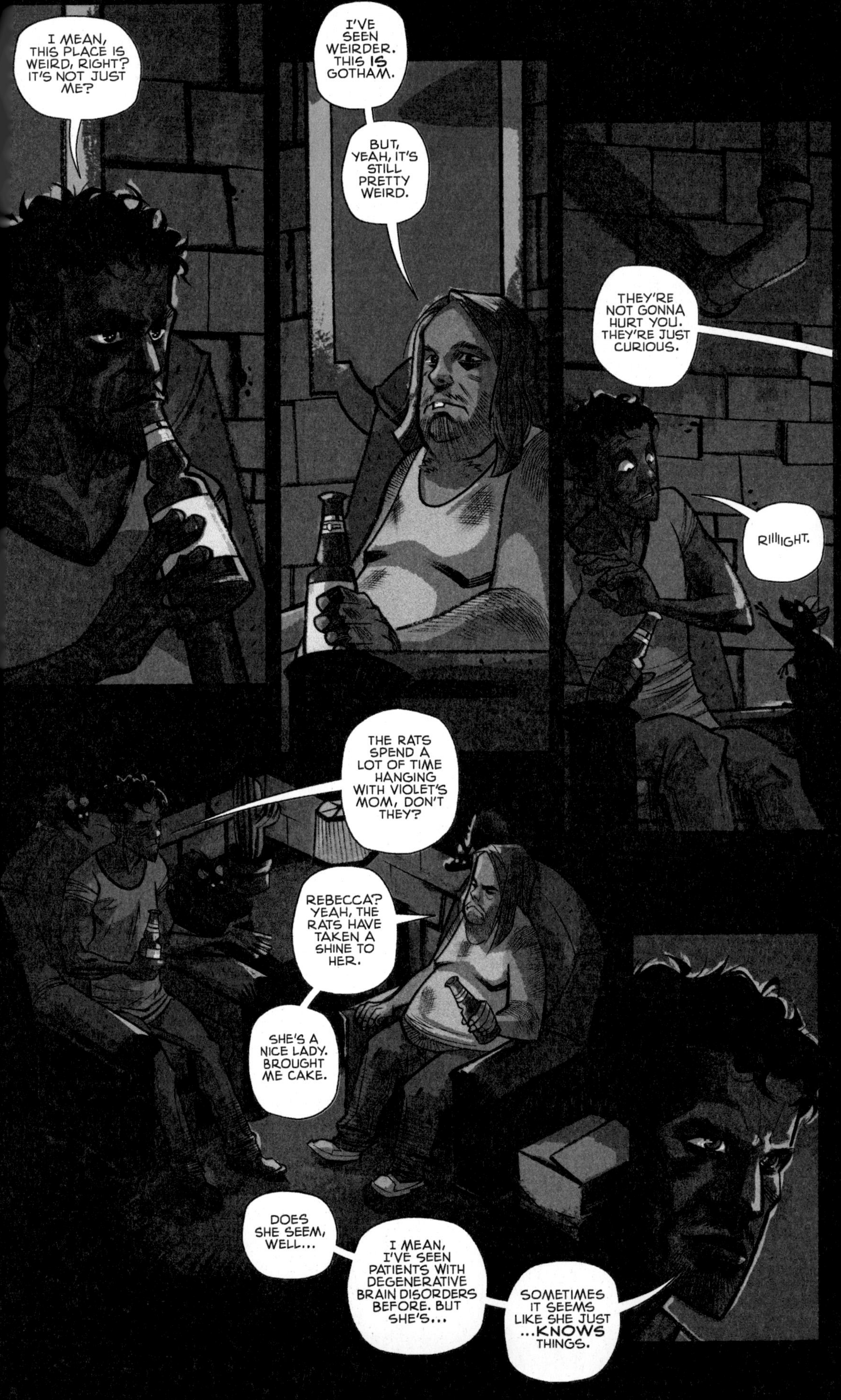
I MEAN, THIS PLACE IS WEIRD, RIGHT? IT'S NOT JUST ME?
I'VE SEEN WEIRDER. THIS **IS** GOTHAM.
BUT, YEAH, IT'S STILL PRETTY WEIRD.
THEY'RE NOT GONNA HURT YOU. THEY'RE JUST CURIOUS.
RIIIIIGHT.
THE RATS SPEND A LOT OF TIME HANGING WITH VIOLET'S MOM, DON'T THEY?
REBECCA? YEAH, THE RATS HAVE TAKEN A SHINE TO HER.
SHE'S A NICE LADY. BROUGHT ME CAKE.
DOES SHE SEEM, WELL...
I MEAN, I'VE SEEN PATIENTS WITH DEGENERATIVE BRAIN DISORDERS BEFORE. BUT SHE'S...
SOMETIMES IT SEEMS LIKE SHE JUST ...**KNOWS** THINGS.

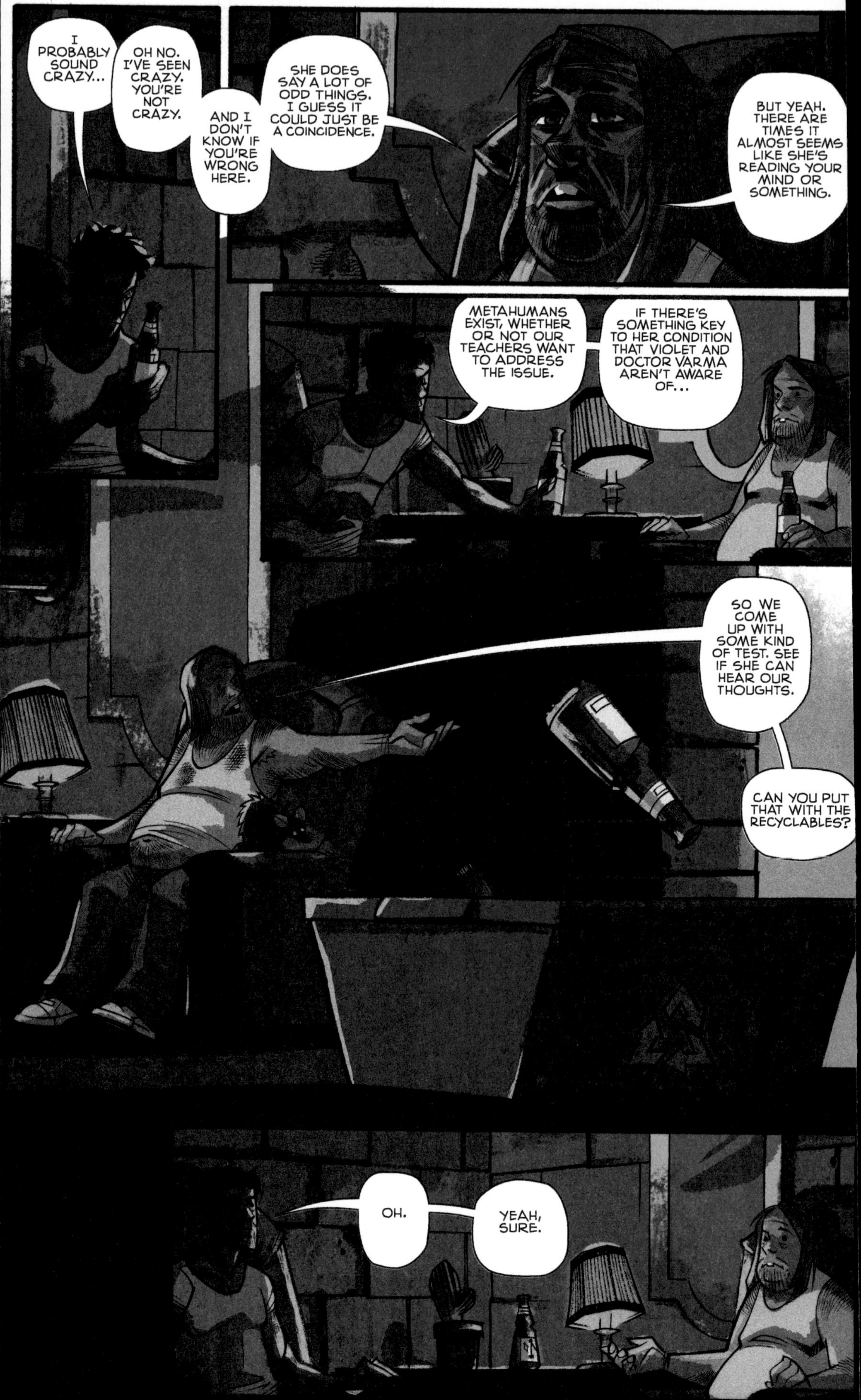
I PROBABLY SOUND CRAZY...
OH NO. I'VE SEEN CRAZY. YOU'RE NOT CRAZY.
AND I DON'T KNOW IF YOU'RE WRONG HERE.
SHE DOES SAY A LOT OF ODD THINGS. I GUESS IT COULD JUST BE A COINCIDENCE.
BUT YEAH. THERE ARE TIMES IT ALMOST SEEMS LIKE SHE'S READING YOUR MIND OR SOMETHING.
METAHUMANS EXIST, WHETHER OR NOT OUR TEACHERS WANT TO ADDRESS THE ISSUE.
IF THERE'S SOMETHING KEY TO HER CONDITION THAT VIOLET AND DOCTOR VARMA AREN'T AWARE OF...
SO WE COME UP WITH SOME KIND OF TEST. SEE IF SHE CAN HEAR OUR THOUGHTS.
CAN YOU PUT THAT WITH THE RECYCLABLES?
OH.
YEAH, SURE.

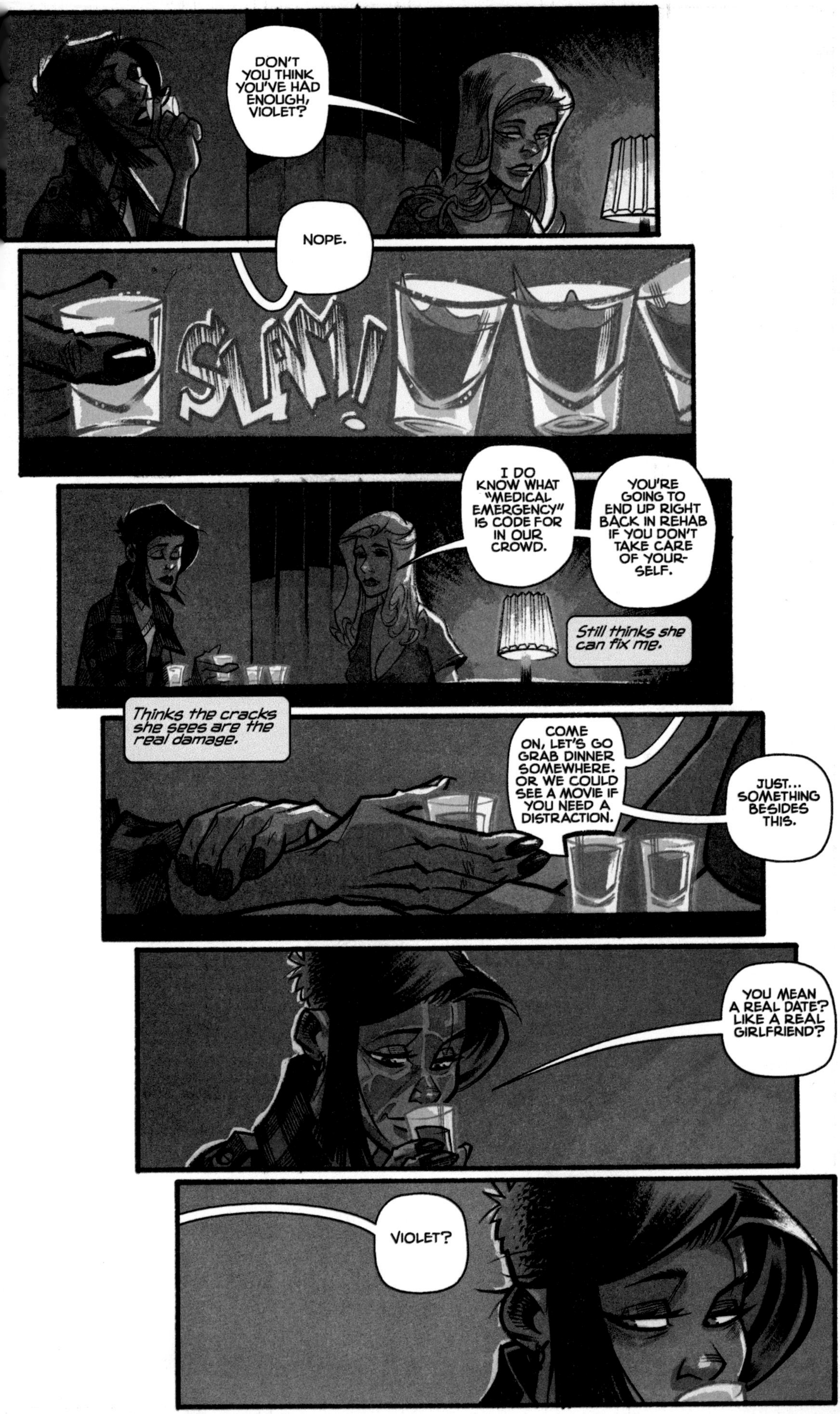

DON'T YOU THINK YOU'VE HAD ENOUGH, VIOLET?
NOPE.
SLAM!
I DO KNOW WHAT "MEDICAL EMERGENCY" IS CODE FOR IN OUR CROWD.
YOU'RE GOING TO END UP RIGHT BACK IN REHAB IF YOU DON'T TAKE CARE OF YOUR-SELF.
Still thinks she can fix me.
Thinks the cracks she sees are the real damage.
COME ON, LET'S GO GRAB DINNER SOMEWHERE. OR WE COULD SEE A MOVIE IF YOU NEED A DISTRACTION.
JUST... SOMETHING BESIDES THIS.
YOU MEAN A REAL DATE? LIKE A REAL GIRLFRIEND?
VIOLET?

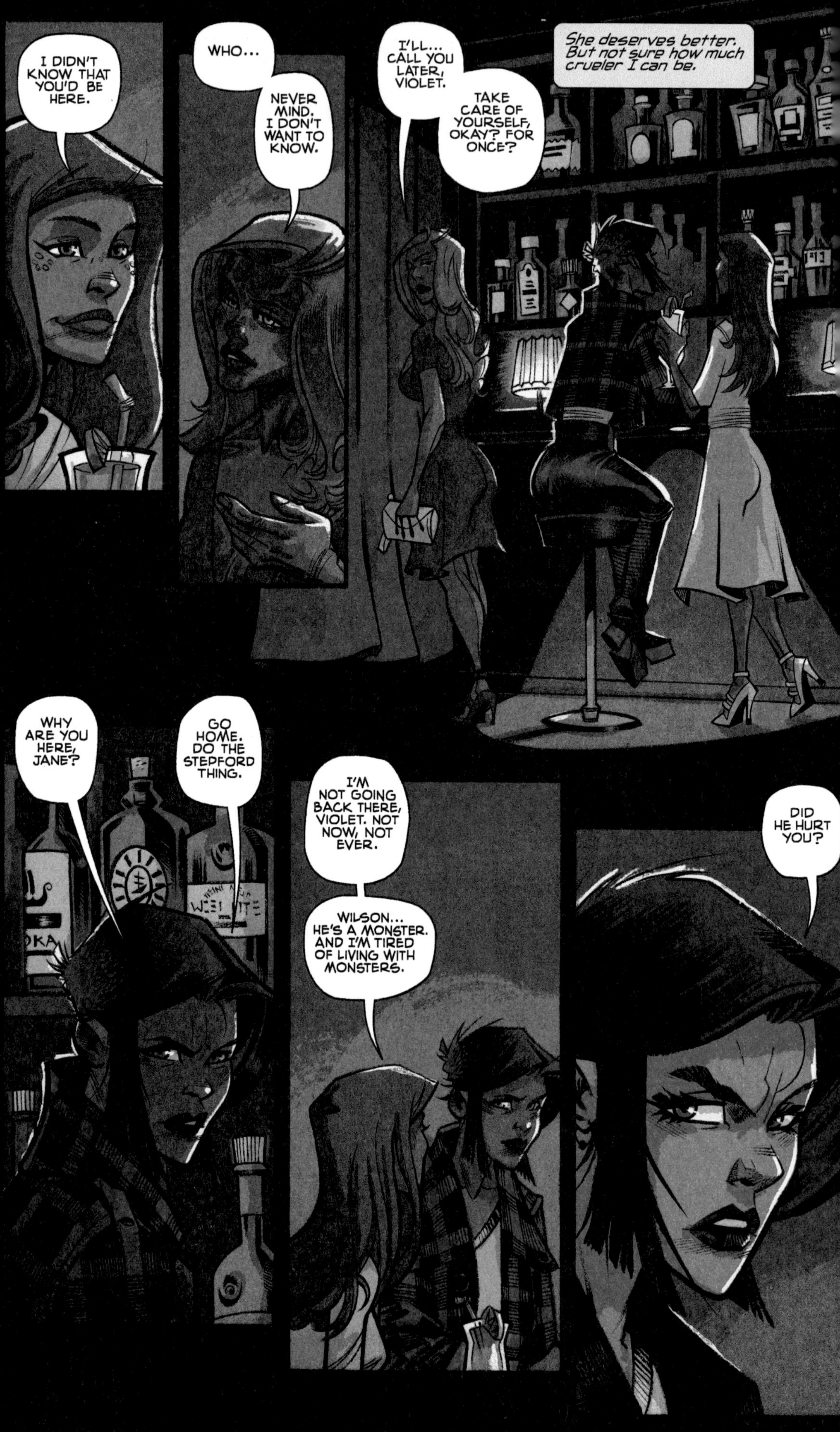
I DIDN'T KNOW THAT YOU'D BE HERE.
WHO...
NEVER MIND. I DON'T WANT TO KNOW.
I'LL... CALL YOU LATER, VIOLET.
TAKE CARE OF YOURSELF, OKAY? FOR ONCE?
She deserves better. But not sure how much crueler I can be.
WHY ARE YOU HERE, JANE?
GO HOME. DO THE STEPFORD THING.
I'M NOT GOING BACK THERE, VIOLET. NOT NOW, NOT EVER.
WILSON... HE'S A MONSTER. AND I'M TIRED OF LIVING WITH MONSTERS.
DID HE HURT YOU?

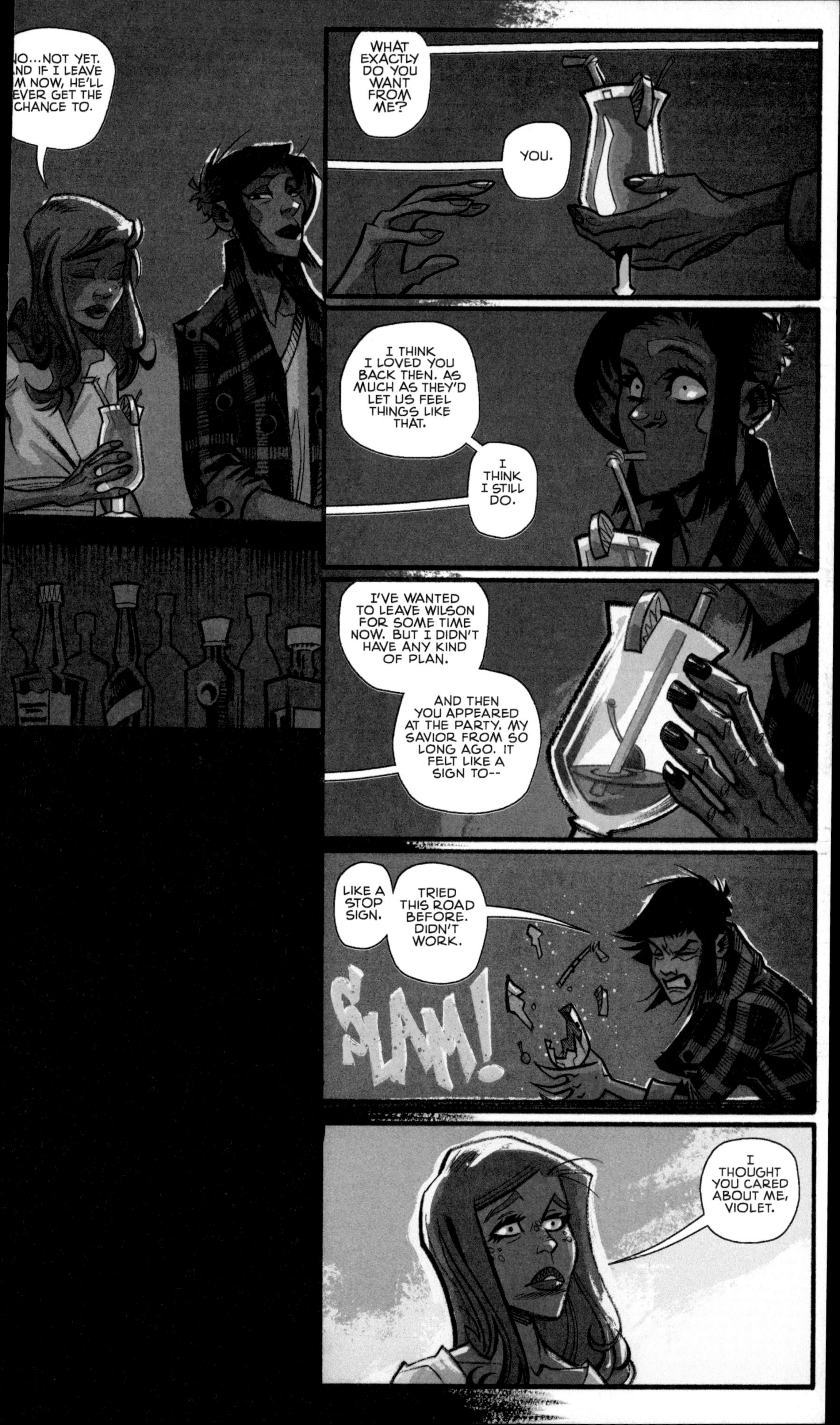
NO...NOT YET. AND IF I LEAVE HIM NOW, HE'LL NEVER GET THE CHANCE TO.
WHAT EXACTLY DO YOU WANT FROM ME?
YOU.
I THINK I LOVED YOU BACK THEN. AS MUCH AS THEY'D LET US FEEL THINGS LIKE THAT.
I THINK I STILL DO.
I'VE WANTED TO LEAVE WILSON FOR SOME TIME NOW. BUT I DIDN'T HAVE ANY KIND OF PLAN.
AND THEN YOU APPEARED AT THE PARTY. MY SAVIOR FROM SO LONG AGO. IT FELT LIKE A SIGN TO--
LIKE A STOP SIGN.
TRIED THIS ROAD BEFORE. DIDN'T WORK.
SLAM!
I THOUGHT YOU CARED ABOUT ME, VIOLET.

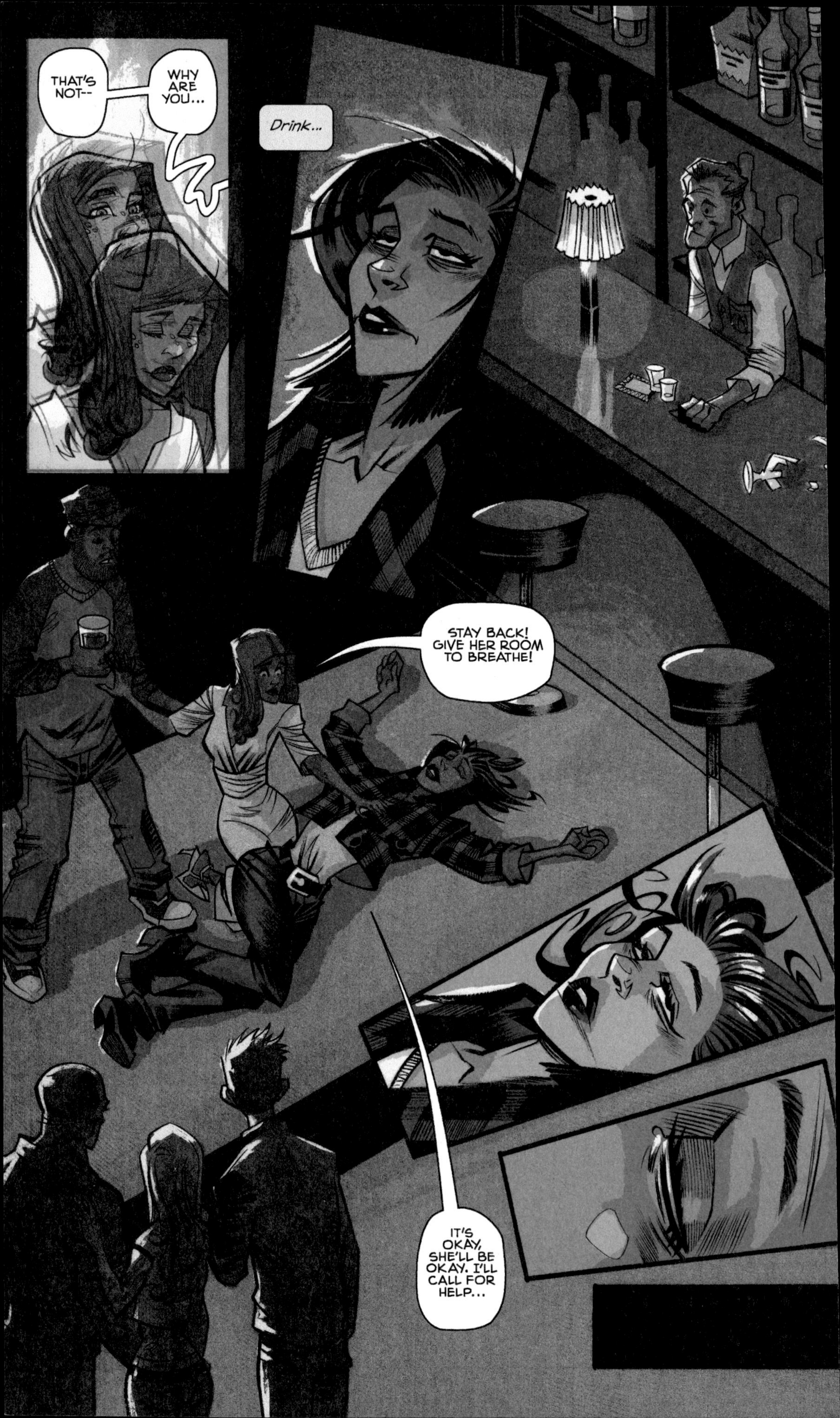
THAT'S NOT--
WHY ARE YOU...
Drink...
STAY BACK! GIVE HER ROOM TO BREATHE!
IT'S OKAY, SHE'LL BE OKAY. I'LL CALL FOR HELP...

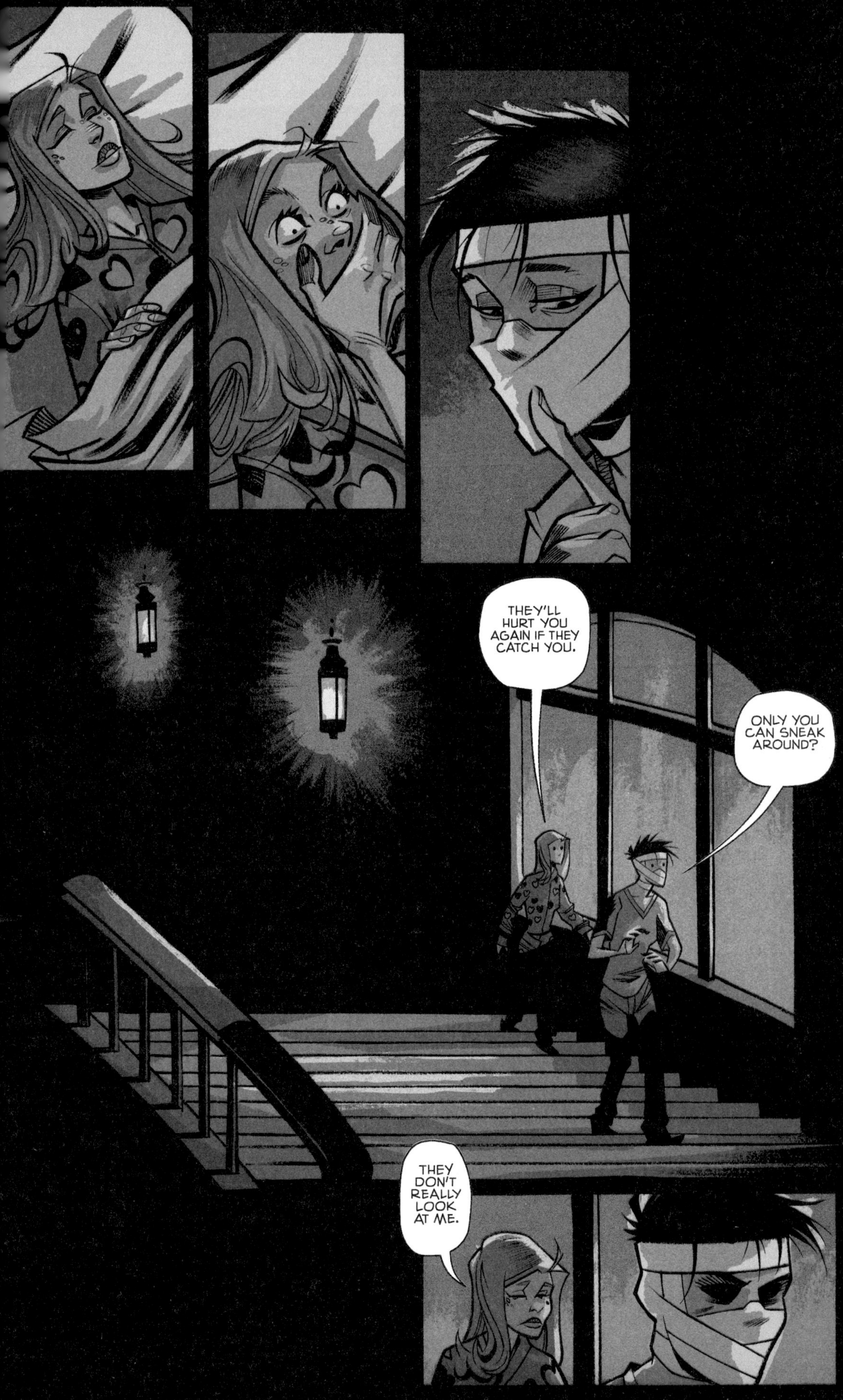
THEY'LL HURT YOU AGAIN IF THEY CATCH YOU.
ONLY YOU CAN SNEAK AROUND?
THEY DON'T REALLY LOOK AT ME.

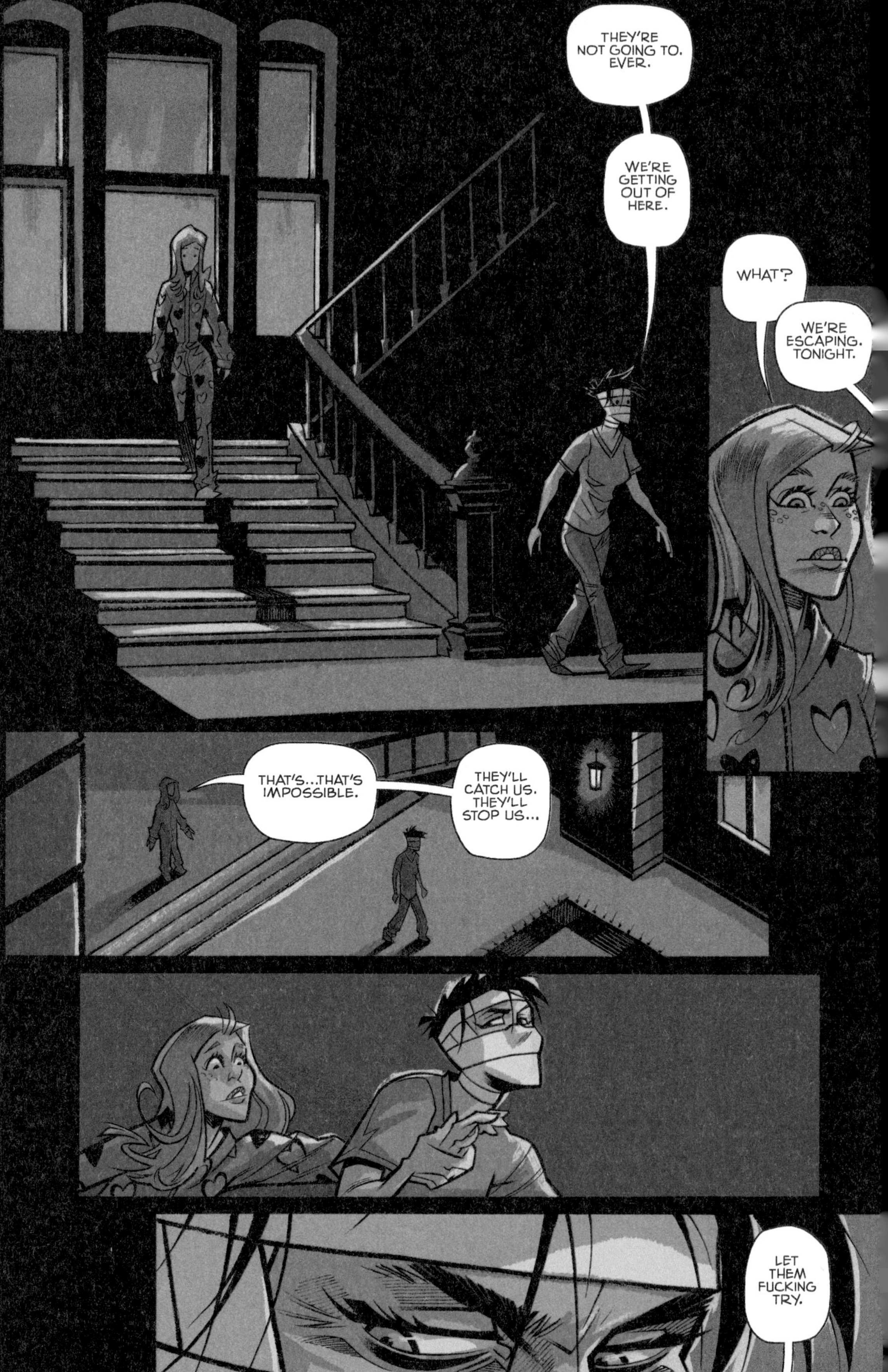
THEY'RE NOT GOING TO. EVER.
WE'RE GETTING OUT OF HERE.
WHAT?
WE'RE ESCAPING. TONIGHT.
THAT'S...THAT'S IMPOSSIBLE.
THEY'LL CATCH US. THEY'LL STOP US...
LET THEM FUCKING TRY.

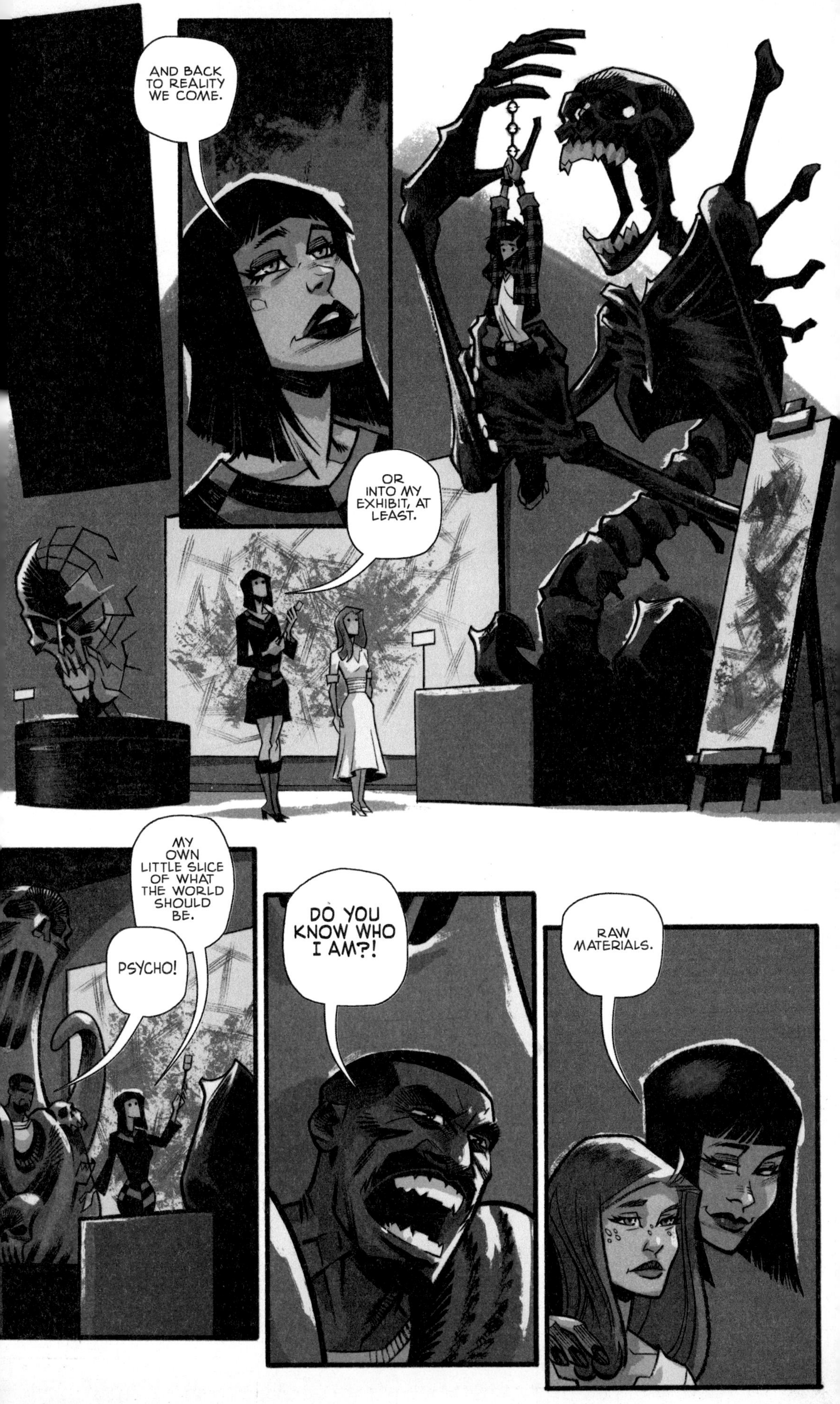
AND BACK TO REALITY WE COME.
OR INTO MY EXHIBIT, AT LEAST.
MY OWN LITTLE SLICE OF WHAT THE WORLD SHOULD BE.
PSYCHO!
DO YOU KNOW WHO I AM?!
RAW MATERIALS.

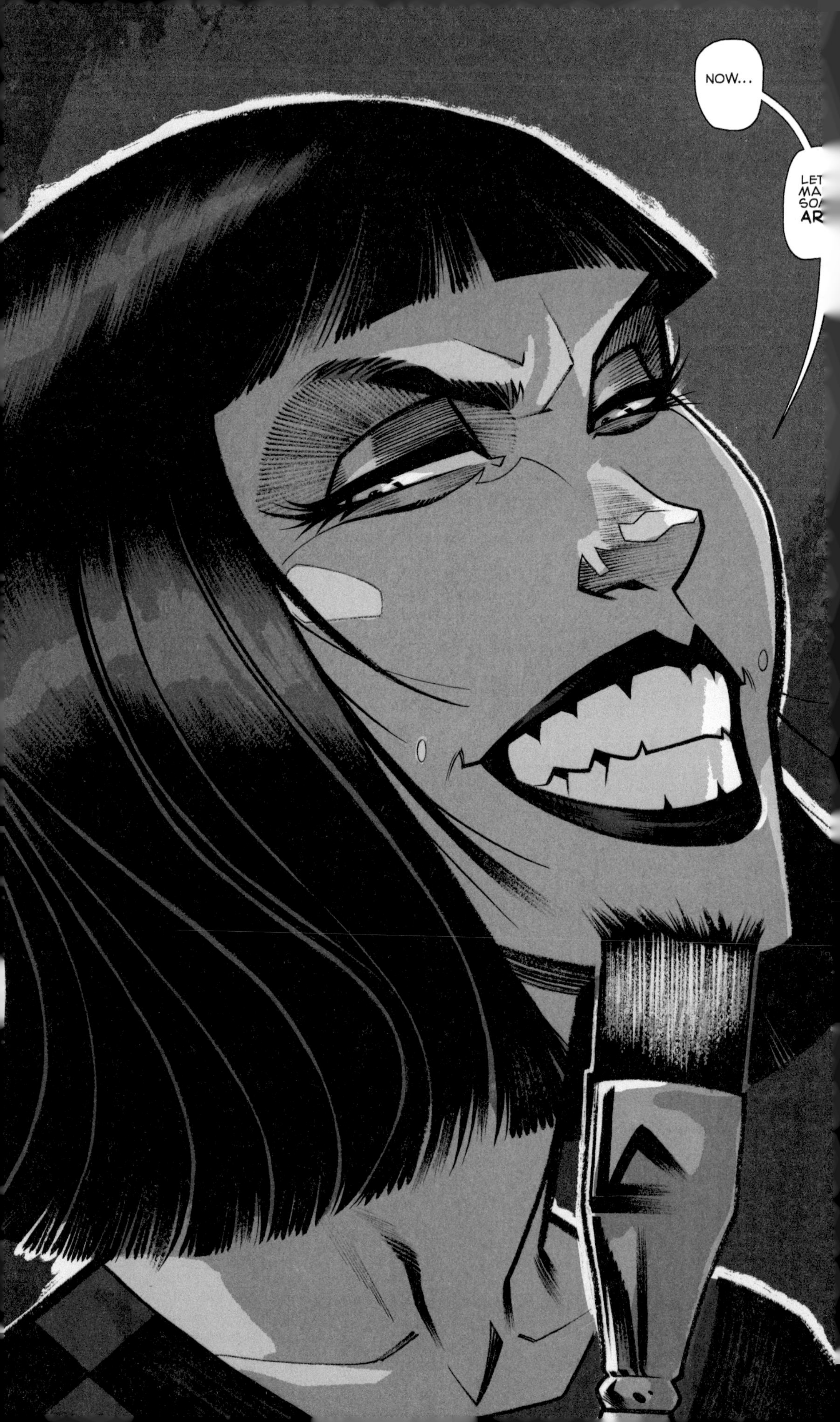
NOW...

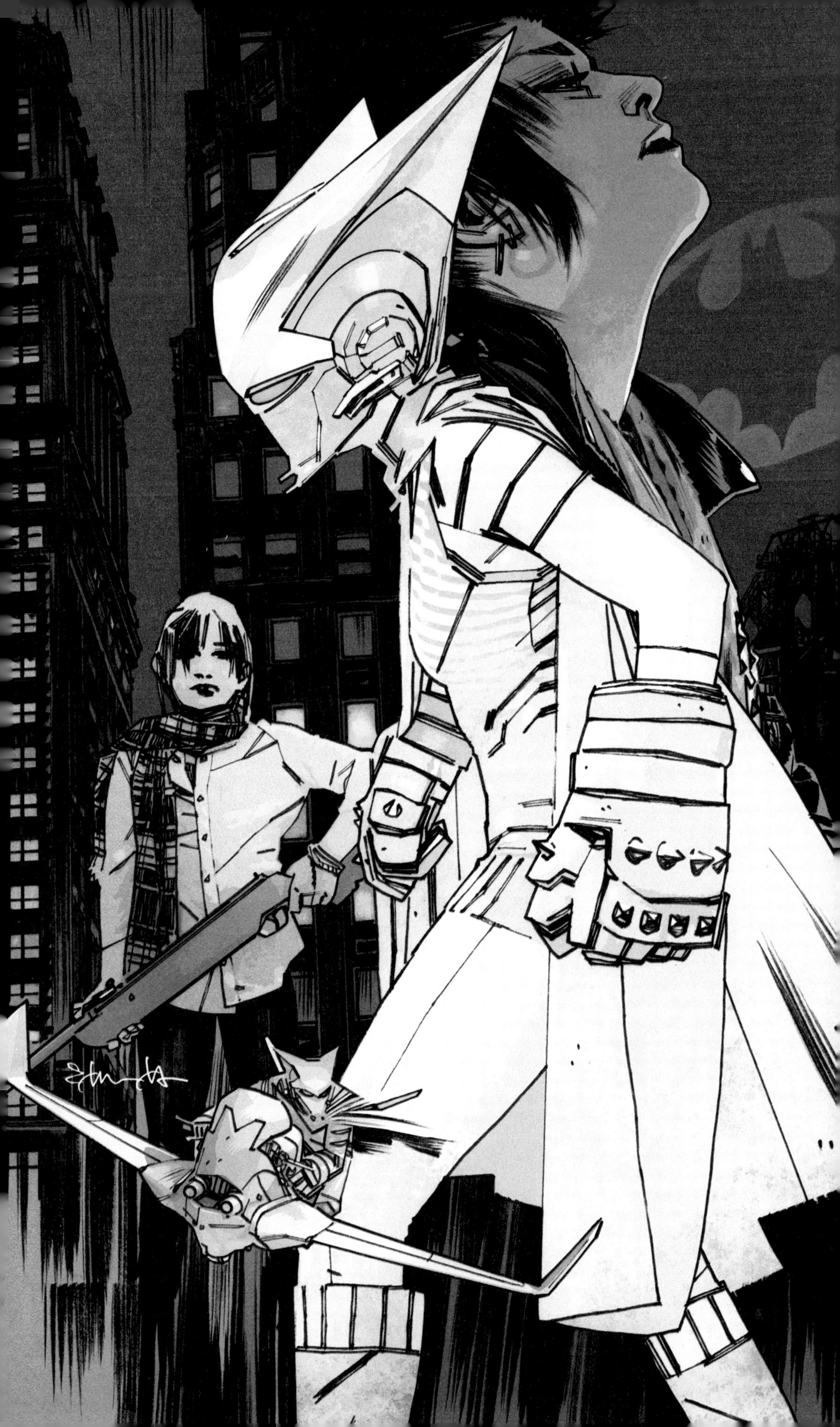

Variant cover art by Joëlle Jones and Laura Allred

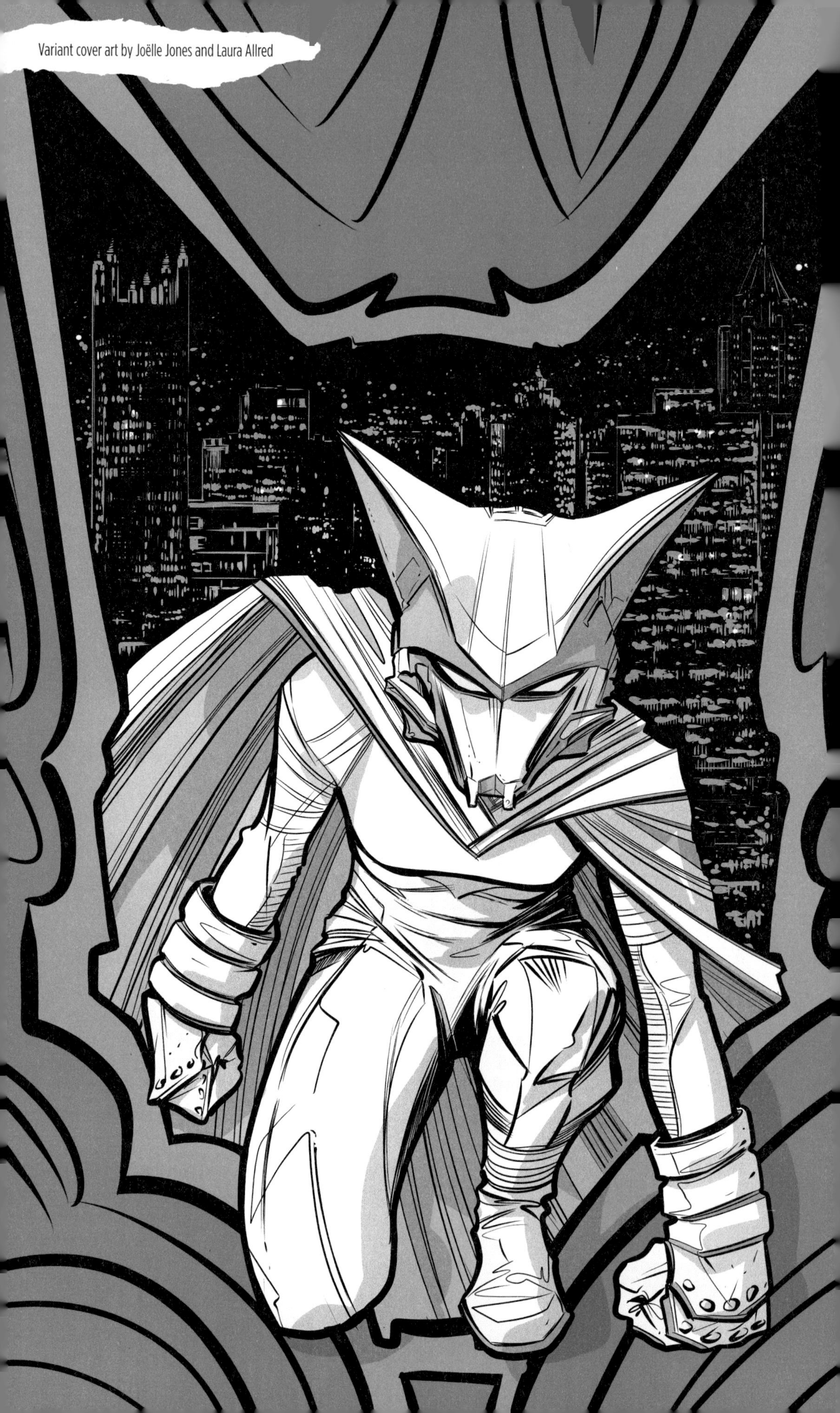

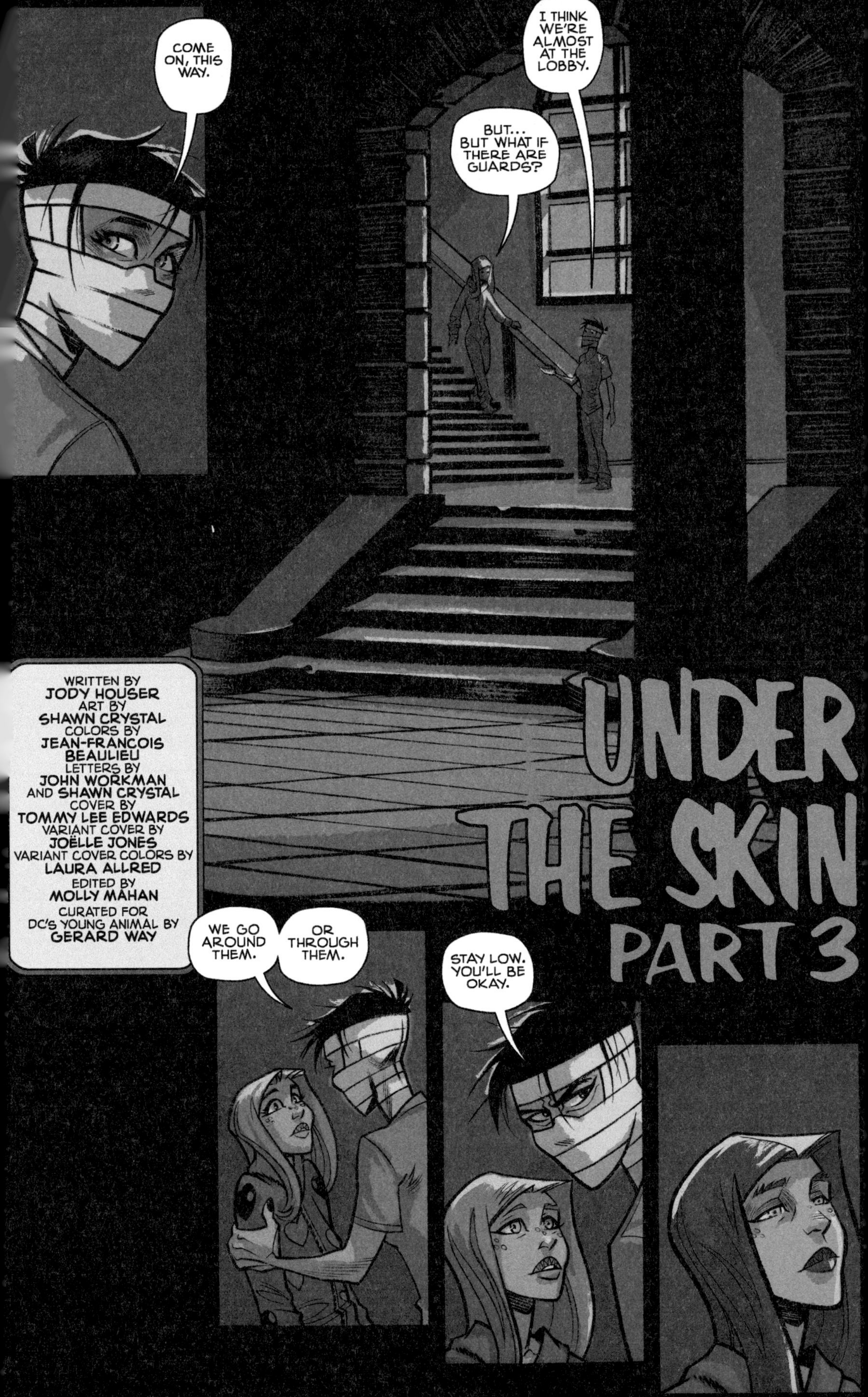
COME ON, THIS WAY.
I THINK WE'RE ALMOST AT THE LOBBY.
BUT... BUT WHAT IF THERE ARE GUARDS?
WRITTEN BY JODY HOUSER
ART BY SHAWN CRYSTAL
COLORS BY JEAN-FRANCOIS BEAULIEU
LETTERS BY JOHN WORKMAN AND SHAWN CRYSTAL
COVER BY TOMMY LEE EDWARDS
VARIANT COVER BY JOËLLE JONES
VARIANT COVER COLORS BY LAURA ALLRED
EDITED BY MOLLY MAHAN
CURATED FOR DC'S YOUNG ANIMAL BY GERARD WAY
UNDER THE SKIN
PART 3
WE GO AROUND THEM.
OR THROUGH THEM.
STAY LOW. YOU'LL BE OKAY.

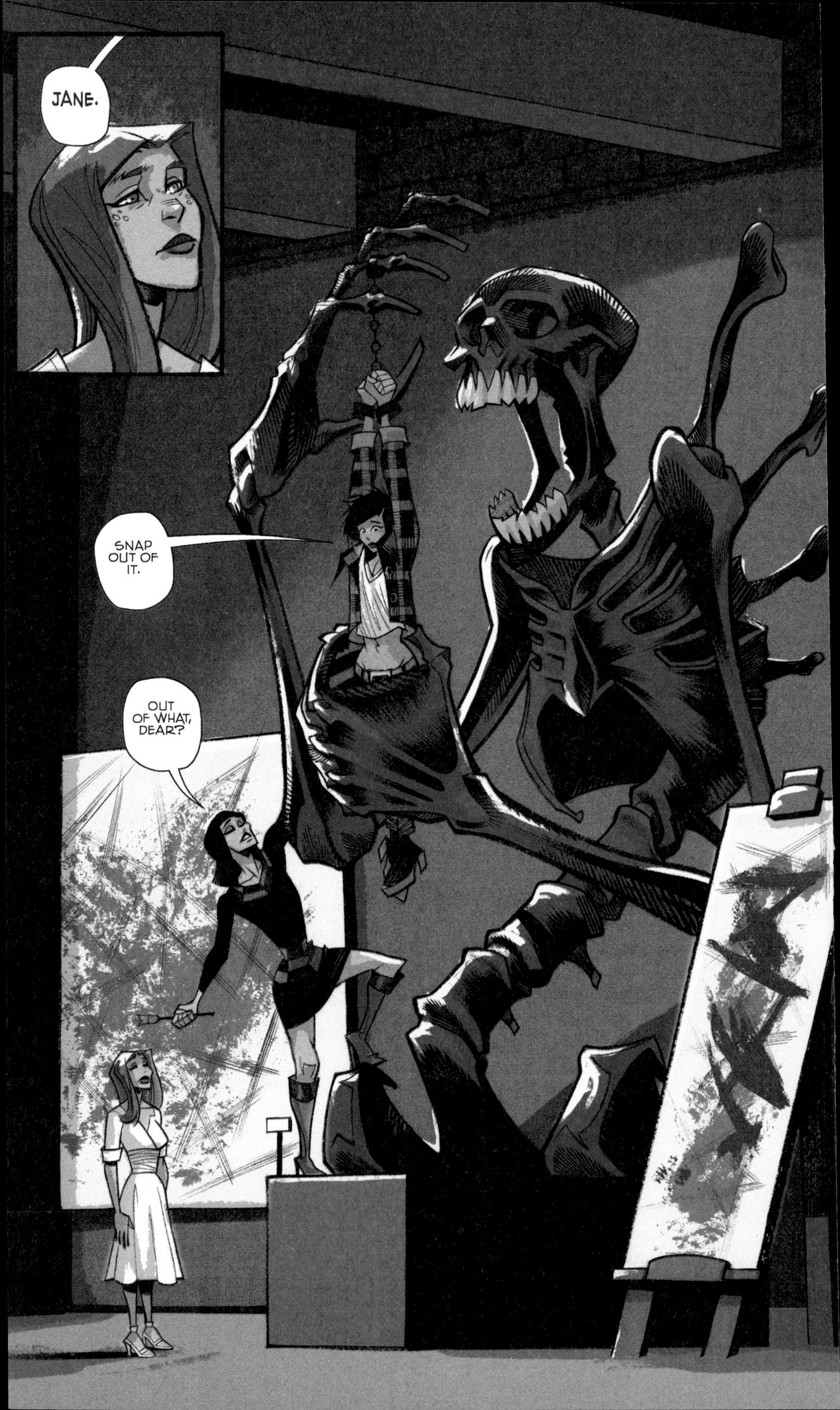
JANE.
SNAP OUT OF IT.
OUT OF WHAT, DEAR?

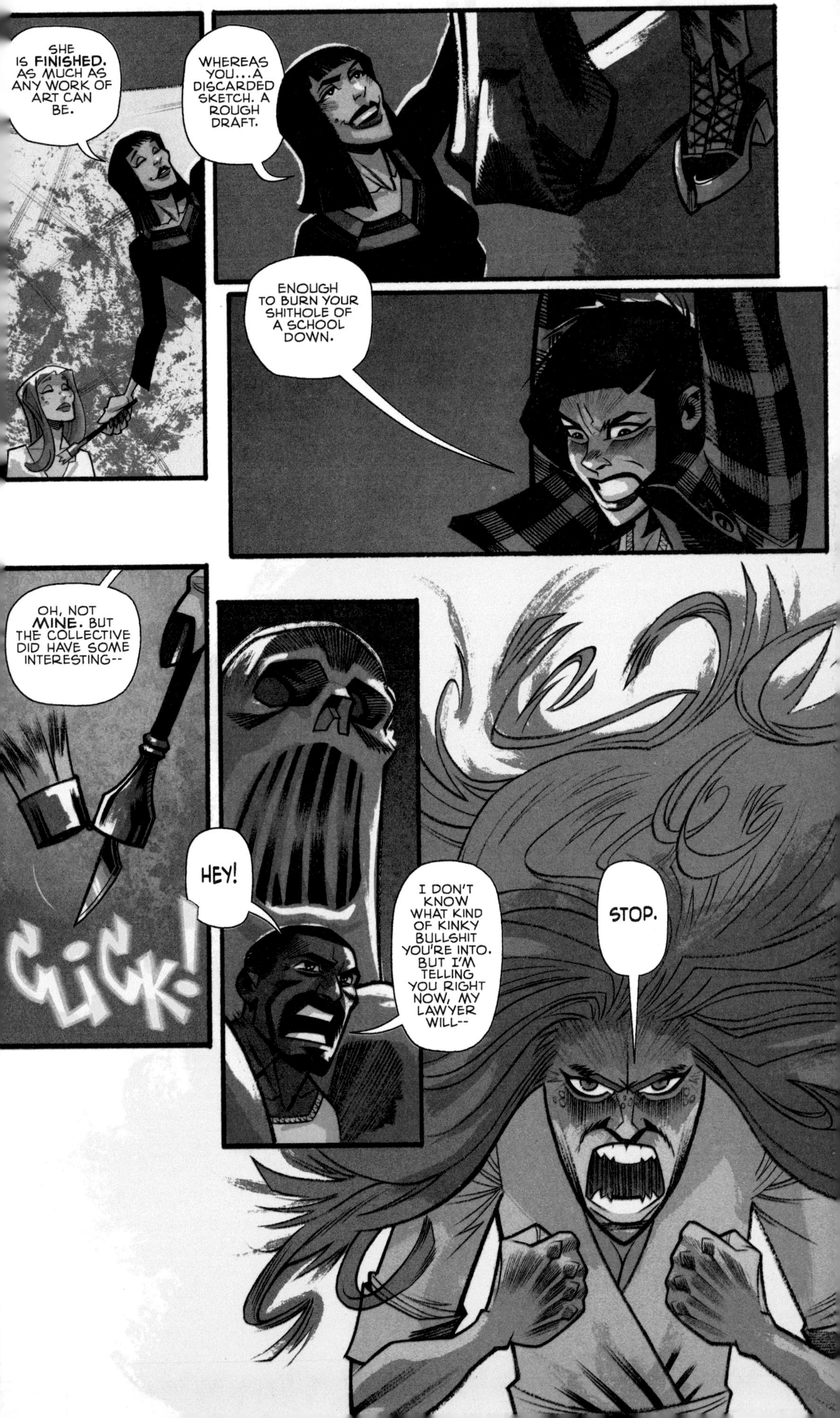
SHE IS FINISHED. AS MUCH AS ANY WORK OF ART CAN BE.
WHEREAS YOU...A DISCARDED SKETCH. A ROUGH DRAFT.
ENOUGH TO BURN YOUR SHITHOLE OF A SCHOOL DOWN.
OH, NOT MINE. BUT THE COLLECTIVE DID HAVE SOME INTERESTING--
CLICK!
HEY!
I DON'T KNOW WHAT KIND OF KINKY BULLSHIT YOU'RE INTO. BUT I'M TELLING YOU RIGHT NOW, MY LAWYER WILL--
STOP.

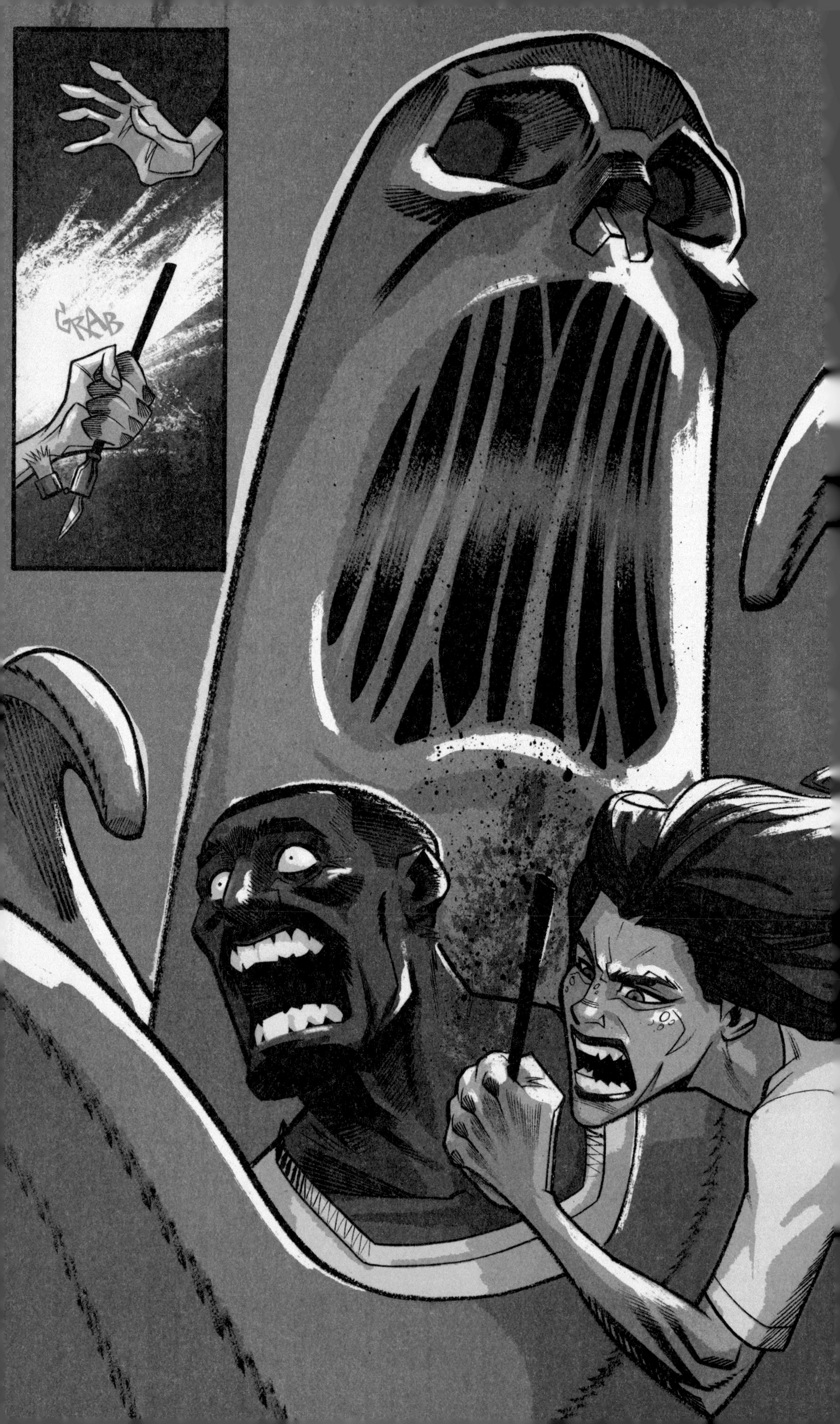
GRAB

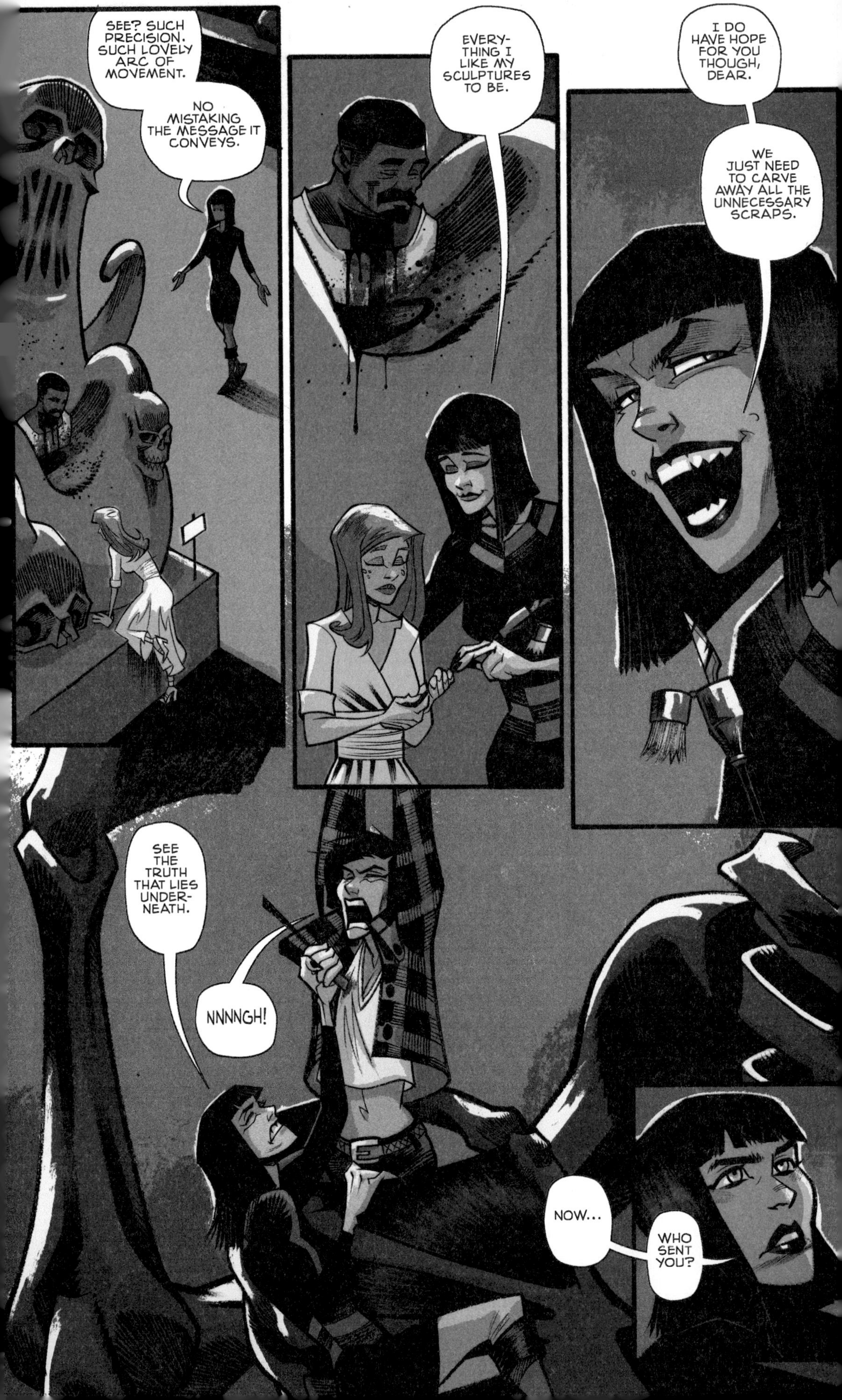
SEE? SUCH PRECISION. SUCH LOVELY ARC OF MOVEMENT.
NO MISTAKING THE MESSAGE IT CONVEYS.
EVERY-THING I LIKE MY SCULPTURES TO BE.
I DO HAVE HOPE FOR YOU THOUGH, DEAR.
WE JUST NEED TO CARVE AWAY ALL THE UNNECESSARY SCRAPS.
SEE THE TRUTH THAT LIES UNDER-NEATH.
NNNNGH!
NOW...
WHO SENT YOU?

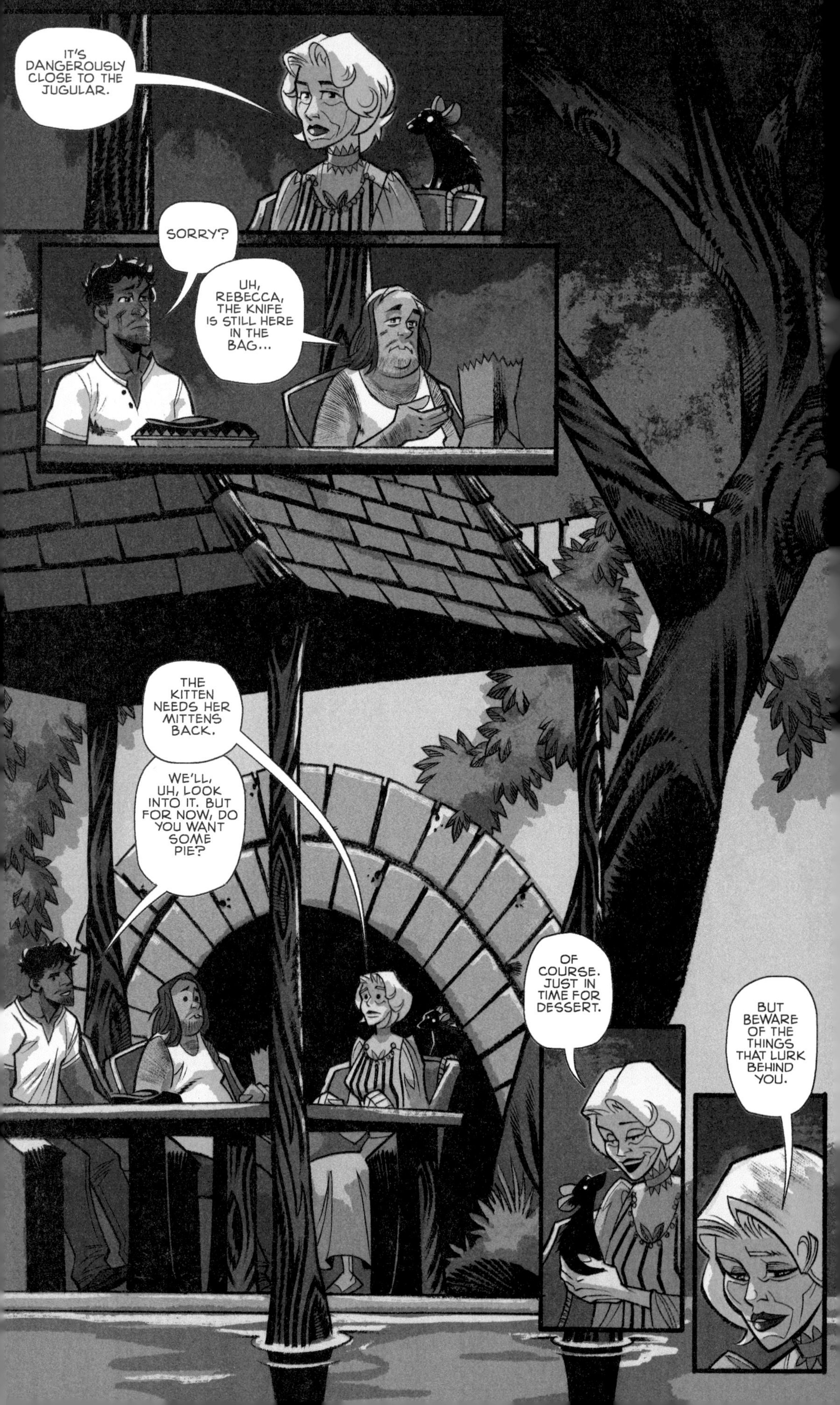
IT'S DANGEROUSLY CLOSE TO THE JUGULAR.
SORRY?
UH, REBECCA, THE KNIFE IS STILL HERE IN THE BAG...
THE KITTEN NEEDS HER MITTENS BACK.
WE'LL, UH, LOOK INTO IT. BUT FOR NOW, DO YOU WANT SOME PIE?
OF COURSE. JUST IN TIME FOR DESSERT.
BUT BEWARE OF THE THINGS THAT LURK BEHIND YOU.

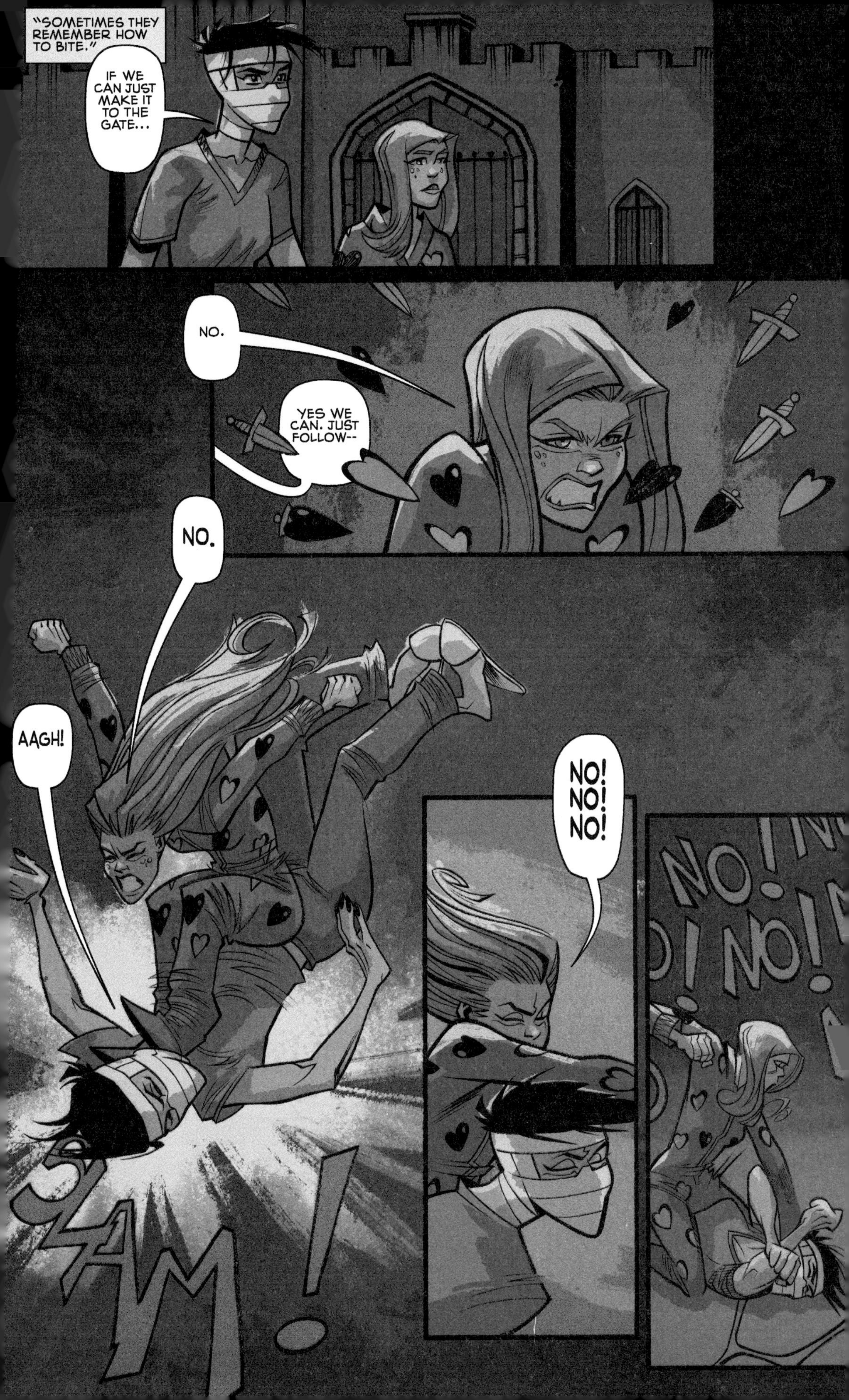
"SOMETIMES THEY REMEMBER HOW TO BITE."
IF WE CAN JUST MAKE IT TO THE GATE...
NO.
YES WE CAN. JUST FOLLOW--
NO.
AAGH!
SLAM!
NO! NO! NO!

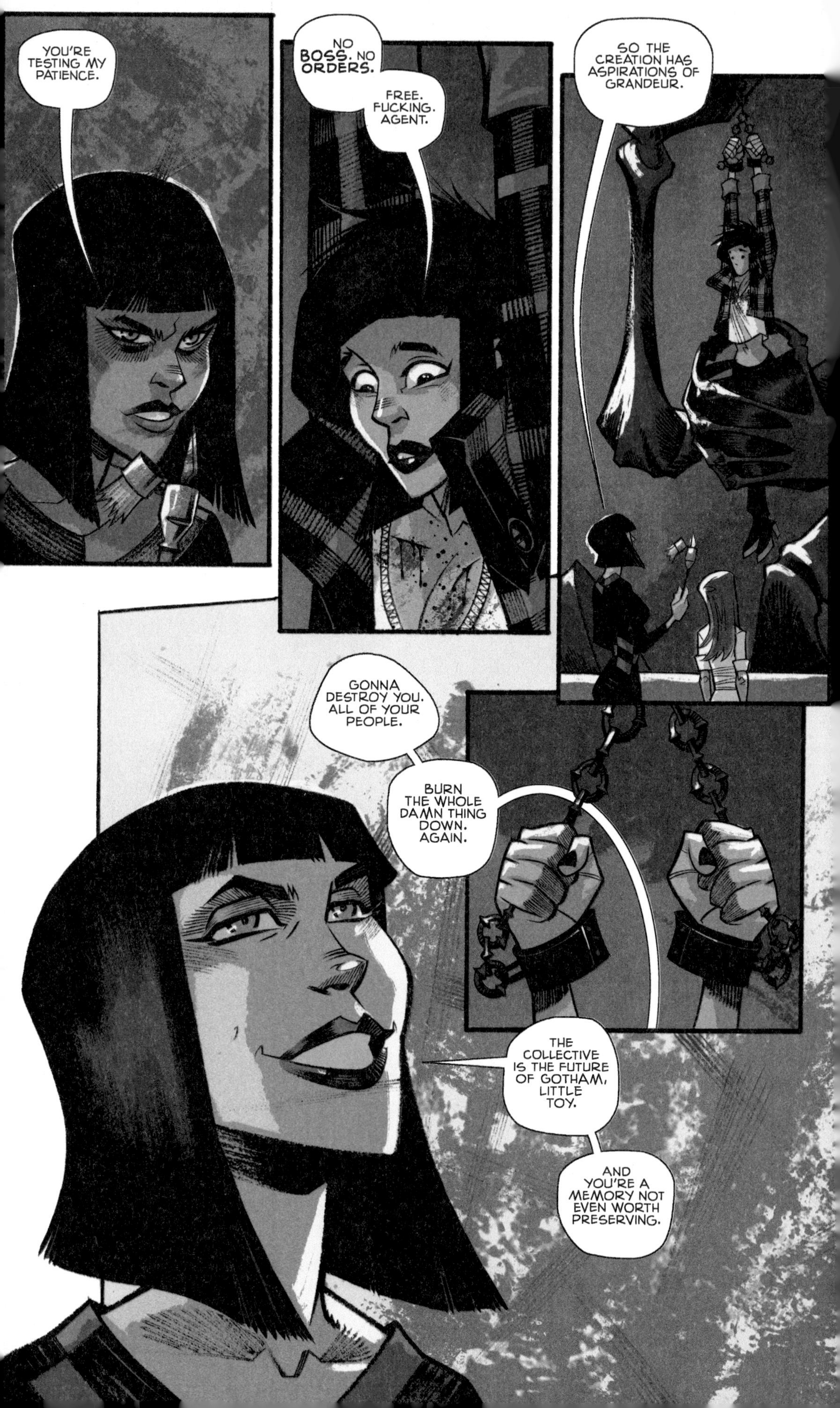

YOU'RE TESTING MY PATIENCE.
NO **BOSS.** NO **ORDERS.**
FREE. FUCKING. AGENT.
SO THE CREATION HAS ASPIRATIONS OF GRANDEUR.
GONNA DESTROY YOU. ALL OF YOUR PEOPLE.
BURN THE WHOLE DAMN THING DOWN. AGAIN.
THE COLLECTIVE IS THE FUTURE OF GOTHAM, LITTLE TOY.
AND YOU'RE A MEMORY NOT EVEN WORTH PRESERVING.

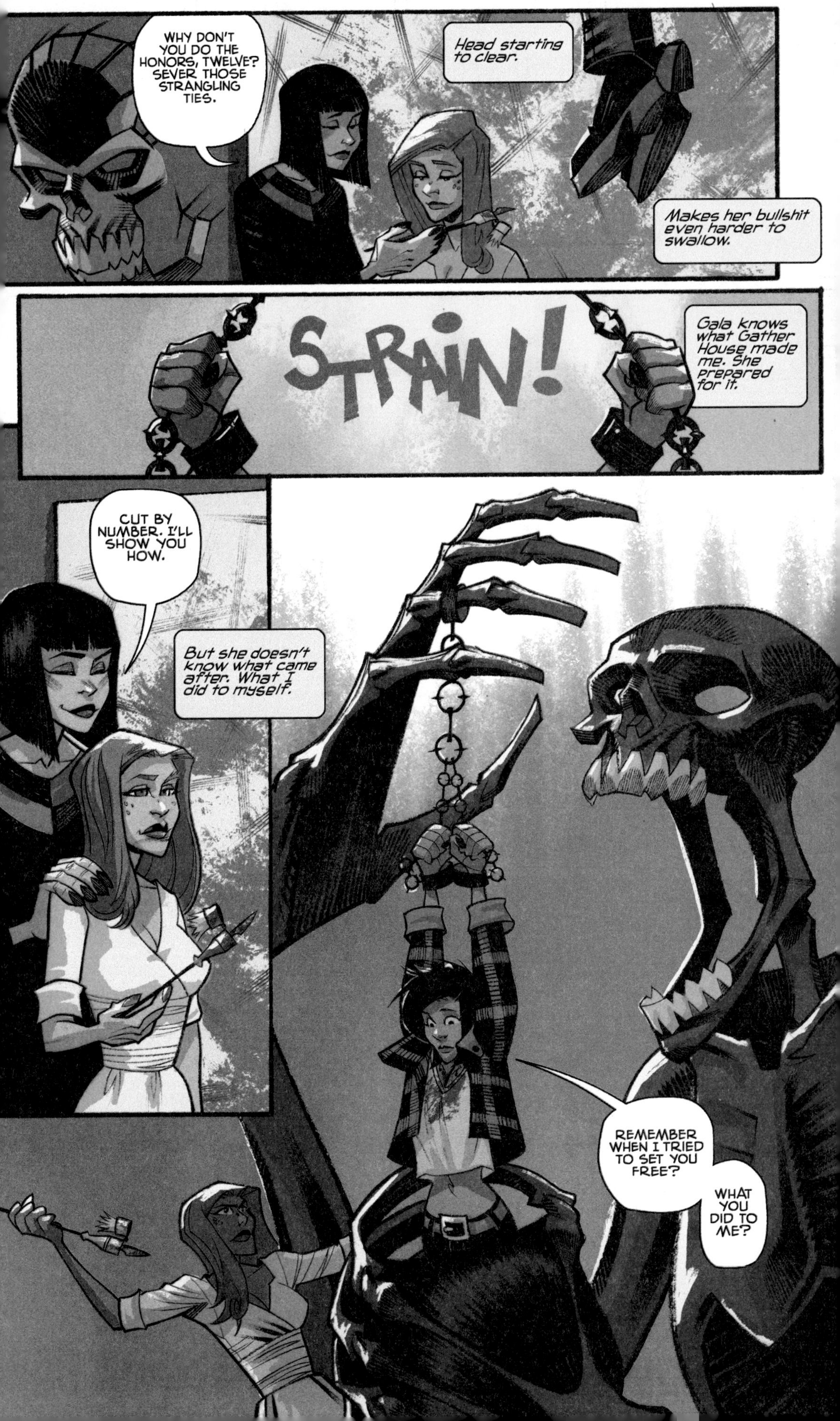

WHY DON'T YOU DO THE HONORS, TWELVE? SEVER THOSE STRANGLING TIES.
Head starting to clear.
Makes her bullshit even harder to swallow.
STRAIN!
Gala knows what Gather House made me. She prepared for it.
CUT BY NUMBER. I'LL SHOW YOU HOW.
But she doesn't know what came after. What I did to myself.
REMEMBER WHEN I TRIED TO SET YOU FREE?
WHAT YOU DID TO ME?

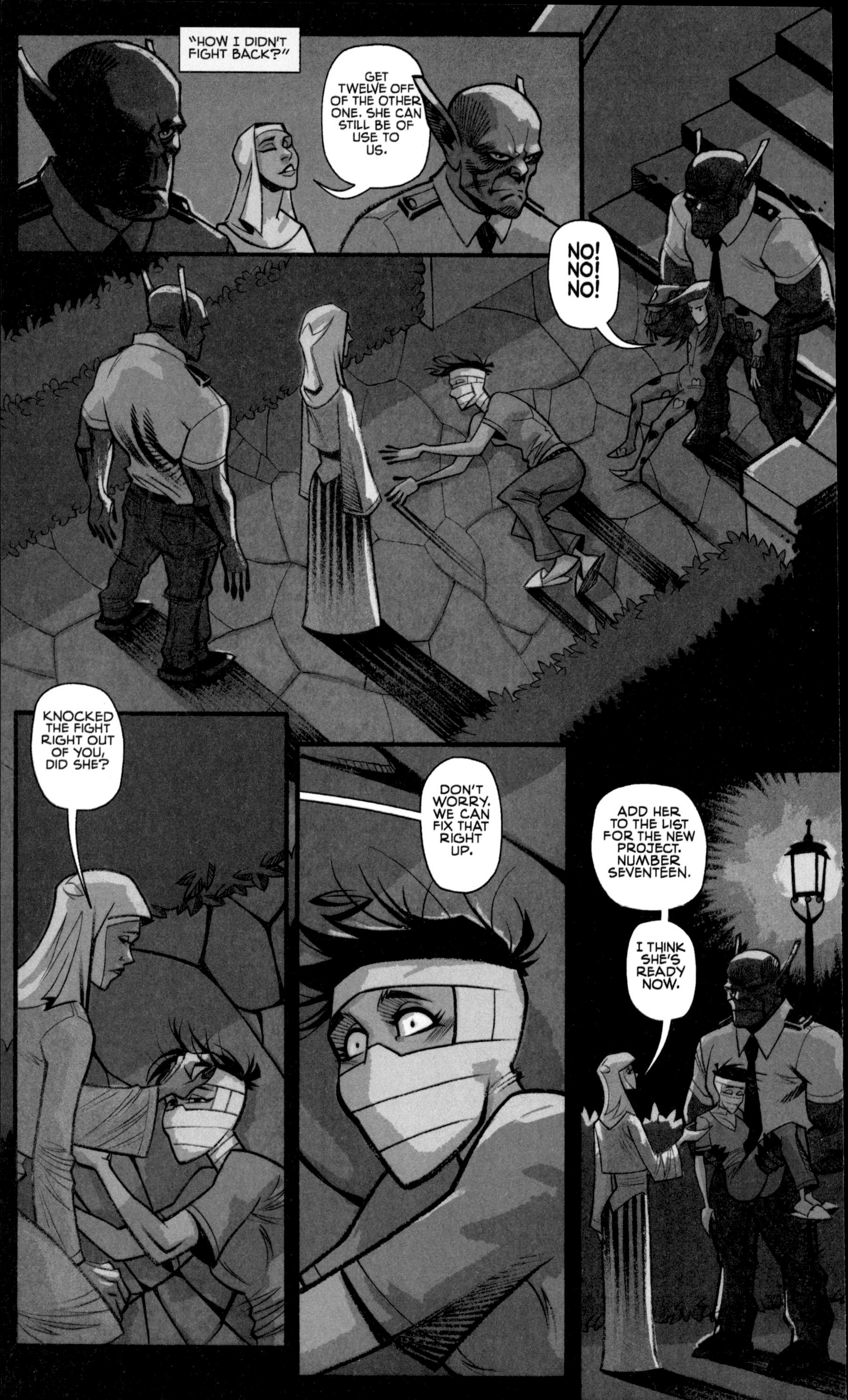
"HOW I DIDN'T FIGHT BACK?"
GET TWELVE OFF OF THE OTHER ONE. SHE CAN STILL BE OF USE TO US.
NO! NO! NO!
KNOCKED THE FIGHT RIGHT OUT OF YOU, DID SHE?
DON'T WORRY. WE CAN FIX THAT RIGHT UP.
ADD HER TO THE LIST FOR THE NEW PROJECT. NUMBER SEVENTEEN.
I THINK SHE'S READY NOW.

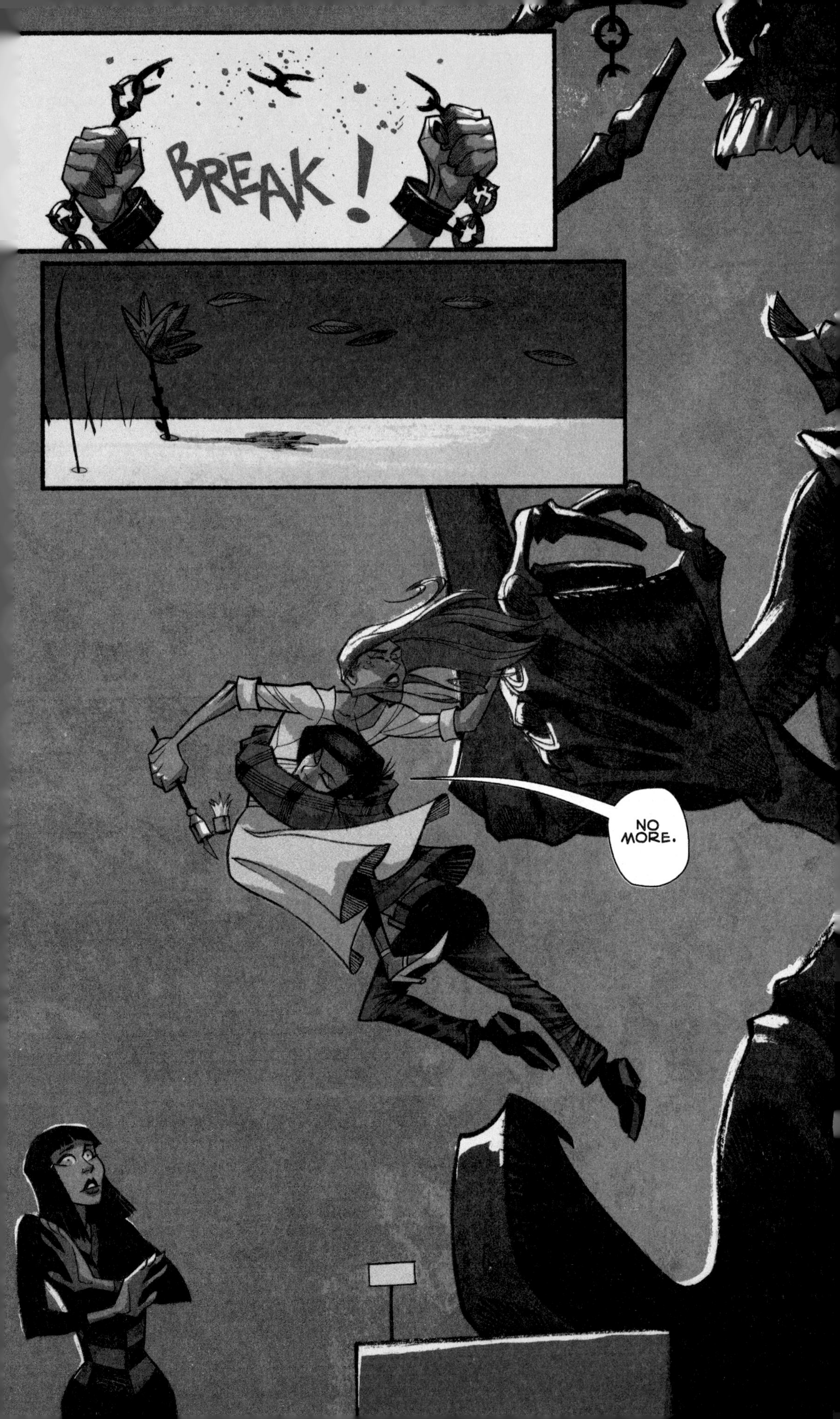
BREAK!
NO MORE.

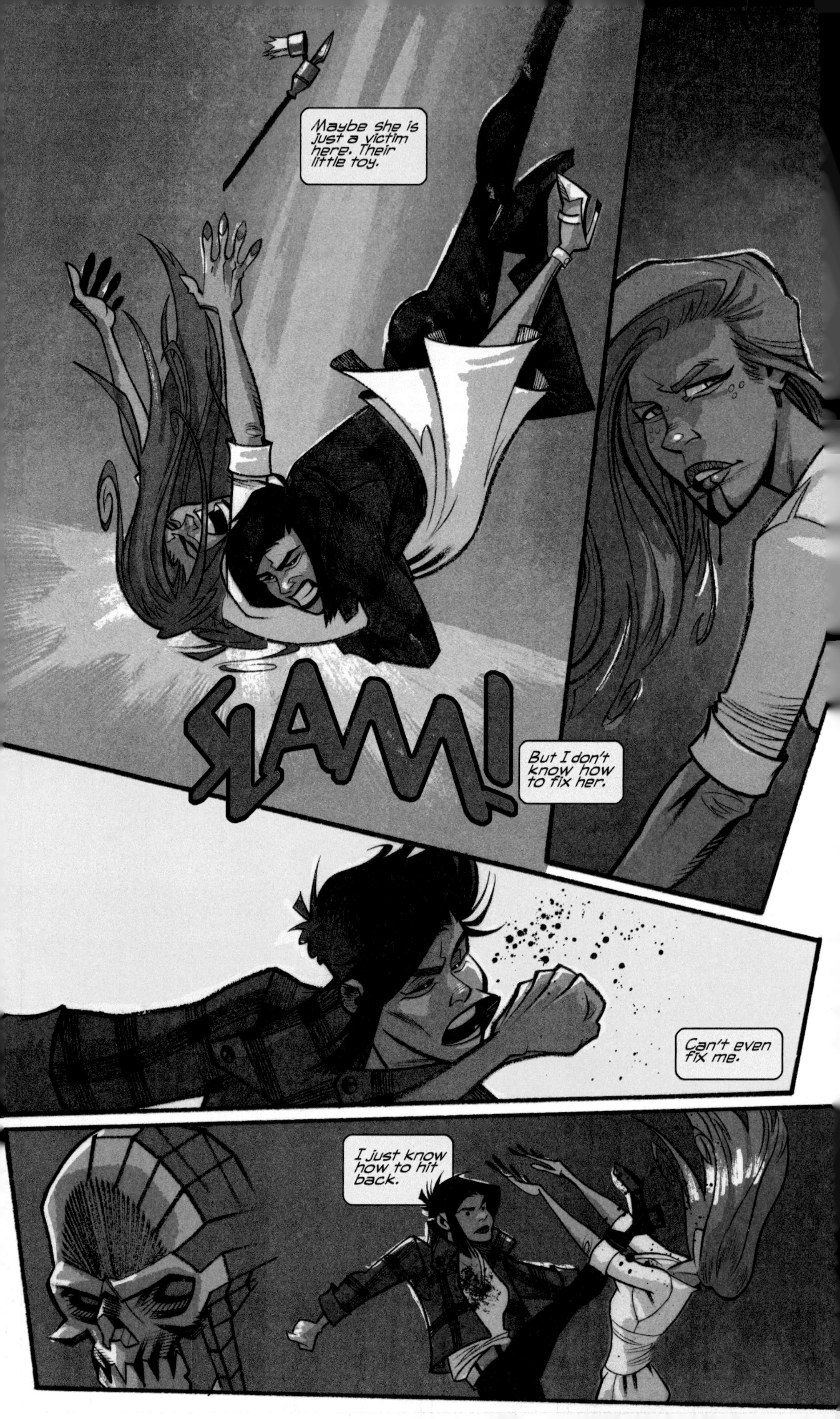
Maybe she is just a victim here. Their little toy.
SLAM!
But I don't know how to fix her.
Can't even fix me.
I just know how to hit back.

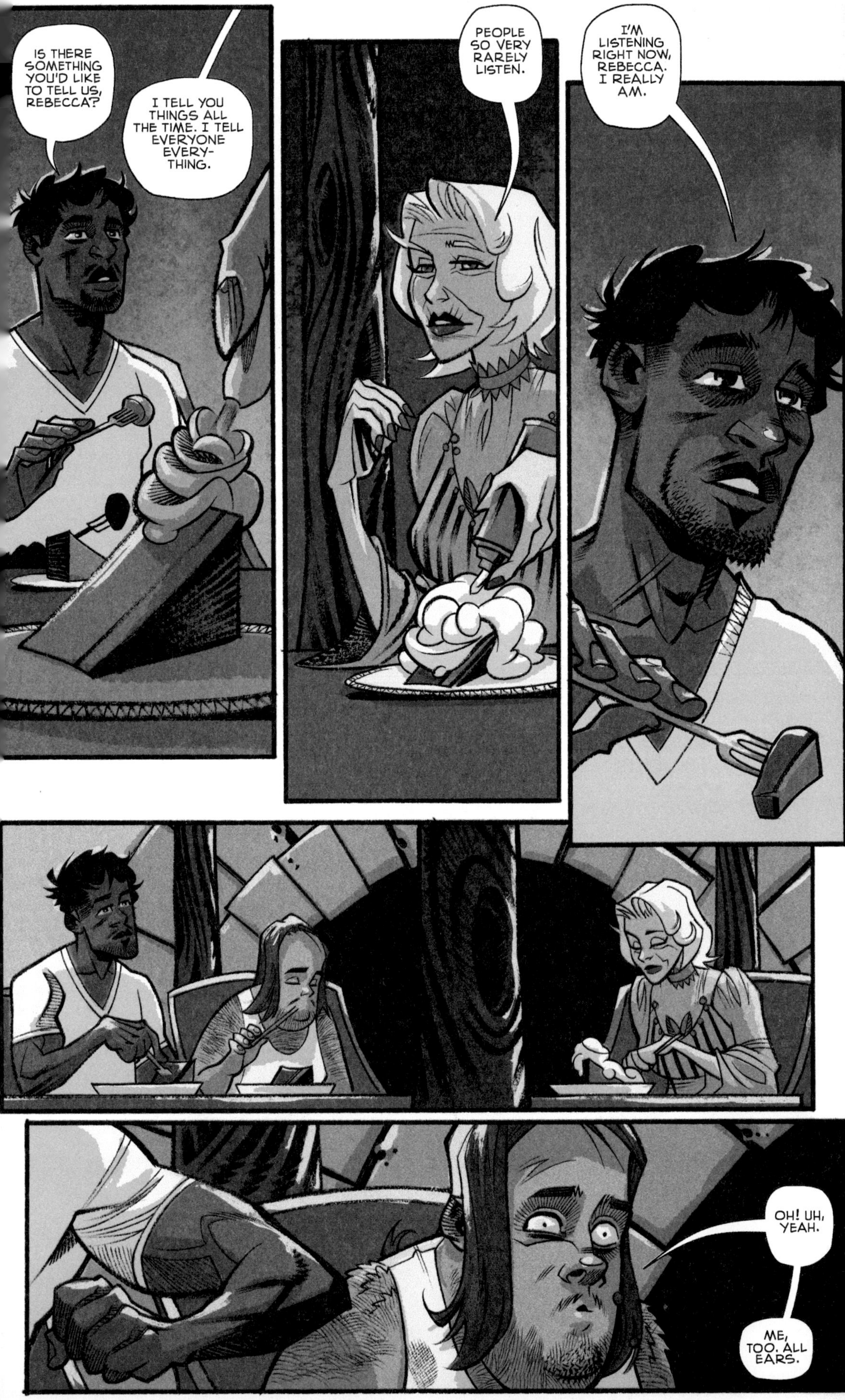
IS THERE SOMETHING YOU'D LIKE TO TELL US, REBECCA?
I TELL YOU THINGS ALL THE TIME. I TELL EVERYONE EVERY-THING.
PEOPLE SO VERY RARELY LISTEN.
I'M LISTENING RIGHT NOW, REBECCA. I REALLY AM.
OH! UH, YEAH.
ME, TOO. ALL EARS.

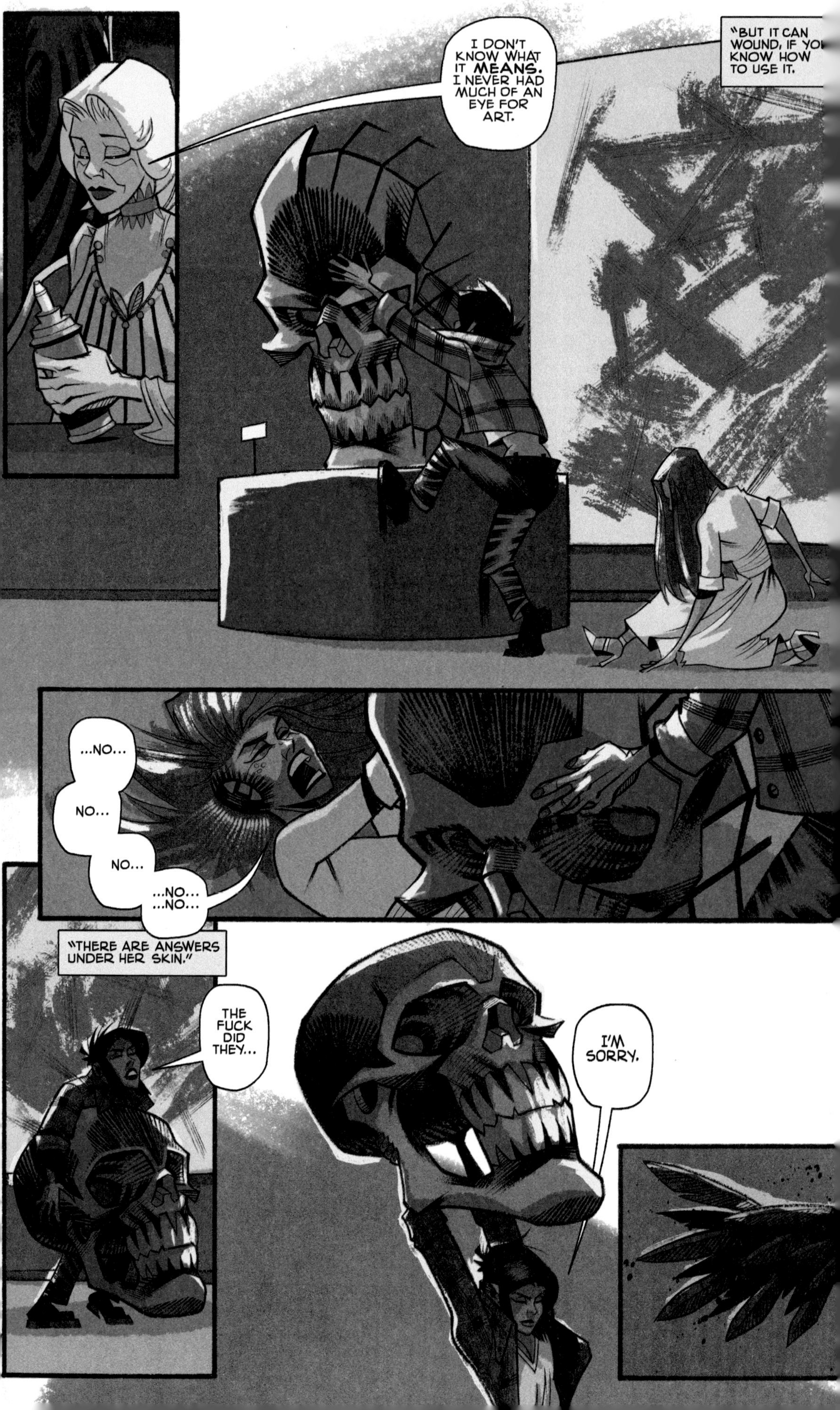
I DON'T KNOW WHAT IT **MEANS.** I NEVER HAD MUCH OF AN EYE FOR ART.
"BUT IT CAN WOUND, IF YO KNOW HOW TO USE IT.
...NO...
NO...
NO...
...NO... ...NO...
"THERE ARE ANSWERS UNDER HER SKIN."
THE FUCK DID THEY...
I'M SORRY.

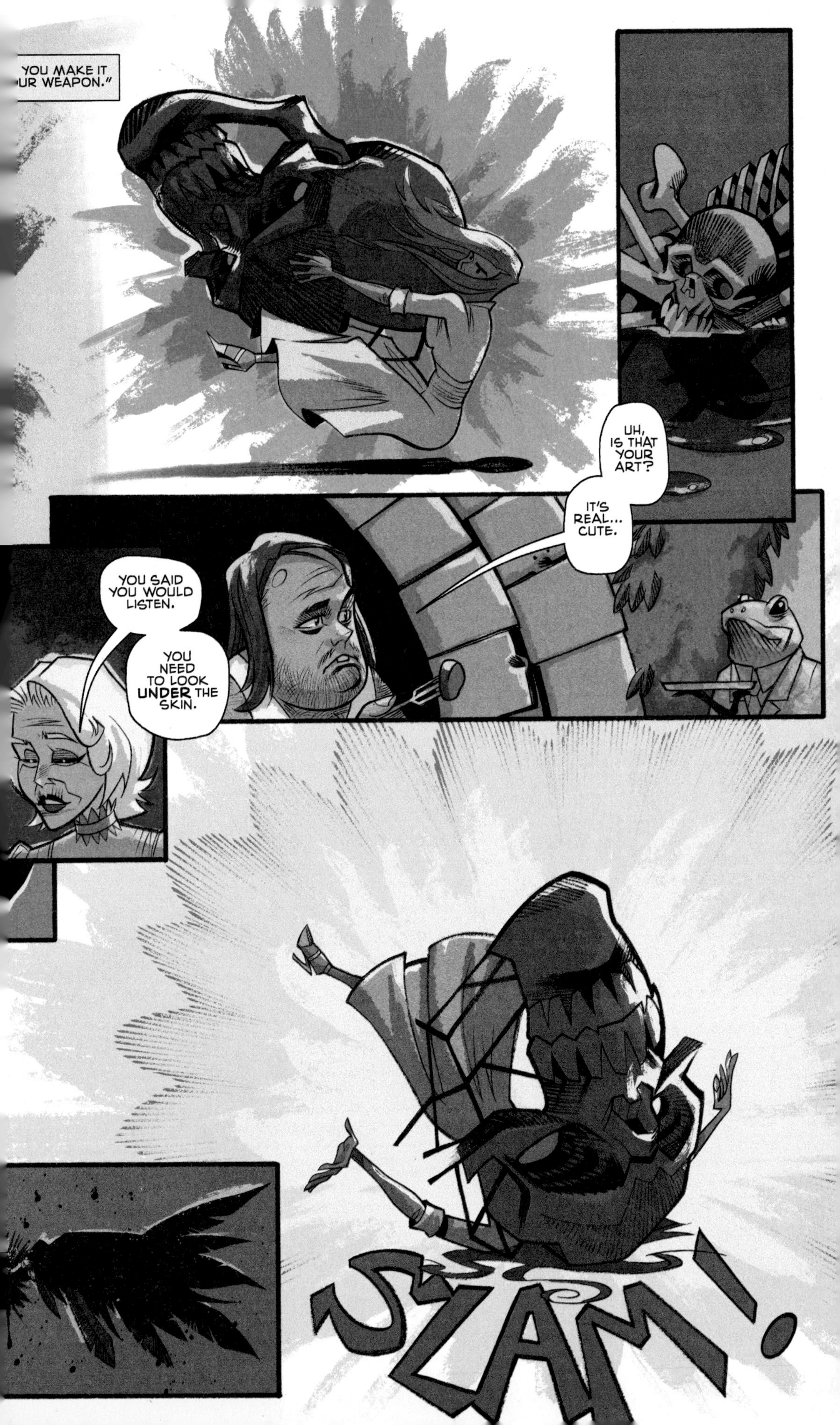
YOU MAKE IT
UR WEAPON."
UH, IS THAT YOUR ART?
IT'S REAL... CUTE.
YOU SAID YOU WOULD LISTEN.
YOU NEED TO LOOK **UNDER** THE SKIN.
SLAM!

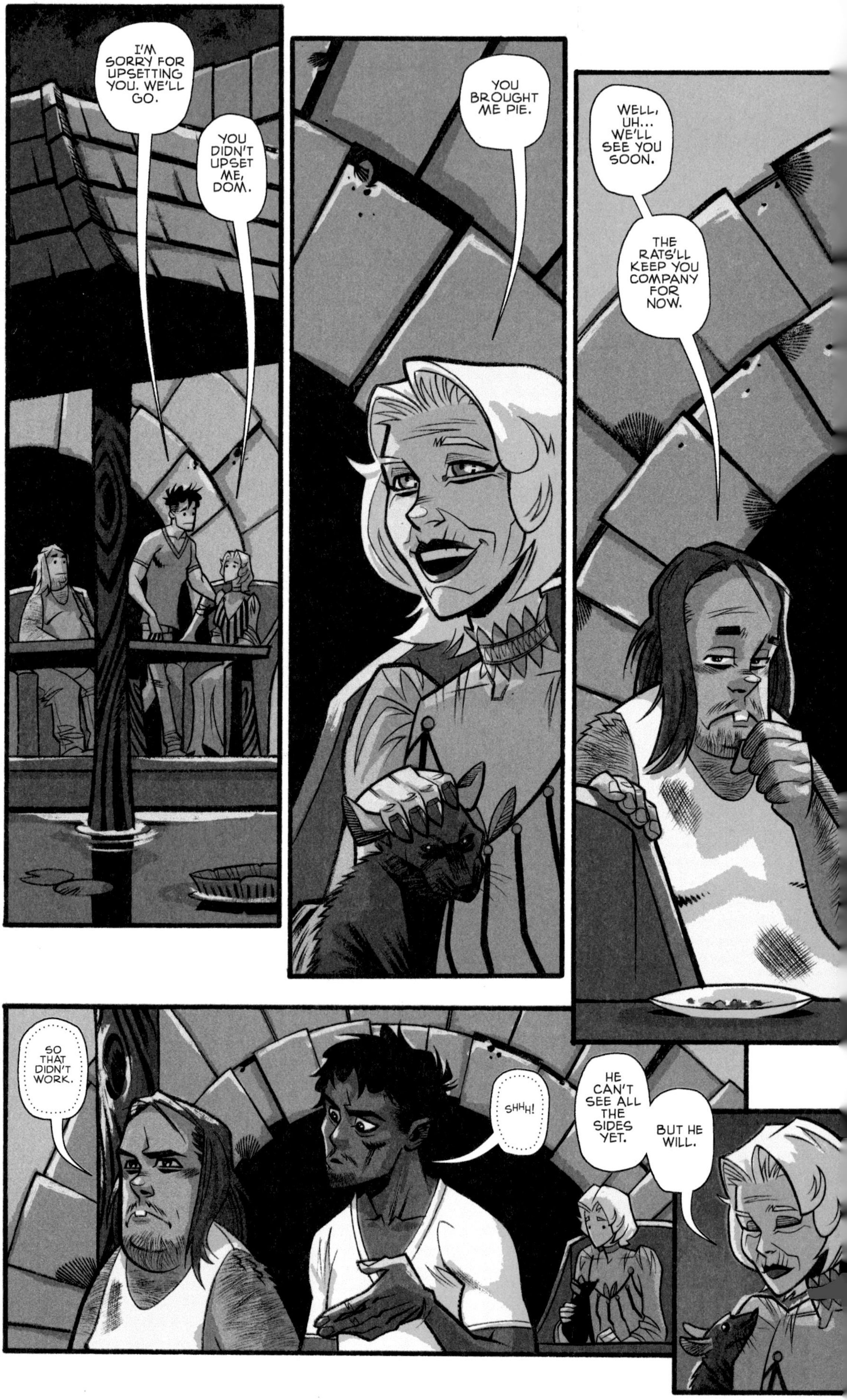
I'M SORRY FOR UPSETTING YOU. WE'LL GO.
YOU DIDN'T UPSET ME, DOM.
YOU BROUGHT ME PIE.
WELL, UH... WE'LL SEE YOU SOON.
THE RATS'LL KEEP YOU COMPANY FOR NOW.
SO THAT DIDN'T WORK.
SHHH!
HE CAN'T SEE ALL THE SIDES YET.
BUT HE WILL.

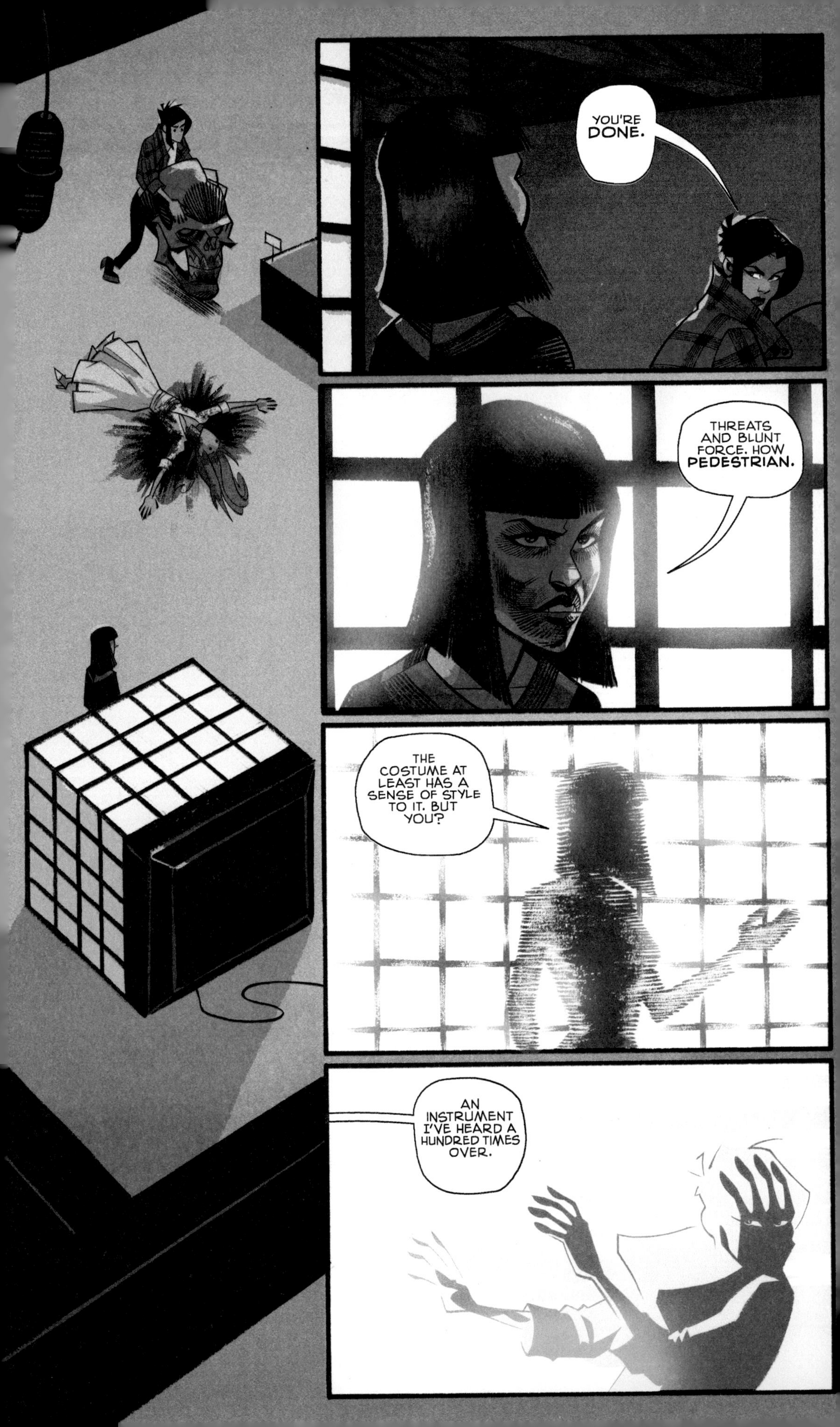
YOU'RE DONE.
THREATS AND BLUNT FORCE. HOW PEDESTRIAN.
THE COSTUME AT LEAST HAS A SENSE OF STYLE TO IT. BUT YOU?
AN INSTRUMENT I'VE HEARD A HUNDRED TIMES OVER.

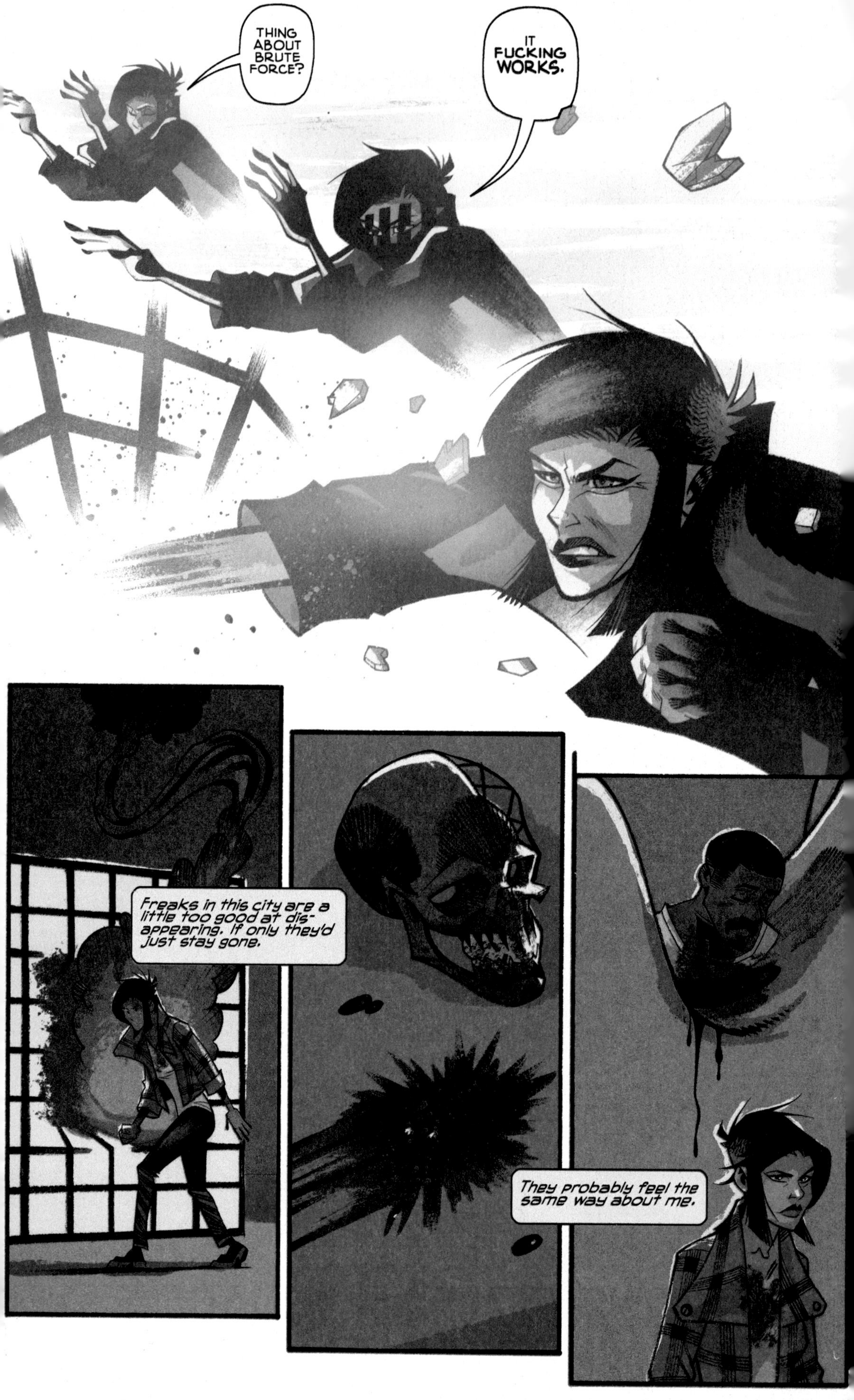
THING ABOUT BRUTE FORCE?
IT FUCKING WORKS.
Freaks in this city are a little too good at dis-appearing. If only they'd just stay gone.
They probably feel the same way about me.

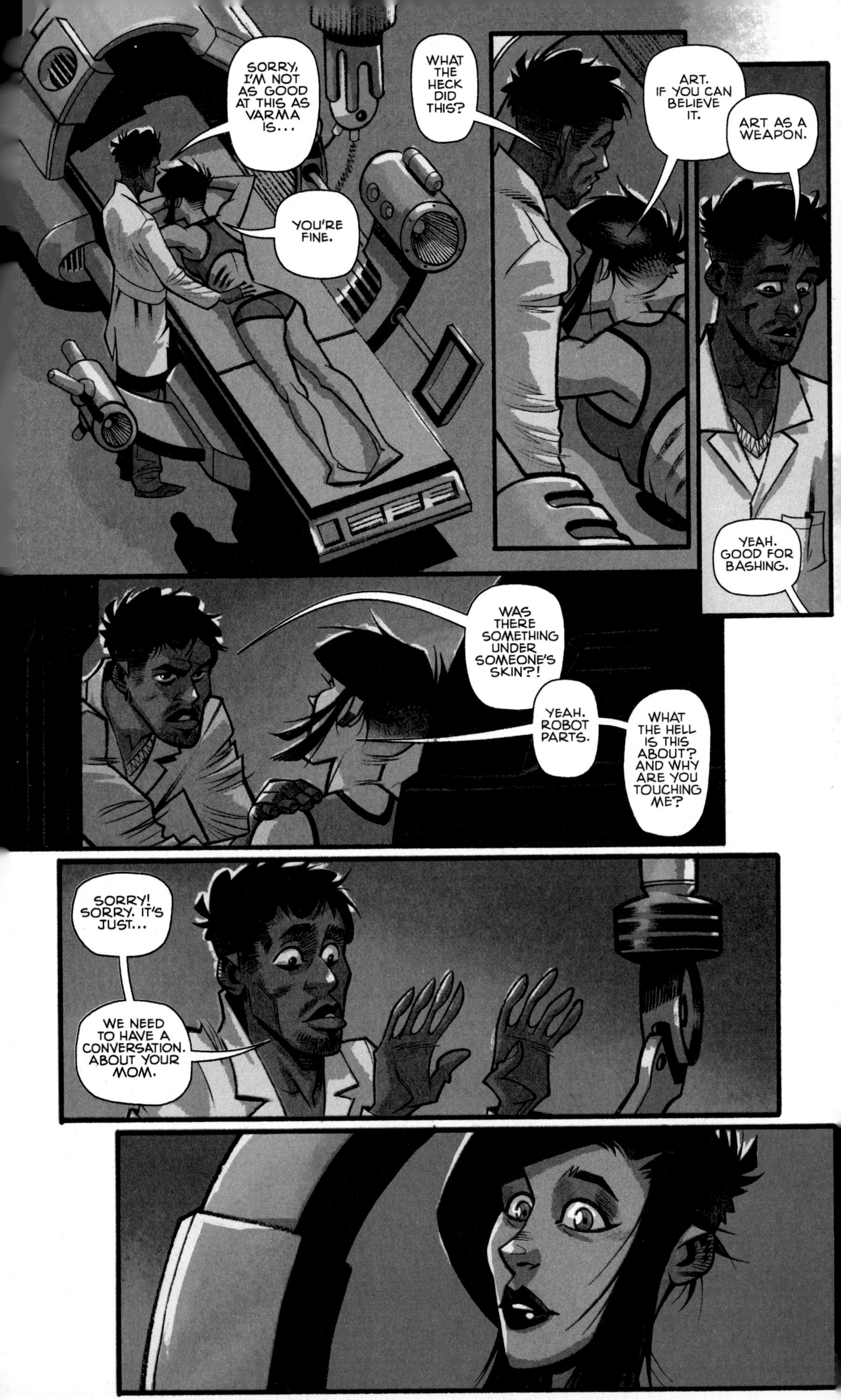
SORRY, I'M NOT AS GOOD AT THIS AS VARMA IS...
YOU'RE FINE.
WHAT THE HECK DID THIS?
ART. IF YOU CAN BELIEVE IT.
ART AS A WEAPON.
YEAH. GOOD FOR BASHING.
WAS THERE SOMETHING UNDER SOMEONE'S SKIN?!
YEAH. ROBOT PARTS.
WHAT THE HELL IS THIS ABOUT? AND WHY ARE YOU TOUCHING ME?
SORRY! SORRY. IT'S JUST...
WE NEED TO HAVE A CONVERSATION. ABOUT YOUR MOM.

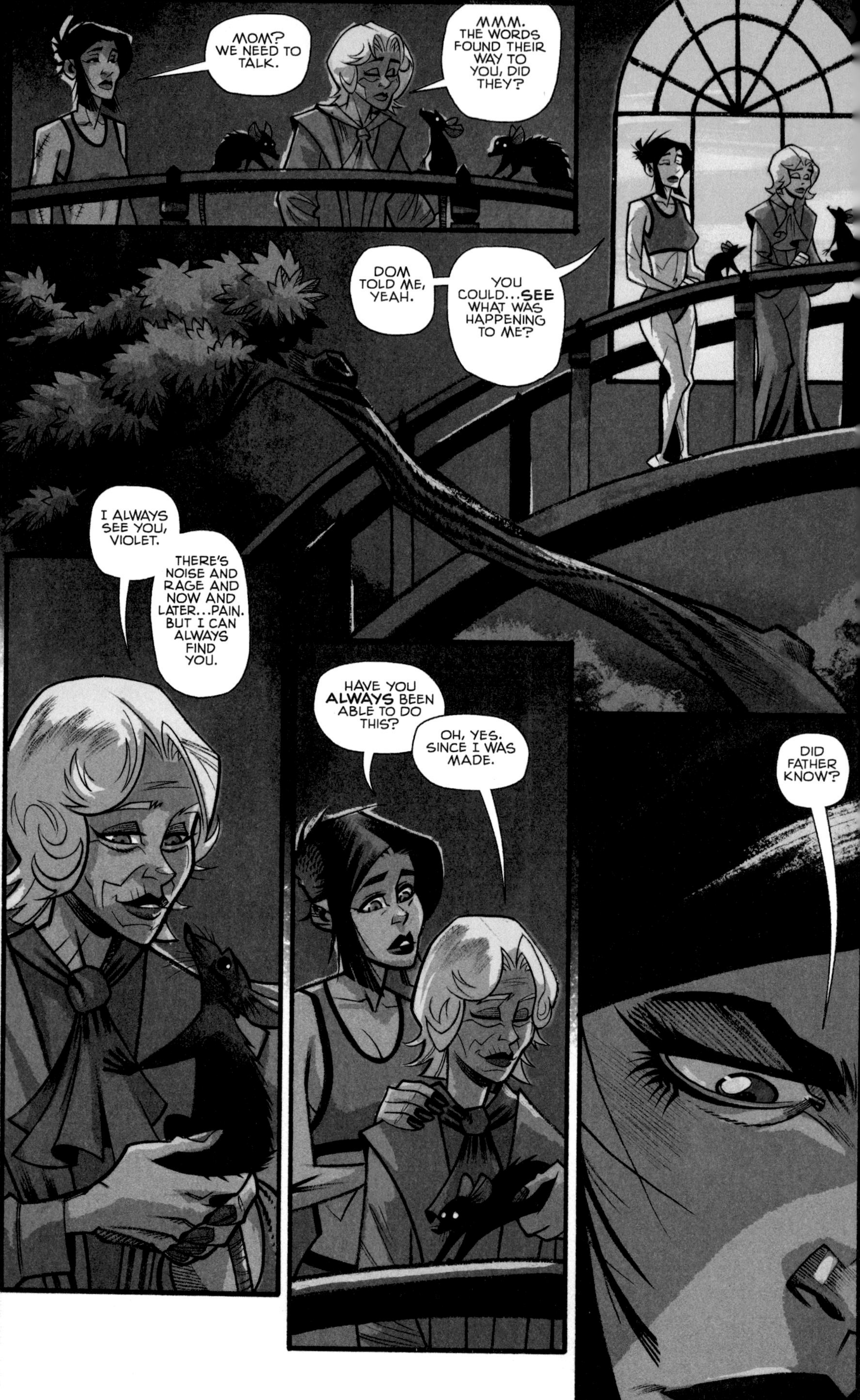
MOM? WE NEED TO TALK.
MMM. THE WORDS FOUND THEIR WAY TO YOU, DID THEY?
DOM TOLD ME, YEAH.
YOU COULD...SEE WHAT WAS HAPPENING TO ME?
I ALWAYS SEE YOU, VIOLET.
THERE'S NOISE AND RAGE AND NOW AND LATER...PAIN. BUT I CAN ALWAYS FIND YOU.
HAVE YOU ALWAYS BEEN ABLE TO DO THIS?
OH, YES. SINCE I WAS MADE.
DID FATHER KNOW?

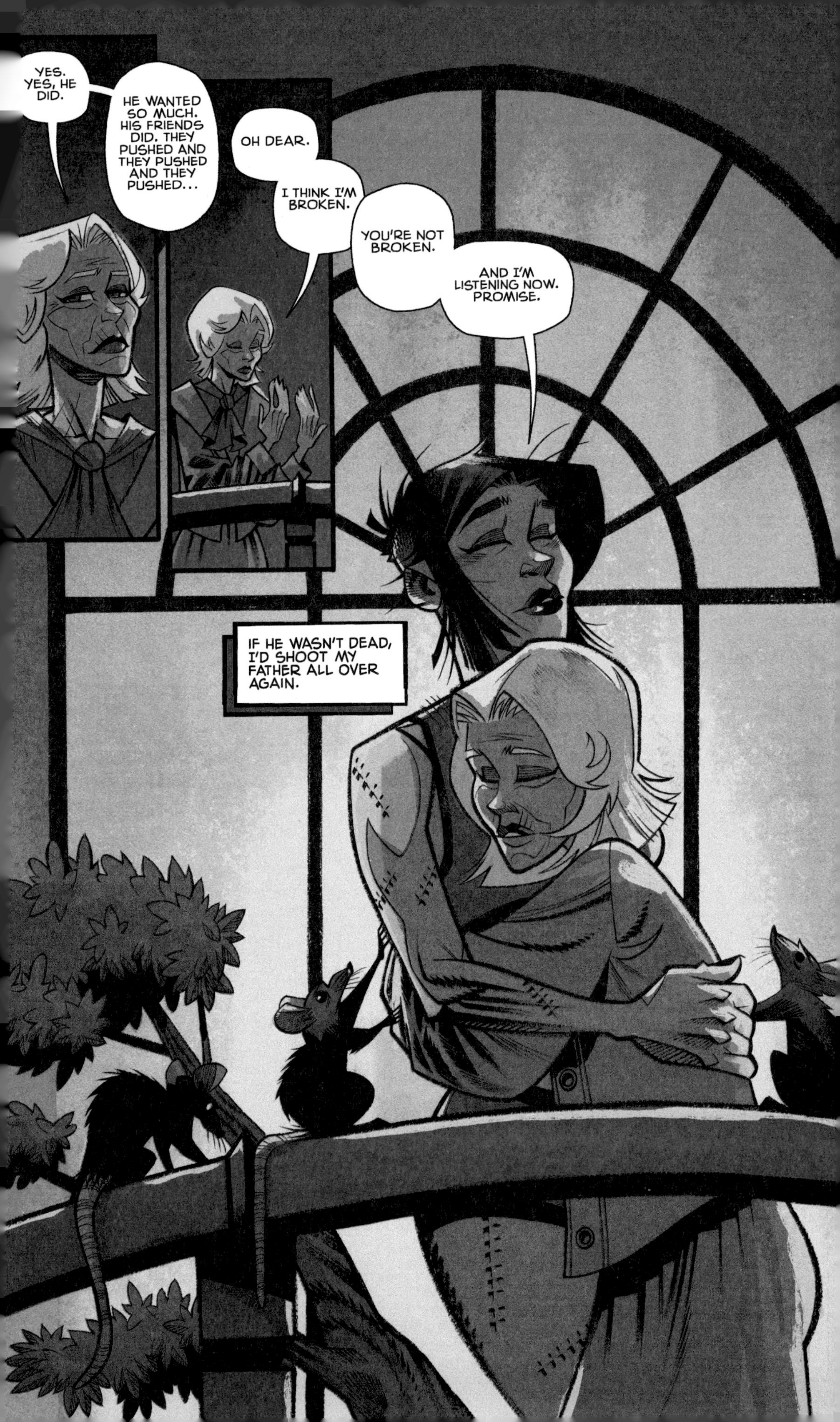
YES. YES, HE DID.
HE WANTED SO MUCH. HIS FRIENDS DID. THEY PUSHED AND THEY PUSHED AND THEY PUSHED...
OH DEAR.
I THINK I'M BROKEN.
YOU'RE NOT BROKEN.
AND I'M LISTENING NOW. PROMISE.
IF HE WASN'T DEAD, I'D SHOOT MY FATHER ALL OVER AGAIN.

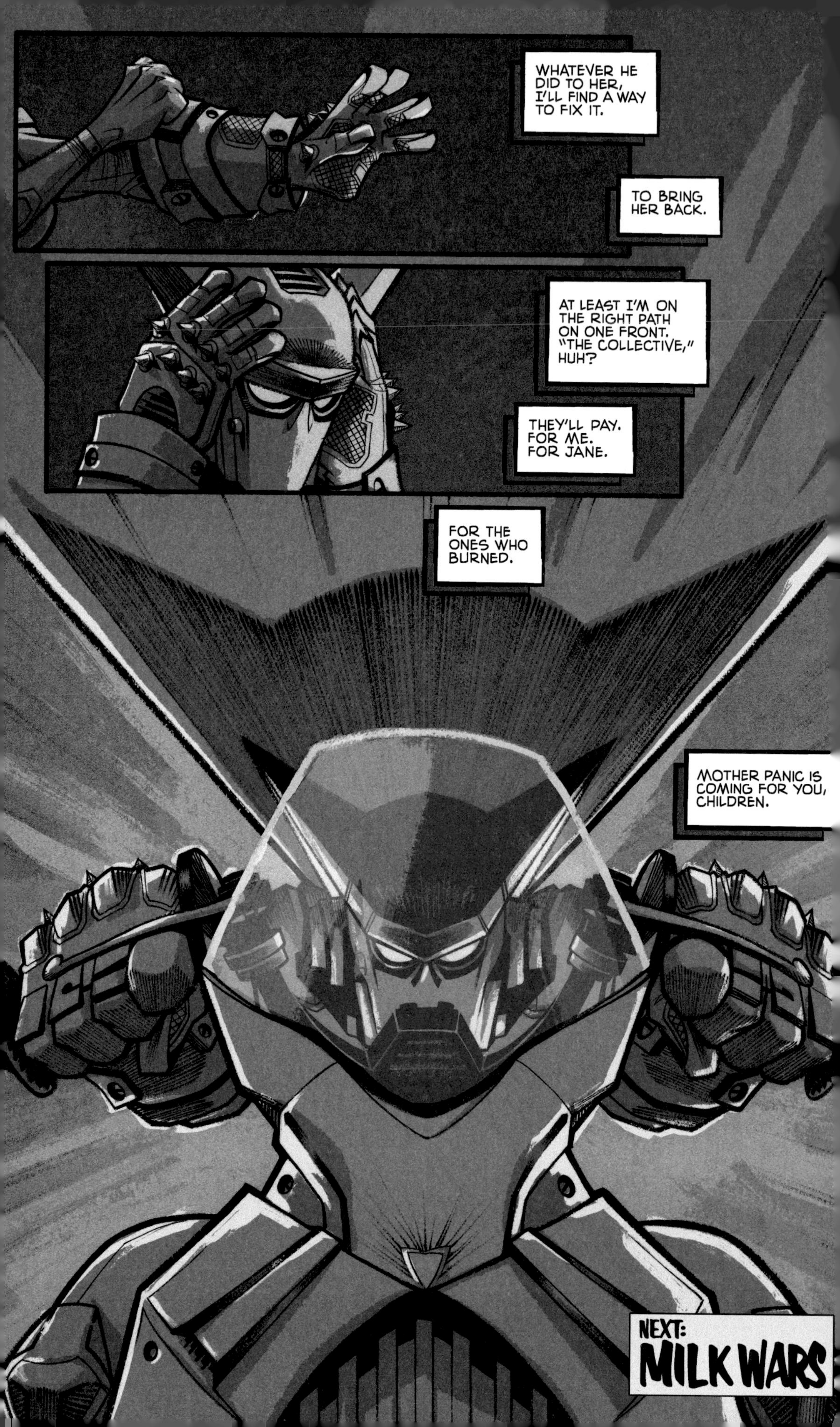
WHATEVER HE DID TO HER, I'LL FIND A WAY TO FIX IT.
TO BRING HER BACK.
AT LEAST I'M ON THE RIGHT PATH ON ONE FRONT. "THE COLLECTIVE," HUH?
THEY'LL PAY. FOR ME. FOR JANE.
FOR THE ONES WHO BURNED.
MOTHER PANIC IS COMING FOR YOU, CHILDREN.
NEXT: MILK WARS

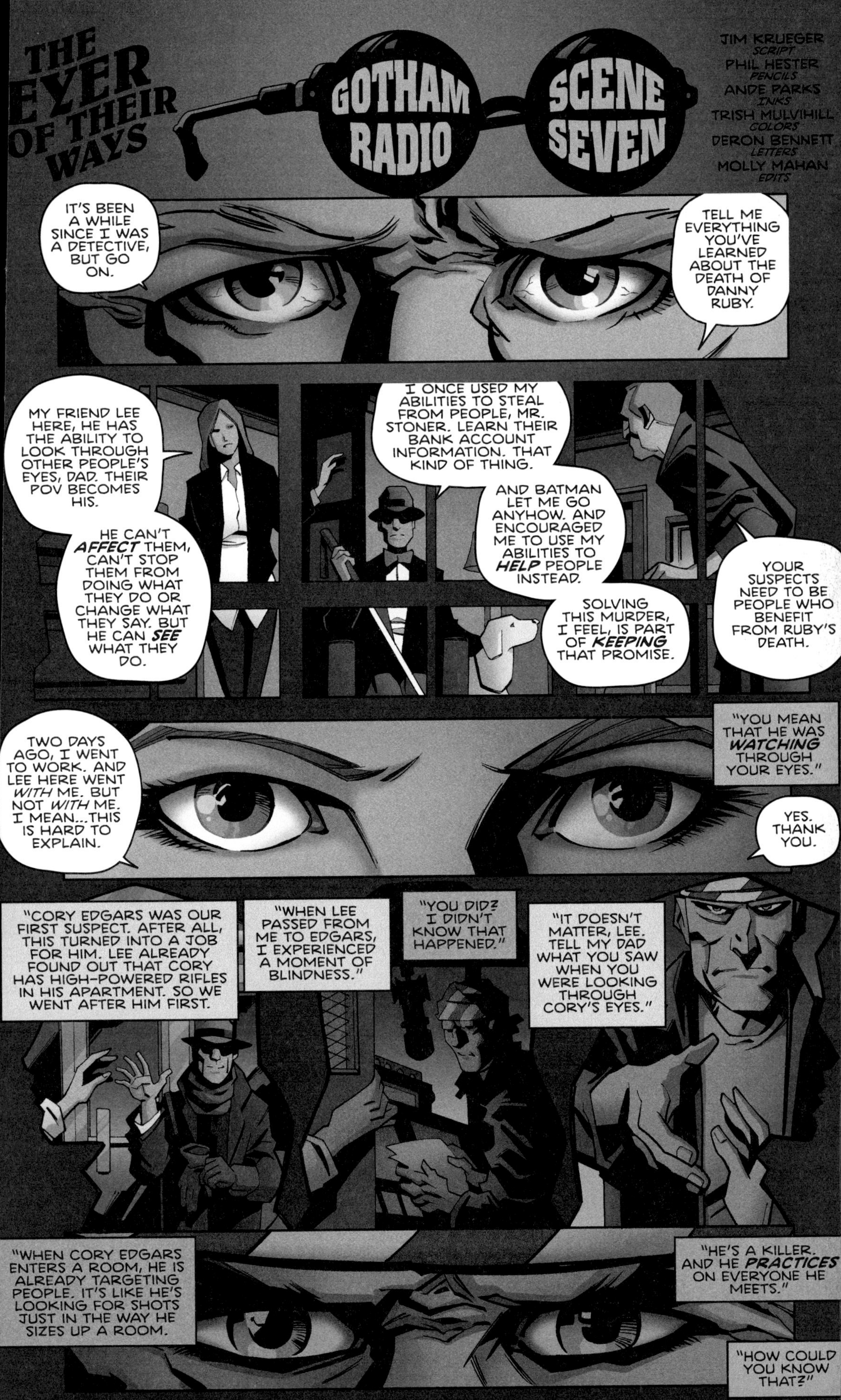
THE EYES OF THEIR WAYS
GOTHAM RADIO
SCENE SEVEN
JIM KRUEGER SCRIPT
PHIL HESTER PENCILS
ANDE PARKS INKS
TRISH MULVIHILL COLORS
DERON BENNETT LETTERS
MOLLY MAHAN EDITS
IT'S BEEN A WHILE SINCE I WAS A DETECTIVE, BUT GO ON.
TELL ME EVERYTHING YOU'VE LEARNED ABOUT THE DEATH OF DANNY RUBY.
MY FRIEND LEE HERE, HE HAS THE ABILITY TO LOOK THROUGH OTHER PEOPLE'S EYES, DAD. THEIR POV BECOMES HIS.
HE CAN'T AFFECT THEM, CAN'T STOP THEM FROM DOING WHAT THEY DO OR CHANGE WHAT THEY SAY. BUT HE CAN SEE WHAT THEY DO.
I ONCE USED MY ABILITIES TO STEAL FROM PEOPLE, MR. STONER. LEARN THEIR BANK ACCOUNT INFORMATION. THAT KIND OF THING.
AND BATMAN LET ME GO ANYHOW. AND ENCOURAGED ME TO USE MY ABILITIES TO HELP PEOPLE INSTEAD.
SOLVING THIS MURDER, I FEEL, IS PART OF KEEPING THAT PROMISE.
YOUR SUSPECTS NEED TO BE PEOPLE WHO BENEFIT FROM RUBY'S DEATH.
TWO DAYS AGO, I WENT TO WORK. AND LEE HERE WENT WITH ME. BUT NOT WITH ME. I MEAN...THIS IS HARD TO EXPLAIN.
"YOU MEAN THAT HE WAS WATCHING THROUGH YOUR EYES."
YES. THANK YOU.
"CORY EDGARS WAS OUR FIRST SUSPECT. AFTER ALL, THIS TURNED INTO A JOB FOR HIM. LEE ALREADY FOUND OUT THAT CORY HAS HIGH-POWERED RIFLES IN HIS APARTMENT. SO WE WENT AFTER HIM FIRST.
"WHEN LEE PASSED FROM ME TO EDGARS, I EXPERIENCED A MOMENT OF BLINDNESS."
"YOU DID? I DIDN'T KNOW THAT HAPPENED."
"IT DOESN'T MATTER, LEE. TELL MY DAD WHAT YOU SAW WHEN YOU WERE LOOKING THROUGH CORY'S EYES."
"WHEN CORY EDGARS ENTERS A ROOM, HE IS ALREADY TARGETING PEOPLE. IT'S LIKE HE'S LOOKING FOR SHOTS JUST IN THE WAY HE SIZES UP A ROOM.
"HE'S A KILLER. AND HE PRACTICES ON EVERYONE HE MEETS."
"HOW COULD YOU KNOW THAT?"

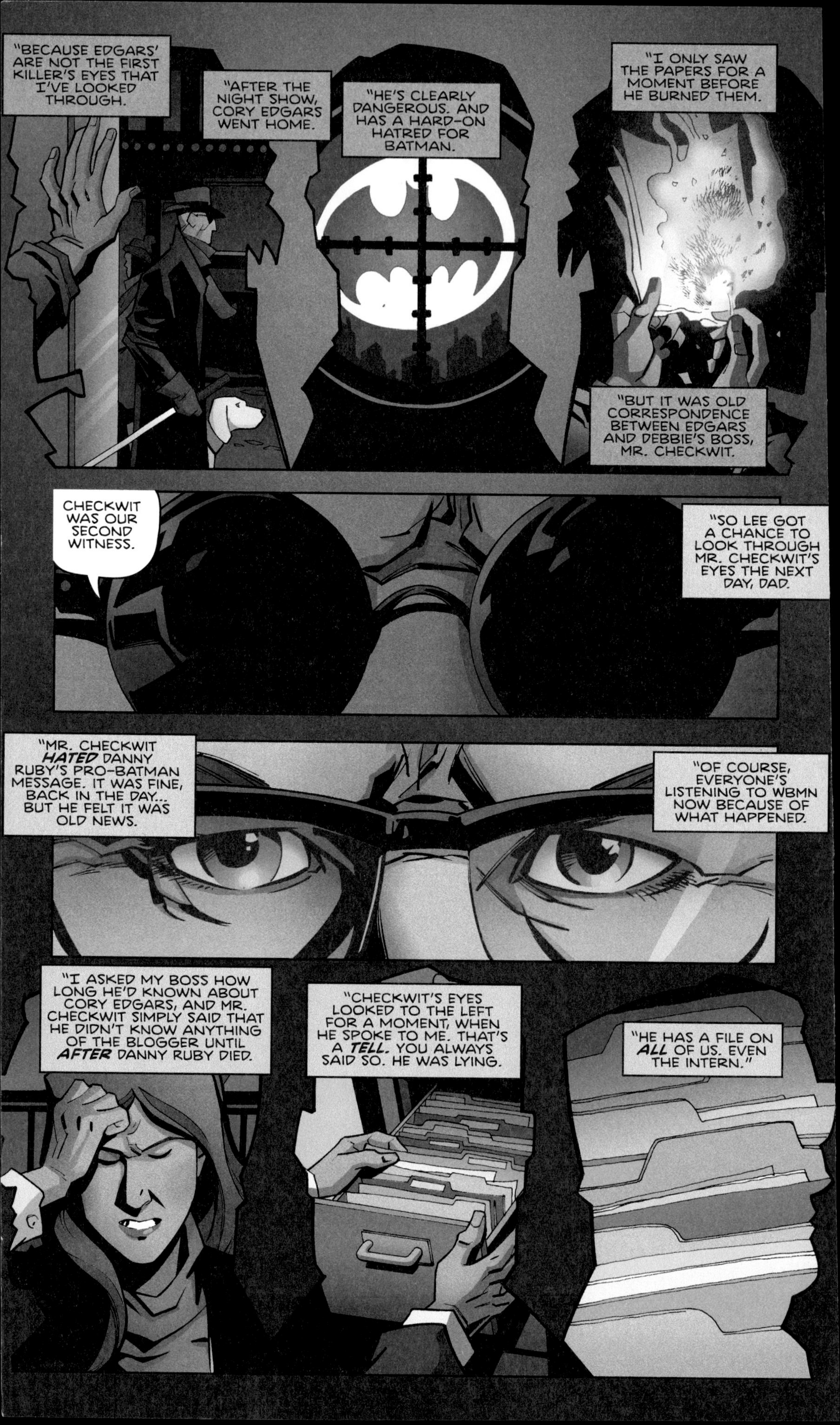
"BECAUSE EDGARS' ARE NOT THE FIRST KILLER'S EYES THAT I'VE LOOKED THROUGH.
"AFTER THE NIGHT SHOW, CORY EDGARS WENT HOME.
"HE'S CLEARLY DANGEROUS. AND HAS A HARD-ON HATRED FOR BATMAN.
"I ONLY SAW THE PAPERS FOR A MOMENT BEFORE HE BURNED THEM.
"BUT IT WAS OLD CORRESPONDENCE BETWEEN EDGARS AND DEBBIE'S BOSS, MR. CHECKWIT.
CHECKWIT WAS OUR SECOND WITNESS.
"SO LEE GOT A CHANCE TO LOOK THROUGH MR. CHECKWIT'S EYES THE NEXT DAY, DAD.
"MR. CHECKWIT *HATED* DANNY RUBY'S PRO-BATMAN MESSAGE. IT WAS FINE, BACK IN THE DAY... BUT HE FELT IT WAS OLD NEWS.
"OF COURSE, EVERYONE'S LISTENING TO WBMN NOW BECAUSE OF WHAT HAPPENED.
"I ASKED MY BOSS HOW LONG HE'D KNOWN ABOUT CORY EDGARS, AND MR. CHECKWIT SIMPLY SAID THAT HE DIDN'T KNOW ANYTHING OF THE BLOGGER UNTIL *AFTER* DANNY RUBY DIED.
"CHECKWIT'S EYES LOOKED TO THE LEFT FOR A MOMENT, WHEN HE SPOKE TO ME. THAT'S A *TELL*. YOU ALWAYS SAID SO. HE WAS LYING.
"HE HAS A FILE ON *ALL* OF US. EVEN THE INTERN."

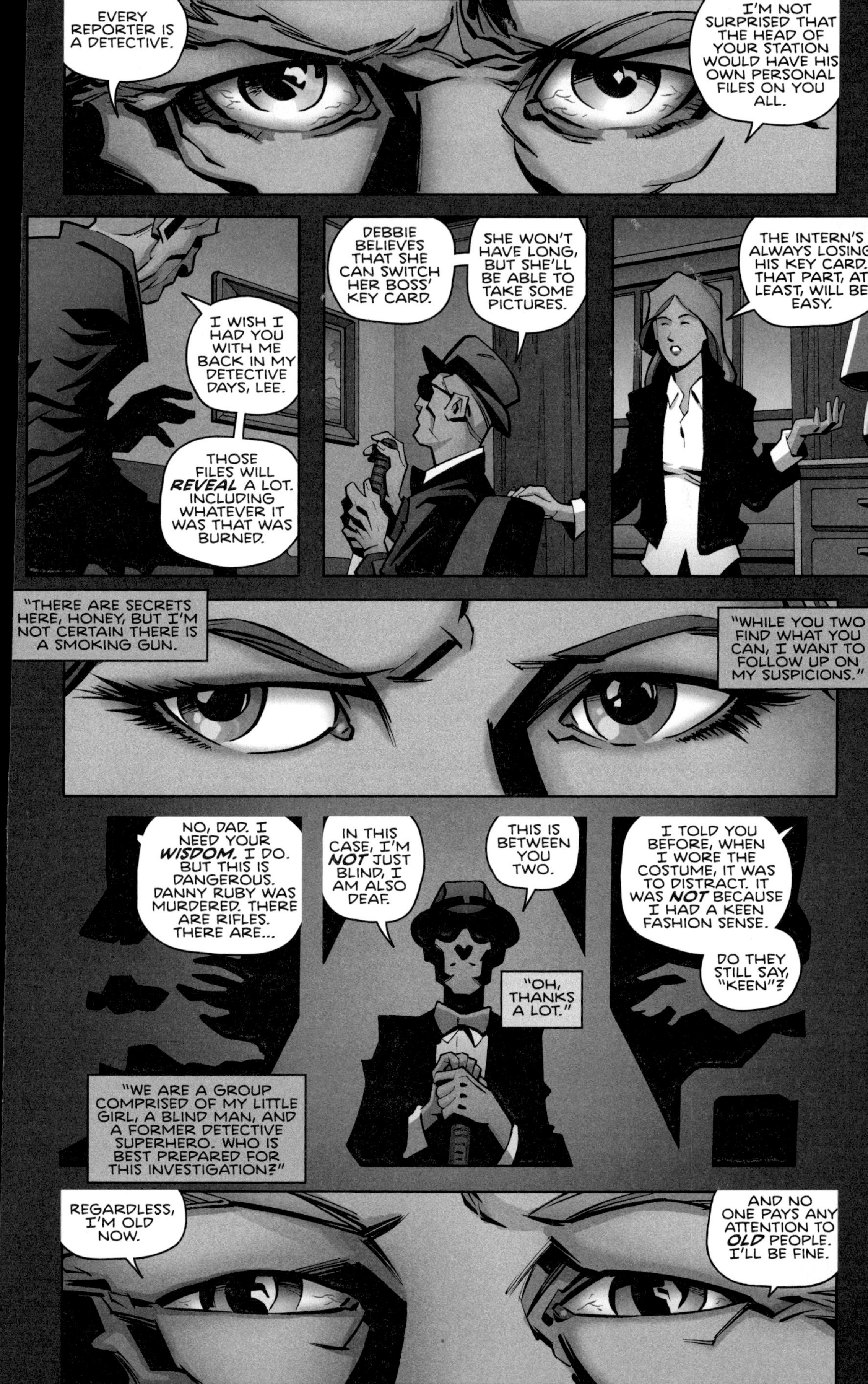
EVERY REPORTER IS A DETECTIVE.
I'M NOT SURPRISED THAT THE HEAD OF YOUR STATION WOULD HAVE HIS OWN PERSONAL FILES ON YOU ALL.
I WISH I HAD YOU WITH ME BACK IN MY DETECTIVE DAYS, LEE.
THOSE FILES WILL *REVEAL* A LOT. INCLUDING WHATEVER IT WAS THAT WAS BURNED.
DEBBIE BELIEVES THAT SHE CAN SWITCH HER BOSS' KEY CARD.
SHE WON'T HAVE LONG, BUT SHE'LL BE ABLE TO TAKE SOME PICTURES.
THE INTERN'S ALWAYS LOSING HIS KEY CARD. THAT PART, AT LEAST, WILL BE EASY.
"THERE ARE SECRETS HERE, HONEY, BUT I'M NOT CERTAIN THERE IS A SMOKING GUN.
"WHILE YOU TWO FIND WHAT YOU CAN, I WANT TO FOLLOW UP ON MY SUSPICIONS."
NO, DAD. I NEED YOUR *WISDOM.* I DO. BUT THIS IS DANGEROUS. DANNY RUBY WAS MURDERED. THERE ARE RIFLES. THERE ARE...
IN THIS CASE, I'M *NOT* JUST BLIND, I AM ALSO DEAF.
THIS IS BETWEEN YOU TWO.
"OH, THANKS A LOT."
I TOLD YOU BEFORE, WHEN I WORE THE COSTUME, IT WAS TO DISTRACT. IT WAS *NOT* BECAUSE I HAD A KEEN FASHION SENSE.
DO THEY STILL SAY, "KEEN"?
"WE ARE A GROUP COMPRISED OF MY LITTLE GIRL, A BLIND MAN, AND A FORMER DETECTIVE SUPERHERO. WHO IS BEST PREPARED FOR THIS INVESTIGATION?"
REGARDLESS, I'M OLD NOW.
AND NO ONE PAYS ANY ATTENTION TO *OLD* PEOPLE. I'LL BE FINE.

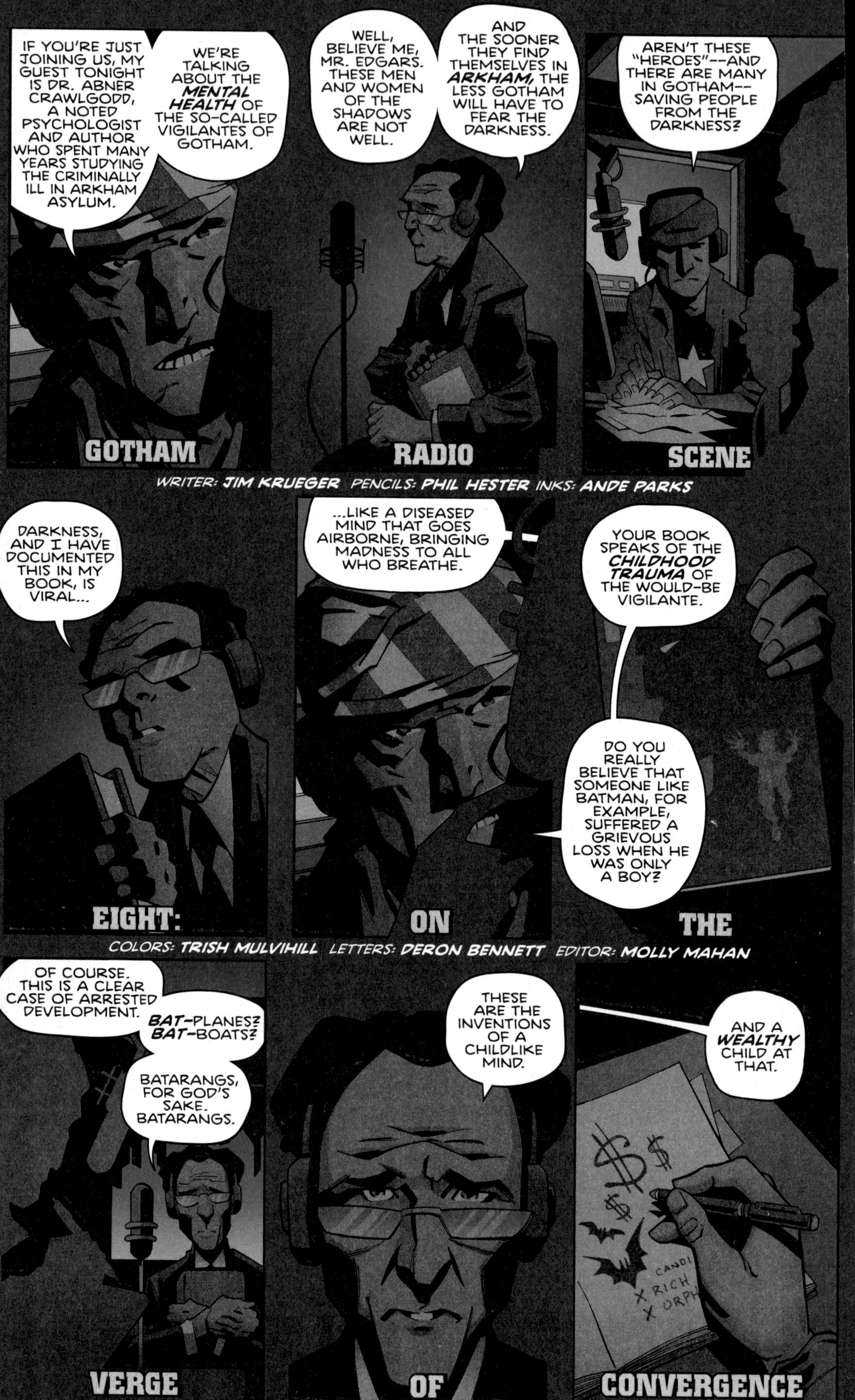
IF YOU'RE JUST JOINING US, MY GUEST TONIGHT IS DR. ABNER CRAWLGODD, A NOTED PSYCHOLOGIST AND AUTHOR WHO SPENT MANY YEARS STUDYING THE CRIMINALLY ILL IN ARKHAM ASYLUM.
WE'RE TALKING ABOUT THE *MENTAL HEALTH* OF THE SO-CALLED VIGILANTES OF GOTHAM.
GOTHAM
WELL, BELIEVE ME, MR. EDGARS. THESE MEN AND WOMEN OF THE SHADOWS ARE NOT WELL.
AND THE SOONER THEY FIND THEMSELVES IN *ARKHAM,* THE LESS GOTHAM WILL HAVE TO FEAR THE DARKNESS.
RADIO
AREN'T THESE "HEROES"--AND THERE ARE MANY IN GOTHAM--SAVING PEOPLE FROM THE DARKNESS?
SCENE
WRITER: JIM KRUEGER PENCILS: PHIL HESTER INKS: ANDE PARKS
DARKNESS, AND I HAVE DOCUMENTED THIS IN MY BOOK, IS VIRAL...
EIGHT:
...LIKE A DISEASED MIND THAT GOES AIRBORNE, BRINGING MADNESS TO ALL WHO BREATHE.
ON
YOUR BOOK SPEAKS OF THE *CHILDHOOD TRAUMA* OF THE WOULD-BE VIGILANTE.
DO YOU REALLY BELIEVE THAT SOMEONE LIKE BATMAN, FOR EXAMPLE, SUFFERED A GRIEVOUS LOSS WHEN HE WAS ONLY A BOY?
THE
COLORS: TRISH MULVIHILL LETTERS: DERON BENNETT EDITOR: MOLLY MAHAN
OF COURSE. THIS IS A CLEAR CASE OF ARRESTED DEVELOPMENT.
BAT-PLANES? *BAT*-BOATS?
BATARANGS, FOR GOD'S SAKE. BATARANGS.
VERGE
THESE ARE THE INVENTIONS OF A CHILDLIKE MIND.
OF
AND A *WEALTHY* CHILD AT THAT.
CANDI
X RICH
X ORPH
CONVERGENCE

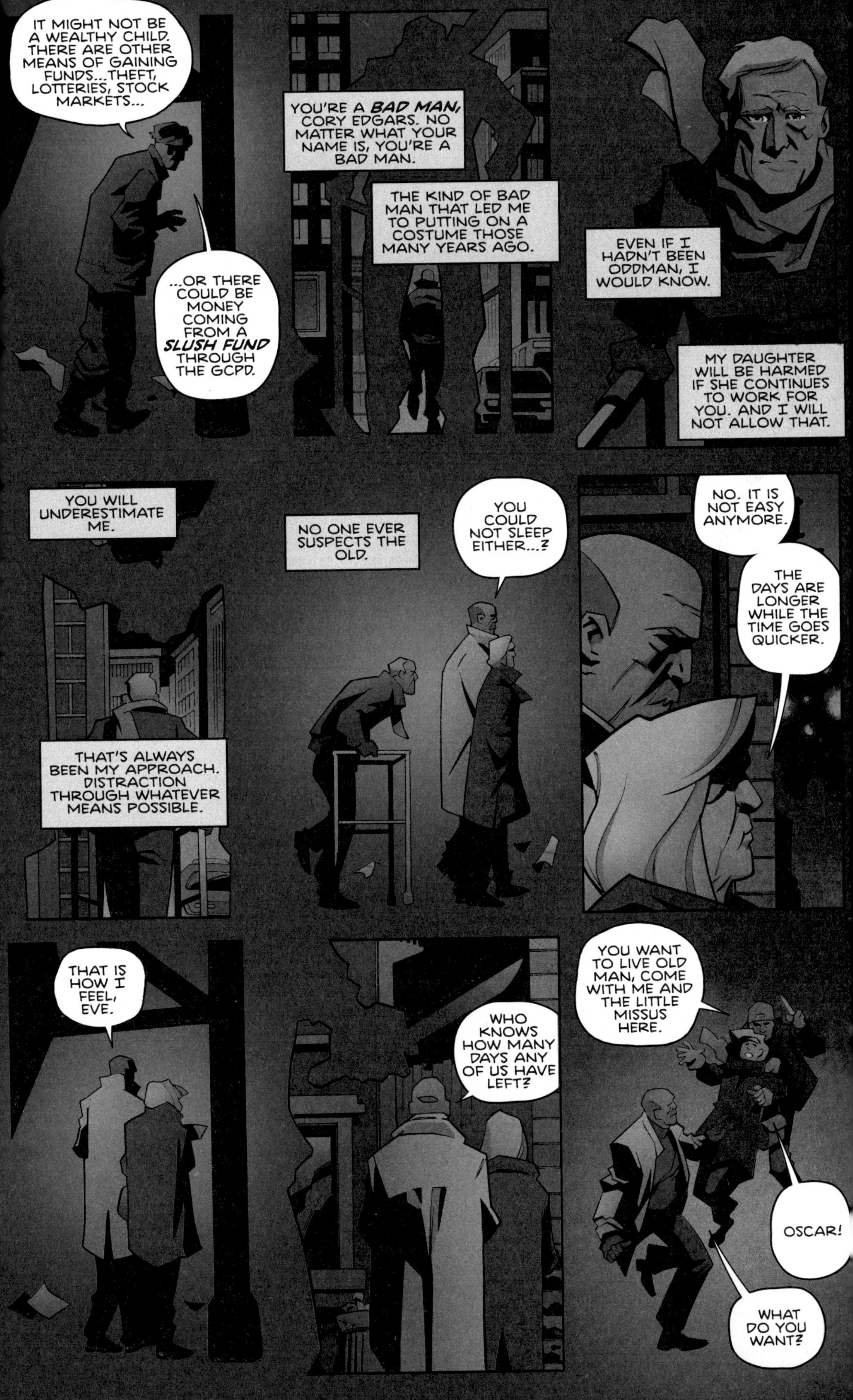
IT MIGHT NOT BE A WEALTHY CHILD. THERE ARE OTHER MEANS OF GAINING FUNDS...THEFT, LOTTERIES, STOCK MARKETS...
...OR THERE COULD BE MONEY COMING FROM A SLUSH FUND THROUGH THE GCPD.
YOU'RE A BAD MAN, CORY EDGARS. NO MATTER WHAT YOUR NAME IS, YOU'RE A BAD MAN.
THE KIND OF BAD MAN THAT LED ME TO PUTTING ON A COSTUME THOSE MANY YEARS AGO.
EVEN IF I HADN'T BEEN ODDMAN, I WOULD KNOW.
MY DAUGHTER WILL BE HARMED IF SHE CONTINUES TO WORK FOR YOU. AND I WILL NOT ALLOW THAT.
YOU WILL UNDERESTIMATE ME.
THAT'S ALWAYS BEEN MY APPROACH. DISTRACTION THROUGH WHATEVER MEANS POSSIBLE.
NO ONE EVER SUSPECTS THE OLD.
YOU COULD NOT SLEEP EITHER...?
NO. IT IS NOT EASY ANYMORE.
THE DAYS ARE LONGER WHILE THE TIME GOES QUICKER.
THAT IS HOW I FEEL, EVE.
WHO KNOWS HOW MANY DAYS ANY OF US HAVE LEFT?
YOU WANT TO LIVE OLD MAN, COME WITH ME AND THE LITTLE MISSUS HERE.
OSCAR!
WHAT DO YOU WANT?

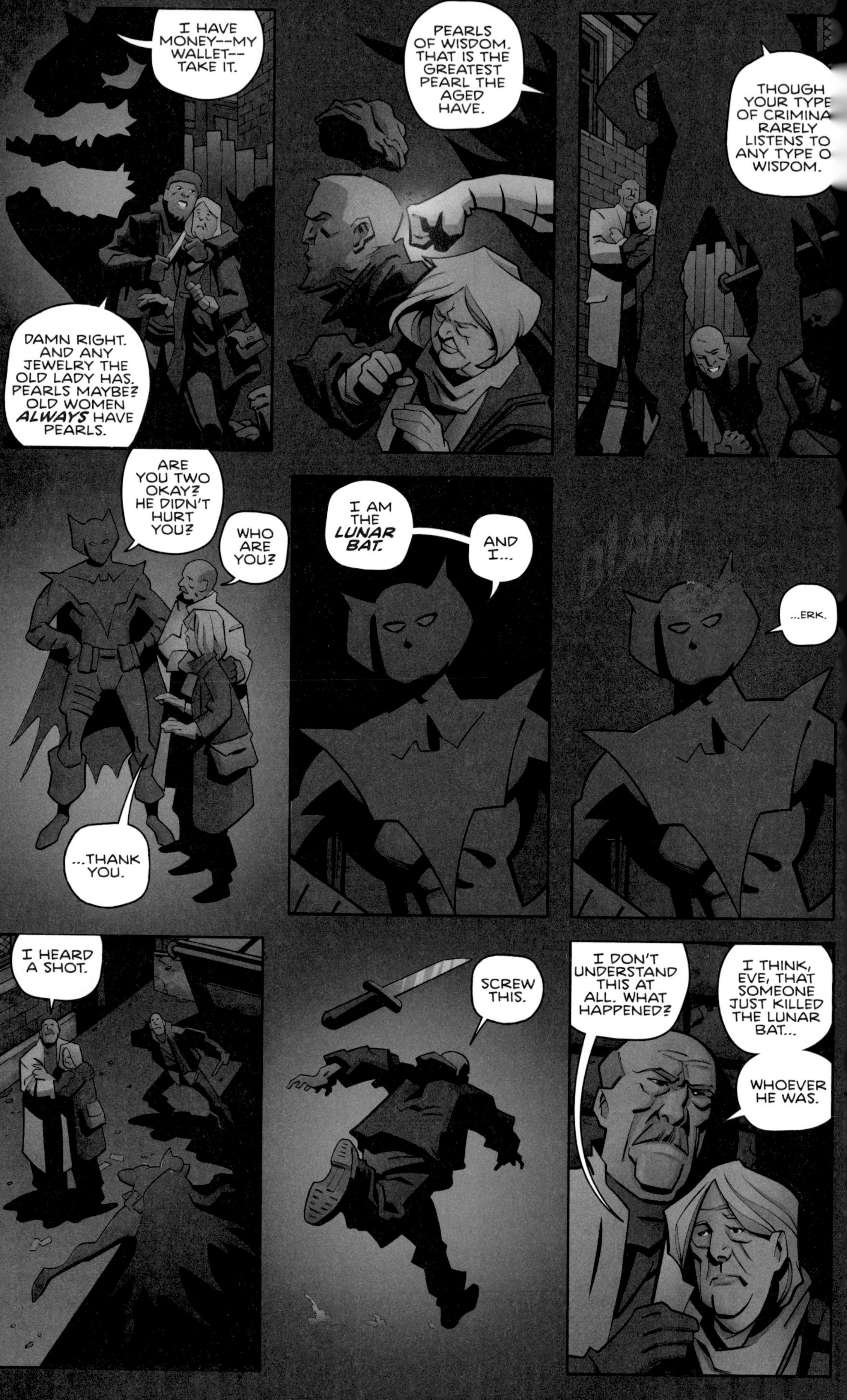
I HAVE MONEY--MY WALLET--TAKE IT.
DAMN RIGHT. AND ANY JEWELRY THE OLD LADY HAS. PEARLS MAYBE? OLD WOMEN *ALWAYS* HAVE PEARLS.
PEARLS OF WISDOM. THAT IS THE GREATEST PEARL THE AGED HAVE.
THOUGH YOUR TYPE OF CRIMINA RARELY LISTENS TO ANY TYPE O WISDOM.
ARE YOU TWO OKAY? HE DIDN'T HURT YOU?
WHO ARE YOU?
...THANK YOU.
I AM THE *LUNAR BAT.*
AND I...
...ERK.
I HEARD A SHOT.
SCREW THIS.
I DON'T UNDERSTAND THIS AT ALL. WHAT HAPPENED?
I THINK, EVE, THAT SOMEONE JUST KILLED THE LUNAR BAT...
WHOEVER HE WAS.

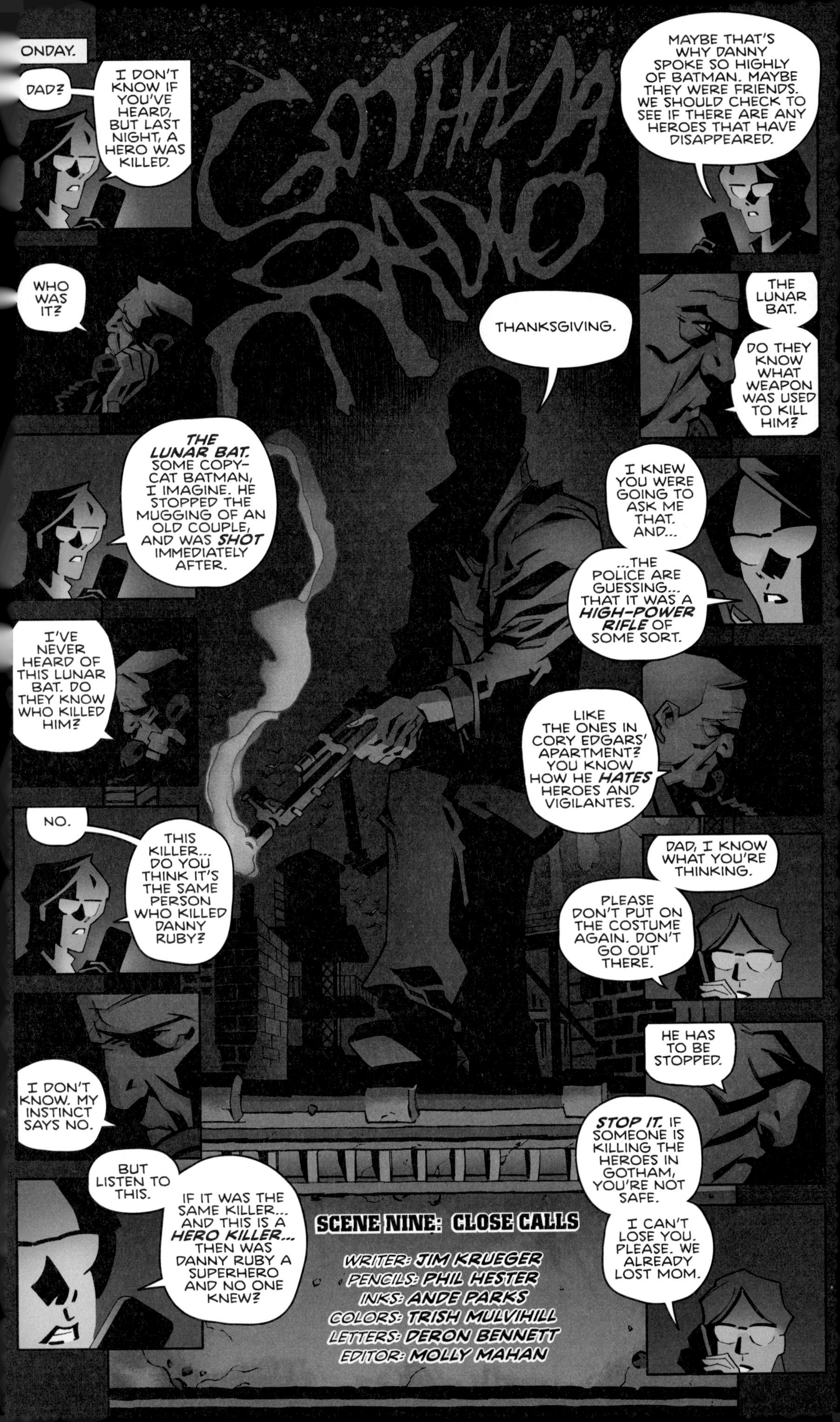
ONDAY.
DAD?
I DON'T KNOW IF YOU'VE HEARD, BUT LAST NIGHT, A HERO WAS KILLED.
WHO WAS IT?
THE LUNAR BAT. SOME COPY-CAT BATMAN, I IMAGINE. HE STOPPED THE MUGGING OF AN OLD COUPLE, AND WAS SHOT IMMEDIATELY AFTER.
I'VE NEVER HEARD OF THIS LUNAR BAT. DO THEY KNOW WHO KILLED HIM?
NO.
THIS KILLER... DO YOU THINK IT'S THE SAME PERSON WHO KILLED DANNY RUBY?
I DON'T KNOW. MY INSTINCT SAYS NO.
BUT LISTEN TO THIS.
IF IT WAS THE SAME KILLER... AND THIS IS A HERO KILLER... THEN WAS DANNY RUBY A SUPERHERO AND NO ONE KNEW?
THANKSGIVING.
MAYBE THAT'S WHY DANNY SPOKE SO HIGHLY OF BATMAN. MAYBE THEY WERE FRIENDS. WE SHOULD CHECK TO SEE IF THERE ARE ANY HEROES THAT HAVE DISAPPEARED.
THE LUNAR BAT.
DO THEY KNOW WHAT WEAPON WAS USED TO KILL HIM?
I KNEW YOU WERE GOING TO ASK ME THAT. AND...
...THE POLICE ARE GUESSING... THAT IT WAS A HIGH-POWER RIFLE OF SOME SORT.
LIKE THE ONES IN CORY EDGARS' APARTMENT? YOU KNOW HOW HE HATES HEROES AND VIGILANTES.
DAD, I KNOW WHAT YOU'RE THINKING.
PLEASE DON'T PUT ON THE COSTUME AGAIN. DON'T GO OUT THERE.
HE HAS TO BE STOPPED.
STOP IT. IF SOMEONE IS KILLING THE HEROES IN GOTHAM, YOU'RE NOT SAFE.
I CAN'T LOSE YOU. PLEASE. WE ALREADY LOST MOM.
SCENE NINE: CLOSE CALLS
WRITER: JIM KRUEGER
PENCILS: PHIL HESTER
INKS: ANDE PARKS
COLORS: TRISH MULVIHILL
LETTERS: DERON BENNETT
EDITOR: MOLLY MAHAN

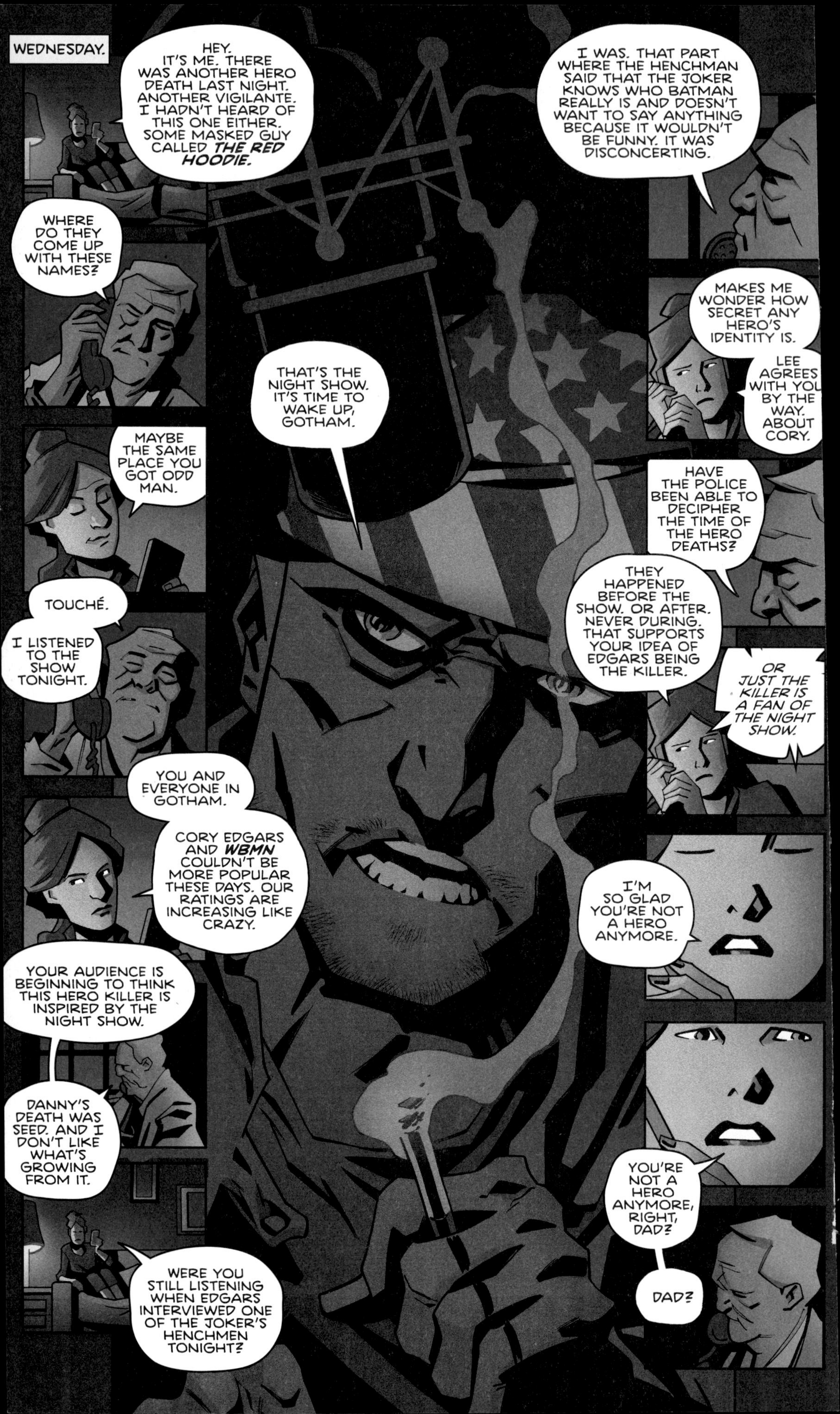

WEDNESDAY.
HEY. IT'S ME. THERE WAS ANOTHER HERO DEATH LAST NIGHT. ANOTHER VIGILANTE. I HADN'T HEARD OF THIS ONE EITHER. SOME MASKED GUY CALLED THE RED HOODIE.
WHERE DO THEY COME UP WITH THESE NAMES?
MAYBE THE SAME PLACE YOU GOT ODD MAN.
TOUCHÉ.
I LISTENED TO THE SHOW TONIGHT.
YOU AND EVERYONE IN GOTHAM.
CORY EDGARS AND WBMN COULDN'T BE MORE POPULAR THESE DAYS. OUR RATINGS ARE INCREASING LIKE CRAZY.
YOUR AUDIENCE IS BEGINNING TO THINK THIS HERO KILLER IS INSPIRED BY THE NIGHT SHOW.
DANNY'S DEATH WAS SEED. AND I DON'T LIKE WHAT'S GROWING FROM IT.
WERE YOU STILL LISTENING WHEN EDGARS INTERVIEWED ONE OF THE JOKER'S HENCHMEN TONIGHT?
THAT'S THE NIGHT SHOW. IT'S TIME TO WAKE UP, GOTHAM.
I WAS. THAT PART WHERE THE HENCHMAN SAID THAT THE JOKER KNOWS WHO BATMAN REALLY IS AND DOESN'T WANT TO SAY ANYTHING BECAUSE IT WOULDN'T BE FUNNY. IT WAS DISCONCERTING.
MAKES ME WONDER HOW SECRET ANY HERO'S IDENTITY IS.
LEE AGREES WITH YOU BY THE WAY. ABOUT CORY.
HAVE THE POLICE BEEN ABLE TO DECIPHER THE TIME OF THE HERO DEATHS?
THEY HAPPENED BEFORE THE SHOW. OR AFTER. NEVER DURING. THAT SUPPORTS YOUR IDEA OF EDGARS BEING THE KILLER.
OR JUST THE KILLER IS A FAN OF THE NIGHT SHOW.
I'M SO GLAD YOU'RE NOT A HERO ANYMORE.
YOU'RE NOT A HERO ANYMORE, RIGHT, DAD?
DAD?

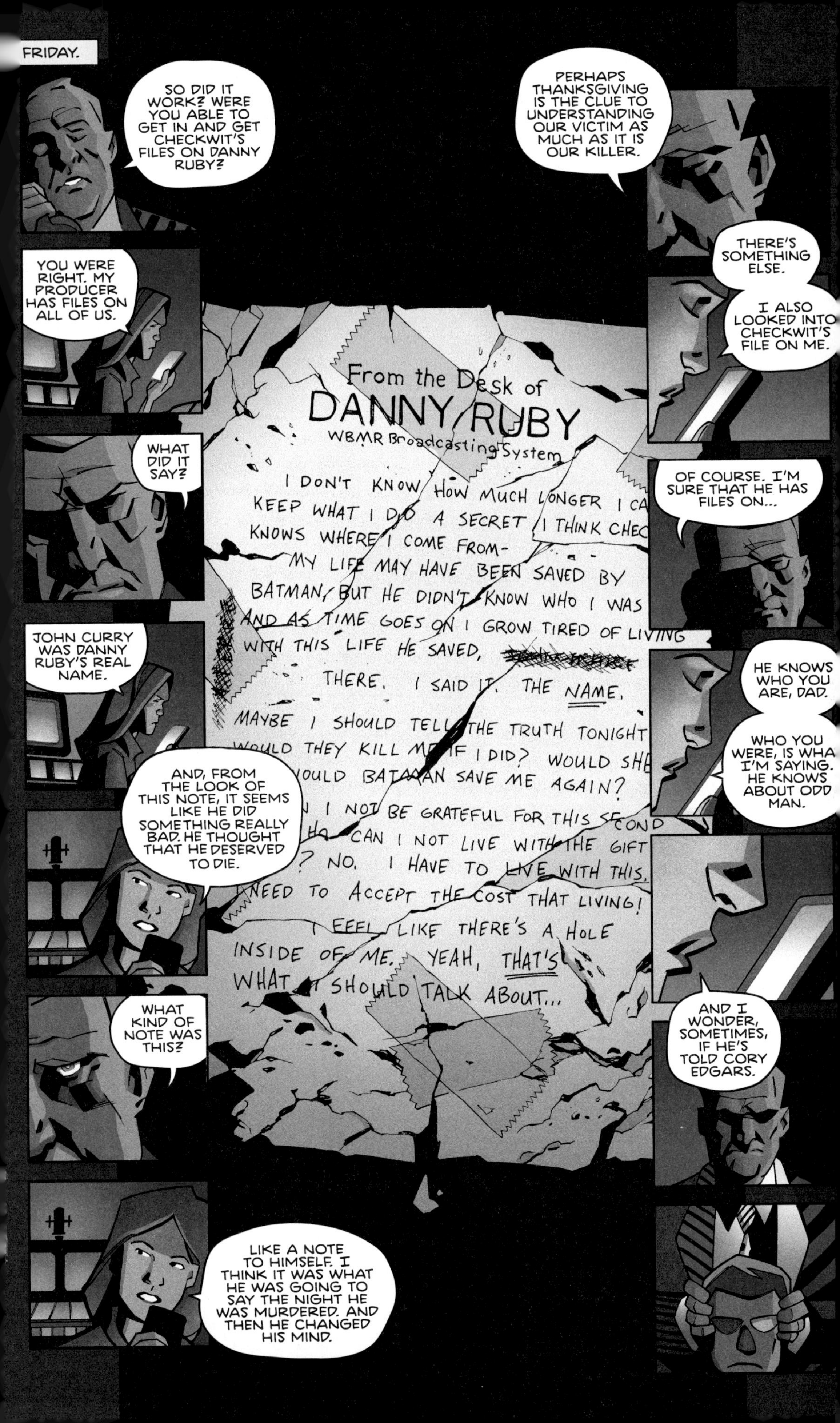
FRIDAY.
SO DID IT WORK? WERE YOU ABLE TO GET IN AND GET CHECKWIT'S FILES ON DANNY RUBY?
YOU WERE RIGHT. MY PRODUCER HAS FILES ON ALL OF US.
WHAT DID IT SAY?
JOHN CURRY WAS DANNY RUBY'S REAL NAME.
AND, FROM THE LOOK OF THIS NOTE, IT SEEMS LIKE HE DID SOMETHING REALLY BAD. HE THOUGHT THAT HE DESERVED TO DIE.
WHAT KIND OF NOTE WAS THIS?
LIKE A NOTE TO HIMSELF. I THINK IT WAS WHAT HE WAS GOING TO SAY THE NIGHT HE WAS MURDERED. AND THEN HE CHANGED HIS MIND.
From the Desk of
DANNY RUBY
WBMR Broadcasting System
I DON'T KNOW HOW MUCH LONGER I CA
KEEP WHAT I DID A SECRET. I THINK CHEC
KNOWS WHERE I COME FROM-
MY LIFE MAY HAVE BEEN SAVED BY
BATMAN, BUT HE DIDN'T KNOW WHO I WAS
AND AS TIME GOES ON I GROW TIRED OF LIVING
WITH THIS LIFE HE SAVED,
THERE. I SAID IT. THE NAME.
MAYBE I SHOULD TELL THE TRUTH TONIGHT
WOULD THEY KILL ME IF I DID? WOULD SHE
WOULD BATMAN SAVE ME AGAIN?
I NOT BE GRATEFUL FOR THIS SECOND
CAN I NOT LIVE WITH THE GIFT
? NO. I HAVE TO LIVE WITH THIS.
NEED TO ACCEPT THE COST THAT LIVING!
I FEEL LIKE THERE'S A HOLE
INSIDE OF ME. YEAH, THAT'S
WHAT I SHOULD TALK ABOUT...
PERHAPS THANKSGIVING IS THE CLUE TO UNDERSTANDING OUR VICTIM AS MUCH AS IT IS OUR KILLER.
THERE'S SOMETHING ELSE.
I ALSO LOOKED INTO CHECKWIT'S FILE ON ME.
OF COURSE. I'M SURE THAT HE HAS FILES ON...
HE KNOWS WHO YOU ARE, DAD.
WHO YOU WERE, IS WHA I'M SAYING. HE KNOWS ABOUT ODD MAN.
AND I WONDER, SOMETIMES, IF HE'S TOLD CORY EDGARS.

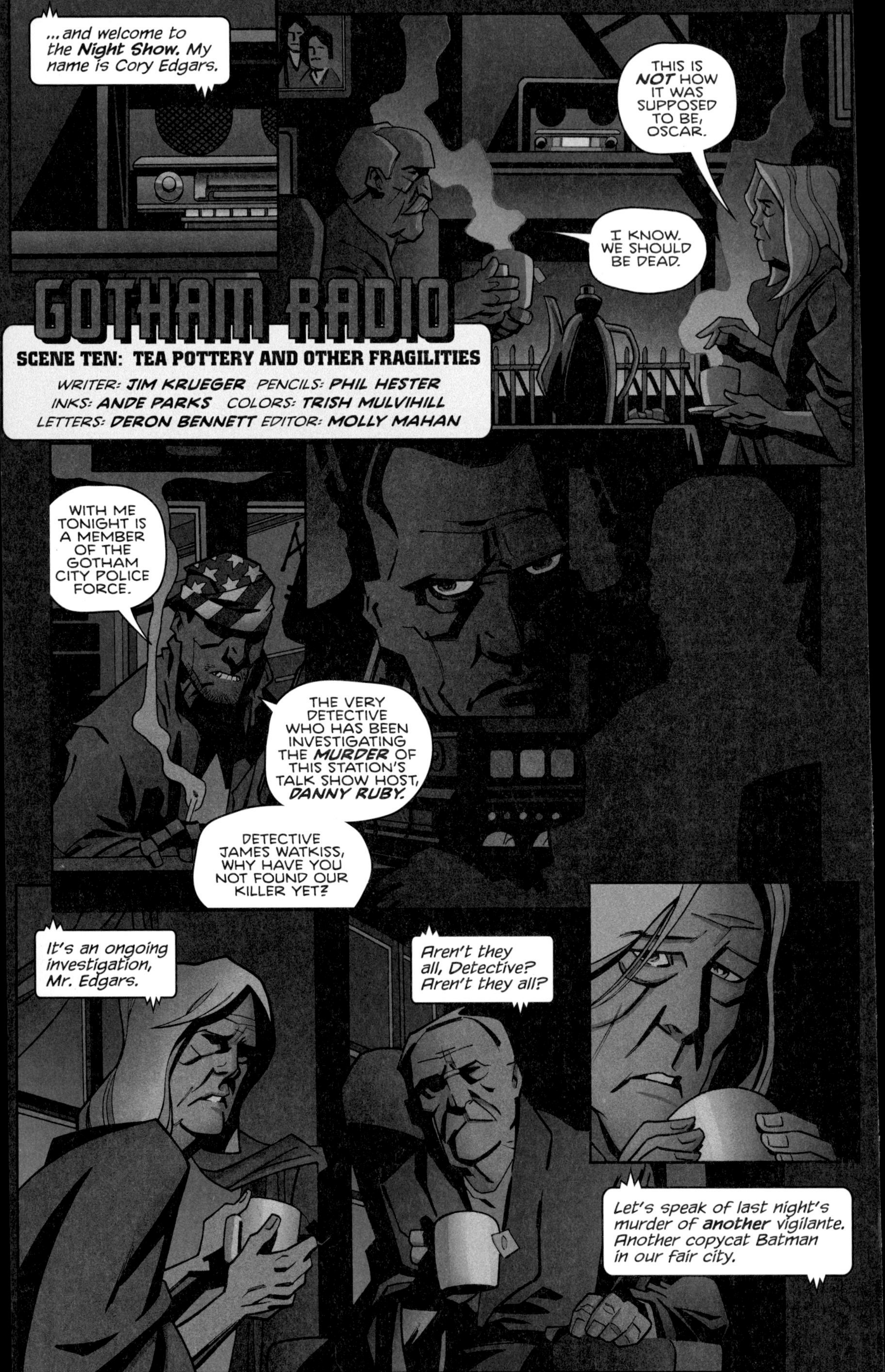
...and welcome to the Night Show. My name is Cory Edgars.
THIS IS NOT HOW IT WAS SUPPOSED TO BE, OSCAR.
I KNOW. WE SHOULD BE DEAD.
GOTHAM RADIO
SCENE TEN: TEA POTTERY AND OTHER FRAGILITIES
WRITER: JIM KRUEGER PENCILS: PHIL HESTER
INKS: ANDE PARKS COLORS: TRISH MULVIHILL
LETTERS: DERON BENNETT EDITOR: MOLLY MAHAN
WITH ME TONIGHT IS A MEMBER OF THE GOTHAM CITY POLICE FORCE.
THE VERY DETECTIVE WHO HAS BEEN INVESTIGATING THE MURDER OF THIS STATION'S TALK SHOW HOST, DANNY RUBY.
DETECTIVE JAMES WATKISS, WHY HAVE YOU NOT FOUND OUR KILLER YET?
It's an ongoing investigation, Mr. Edgars.
Aren't they all, Detective? Aren't they all?
Let's speak of last night's murder of another vigilante. Another copycat Batman in our fair city.

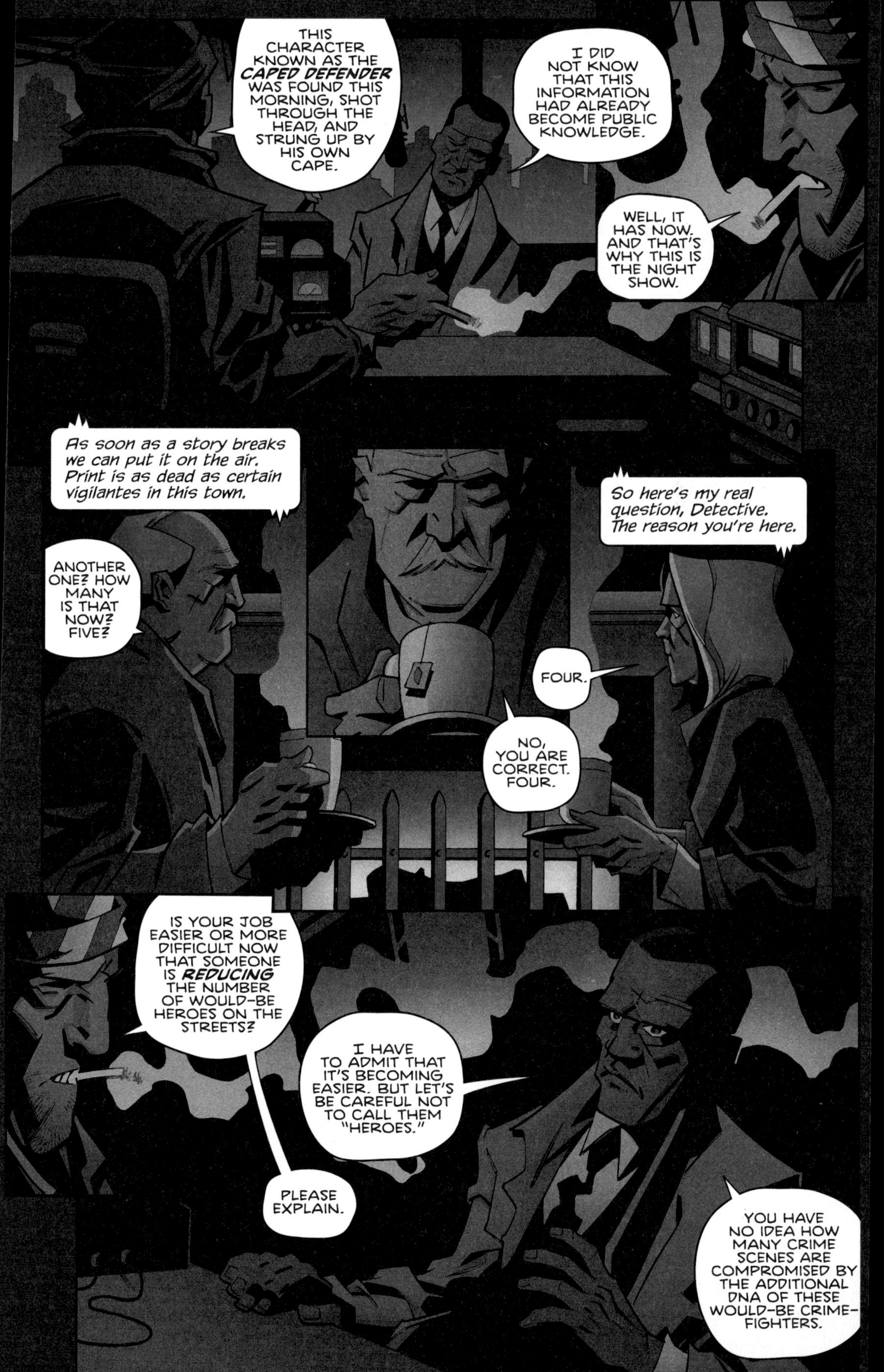
THIS CHARACTER KNOWN AS THE ***CAPED DEFENDER*** WAS FOUND THIS MORNING, SHOT THROUGH THE HEAD, AND STRUNG UP BY HIS OWN CAPE.
I DID NOT KNOW THAT THIS INFORMATION HAD ALREADY BECOME PUBLIC KNOWLEDGE.
WELL, IT HAS NOW. AND THAT'S WHY THIS IS THE NIGHT SHOW.
As soon as a story breaks we can put it on the air. Print is as dead as certain vigilantes in this town.
So here's my real question, Detective. The reason you're here.
ANOTHER ONE? HOW MANY IS THAT NOW? FIVE?
FOUR.
NO, YOU ARE CORRECT. FOUR.
IS YOUR JOB EASIER OR MORE DIFFICULT NOW THAT SOMEONE IS ***REDUCING*** THE NUMBER OF WOULD-BE HEROES ON THE STREETS?
I HAVE TO ADMIT THAT IT'S BECOMING EASIER. BUT LET'S BE CAREFUL NOT TO CALL THEM "HEROES."
PLEASE EXPLAIN.
YOU HAVE NO IDEA HOW MANY CRIME SCENES ARE COMPROMISED BY THE ADDITIONAL DNA OF THESE WOULD-BE CRIME-FIGHTERS.

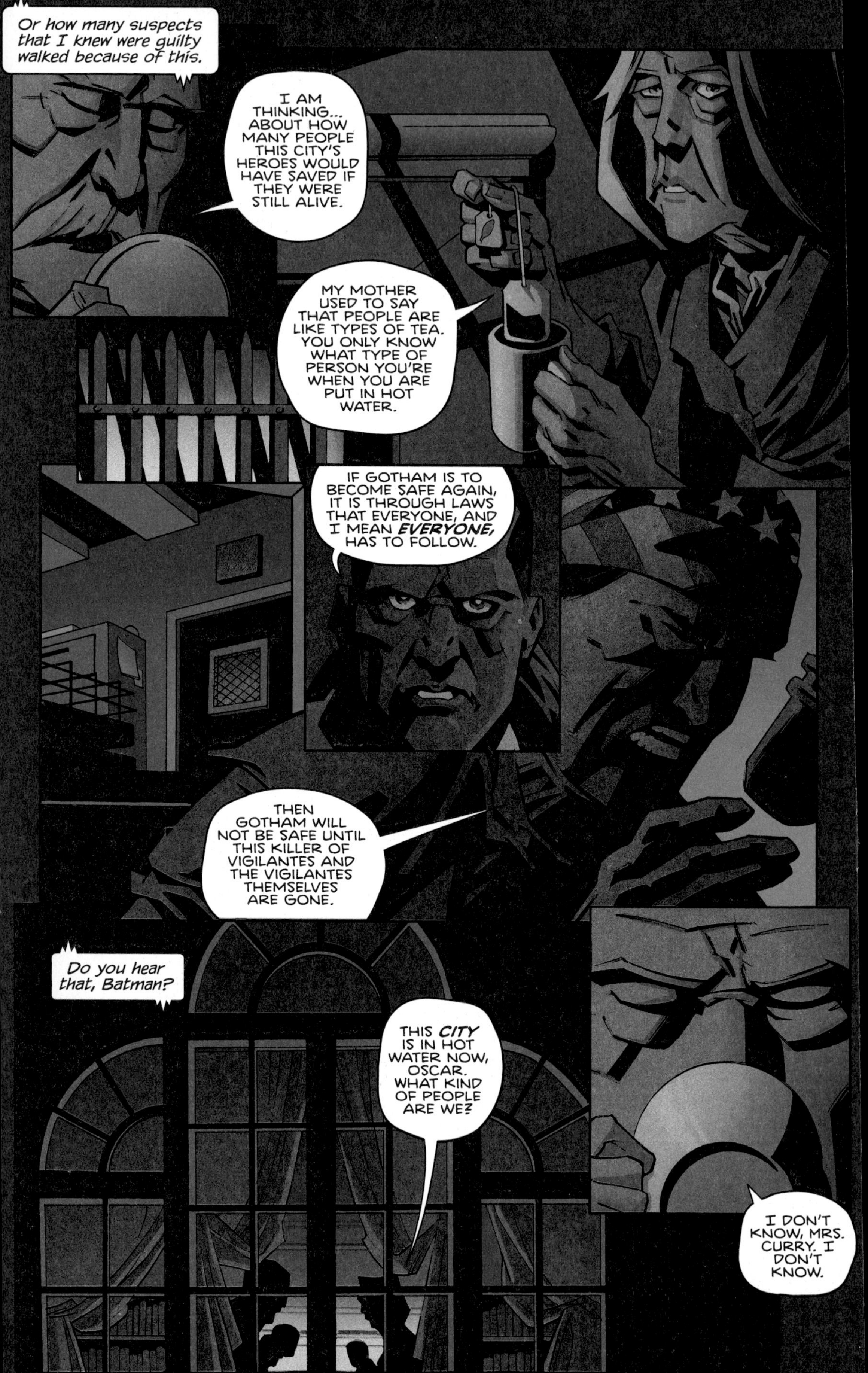
Or how many suspects that I knew were guilty walked because of this.
I AM THINKING... ABOUT HOW MANY PEOPLE THIS CITY'S HEROES WOULD HAVE SAVED IF THEY WERE STILL ALIVE.
MY MOTHER USED TO SAY THAT PEOPLE ARE LIKE TYPES OF TEA. YOU ONLY KNOW WHAT TYPE OF PERSON YOU'RE WHEN YOU ARE PUT IN HOT WATER.
IF GOTHAM IS TO BECOME SAFE AGAIN, IT IS THROUGH LAWS THAT EVERYONE, AND I MEAN EVERYONE, HAS TO FOLLOW.
THEN GOTHAM WILL NOT BE SAFE UNTIL THIS KILLER OF VIGILANTES AND THE VIGILANTES THEMSELVES ARE GONE.
Do you hear that, Batman?
THIS CITY IS IN HOT WATER NOW, OSCAR. WHAT KIND OF PEOPLE ARE WE?
I DON'T KNOW, MRS. CURRY. I DON'T KNOW.

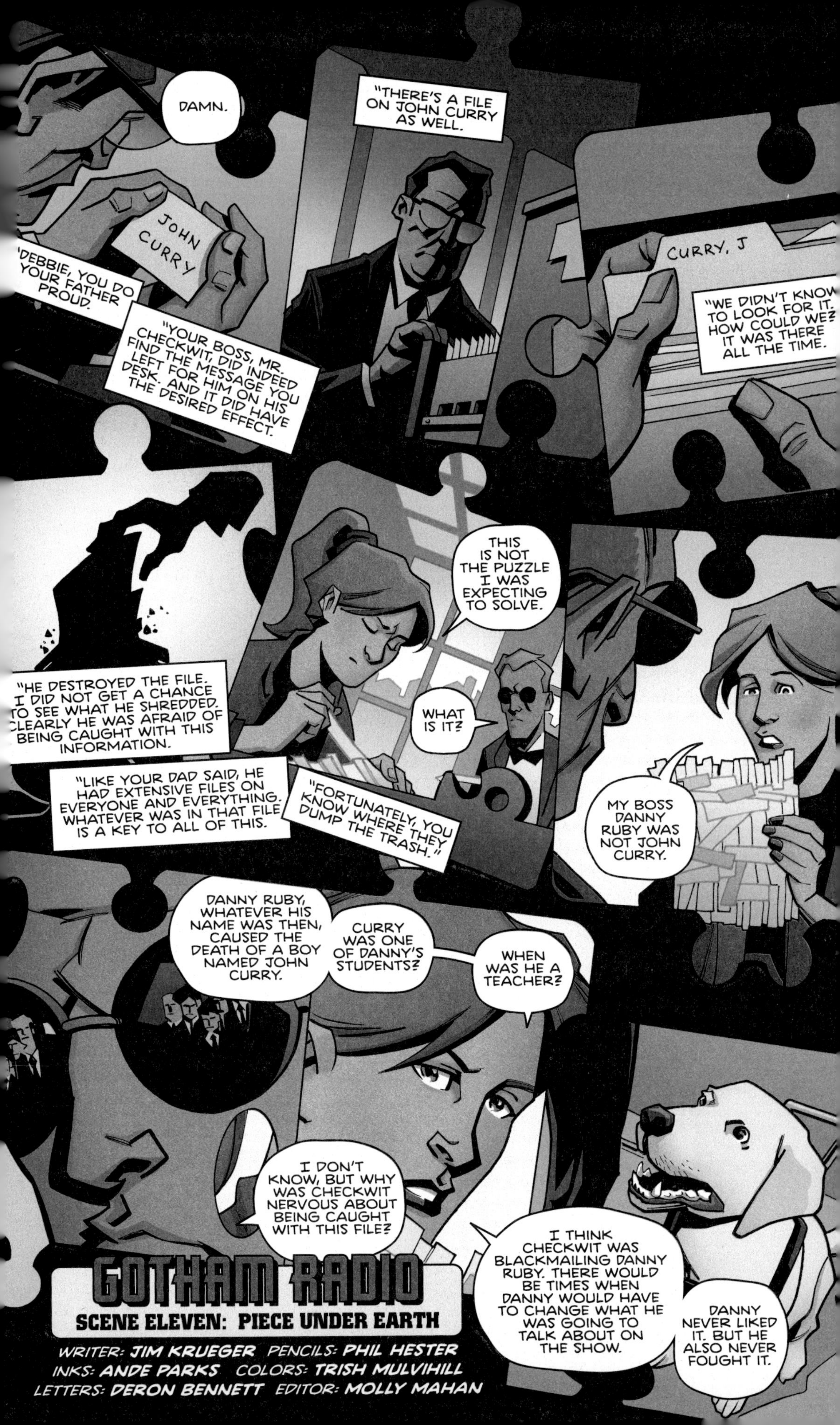
DAMN.
"THERE'S A FILE ON JOHN CURRY AS WELL.
JOHN CURRY
"DEBBIE, YOU DO YOUR FATHER PROUD.
"YOUR BOSS, MR. CHECKWIT, DID INDEED FIND THE MESSAGE YOU LEFT FOR HIM ON HIS DESK. AND IT DID HAVE THE DESIRED EFFECT.
CURRY, J
"WE DIDN'T KNOW TO LOOK FOR IT. HOW COULD WE? IT WAS THERE ALL THE TIME.
"HE DESTROYED THE FILE. I DID NOT GET A CHANCE TO SEE WHAT HE SHREDDED. CLEARLY HE WAS AFRAID OF BEING CAUGHT WITH THIS INFORMATION.
THIS IS NOT THE PUZZLE I WAS EXPECTING TO SOLVE.
WHAT IS IT?
"LIKE YOUR DAD SAID, HE HAD EXTENSIVE FILES ON EVERYONE AND EVERYTHING. WHATEVER WAS IN THAT FILE IS A KEY TO ALL OF THIS.
"FORTUNATELY, YOU KNOW WHERE THEY DUMP THE TRASH."
MY BOSS DANNY RUBY WAS NOT JOHN CURRY.
DANNY RUBY, WHATEVER HIS NAME WAS THEN, CAUSED THE DEATH OF A BOY NAMED JOHN CURRY.
CURRY WAS ONE OF DANNY'S STUDENTS?
WHEN WAS HE A TEACHER?
I DON'T KNOW, BUT WHY WAS CHECKWIT NERVOUS ABOUT BEING CAUGHT WITH THIS FILE?
I THINK CHECKWIT WAS BLACKMAILING DANNY RUBY. THERE WOULD BE TIMES WHEN DANNY WOULD HAVE TO CHANGE WHAT HE WAS GOING TO TALK ABOUT ON THE SHOW.
DANNY NEVER LIKED IT. BUT HE ALSO NEVER FOUGHT IT.
GOTHAM RADIO
SCENE ELEVEN: PIECE UNDER EARTH
WRITER: JIM KRUEGER PENCILS: PHIL HESTER
INKS: ANDE PARKS COLORS: TRISH MULVIHILL
LETTERS: DERON BENNETT EDITOR: MOLLY MAHAN

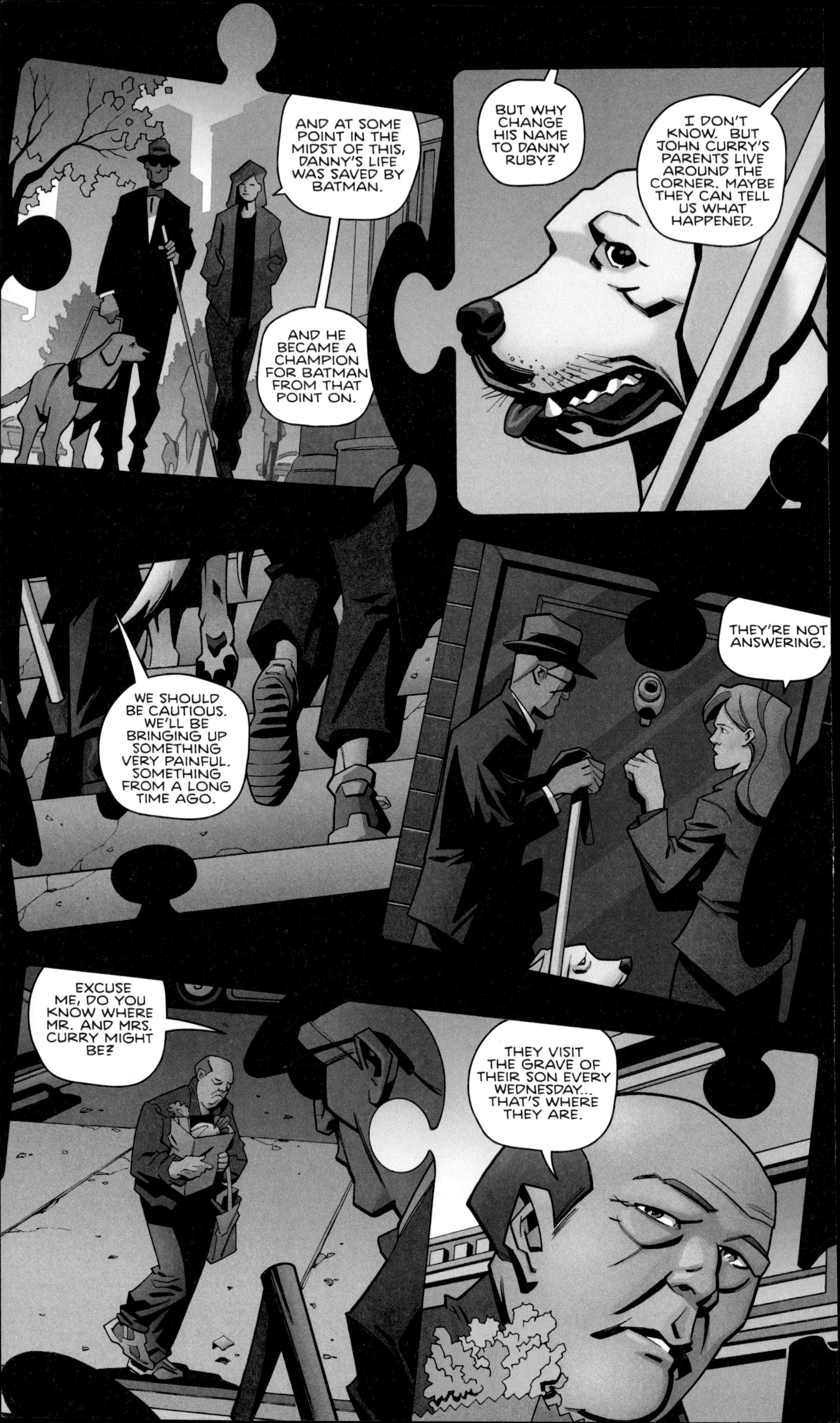
AND AT SOME POINT IN THE MIDST OF THIS, DANNY'S LIFE WAS SAVED BY BATMAN.
AND HE BECAME A CHAMPION FOR BATMAN FROM THAT POINT ON.
BUT WHY CHANGE HIS NAME TO DANNY RUBY?
I DON'T KNOW. BUT JOHN CURRY'S PARENTS LIVE AROUND THE CORNER. MAYBE THEY CAN TELL US WHAT HAPPENED.
WE SHOULD BE CAUTIOUS. WE'LL BE BRINGING UP SOMETHING VERY PAINFUL. SOMETHING FROM A LONG TIME AGO.
THEY'RE NOT ANSWERING.
EXCUSE ME, DO YOU KNOW WHERE MR. AND MRS. CURRY MIGHT BE?
THEY VISIT THE GRAVE OF THEIR SON EVERY WEDNESDAY... THAT'S WHERE THEY ARE.

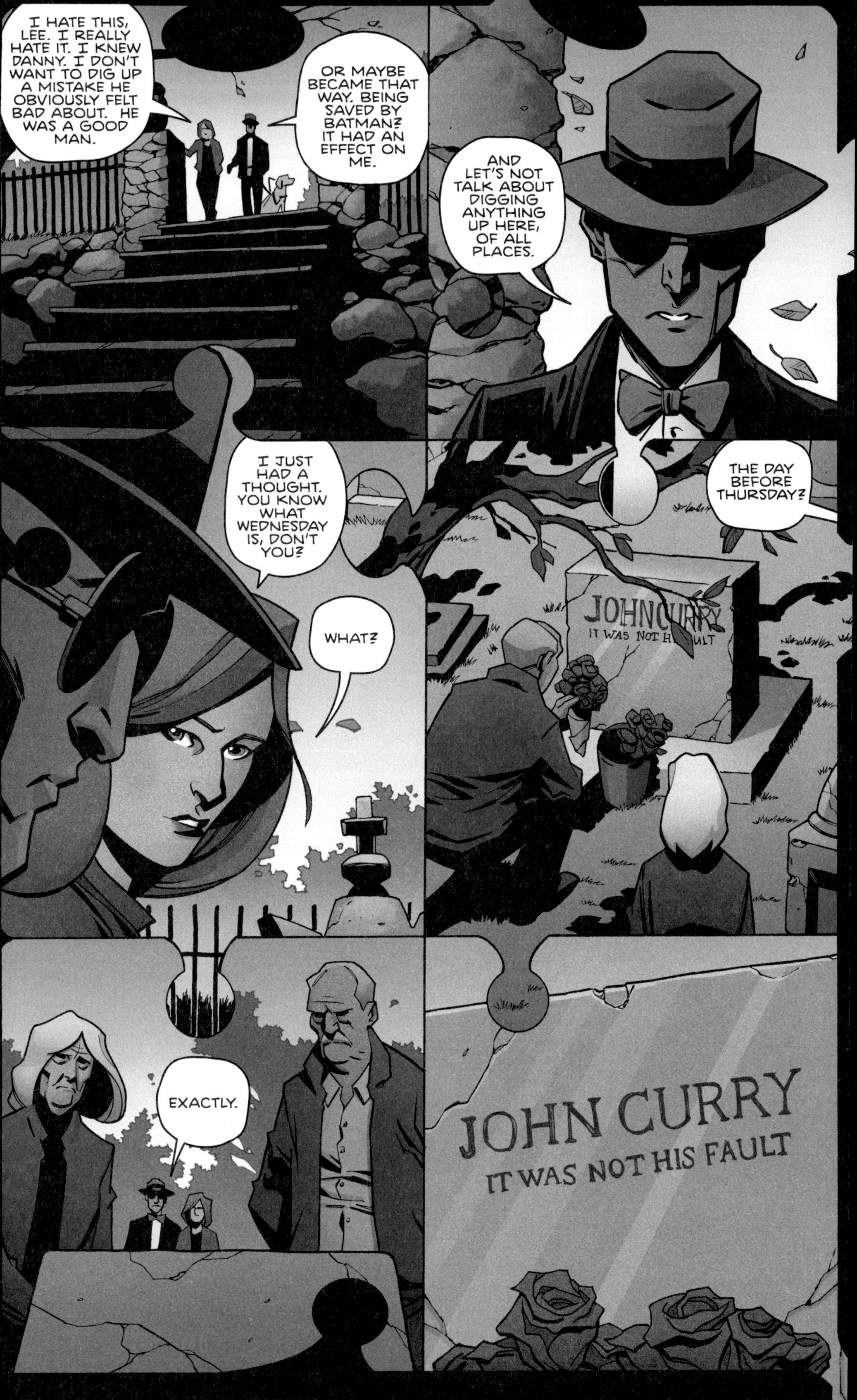
I HATE THIS, LEE. I REALLY HATE IT. I KNEW DANNY. I DON'T WANT TO DIG UP A MISTAKE HE OBVIOUSLY FELT BAD ABOUT. HE WAS A GOOD MAN.
OR MAYBE BECAME THAT WAY. BEING SAVED BY BATMAN? IT HAD AN EFFECT ON ME.
AND LET'S NOT TALK ABOUT DIGGING ANYTHING UP HERE, OF ALL PLACES.
I JUST HAD A THOUGHT. YOU KNOW WHAT WEDNESDAY IS, DON'T YOU?
THE DAY BEFORE THURSDAY?
WHAT?
EXACTLY.
JOHN CURRY
IT WAS NOT HIS FAULT

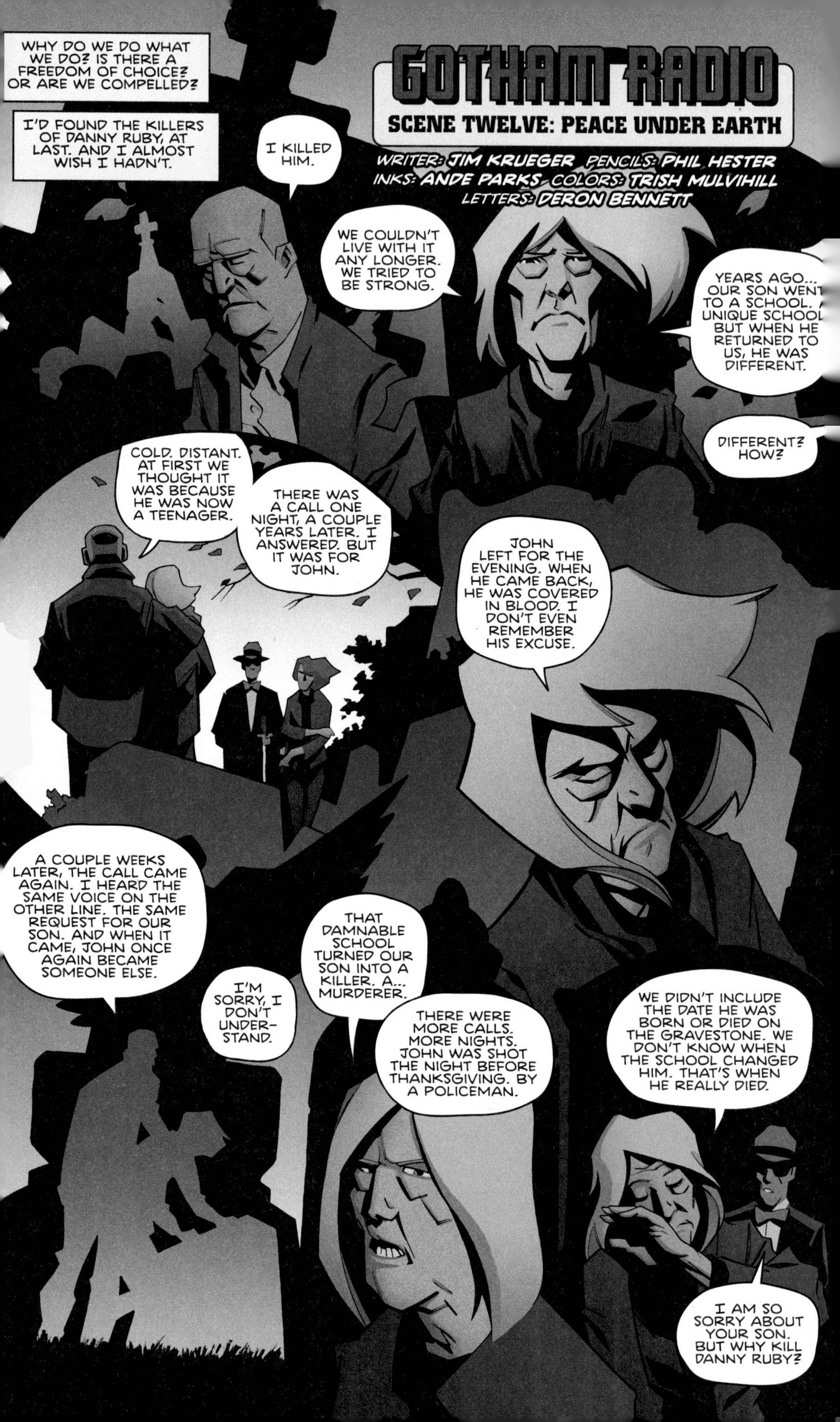
GOTHAM RADIO
SCENE TWELVE: PEACE UNDER EARTH
WRITER: JIM KRUEGER PENCILS: PHIL HESTER
INKS: ANDE PARKS COLORS: TRISH MULVIHILL
LETTERS: DERON BENNETT
WHY DO WE DO WHAT WE DO? IS THERE A FREEDOM OF CHOICE? OR ARE WE COMPELLED?
I'D FOUND THE KILLERS OF DANNY RUBY, AT LAST. AND I ALMOST WISH I HADN'T.
I KILLED HIM.
WE COULDN'T LIVE WITH IT ANY LONGER. WE TRIED TO BE STRONG.
YEARS AGO... OUR SON WENT TO A SCHOOL. A UNIQUE SCHOOL BUT WHEN HE RETURNED TO US, HE WAS DIFFERENT.
DIFFERENT? HOW?
COLD. DISTANT. AT FIRST WE THOUGHT IT WAS BECAUSE HE WAS NOW A TEENAGER.
THERE WAS A CALL ONE NIGHT, A COUPLE YEARS LATER. I ANSWERED. BUT IT WAS FOR JOHN.
JOHN LEFT FOR THE EVENING. WHEN HE CAME BACK, HE WAS COVERED IN BLOOD. I DON'T EVEN REMEMBER HIS EXCUSE.
A COUPLE WEEKS LATER, THE CALL CAME AGAIN. I HEARD THE SAME VOICE ON THE OTHER LINE. THE SAME REQUEST FOR OUR SON. AND WHEN IT CAME, JOHN ONCE AGAIN BECAME SOMEONE ELSE.
I'M SORRY, I DON'T UNDER-STAND.
THAT DAMNABLE SCHOOL TURNED OUR SON INTO A KILLER. A... MURDERER.
THERE WERE MORE CALLS. MORE NIGHTS. JOHN WAS SHOT THE NIGHT BEFORE THANKSGIVING. BY A POLICEMAN.
WE DIDN'T INCLUDE THE DATE HE WAS BORN OR DIED ON THE GRAVESTONE. WE DON'T KNOW WHEN THE SCHOOL CHANGED HIM. THAT'S WHEN HE REALLY DIED.
I AM SO SORRY ABOUT YOUR SON. BUT WHY KILL DANNY RUBY?

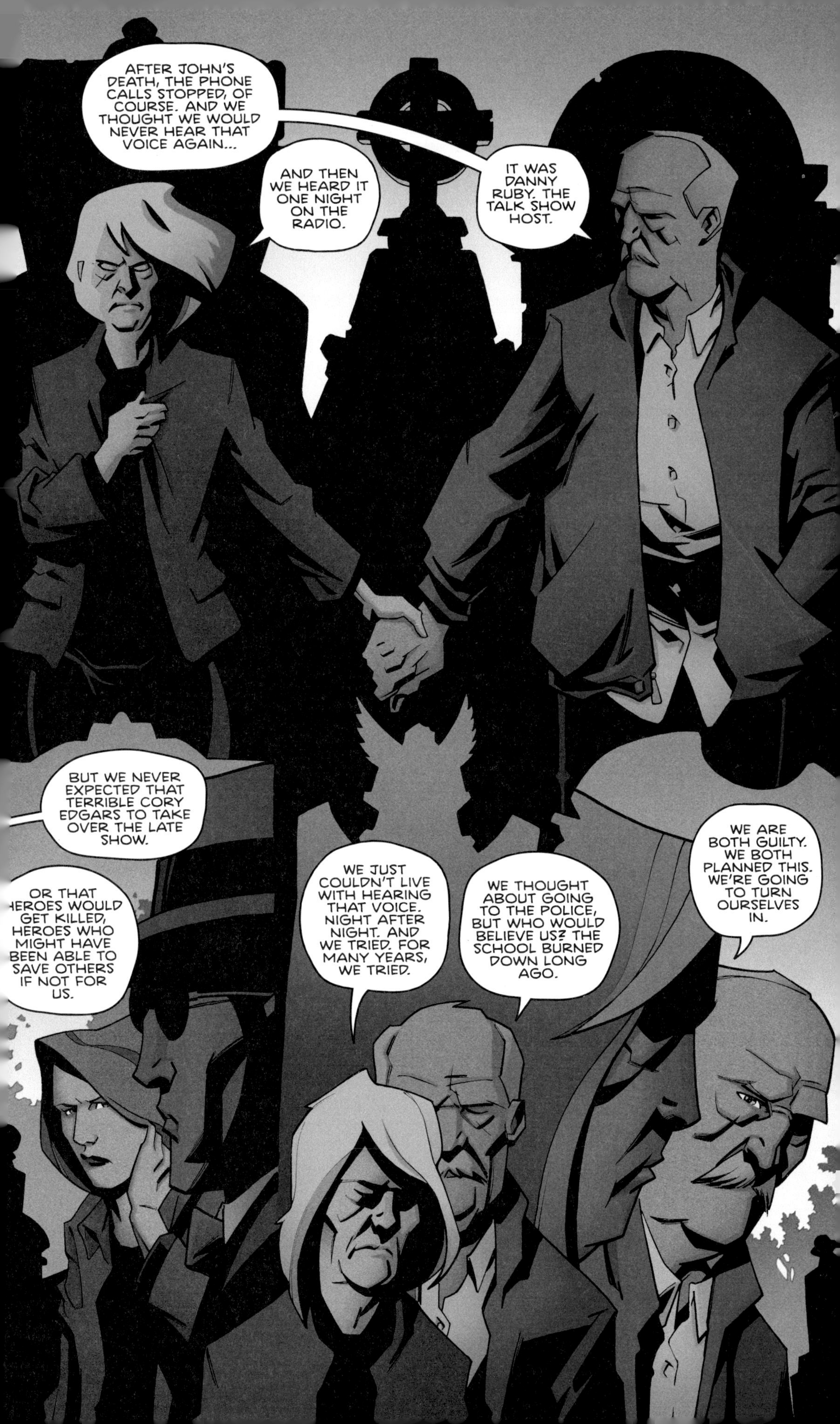
AFTER JOHN'S DEATH, THE PHONE CALLS STOPPED, OF COURSE. AND WE THOUGHT WE WOULD NEVER HEAR THAT VOICE AGAIN...
AND THEN WE HEARD IT ONE NIGHT ON THE RADIO.
IT WAS DANNY RUBY. THE TALK SHOW HOST.
BUT WE NEVER EXPECTED THAT TERRIBLE CORY EDGARS TO TAKE OVER THE LATE SHOW.
OR THAT HEROES WOULD GET KILLED, HEROES WHO MIGHT HAVE BEEN ABLE TO SAVE OTHERS IF NOT FOR US.
WE JUST COULDN'T LIVE WITH HEARING THAT VOICE. NIGHT AFTER NIGHT. AND WE TRIED. FOR MANY YEARS, WE TRIED.
WE THOUGHT ABOUT GOING TO THE POLICE, BUT WHO WOULD BELIEVE US? THE SCHOOL BURNED DOWN LONG AGO.
WE ARE BOTH GUILTY. WE BOTH PLANNED THIS. WE'RE GOING TO TURN OURSELVES IN.

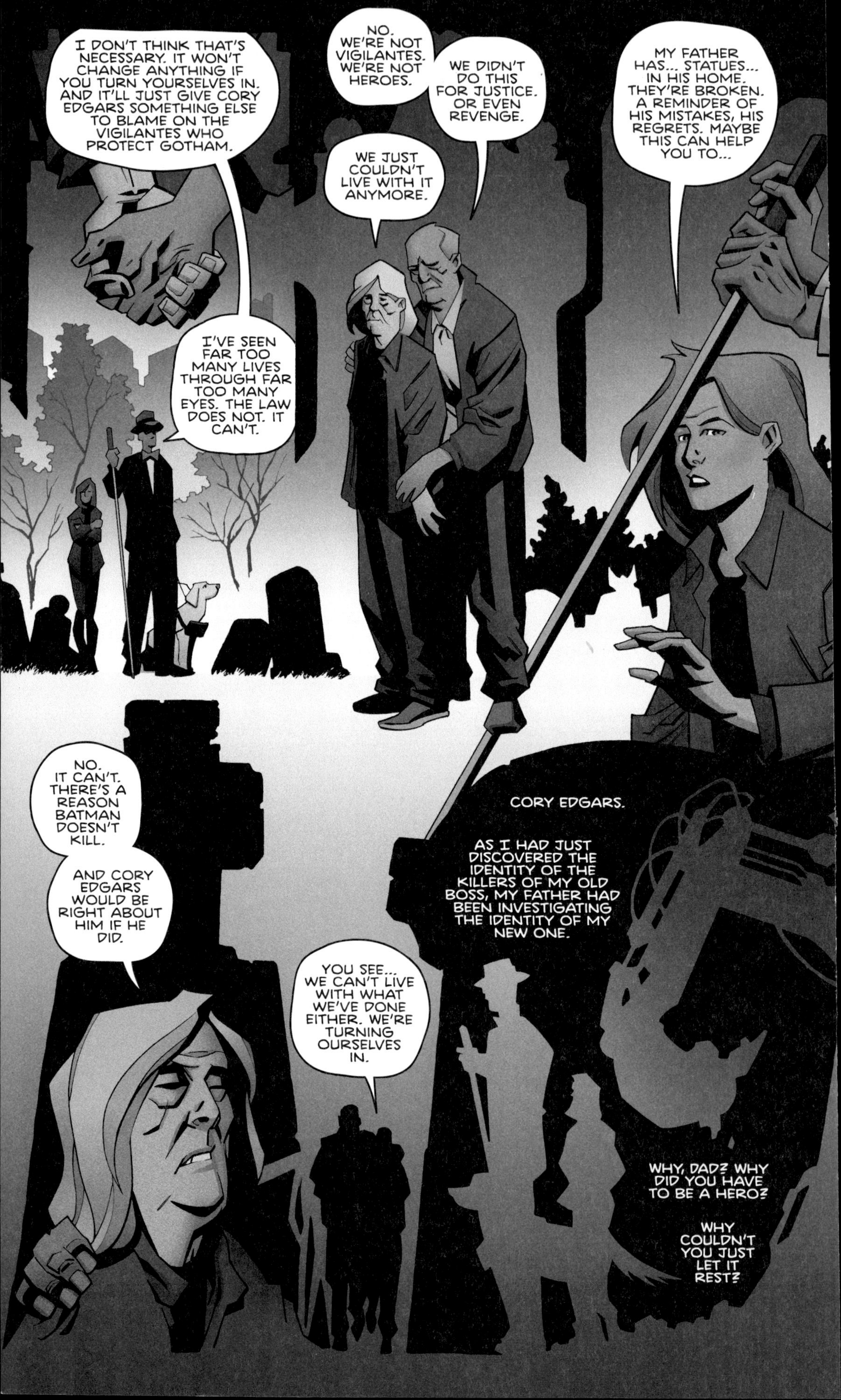
I DON'T THINK THAT'S NECESSARY. IT WON'T CHANGE ANYTHING IF YOU TURN YOURSELVES IN. AND IT'LL JUST GIVE CORY EDGARS SOMETHING ELSE TO BLAME ON THE VIGILANTES WHO PROTECT GOTHAM.
I'VE SEEN FAR TOO MANY LIVES THROUGH FAR TOO MANY EYES. THE LAW DOES NOT. IT CAN'T.
NO. WE'RE NOT VIGILANTES. WE'RE NOT HEROES.
WE DIDN'T DO THIS FOR JUSTICE. OR EVEN REVENGE.
WE JUST COULDN'T LIVE WITH IT ANYMORE.
MY FATHER HAS... STATUES... IN HIS HOME. THEY'RE BROKEN. A REMINDER OF HIS MISTAKES, HIS REGRETS. MAYBE THIS CAN HELP YOU TO...
NO. IT CAN'T. THERE'S A REASON BATMAN DOESN'T KILL.
AND CORY EDGARS WOULD BE RIGHT ABOUT HIM IF HE DID.
YOU SEE... WE CAN'T LIVE WITH WHAT WE'VE DONE EITHER. WE'RE TURNING OURSELVES IN.
CORY EDGARS.
AS I HAD JUST DISCOVERED THE IDENTITY OF THE KILLERS OF MY OLD BOSS, MY FATHER HAD BEEN INVESTIGATING THE IDENTITY OF MY NEW ONE.
WHY, DAD? WHY DID YOU HAVE TO BE A HERO?
WHY COULDN'T YOU JUST LET IT REST?

Who's Who
DC's Young Animal

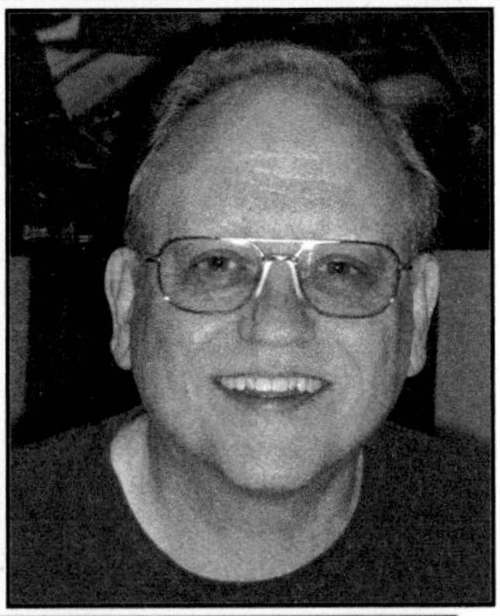

PERSONAL DATA

Name: John Workman
Occupation: Comics editor, writer, penciller, inker, letterer, colorist, designer, production director
Occupation for MOTHER PANIC: Letterer
First DC Appearance: DETECTIVE COMICS #455 in 1975
First DC's Young Animal Appearance: MOTHER PANIC #1

HISTORY

When I was eleven years old, I gave up wanting to be a lawyer (in pursuit of which I actually learned valuable lessons about writing) and decided that I would devote my life to the creation of comic book stories. After making a living doing advertising writing and art and having my stuff pop up in various fan and pro magazines, I started working on staff for DC Comics in 1975. Two years later, I was at *Heavy Metal* Magazine as its art director. Great fun. I got to write, draw, letter, color, and do several other things…all for an audience of a million readers. All these years later, I'm still working in comics, though I'm now known primarily as a letterer. Always hated to be placed in a category, but….

ONE OF MANY WAYS TO LETTER COMICS...

I drew, lettered, and inked this page years ago for a DC "Secret Origins" story. At that time, comics art and lettering were both done in ink on the same piece of art board. The images were first drawn in pencil, then the lettering was done in ink (including balloons, panel borders, and sound effects). The remaining art was then rendered in ink, and the pencil lines for both art and lettering were erased.

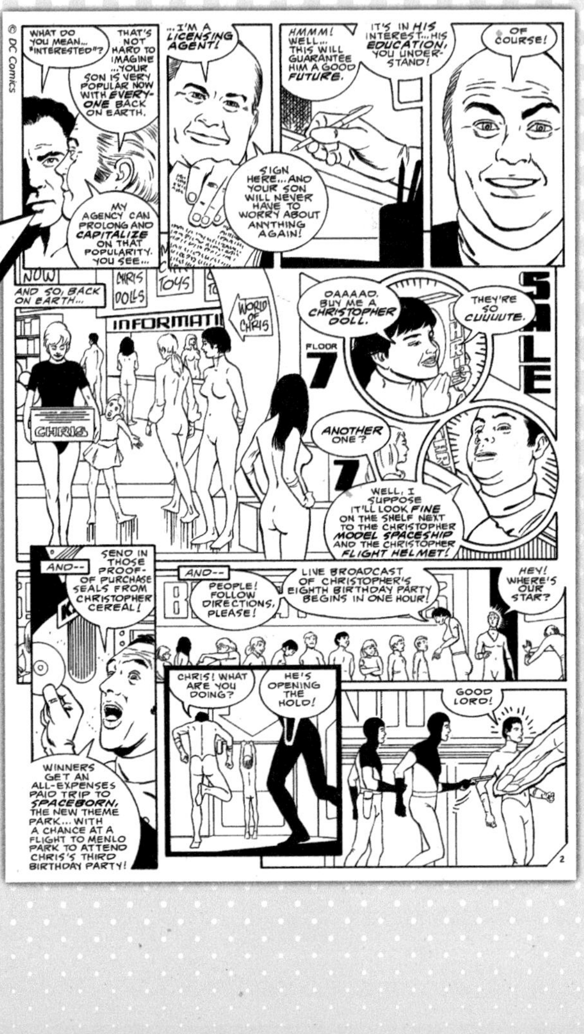
© DC Comics
WHAT DO YOU MEAN... "INTERESTED"?
THAT'S NOT HARD TO IMAGINE ...YOUR SON IS VERY POPULAR NOW WITH EVERY-ONE BACK ON EARTH.
MY AGENCY CAN PROLONG AND CAPITALIZE ON THAT POPULARITY. YOU SEE...
...I'M A LICENSING AGENT!
SIGN HERE...AND YOUR SON WILL NEVER HAVE TO WORRY ABOUT ANYTHING AGAIN!
HMMM! WELL... THIS WILL GUARANTEE HIM A GOOD FUTURE.
IT'S IN HIS INTEREST...HIS EDUCATION, YOU UNDER-STAND!
OF COURSE!
AND SO, BACK ON EARTH...
NOW
CHRIS DOLLS
TOYS
INFORMATI
WORLD OF CHRIS
CHRIS
DAAAAD. BUY ME A CHRISTOPHER DOLL.
THEY'RE SO CUUUUTE.
FLOOR 7
SALE
ANOTHER ONE?
WELL, I SUPPOSE IT'LL LOOK FINE ON THE SHELF NEXT TO THE CHRISTOPHER MODEL SPACESHIP AND THE CHRISTOPHER FLIGHT HELMET!
AND--
SEND IN THOSE PROOF-OF PURCHASE SEALS FROM CHRISTOPHER CEREAL!
WINNERS GET AN ALL-EXPENSES PAID TRIP TO SPACEBORN, THE NEW THEME PARK... WITH A CHANCE AT A FLIGHT TO MENLO PARK TO ATTEND CHRIS'S THIRD BIRTHDAY PARTY!
AND--
PEOPLE! FOLLOW DIRECTIONS, PLEASE!
LIVE BROADCAST OF CHRISTOPHER'S EIGHTH BIRTHDAY PARTY BEGINS IN ONE HOUR!
HEY! WHERE'S OUR STAR?
CHRIS! WHAT ARE YOU DOING?
HE'S OPENING THE HOLD!
GOOD LORD!
2

THE PROCESS OF LETTERING MOTHER PANIC

For the most part, comics have always begun with words. In this case, the script by Jody Houser.

PAGE 1
Panel 1 (Semi-Splash) - A club scene, lights, dancing. Looks loud. Wearing a party outfit including a boned corset top, Violet sits at the prime table, sipping a cocktail and watching the crowd like a queen surveys her people.
CAPTION (VIOLET)
Celebrity of the moment. Tell a sad story. Shed a few tears.
CAPTION (VIOLET)
All a lie, of course. But people like a tragic hero more than the monster.
violet
violet
violet
violet
young man
violet
violet
young man
violet
violet

John Paul Leon takes Jody's script and creates the visuals based on her descriptions. He also has to be aware of the dialogue and narrative balloons, and usually works out a rough placement for them when doing his layouts. It's at this point that I come into the picture.

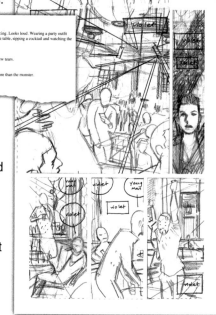

Based on JP's layouts, I figure out the area to be devoted to the words and plan the size and shape of the balloons accordingly. I do the actual lettering by using a Wacom tablet and pen. For some books I do, depending on my pay and the deadline, I type the letters, making use of commercial typefaces that have a hand-lettered look. Not so with MOTHER PANIC. For MP, the letters are drawn freehand directly into the computer on a file page that features gray guidelines, balloons, and various kinds of balloon tails. These elements are sized at about 150% of the final printed size…similar to the on-the-art lettering that was a constant for so many years. I find that, in creating the lettering, I have to be deliberately "messy" in order to give those letters a much-needed feeling of humanity and to make their lack of perfection visually interesting. I obliterate the gray guidelines, leaving a nice batch of balloons, and wait for scans of JP's final inked art to come my way.

Serving myself up as bait for a creep in a body bag. A murderer.
Still waiting for a bite.
LOOKING LONELY THERE, VI. COME ON, HAVE SOME FUN.
PREFER TO WATCH TONIGHT.
SHOW ME WHAT YOU GOT?
OH, YEAH.
Not a fan of the sidelines. But I don't have a choice right now.
Some of the cybernetics that hold me together crapped out.

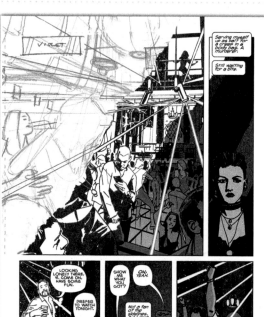

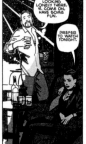

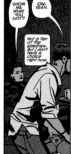

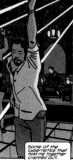

When scans of JP's final art are set up and sent to both me and the colorist (artwork has to be at the same down-to-the-pixel size for both creators) …

...I whip up an overlay that "floats" directly on top of JP's art, securing the overlay with a thin black line on its outer borders. Then I drop in place on the overlay the lettering and the balloons, reduced to 67% of their original size. To simplify things, I then obliterate the artwork, leaving the still-floating overlay. This, along with a low-resolution proof showing the combined art and lettering, is then sent to DC where …

… the overlay and the colored art are merged. Voila! Comics!

All during this process, I send along low-rez versions of the proofs to editor Molly Mahan and to everyone involved in the project. This makes for such great camaraderie and such hilarious e-mail conversations. It's always good to have other eyes looking at your stuff. When others make worthwhile suggestions, catch mistakes, and even (as often happens) offer praise for your efforts, the final pages that appear before the reader are made so much better.

I've been very lucky over the years to have worked with such wonderful people and such talented creators. That happy circumstance continues with the crew of MOTHER PANIC.